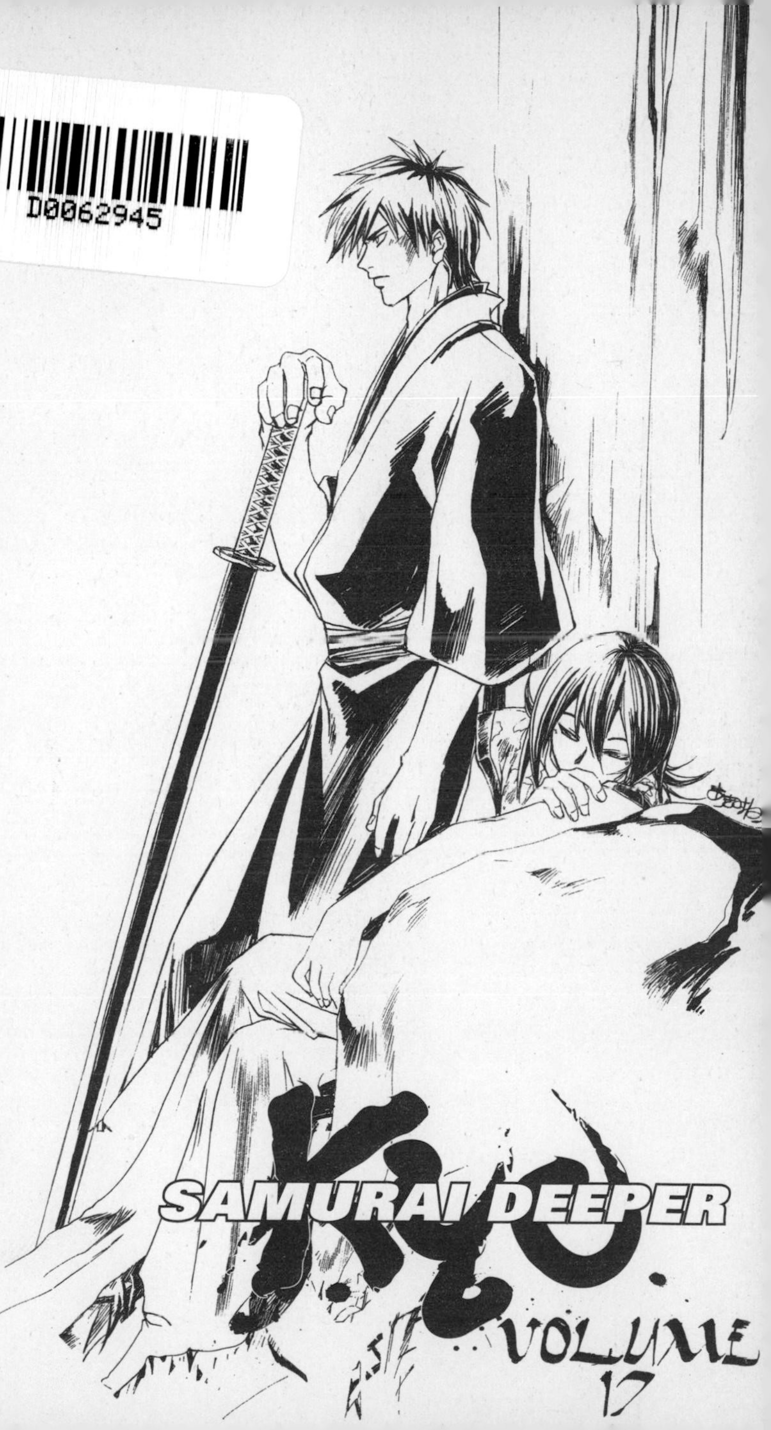
SAMURAI DEEPER
KYO
VOLUME
17

Samurai Deeper Kyo Vol. 17
Created by Akimine Kamijyo

Translation - Alexander O. Smith
Copy Editor - Hope Donovan
Retouch and Lettering - Jennifer Carbajal
Production Artist - Jennifer Carbajal
Cover Design - Seth Cable

Editor - Aaron Suhr
Digital Imaging Manager - Chris Buford
Production Managers - Jennifer Miller and Mutsumi Miyazaki
Managing Editor - Lindsey Johnston
VP of Production - Ron Klamert
Publisher and E.I.C. - Mike Kiley
President and C.O.O. - John Parker
C.E.O. - Stuart Levy

A  Manga

TOKYOPOP Inc.
5900 Wilshire Blvd. Suite 2000
Los Angeles, CA 90036

E-mail: info@TOKYOPOP.com
Come visit us online at www.TOKYOPOP.com

ISBN: 1-59532-457-7

First TOKYOPOP printing: February 2006
10 9 8 7 6 5 4 3 2 1
Printed in the USA

SAMURAI DEEPER K.yo.

Vol. 17
by Akimine Kamijyo

TOKYOPOP®

HAMBURG // LONDON // LOS ANGELES // TOKYO

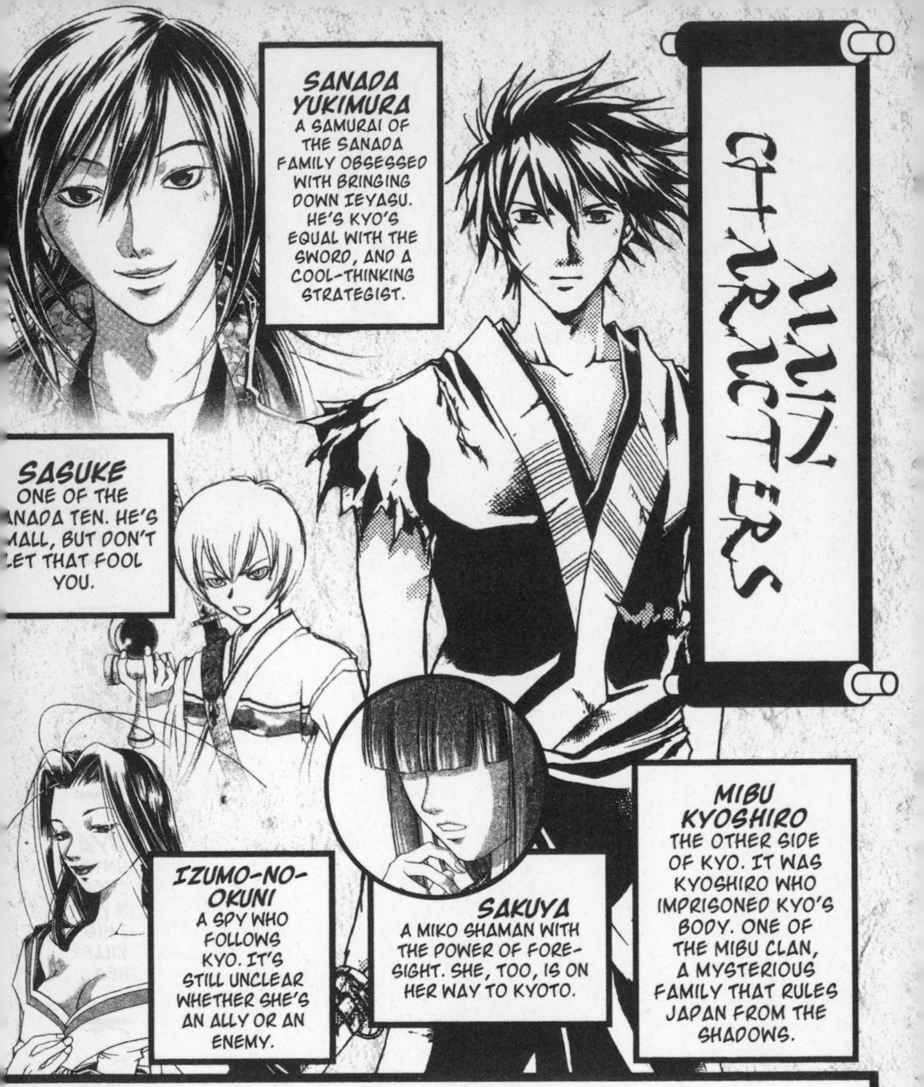
MAIN CHARACTERS
SANADA YUKIMURA
A SAMURAI OF THE SANADA FAMILY OBSESSED WITH BRINGING DOWN IEYASU. HE'S KYO'S EQUAL WITH THE SWORD, AND A COOL-THINKING STRATEGIST.
SASUKE
ONE OF THE ANADA TEN. HE'S MALL, BUT DON'T ET THAT FOOL YOU.
MIBU KYOSHIRO
THE OTHER SIDE OF KYO. IT WAS KYOSHIRO WHO IMPRISONED KYO'S BODY. ONE OF THE MIBU CLAN, A MYSTERIOUS FAMILY THAT RULES JAPAN FROM THE SHADOWS.
SAKUYA
A MIKO SHAMAN WITH THE POWER OF FORE-SIGHT. SHE, TOO, IS ON HER WAY TO KYOTO.
IZUMO-NO-OKUNI
A SPY WHO FOLLOWS KYO. IT'S STILL UNCLEAR WHETHER SHE'S AN ALLY OR AN ENEMY.

THE STORY

KYO AND FRIENDS HEAD INTO THE LAND OF THE MIBU TO SAVE YUYA, WHO ONLY HAS 12 HOURS BEFORE SHINREI AND SAISEI'S SECRET TECHNIQUES KILL HER. THEY SEEK THE FORMER CRIMSON KING, WHO HOLDS THE KEY TO YUYA'S LIFE AND THE SECRET OF KYO'S BIRTH!

THE GOING IS ROUGH. BONTENMARU AND AKIRA FALL INTO A MIBU TRAP AND ARE SEPARATED FROM THE OTHERS, LEAVING KYO AND YUYA TO FACE THE GUARDIAN OF THE FIRST SHINING GATE, KEIKOKU OF THE FIVE STARS (FORMERLY HOTARU OF THE FOUR EMPERORS).

HOTARU HAS LITTLE LOVE FOR THE MIBU, ESPECIALLY HIS HALF-BROTHER SHINREI, AND HE SEEKS TO BEST THEM ALL BY BECOMING THE STRONGEST MAN ALIVE. A FIERCE BATTLE ERUPTS BETWEEN HOTARU, MASTER OF FIRE, AND KYO, WITH HIS NEWLY-ACQUIRED TRUE MUMYOJINPU SCHOOL TECHNIQUES. KYO WINS, BUT IS GRAVELY WOUNDED IN THE CLOSE CONTEST.

REUNITED ONCE AGAIN WITH BONTENMARU AND AKIRA, KYO'S PARTY HEADS TOWARD THE SECOND GATE, WHERE WAIT THE DEVILS IN WHITE, SAISHI AND SAISEI, AND YUKIMURA, WHO HAS THROWN HIS LOT IN WITH THE MIBU!

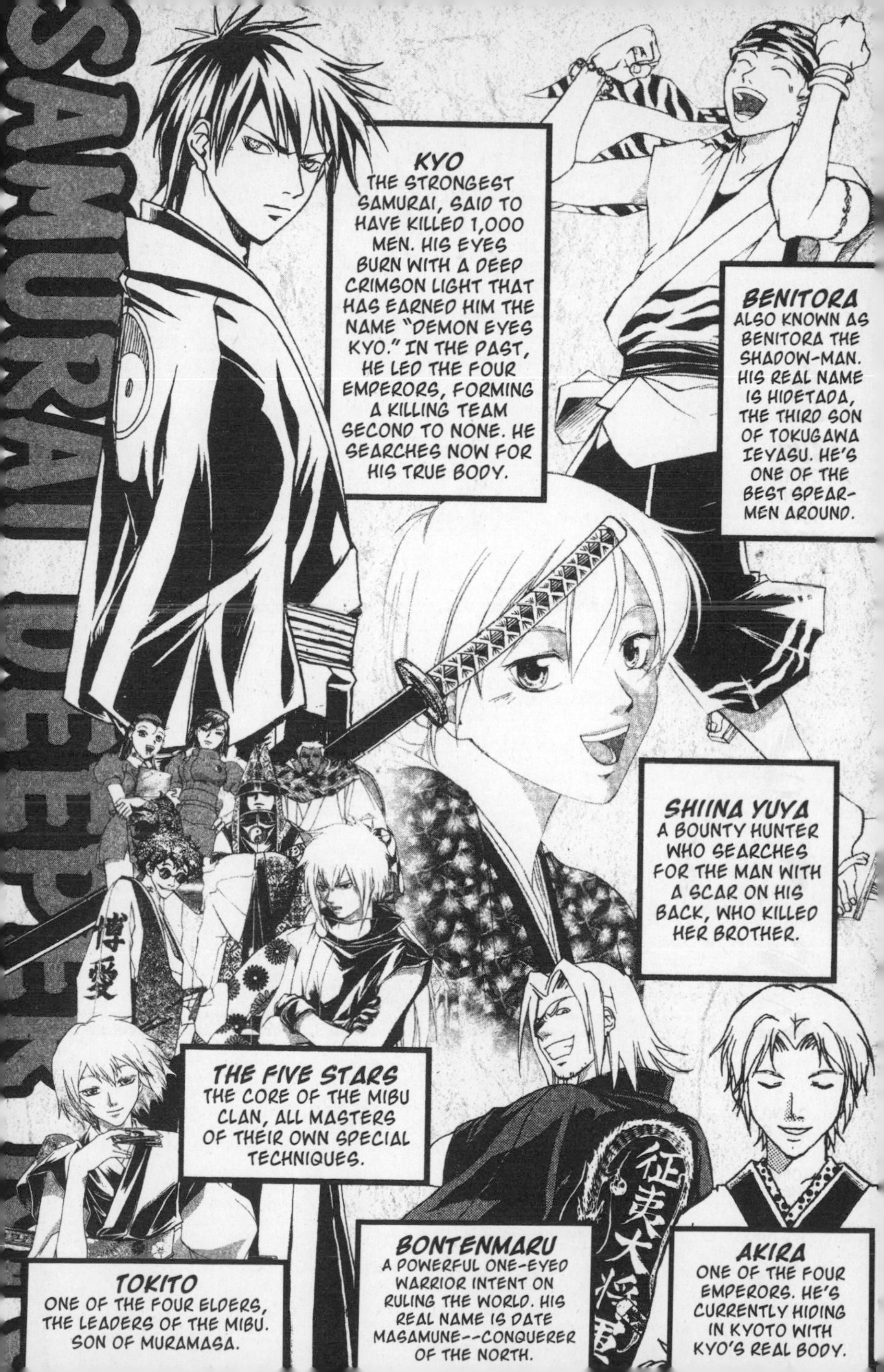
SAMURAI DEEPER KYO
KYO
THE STRONGEST SAMURAI, SAID TO HAVE KILLED 1,000 MEN. HIS EYES BURN WITH A DEEP CRIMSON LIGHT THAT HAS EARNED HIM THE NAME "DEMON EYES KYO." IN THE PAST, HE LED THE FOUR EMPERORS, FORMING A KILLING TEAM SECOND TO NONE. HE SEARCHES NOW FOR HIS TRUE BODY.
BENITORA
ALSO KNOWN AS BENITORA THE SHADOW-MAN. HIS REAL NAME IS HIDETADA, THE THIRD SON OF TOKUGAWA IEYASU. HE'S ONE OF THE BEST SPEAR-MEN AROUND.
SHIINA YUYA
A BOUNTY HUNTER WHO SEARCHES FOR THE MAN WITH A SCAR ON HIS BACK, WHO KILLED HER BROTHER.
THE FIVE STARS
THE CORE OF THE MIBU CLAN, ALL MASTERS OF THEIR OWN SPECIAL TECHNIQUES.
AKIRA
ONE OF THE FOUR EMPERORS. HE'S CURRENTLY HIDING IN KYOTO WITH KYO'S REAL BODY.
BONTENMARU
A POWERFUL ONE-EYED WARRIOR INTENT ON RULING THE WORLD. HIS REAL NAME IS DATE MASAMUNE--CONQUERER OF THE NORTH.
TOKITO
ONE OF THE FOUR ELDERS, THE LEADERS OF THE MIBU. SON OF MURAMASA.

WHERE DID KYO MEET ALL HIS FRIENDS? WHO DID THEY FIGHT? SWIFTER THAN KYO CAN SWING HIS SWORD, HERE'S A RECAP OF ALL THAT'S HAPPENED IN SDK SO FAR!

F KYO!

(1) THE JOURNEY OF KYOSHIRO AND YUYA BEGINS! (SDK VOL. 1)

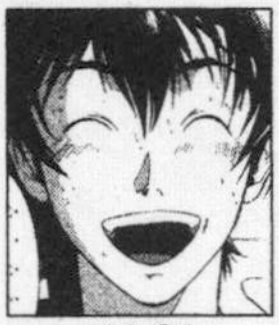

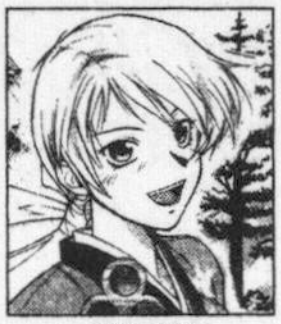

▲ MIBU KYOSHIRO

▲ SHIINA YUYA

THE BEAUTIFUL BOUNTY HUNTER YUYA MEETS MIBU KYOSHIRO BY CHANCE (OR WAS IT FATE?!). WHEN THEY FOUGHT THE BANTOUJI BROTHERS, KYOSHIRO'S OTHER SIDE WAS REVEALED: THAT OF DEMON EYES KYO!

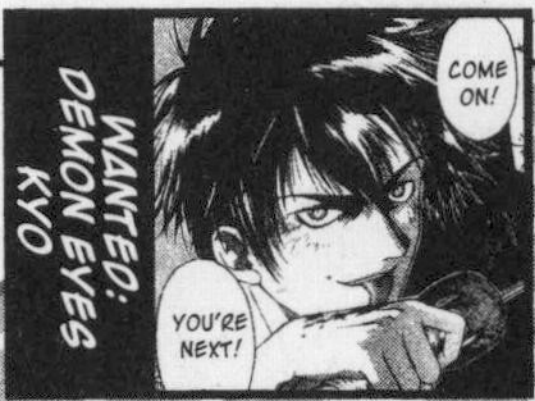

WANTED: DEMON EYES KYO
COME ON!
YOU'RE NEXT!

(2) THE WOMAN IZUMO-NO-OKUNI (SDK VOL. 1-2)

THEY MEET THE WOMAN IZUMO-NO-OKUNI AT AN INN TOWN--AND SHE SEEMS TO KNOW A LOT ABOUT KYO AND KYOSHIRO'S PAST. THEN, IN THE VILLAGE OF DESERTERS, KYO AWAKENS AND SHOWS HIS FULL STRENGTH!

TOUGE (THE PASS)
ZENGEN VILLAGE
INN VILLAGE
OCHUDOMURA (VILLAGE OF DESERTERS)
IN THE IPPONZAKURA MOUNTAINS (LONE CHERRY MOUNTAINS)
TEAHOUSE IN THE PASS
EDO
THE FOREST OF AOKIGAHARA
HAKONE
MT. FUJI

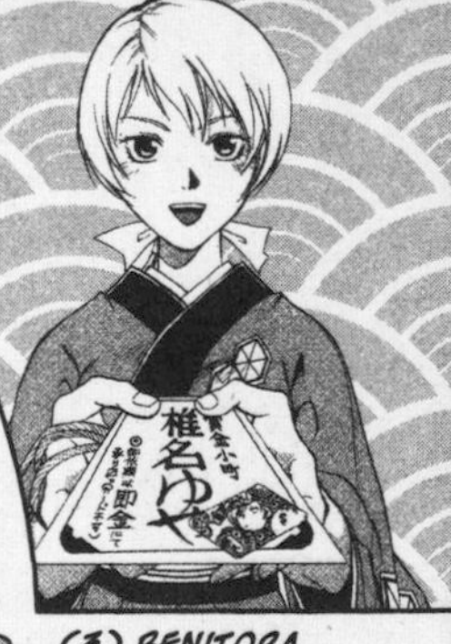

(3) BENITORA JOINS THE PARTY! (SDK VOL. 2-3)

THE PARTY GETS INTO A FIGHT WITH A TREASURE-SEEKING GROUP OF ASSASSINS KNOWN AS THE KITOU FAMILY SANSAISHU. ONE OF THEIR NUMBER, BENITORA, ENDS UP JOINING SIDES WITH KYO. KYO FIGHTS THE SHIROKARASU (WHITE CROW) AND FULLY AWAKENS! KYOSHIRO, HOWEVER, IS NOWHERE TO BE SEEN.

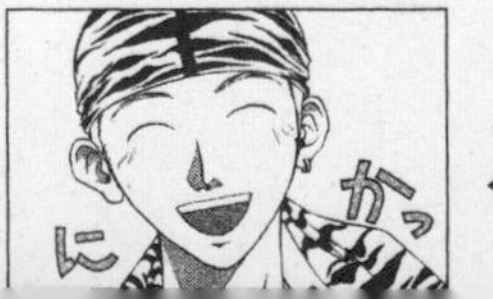

▲ BENITORA

(4) KYO AND YUKIMURA MEET! (SDK VOL. 3)

A DRUNK CALLS OUT TO THEM AT A TEAHOUSE--AND TURNS OUT TO BE A SWORDSMAN OF SUCH SKILL, HE CAN SLIP PAST EVEN KYO'S DEFENSES!

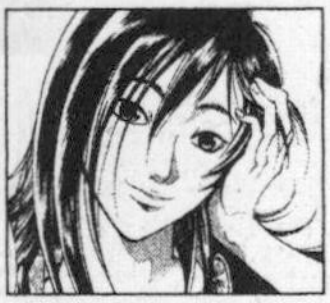

▶ SANADA YUKIMURA

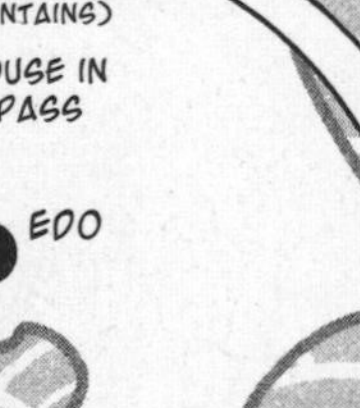

▲ THE REAL TOKUGAWA IEYASU

(5) FIGHT BEFORE THE SHOGUN! (SDK VOL. 3-5)

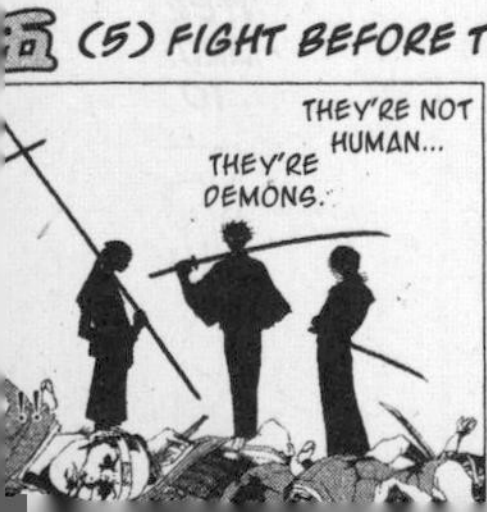

THEY'RE NOT HUMAN...
THEY'RE DEMONS.

KYO, YUKIMURA, AND BENITORA ENTER A TOURNEY HELD BY THE RULER OF THE LAND, TOKUGAWA IEYASU. BUT THE TOURNEY WAS A TRAP! SET UPON BY TOKUGAWA'S ELITES, THE THREE MANAGE TO DESTROY THEM ALL WITHOUT BREAKING A SWEAT! THEN YUKIMURA TELLS KYO A SECRET: THE LOCATION OF HIS BODY!

IN JUST 3 MINUTES!

LEARN THE LEGEND

六 (6) MORTAL COMBAT VERSUS ODA NOBUNAGA AND THE TWELVE GOD SHOGUNS! (SDK VOL. 5-10)

KYO'S BODY LIES HIDDEN IN THE DEEPEST REACHES OF THE AOKIGAHARA FOREST AT THE FOOT OF MT. FUJI. BUT BETWEEN KYO AND HIS BODY STAND THE TWELVE--GUARDIANS OF THE MASTER, ODA NOBUNAGA. AFTER A STRING OF BLOODY BATTLES, KYO'S DEMONBLADE, MURAMASA, RELIEVES NOBUNAGA'S BODY OF ITS HEAD, BUT AKIRA MAKES HIS ESCAPE WITH KYO'S BODY!

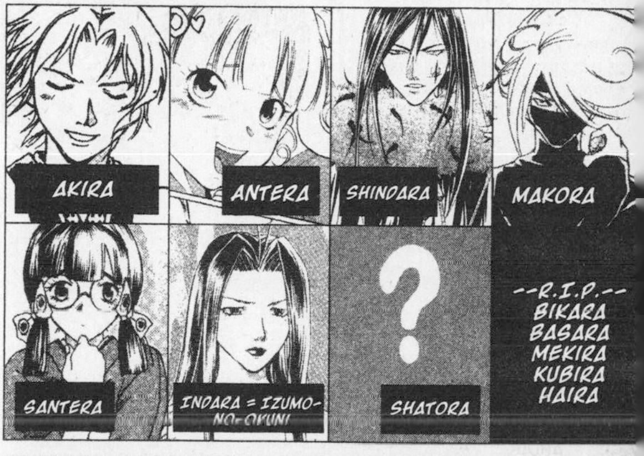
AKIRA
ANTERA
SHINDARA
MAKORA
SANTERA
INDARA = IZUMO-NO-OKUNI
?
SHATORA
--R.I.P.--
BIKARA
BASARA
MEKIRA
KUBIRA
HAIRA

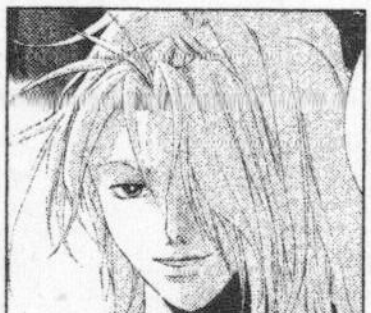

NOBUNAGA AWAITS THE TIME OF HIS RESURRECTION IN THE VILLAGE OF THE MIBU, DEEP WITHIN THE LAND OF THE FIRE LOTUS.

▲ ODA NOBUNAGA

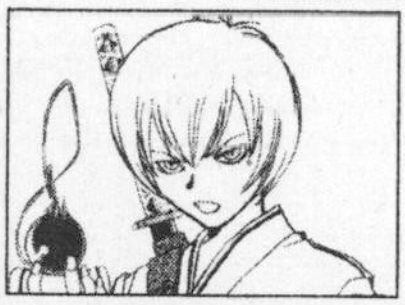

◀ SASUKE

ONE OF THE SANADA TEN. HE RETURNED TO THE FOREST WHERE HE WAS BORN ON YUKIMURA'S ORDERS.

八 (8) FIERCE FIGHTING AGAINST THE PRIDE OF THE MIBU CLAN! (SDK VOL. 11-)

THE ENIGMATIC MIBU FAMILY HOLDS THE KEY TO THE MYSTERY BEHIND KYO'S BIRTH. AFTER HOLDING THE POWER TO CONTROL JAPAN'S HISTORY FROM THE DARK SIDE, SUDDENLY THE FACE-TO-FACE SHOWDOWN HAS BEGUN! AT THE SAME TIME, THE POWER TO SAVE YUYA'S LIFE LIES WITH THE ENEMY. KYO HAS CONFRONTED THE FIVE STARS, THE FOUR EMPERORS AND, MOST RECENTLY, THE CRIMSON KING (AKA NO OU), HIS LATEST ULTIMATELY STRONG FOE. ON THE OTHER HAND, KYO IS MARCHING INTO ENEMY TERRITORY ARMED WITH THE MUMYO JINPU TECHNIQUE THAT MURAMASA TRADED HIS LIFE TO OBTAIN.

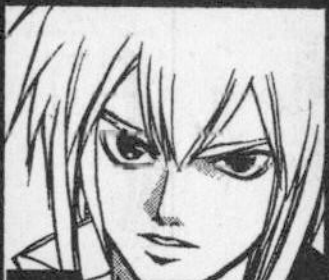

SHINREI

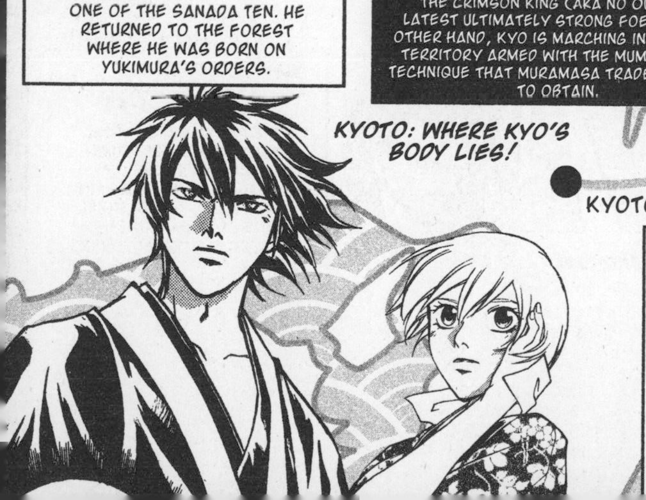
KYOTO: WHERE KYO'S BODY LIES!
NAKASENDO ROAD
TOKAIDO ROAD
OWARI
KYOTO

七 (7) ENTER BONTENMARU! (SDK VOL. 10)

THE ONE-EYED DATE MASAMUNE APPEARS BEFORE KYO AND LEADS THE PARTY TO KYO'S MASTER, MURAMASA.

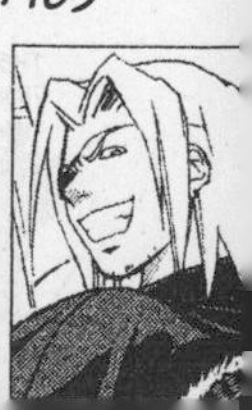

SOME SKETCHES FOR A FLIPBOOK STYLE MANGA. IT GOES 1-2-3 AND BACK TO 1!

SAMURAI DEEPER KYO

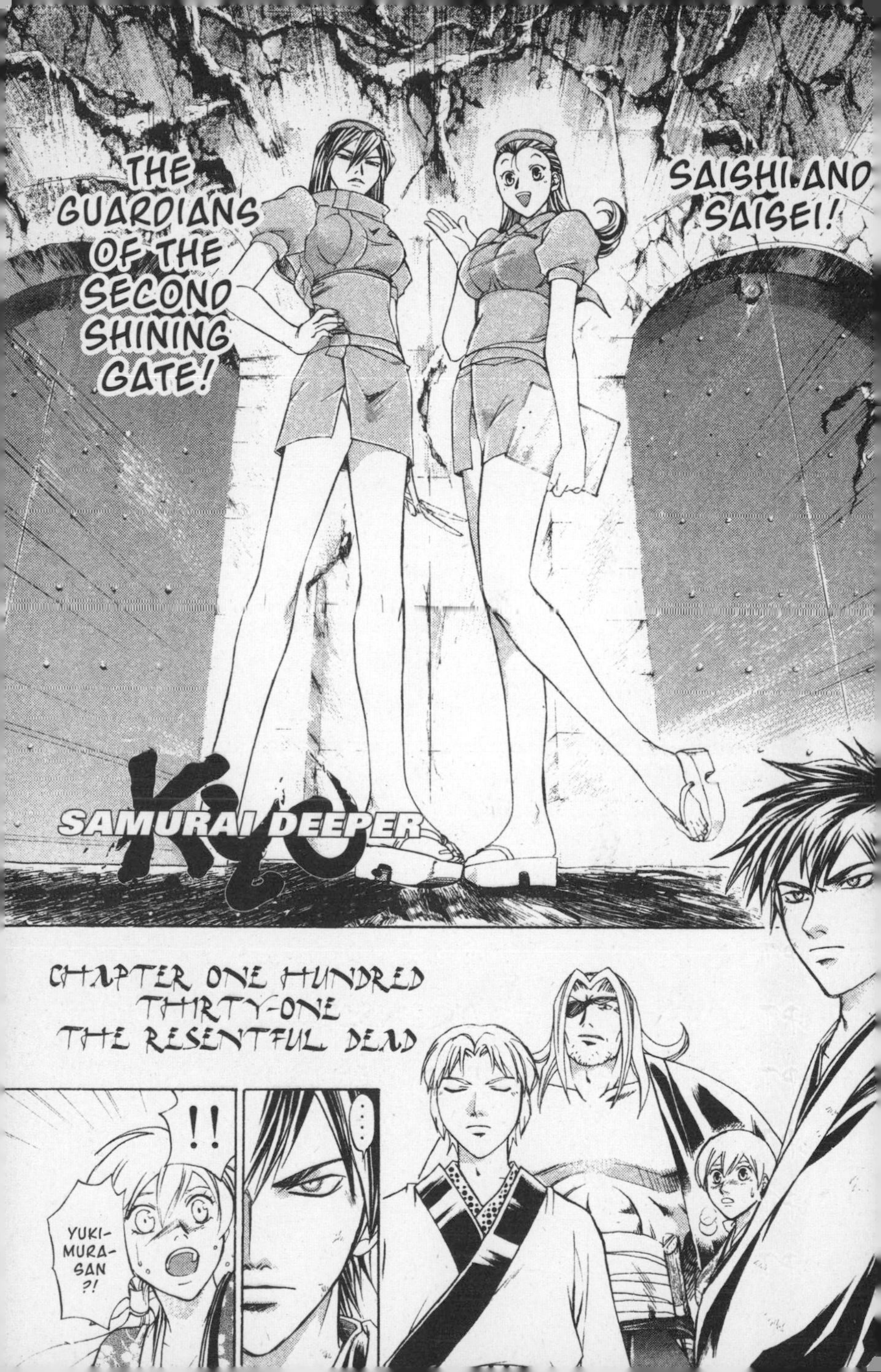
SAISHI AND SAISEI!
THE GUARDIANS OF THE SECOND SHINING GATE!
SAMURAI DEEPER KYO
CHAPTER ONE HUNDRED THIRTY-ONE
THE RESENTFUL DEAD
...
!!
YUKIMURA-SAN?!

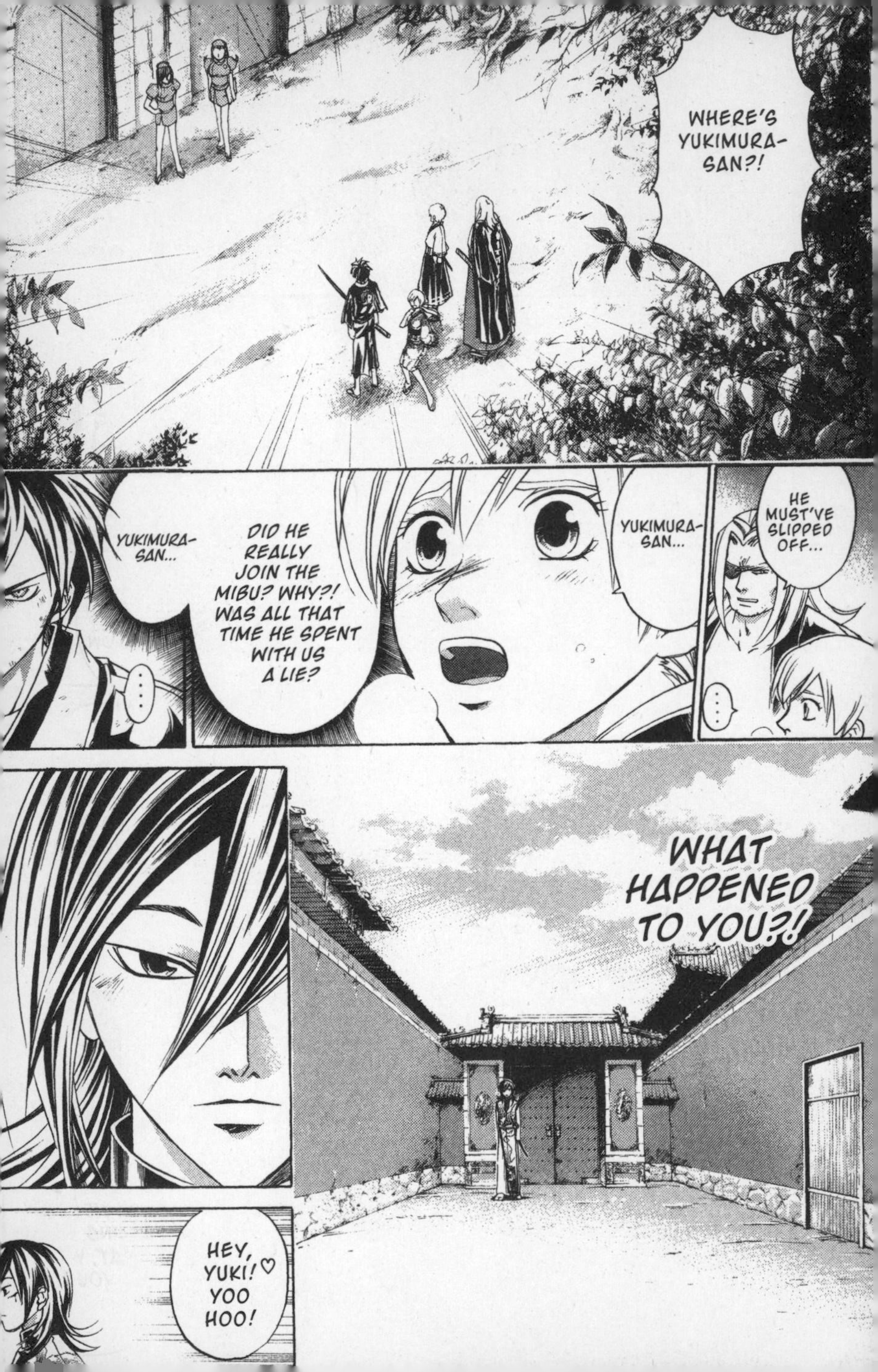
WHERE'S YUKIMURA-SAN?!
HE MUST'VE SLIPPED OFF...
...
YUKIMURA-SAN...
DID HE REALLY JOIN THE MIBU? WHY?! WAS ALL THAT TIME HE SPENT WITH US A LIE?
YUKIMURA-SAN...
...
WHAT HAPPENED TO YOU?!
HEY, YUKI! ♡ YOO HOO!

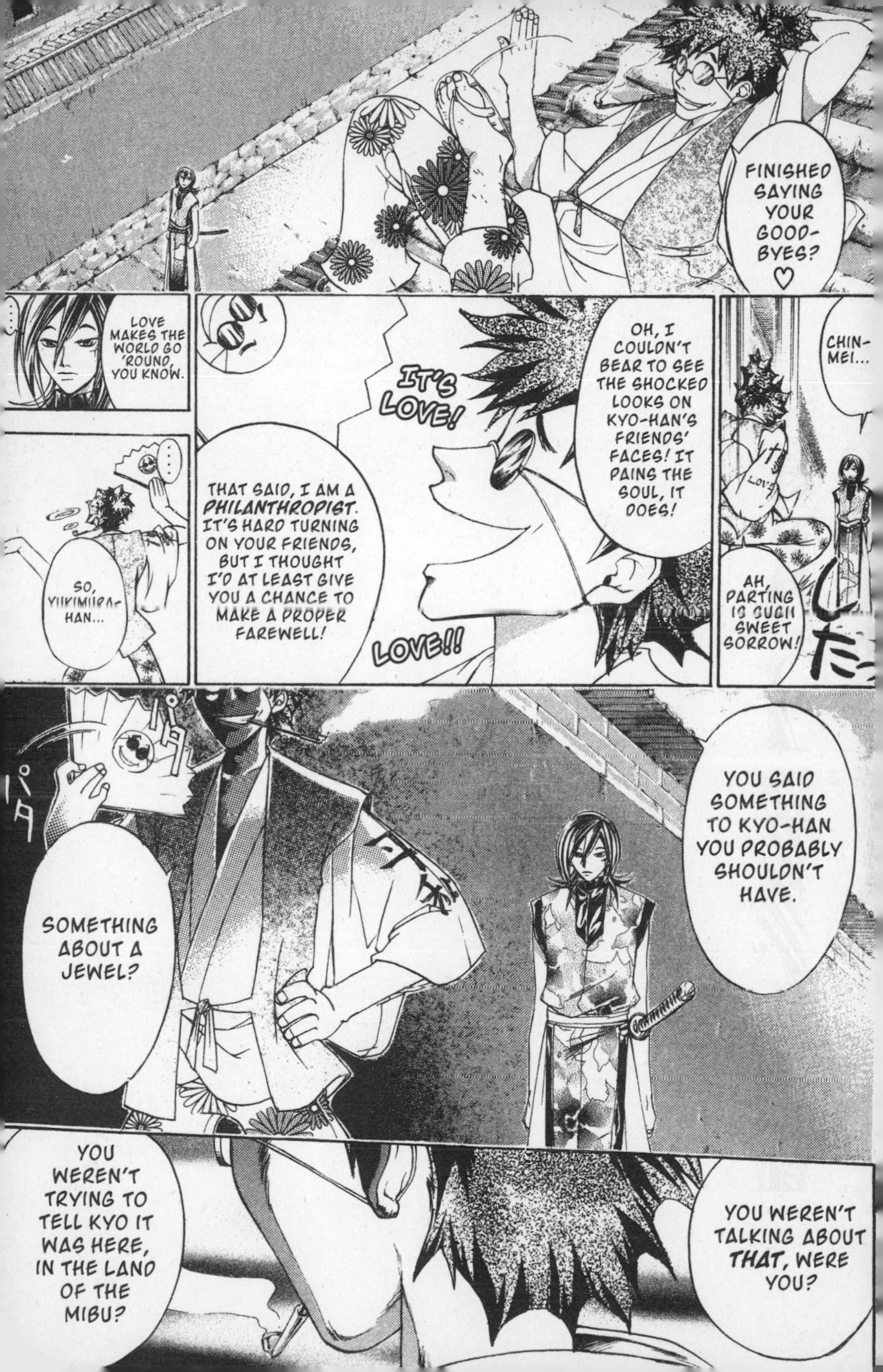
FINISHED SAYING YOUR GOOD-BYES? ♡
CHIN-MEI...
AH, PARTING IS SUCH SWEET SORROW!
OH, I COULDN'T BEAR TO SEE THE SHOCKED LOOKS ON KYO-HAN'S FRIENDS' FACES! IT PAINS THE SOUL, IT DOES!
IT'S LOVE!
THAT SAID, I AM A *PHILANTHROPIST*. IT'S HARD TURNING ON YOUR FRIENDS, BUT I THOUGHT I'D AT LEAST GIVE YOU A CHANCE TO MAKE A PROPER FAREWELL!
LOVE!!
...
LOVE MAKES THE WORLD GO 'ROUND, YOU KNOW.
...
SO, YUKIMURA-HAN...
YOU SAID SOMETHING TO KYO-HAN YOU PROBABLY SHOULDN'T HAVE.
SOMETHING ABOUT A JEWEL?
YOU WEREN'T TALKING ABOUT *THAT*, WERE YOU?
YOU WEREN'T TRYING TO TELL KYO IT WAS HERE, IN THE LAND OF THE MIBU?

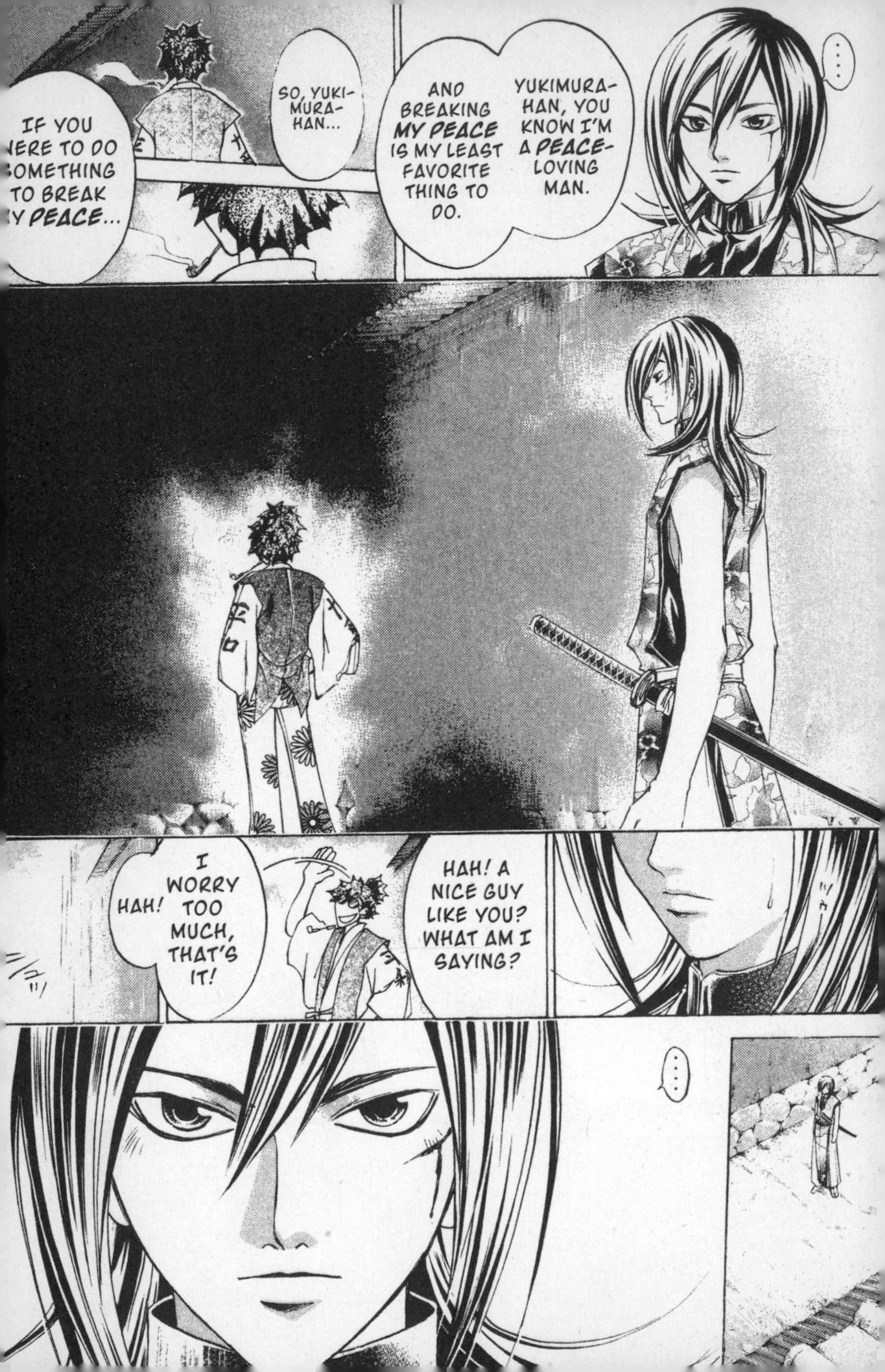
....
YUKIMURA-HAN, YOU KNOW I'M A PEACE-LOVING MAN.
AND BREAKING MY PEACE IS MY LEAST FAVORITE THING TO DO.
SO, YUKI-MURA-HAN...
IF YOU ERE TO DO OMETHING TO BREAK Y PEACE...
HAH! A NICE GUY LIKE YOU? WHAT AM I SAYING?
I WORRY TOO MUCH, THAT'S IT!
HAH!
....

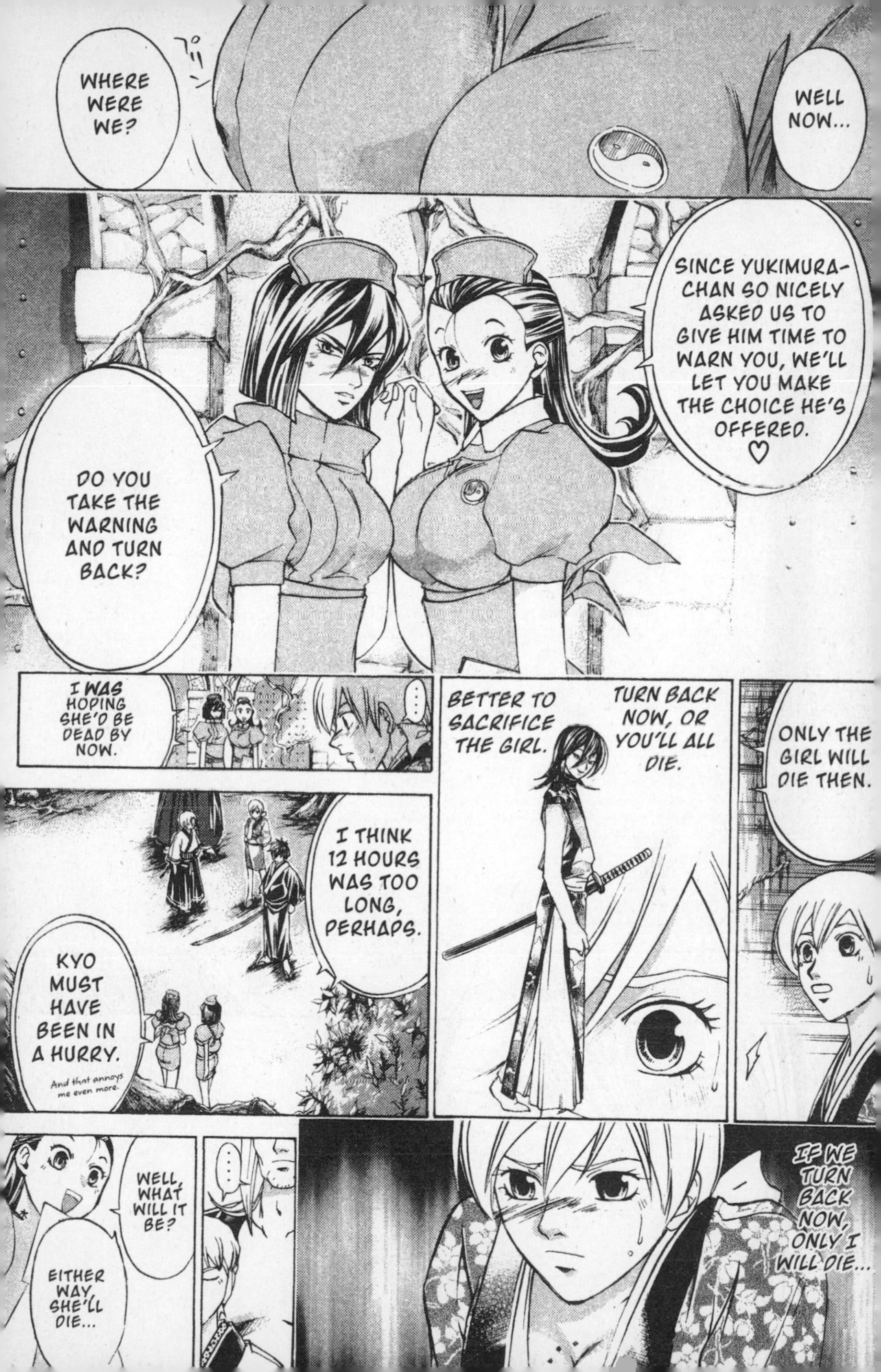
WELL NOW...
WHERE WERE WE?
SINCE YUKIMURA-CHAN SO NICELY ASKED US TO GIVE HIM TIME TO WARN YOU, WE'LL LET YOU MAKE THE CHOICE HE'S OFFERED. ♡
DO YOU TAKE THE WARNING AND TURN BACK?
ONLY THE GIRL WILL DIE THEN.
TURN BACK NOW, OR YOU'LL ALL DIE.
BETTER TO SACRIFICE THE GIRL.
...
I WAS HOPING SHE'D BE DEAD BY NOW.
I THINK 12 HOURS WAS TOO LONG, PERHAPS.
KYO MUST HAVE BEEN IN A HURRY.
And that annoys me even more.
IF WE TURN BACK NOW, ONLY I WILL DIE...
...
WELL, WHAT WILL IT BE?
EITHER WAY, SHE'LL DIE...

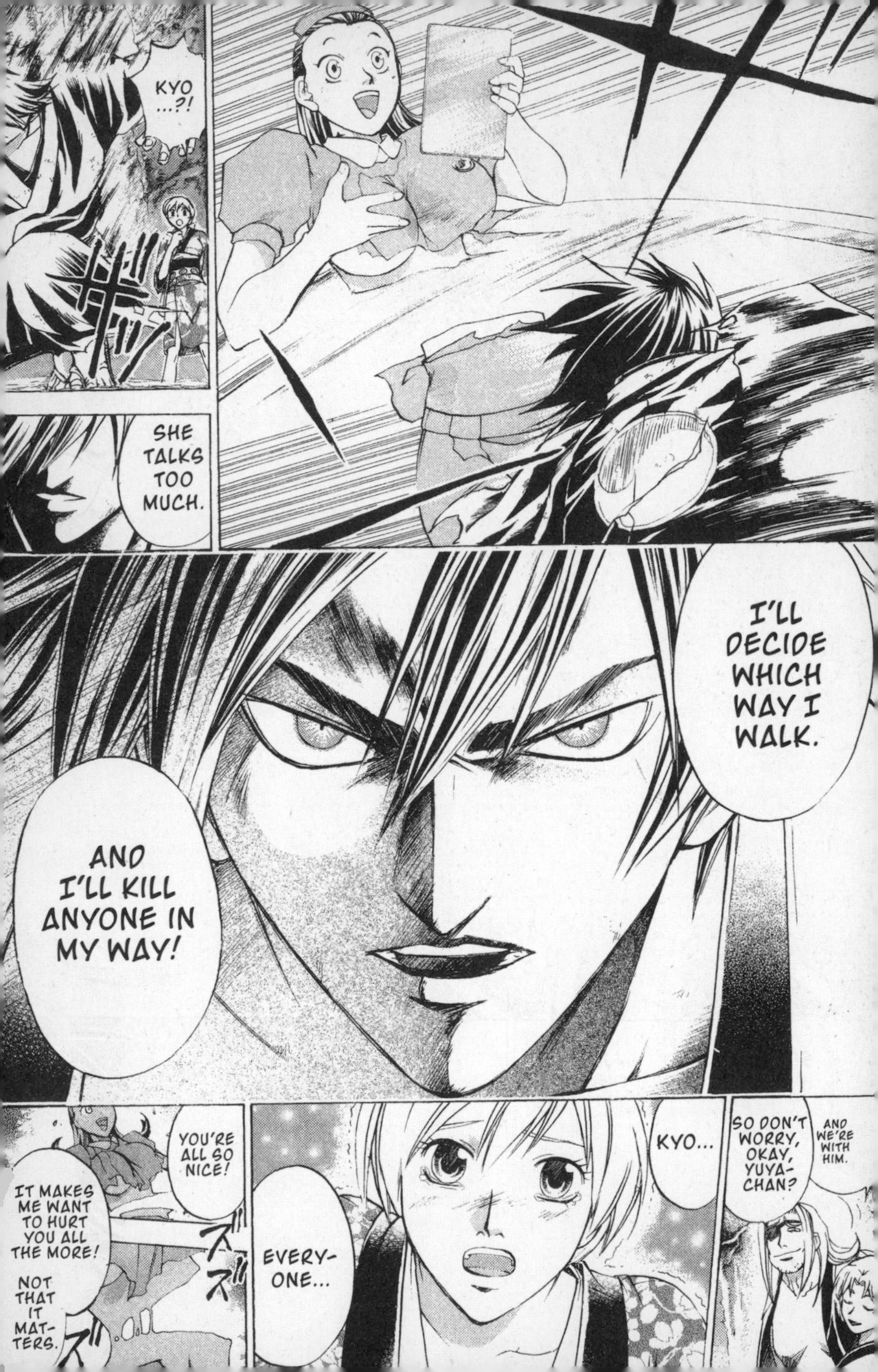
KYO ...?!
SHE TALKS TOO MUCH.
I'LL DECIDE WHICH WAY I WALK.
AND I'LL KILL ANYONE IN MY WAY!
AND WE'RE WITH HIM.
SO DON'T WORRY, OKAY, YUYA-CHAN?
KYO...
EVERY-ONE...
YOU'RE ALL SO NICE!
IT MAKES ME WANT TO HURT YOU ALL THE MORE!
NOT THAT IT MATTERS.

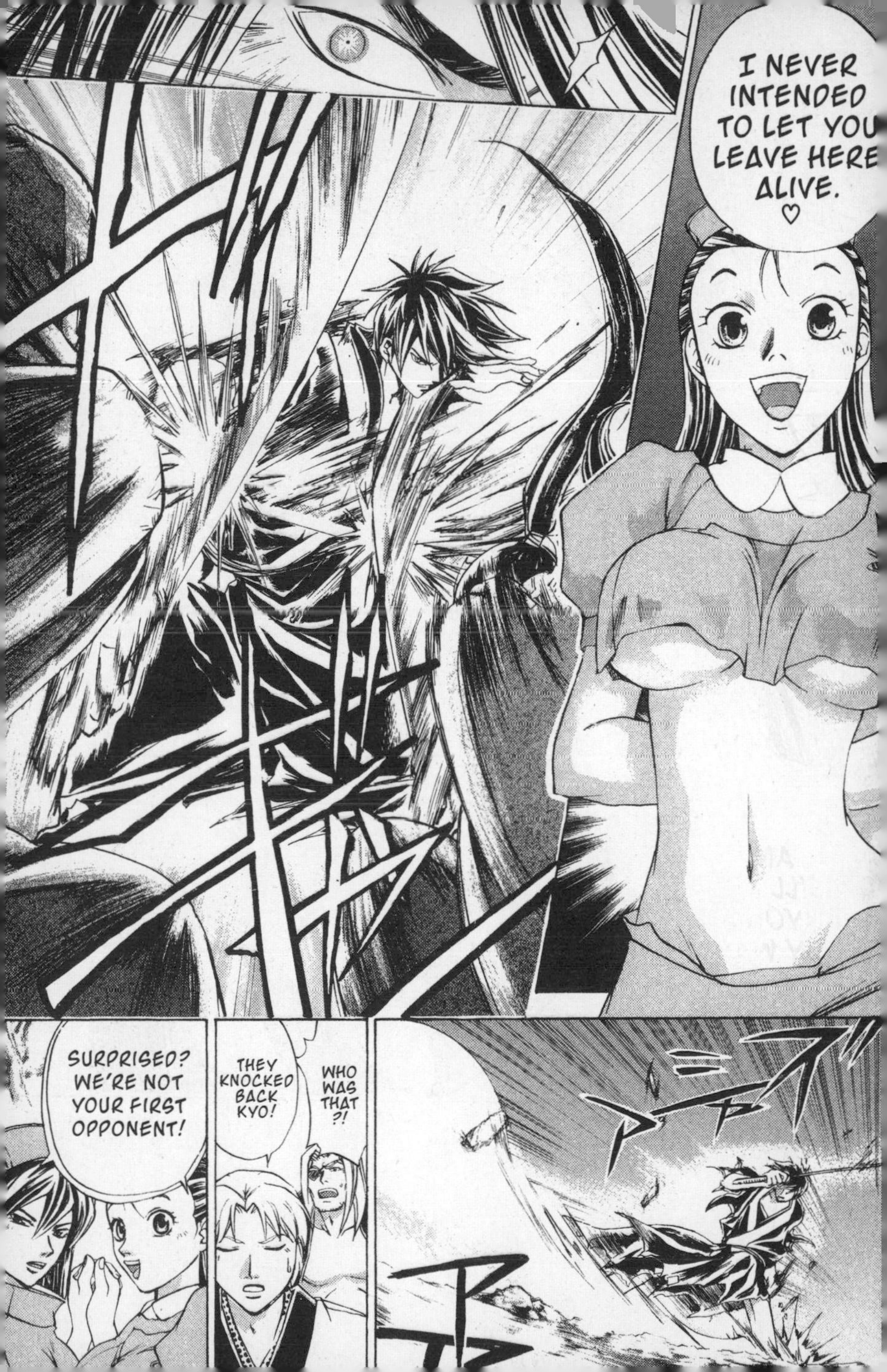
I NEVER INTENDED TO LET YOU LEAVE HERE ALIVE. ♡
WHO WAS THAT?!
THEY KNOCKED BACK KYO!
SURPRISED? WE'RE NOT YOUR FIRST OPPONENT!

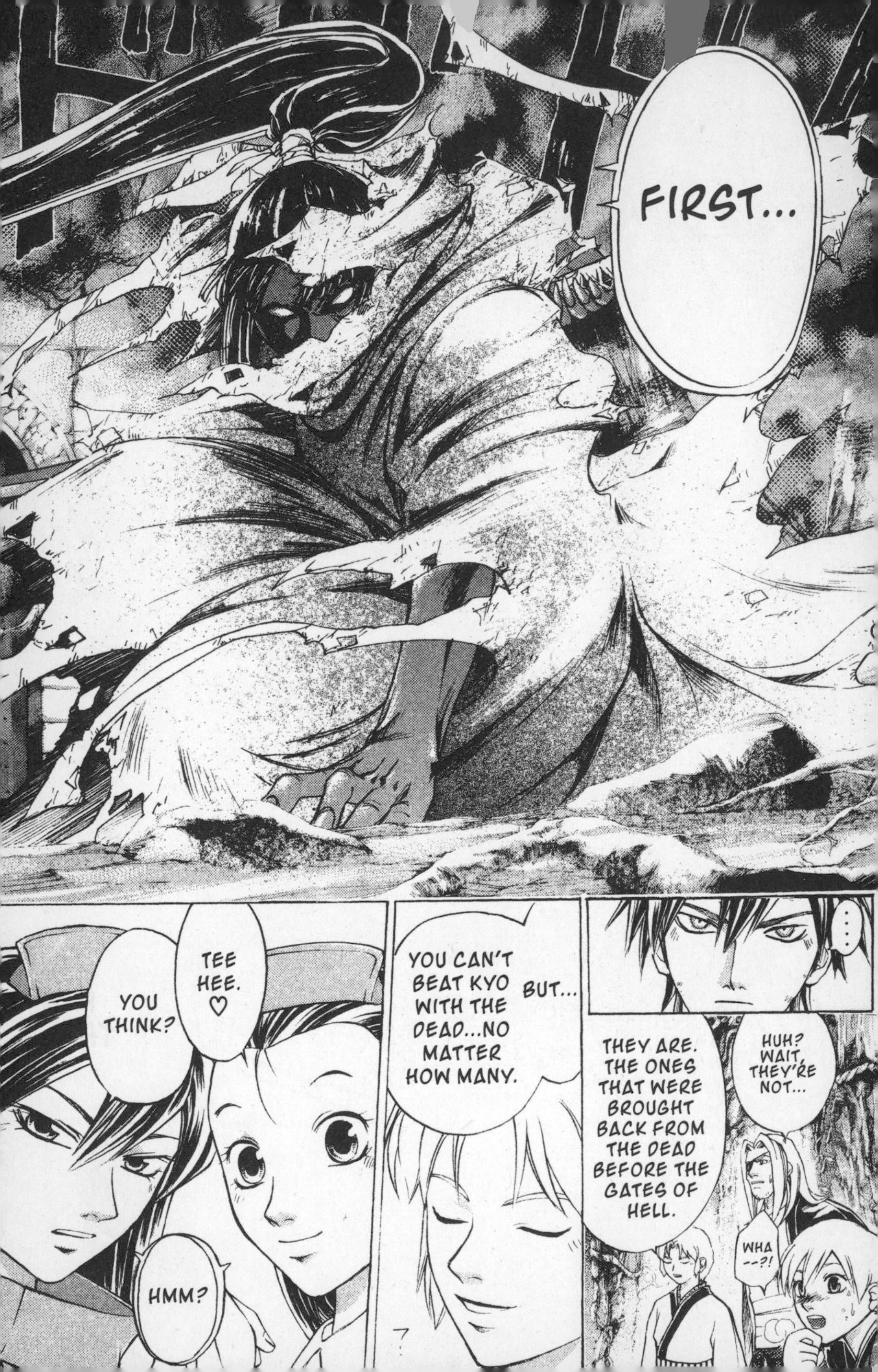
FIRST...
...
HUH? WAIT, THEY'RE NOT...
THEY ARE. THE ONES THAT WERE BROUGHT BACK FROM THE DEAD BEFORE THE GATES OF HELL.
WHA--?!
BUT...
YOU CAN'T BEAT KYO WITH THE DEAD...NO MATTER HOW MANY.
TEE HEE. ♡
YOU THINK?
HMM?

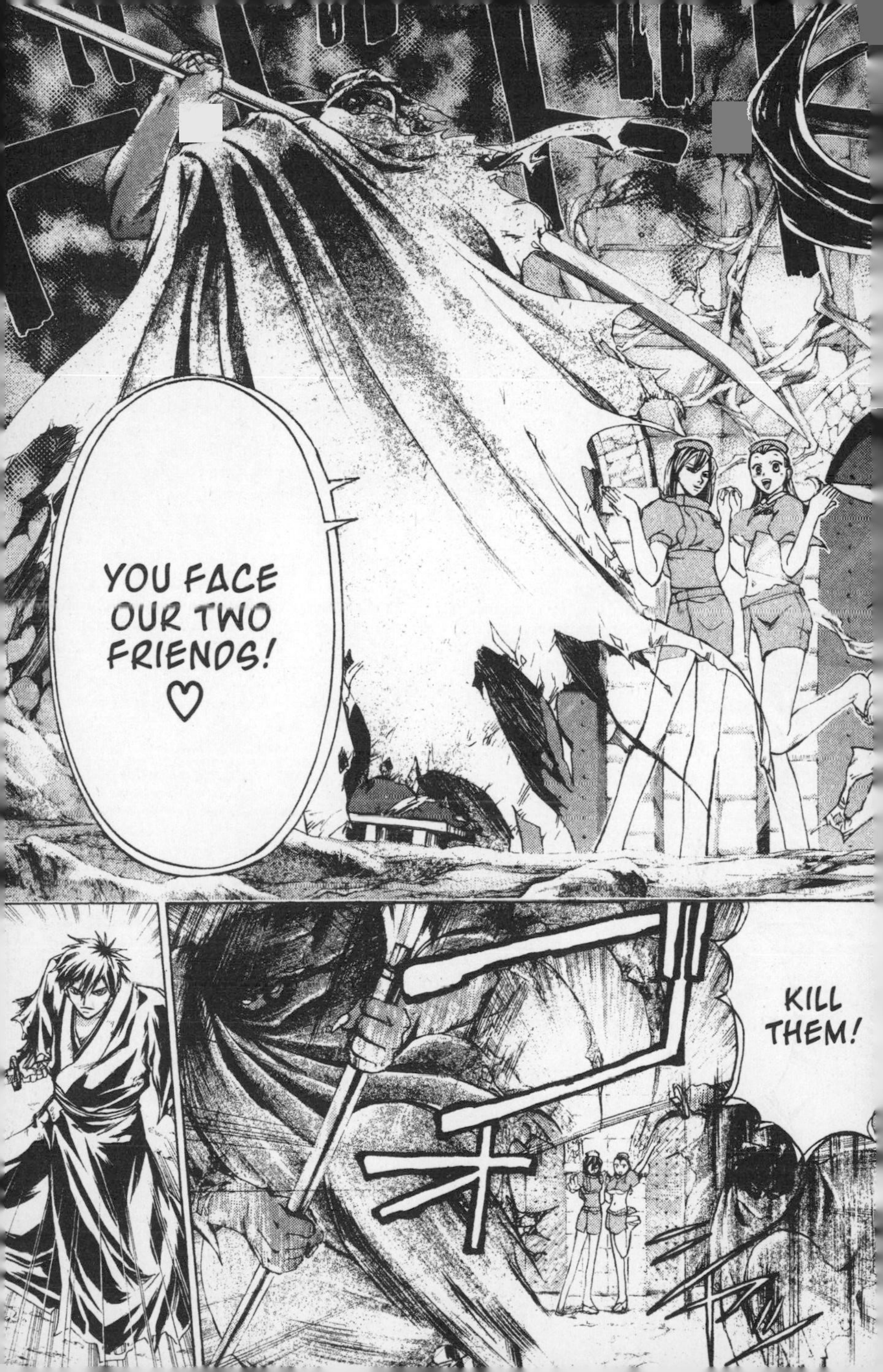
YOU FACE OUR TWO FRIENDS! ♡
KILL THEM!

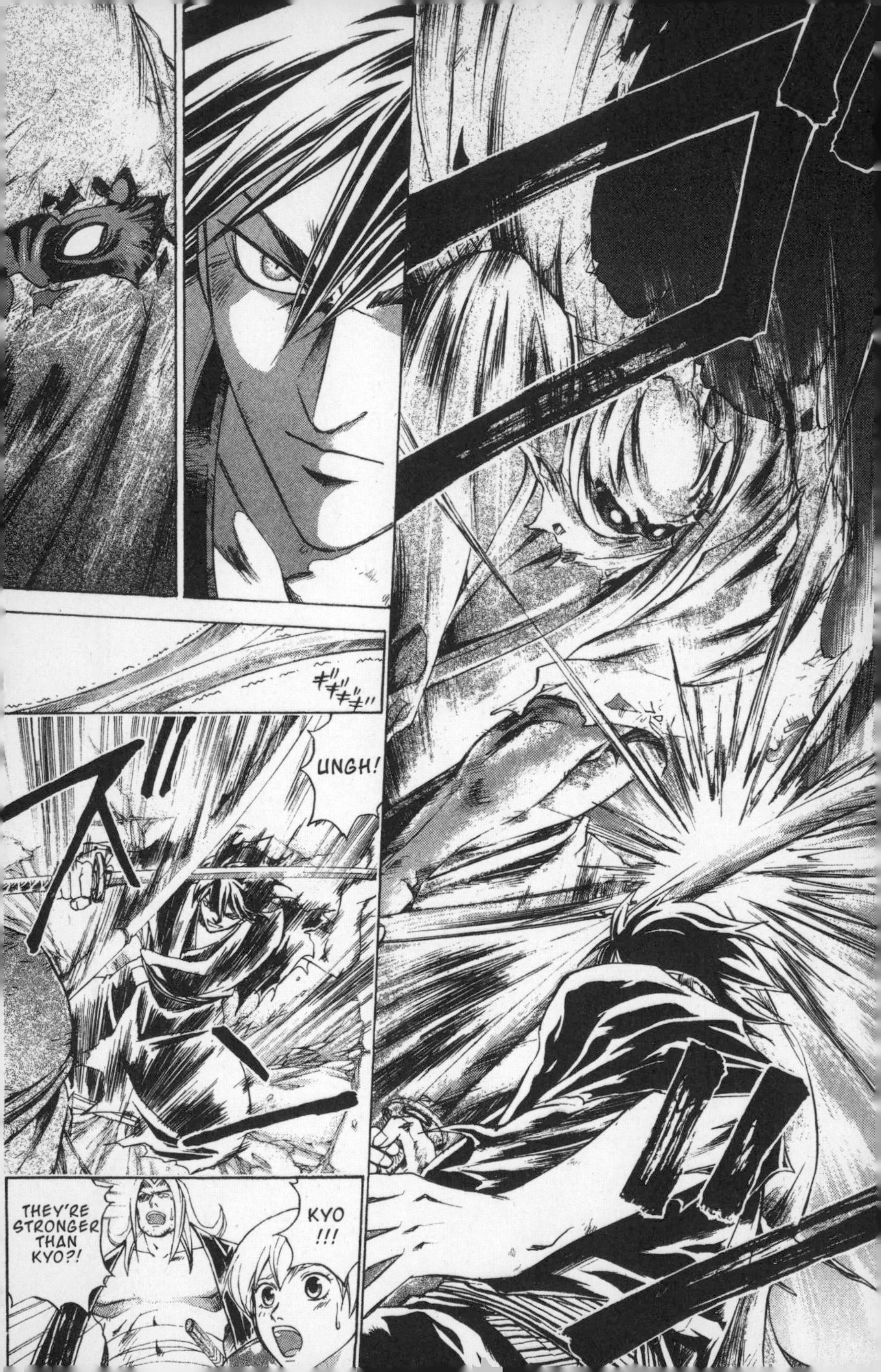
ギギギギ
UNGH!
KYO !!!
THEY'RE STRONGER THAN KYO?!

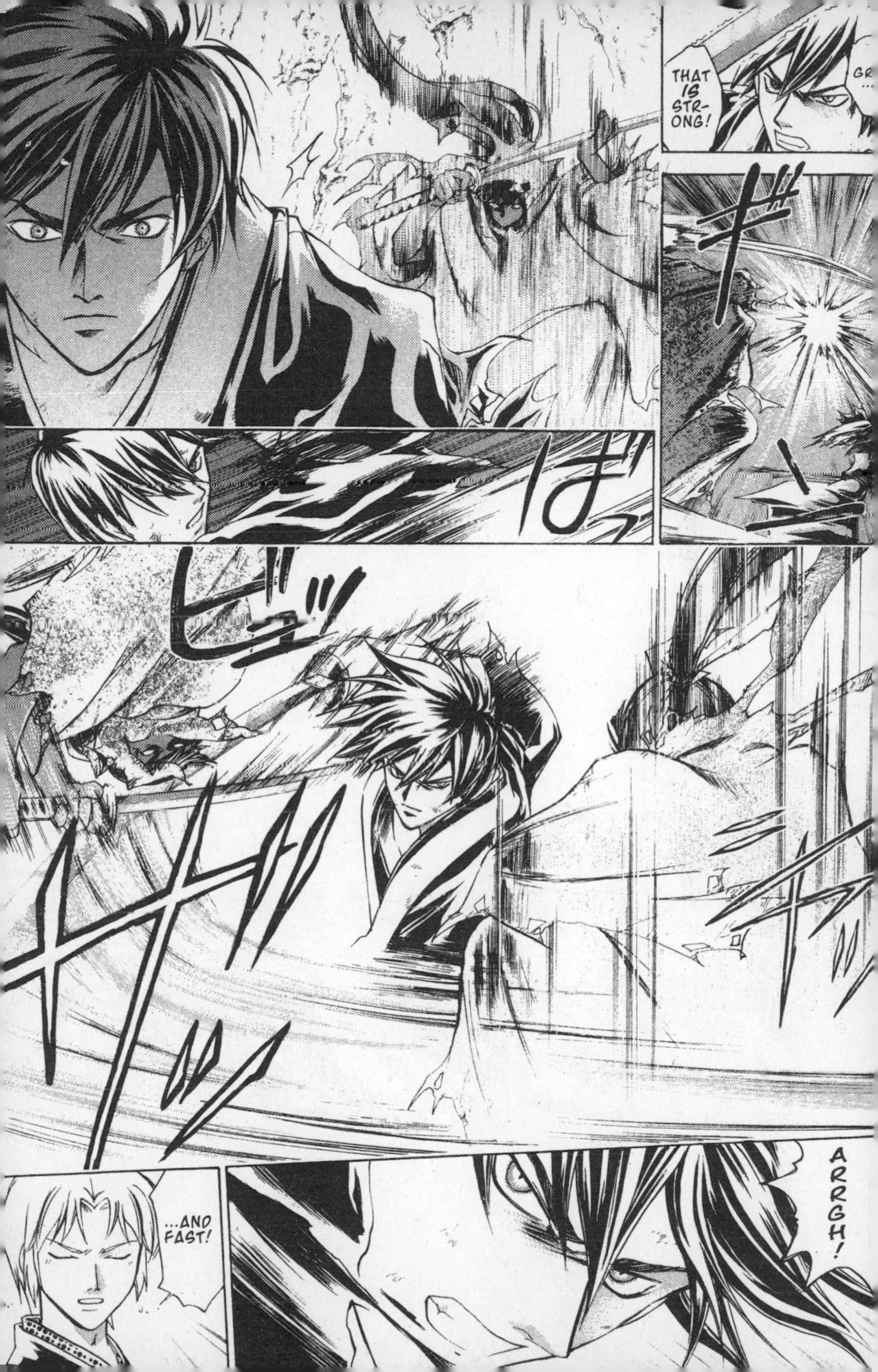
GR...
THAT IS STR-ONG!
ばっ
ARRGH!
...AND FAST!

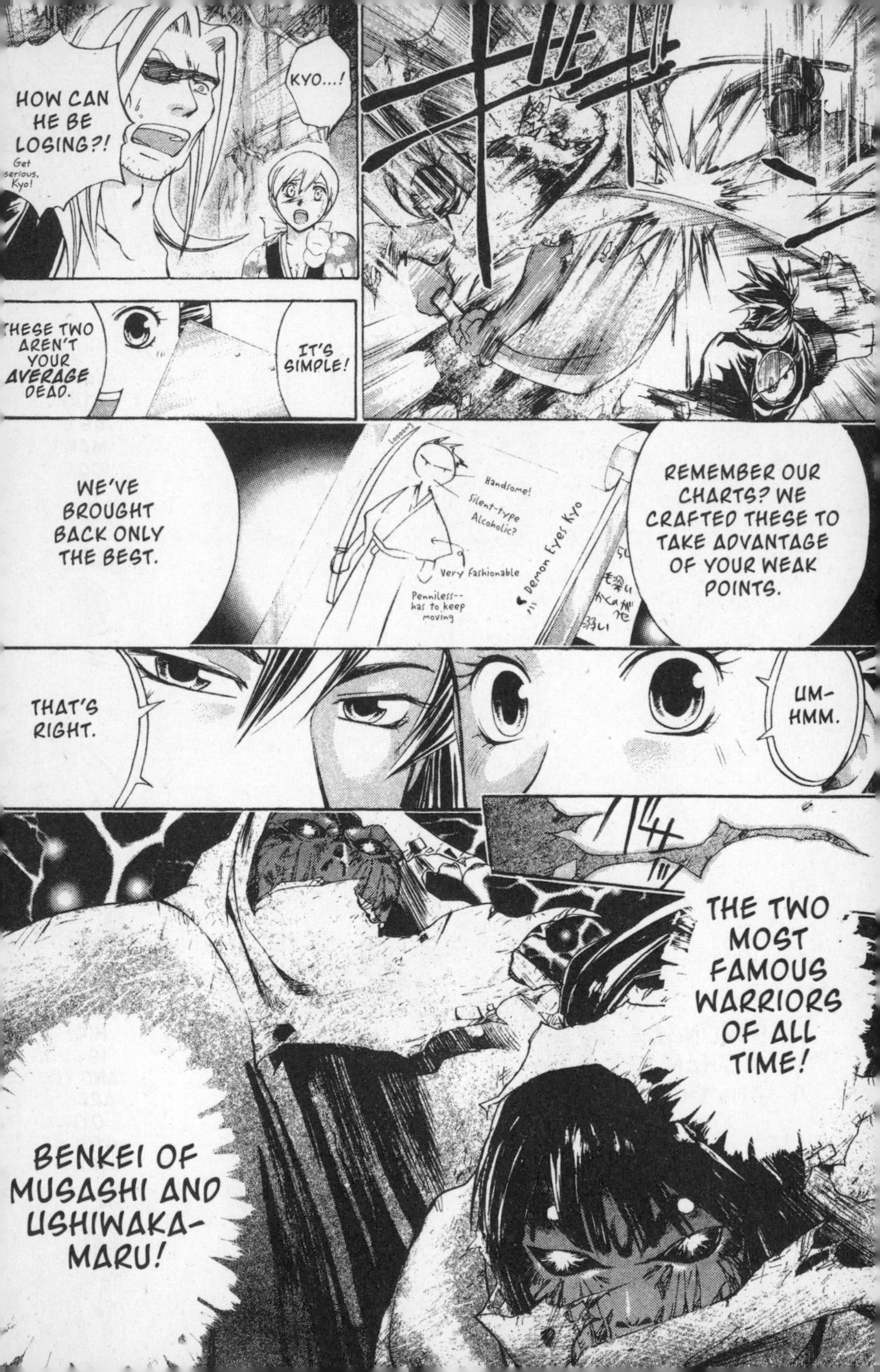
KYO...!
HOW CAN HE BE LOSING?!
Get serious, Kyo!
IT'S SIMPLE!
THESE TWO AREN'T YOUR AVERAGE DEAD.
REMEMBER OUR CHARTS? WE CRAFTED THESE TO TAKE ADVANTAGE OF YOUR WEAK POINTS.
Looooong
Handsome!
Silent-type
Alcoholic?
Very fashionable
Penniless-- has to keep moving
Demon Eyes Kyo
WE'VE BROUGHT BACK ONLY THE BEST.
UM-HMM.
THAT'S RIGHT.
THE TWO MOST FAMOUS WARRIORS OF ALL TIME!
BENKEI OF MUSASHI AND USHIWAKA-MARU!

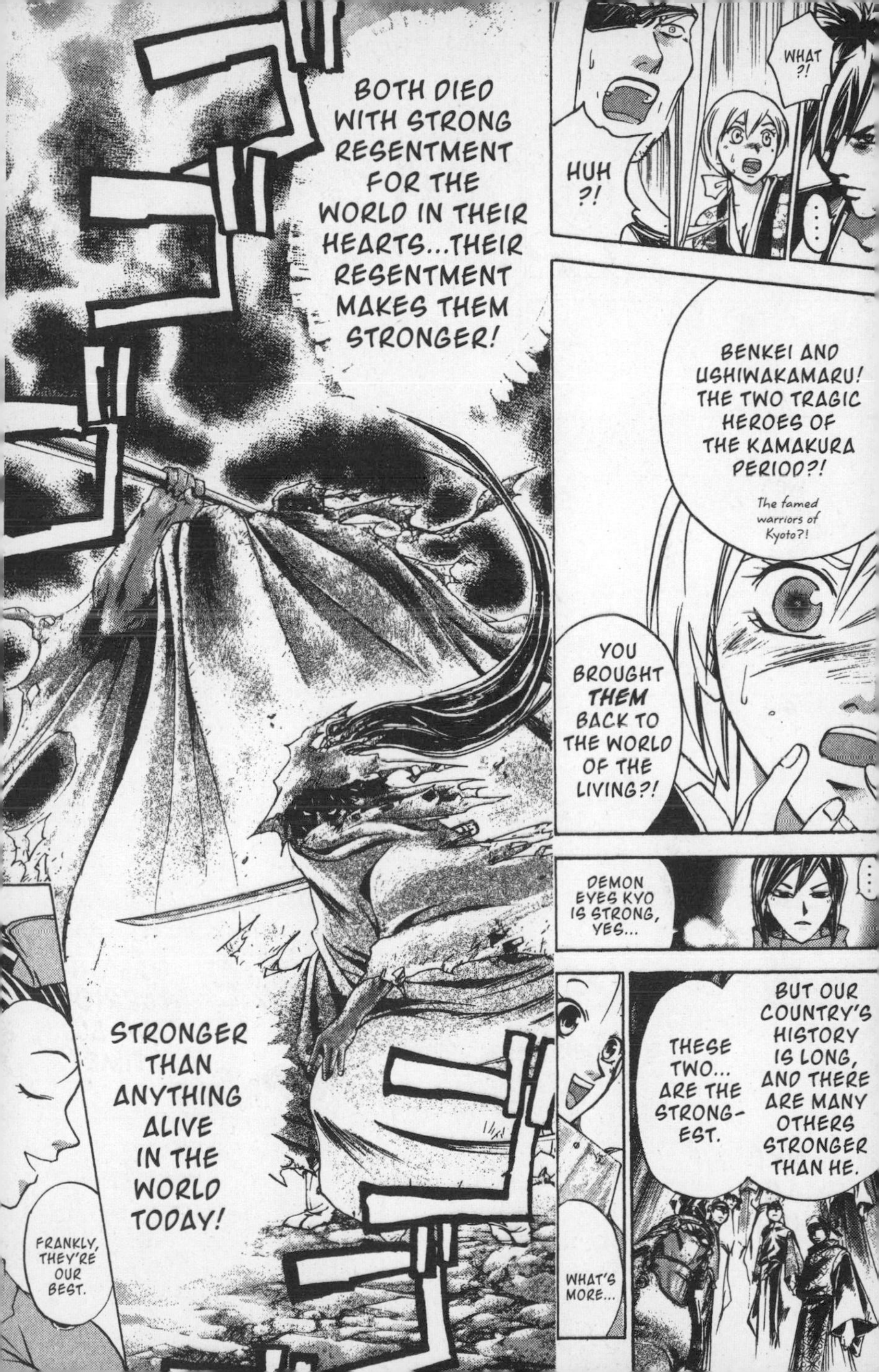
WHAT?!
...
HUH?!
BENKEI AND USHIWAKAMARU! THE TWO TRAGIC HEROES OF THE KAMAKURA PERIOD?!
The famed warriors of Kyoto?!
YOU BROUGHT *THEM* BACK TO THE WORLD OF THE LIVING?!
...
DEMON EYES KYO IS STRONG, YES...
BUT OUR COUNTRY'S HISTORY IS LONG, AND THERE ARE MANY OTHERS STRONGER THAN HE.
THESE TWO... ARE THE STRONG-EST.
WHAT'S MORE...
BOTH DIED WITH STRONG RESENTMENT FOR THE WORLD IN THEIR HEARTS...THEIR RESENTMENT MAKES THEM STRONGER!
STRONGER THAN ANYTHING ALIVE IN THE WORLD TODAY!
FRANKLY, THEY'RE OUR BEST.

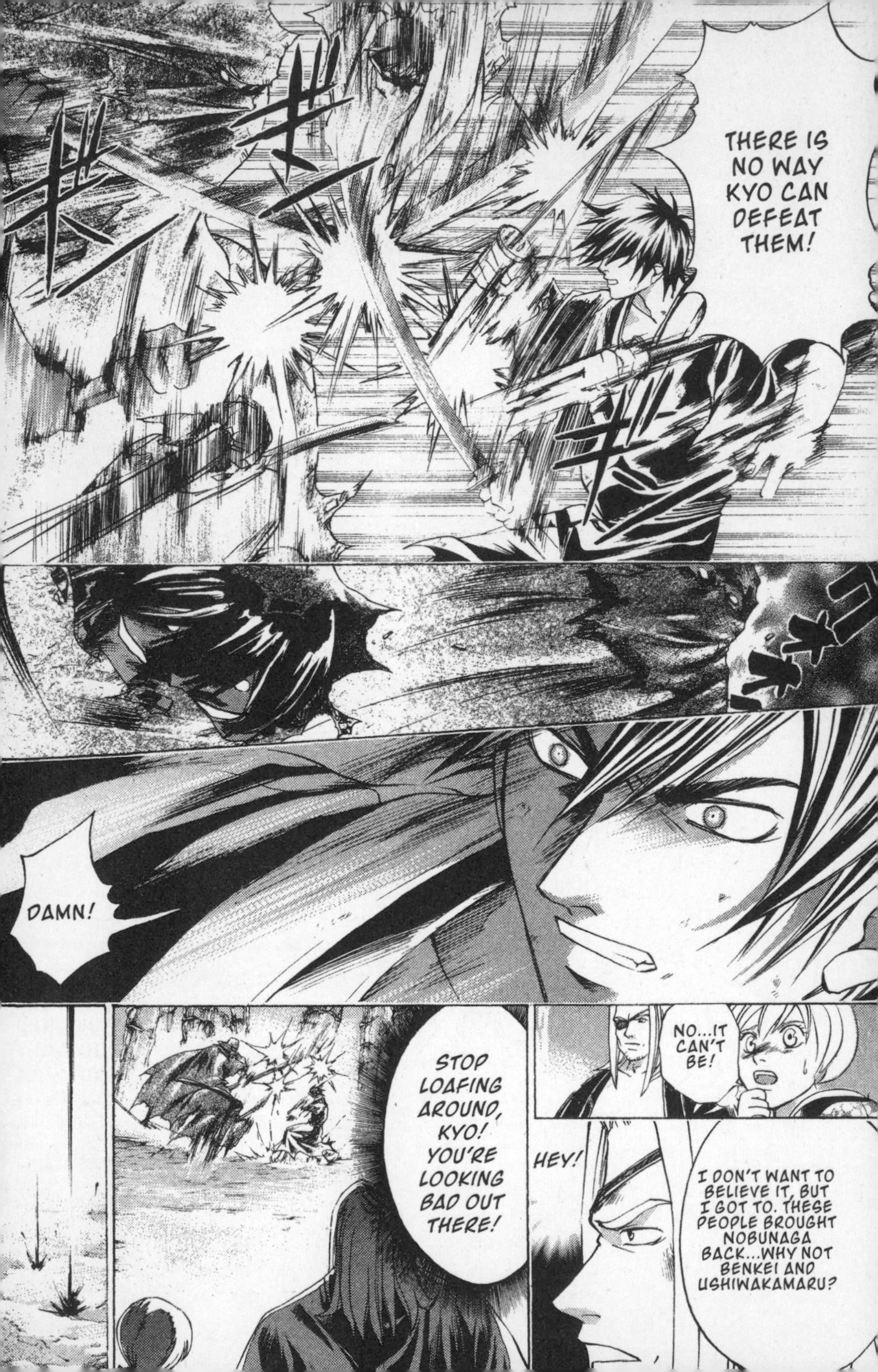
THERE IS NO WAY KYO CAN DEFEAT THEM!
DAMN!
NO...IT CAN'T BE!
STOP LOAFING AROUND, KYO! YOU'RE LOOKING BAD OUT THERE!
I DON'T WANT TO BELIEVE IT, BUT I GOT TO. THESE PEOPLE BROUGHT NOBUNAGA BACK...WHY NOT BENKEI AND USHIWAKAMARU?
HEY!

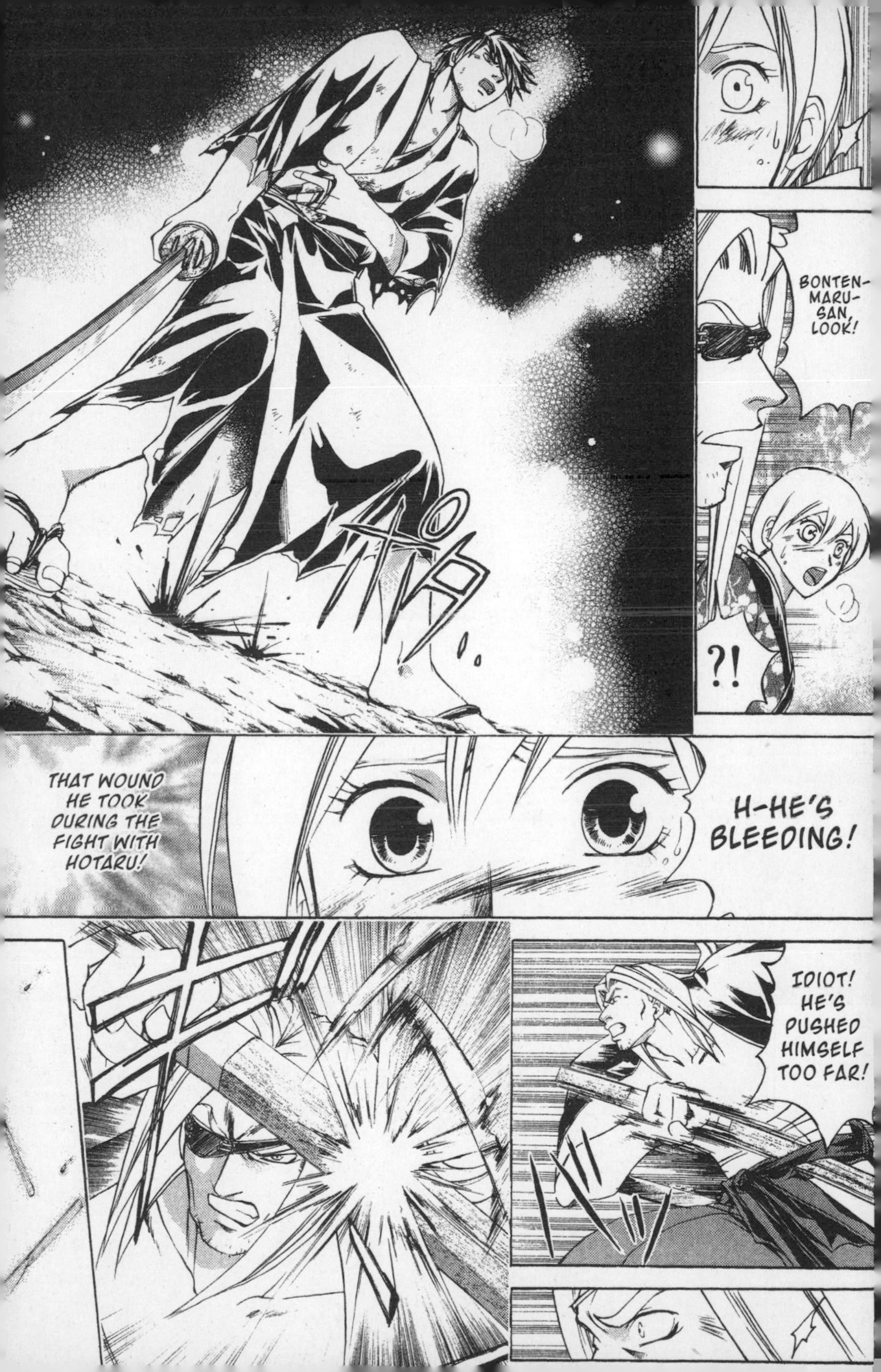
BONTEN-MARU-SAN, LOOK!
?!
H-HE'S BLEEDING!
THAT WOUND HE TOOK DURING THE FIGHT WITH HOTARU!
IDIOT! HE'S PUSHED HIMSELF TOO FAR!

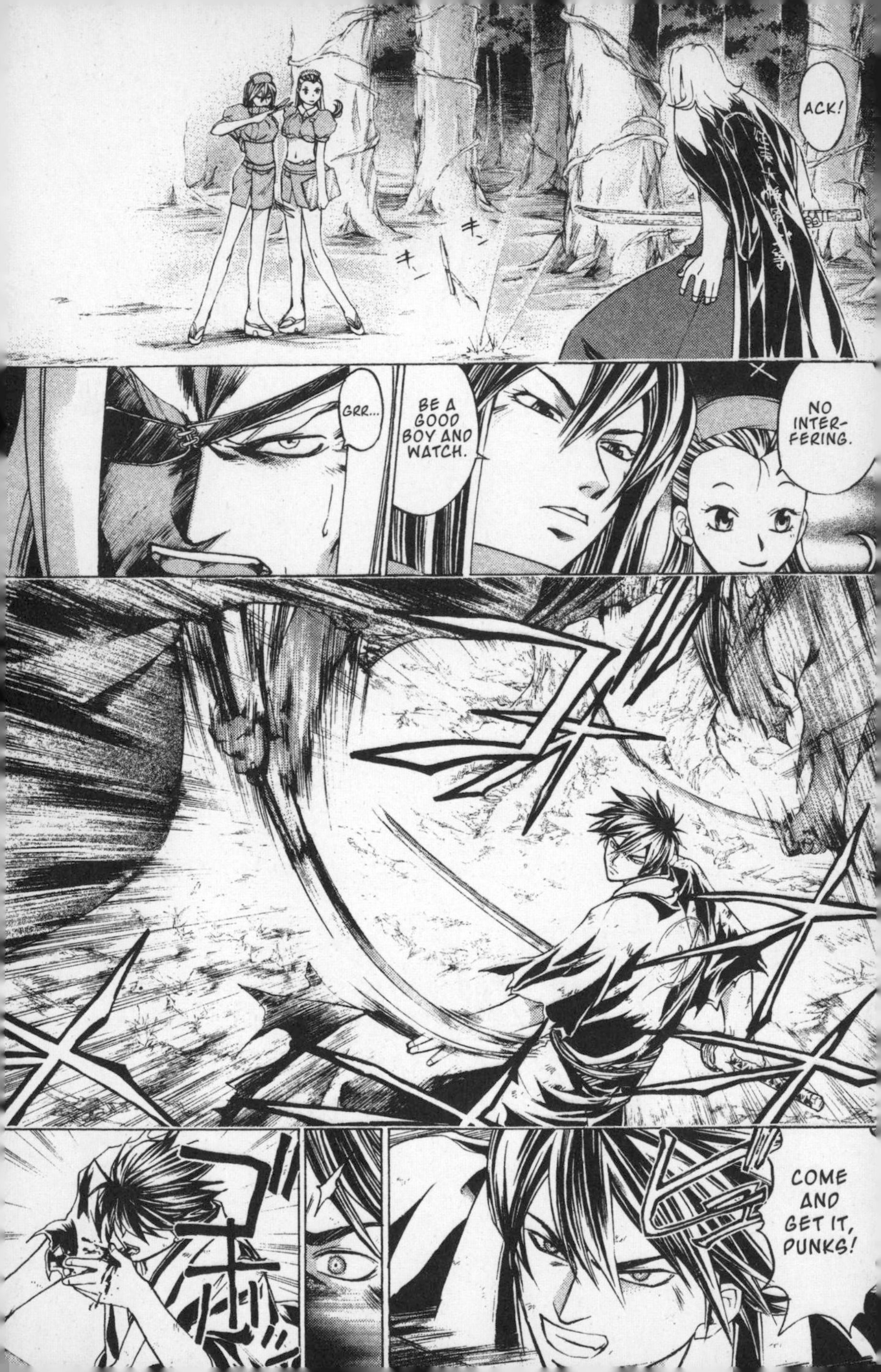
ACK!
キン
キン
NO INTER-FERING.
BE A GOOD BOY AND WATCH.
GRR...
COME AND GET IT, PUNKS!

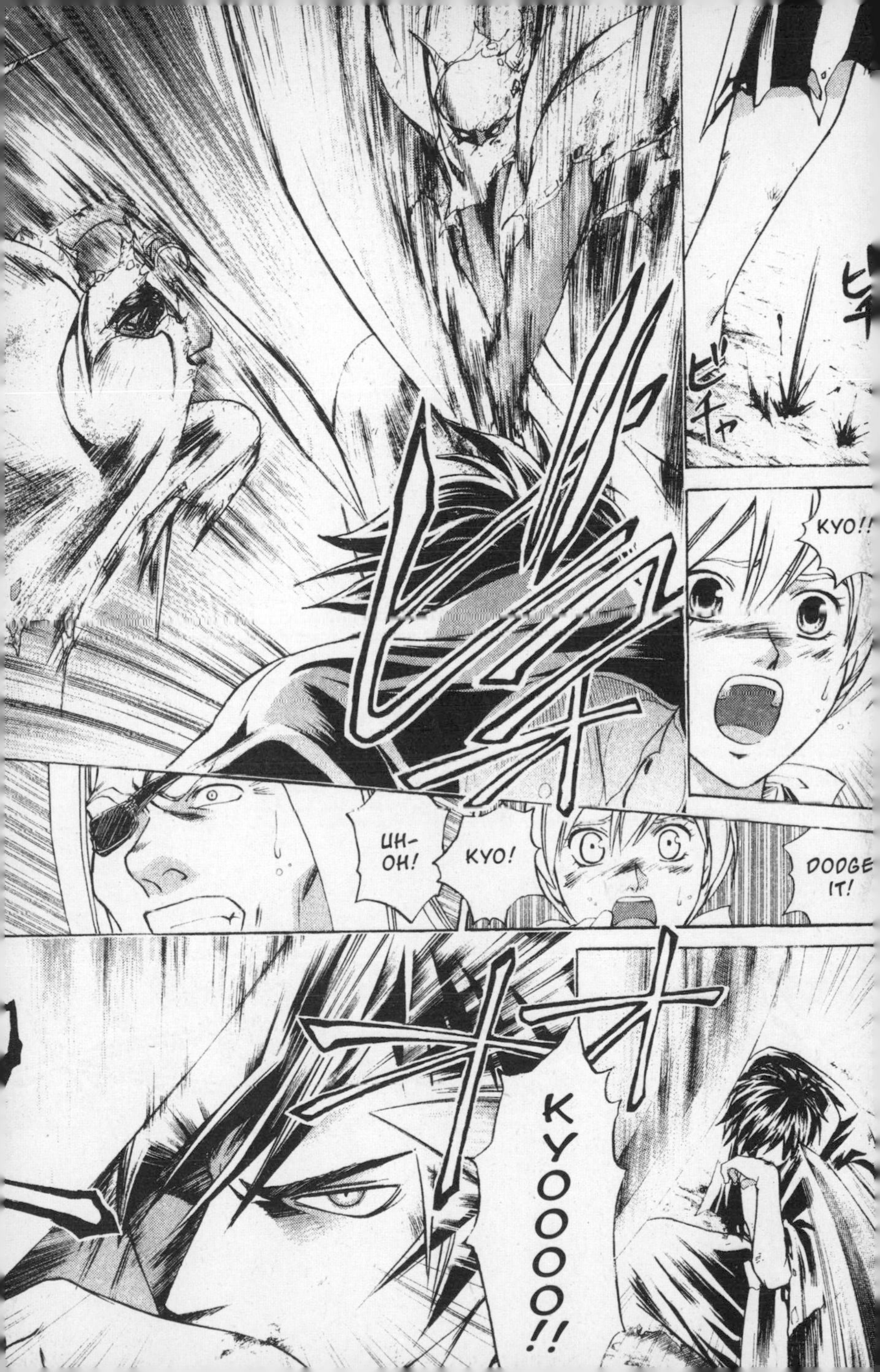
ビチャ
KYO!!
DODGE IT!
KYO!
UH-OH!
KYOOOOO!!

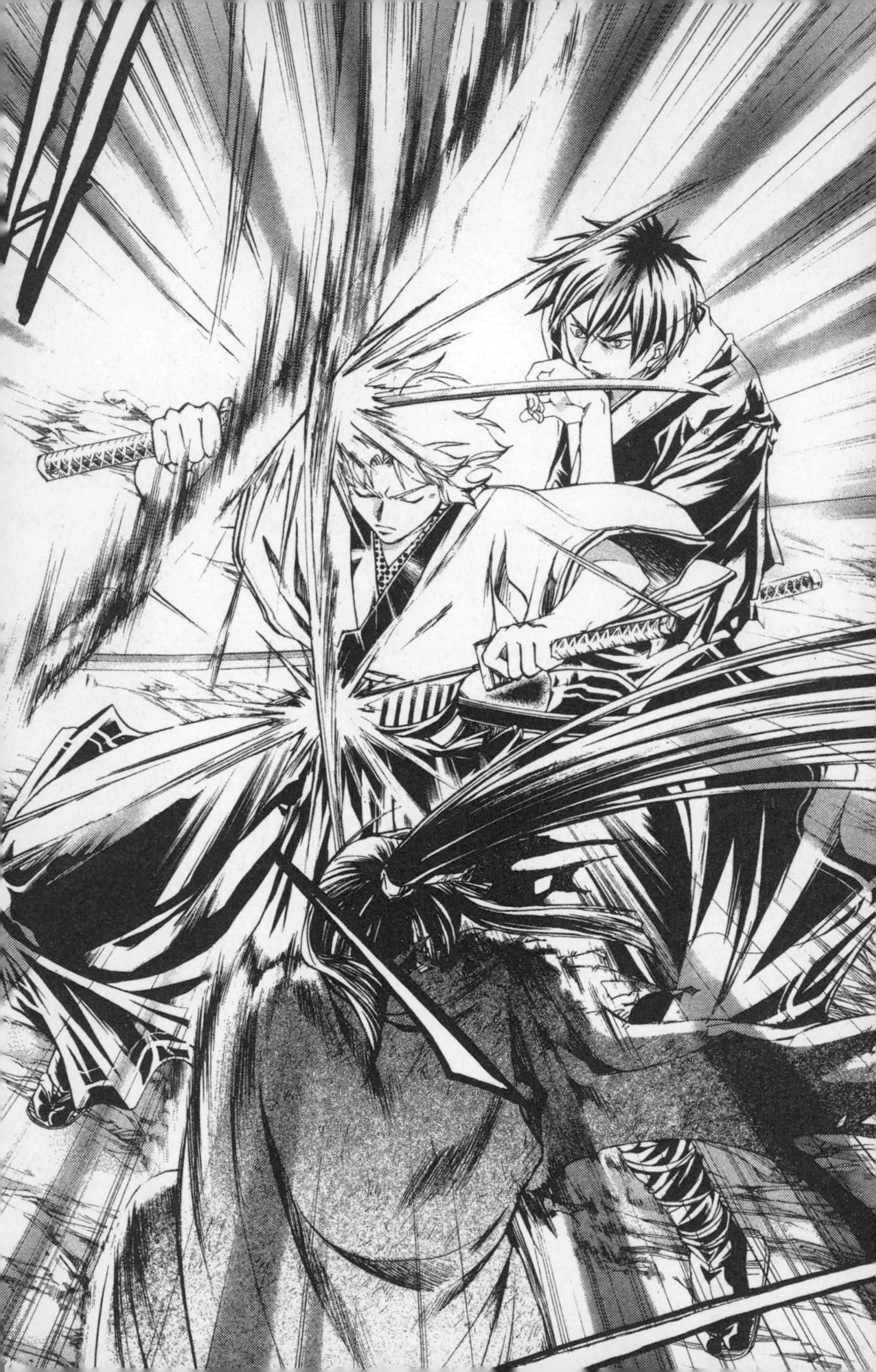

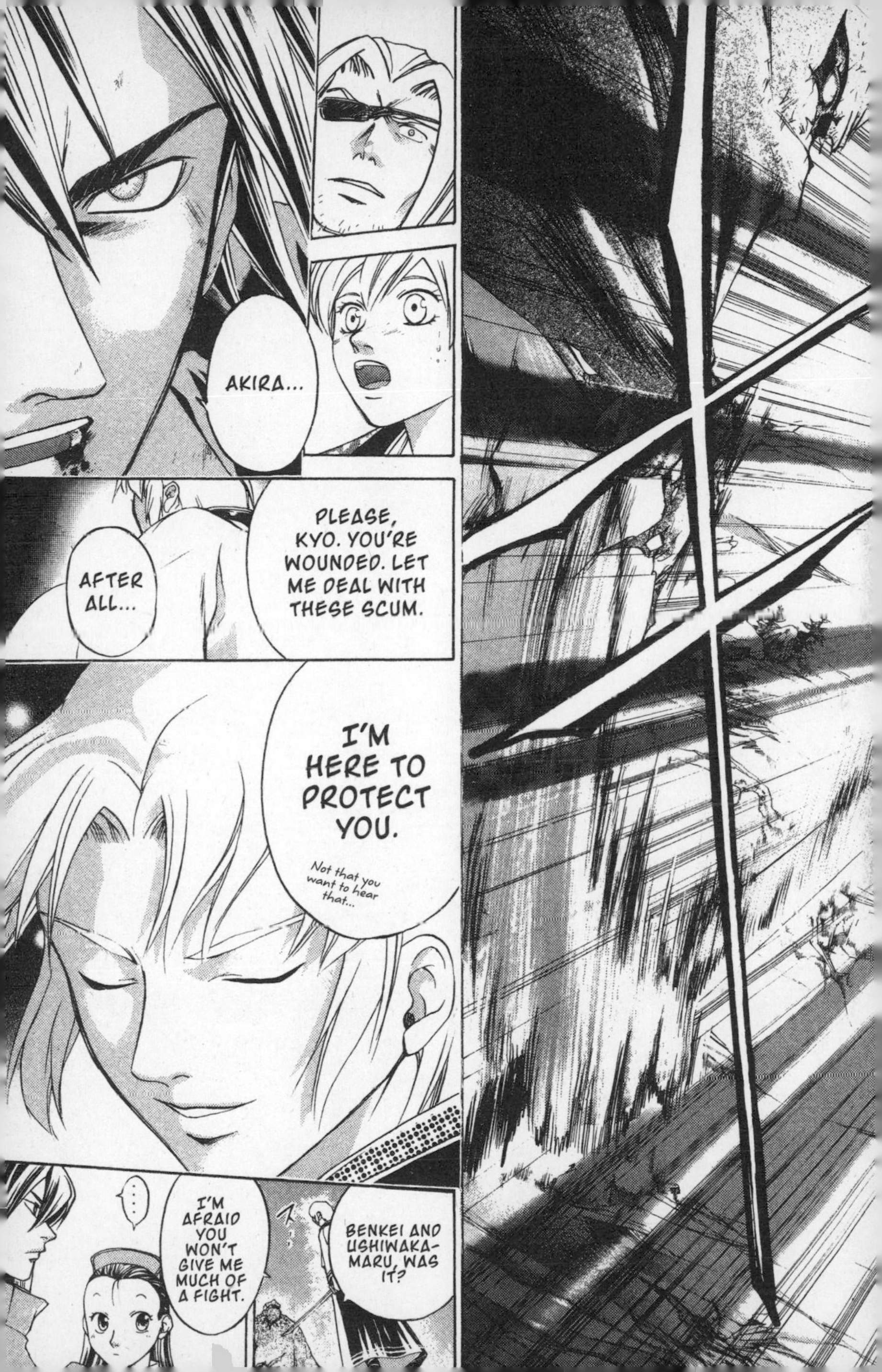
AKIRA...
PLEASE, KYO. YOU'RE WOUNDED. LET ME DEAL WITH THESE SCUM.
AFTER ALL...
I'M HERE TO PROTECT YOU.
Not that you want to hear that...
BENKEI AND USHIWAKA-MARU, WAS IT?
I'M AFRAID YOU WON'T GIVE ME MUCH OF A FIGHT.
...

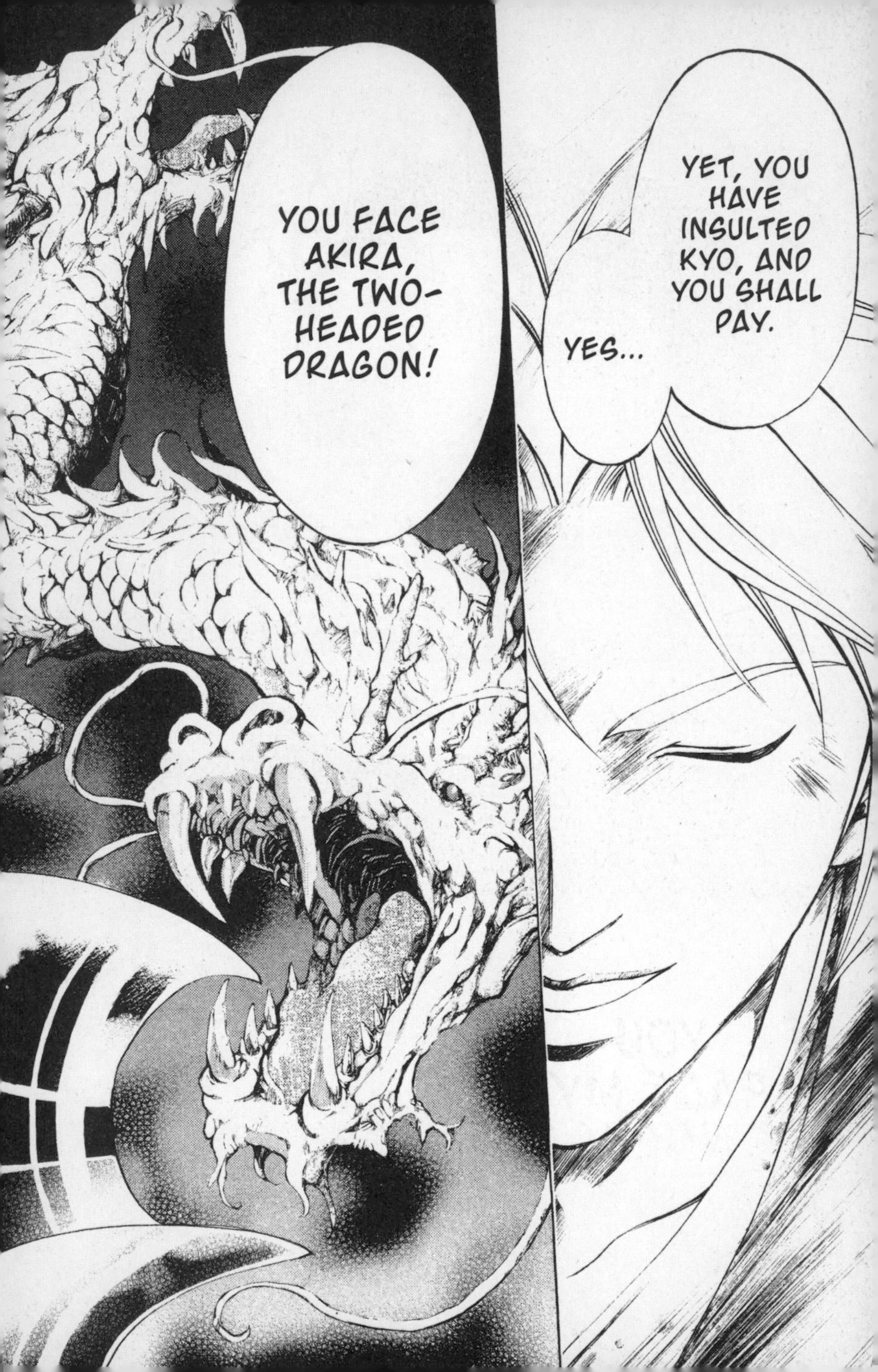
YES...
YET, YOU HAVE INSULTED KYO, AND YOU SHALL PAY.
YOU FACE AKIRA, THE TWO-HEADED DRAGON!

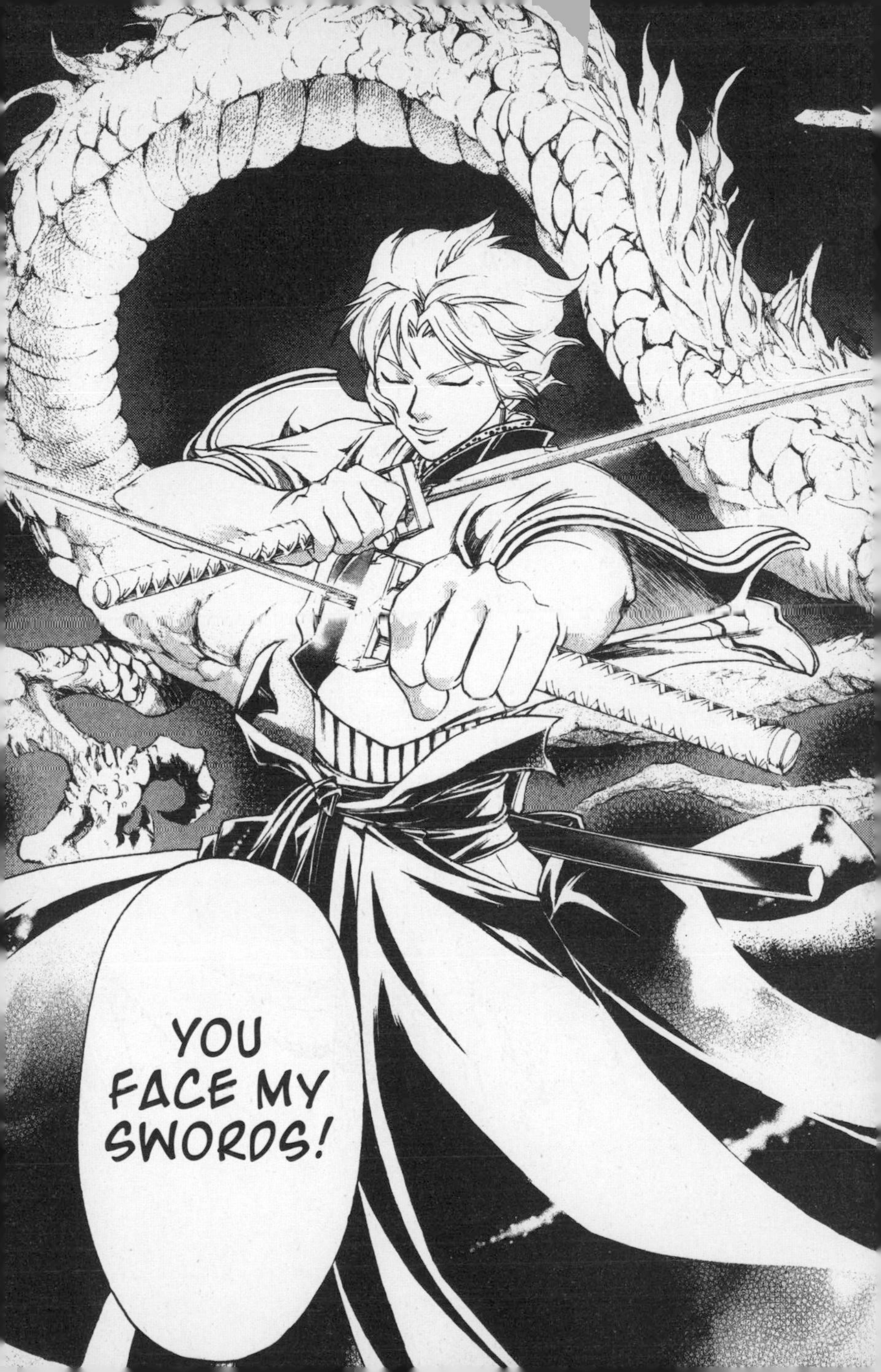
YOU FACE MY SWORDS!

The Kamijyo Report

Yo, Kamijyo here. Thanks to you, the reader, I have 17 volumes of SDK sitting here on my shelf. 17! That's a lot. Long, but oddly enough, only recently did I really realize, "Hey! I'm a manga artist!" (slow, I know.) For me, this is only the beginning! Let's do it!

That said, the cover for this month's volume isn't original--it was the color inside illustration from chapter 138. "No fair! That's recycling!" you might say, but I just wanted that picture in there. "Is it really that great a picture?" you ask? Yeah, well, it was fun to draw, okay?

THE SECRET OF SHINREI

A WHILE AGO, I GOT LOTS OF LETTERS SAYING, "WE LIKE SHINREI!"
HUH? SHINREI?! NEVER WOULDA GUESSED.
DOESN'T HIS HEAD KINDA LOOK LIKE A TIGER MASK?
I WONDER WHAT THEY LIKE ABOUT HIM?
THEN AGAIN, HE IS PRETTY STRONG...HIS EVERY MOVE, A WORK OF ART!
HIS TECHNIQUES ARE WELL-NAMED, AND HE'S A GOOD GUY, SO I GUESS IT'S ONLY NATURAL...
YEAH YEAH!
THAT'S RIGHT! SIS LIKED HIM, TOO. I'LL ASK HER WHY.
天狗
SHINREI? YEAH, HE'S GREAT!
BOASTER
YEAH, YEAH, I KNOW. BUT WHY?
WHA-AAT?
IT'S HIS FACE, OF COURSE!
ボキッ
...
YOU SURE?
SHOULD I BE HAPPY? OR DEPRESSED?

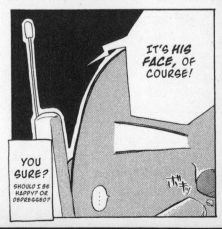

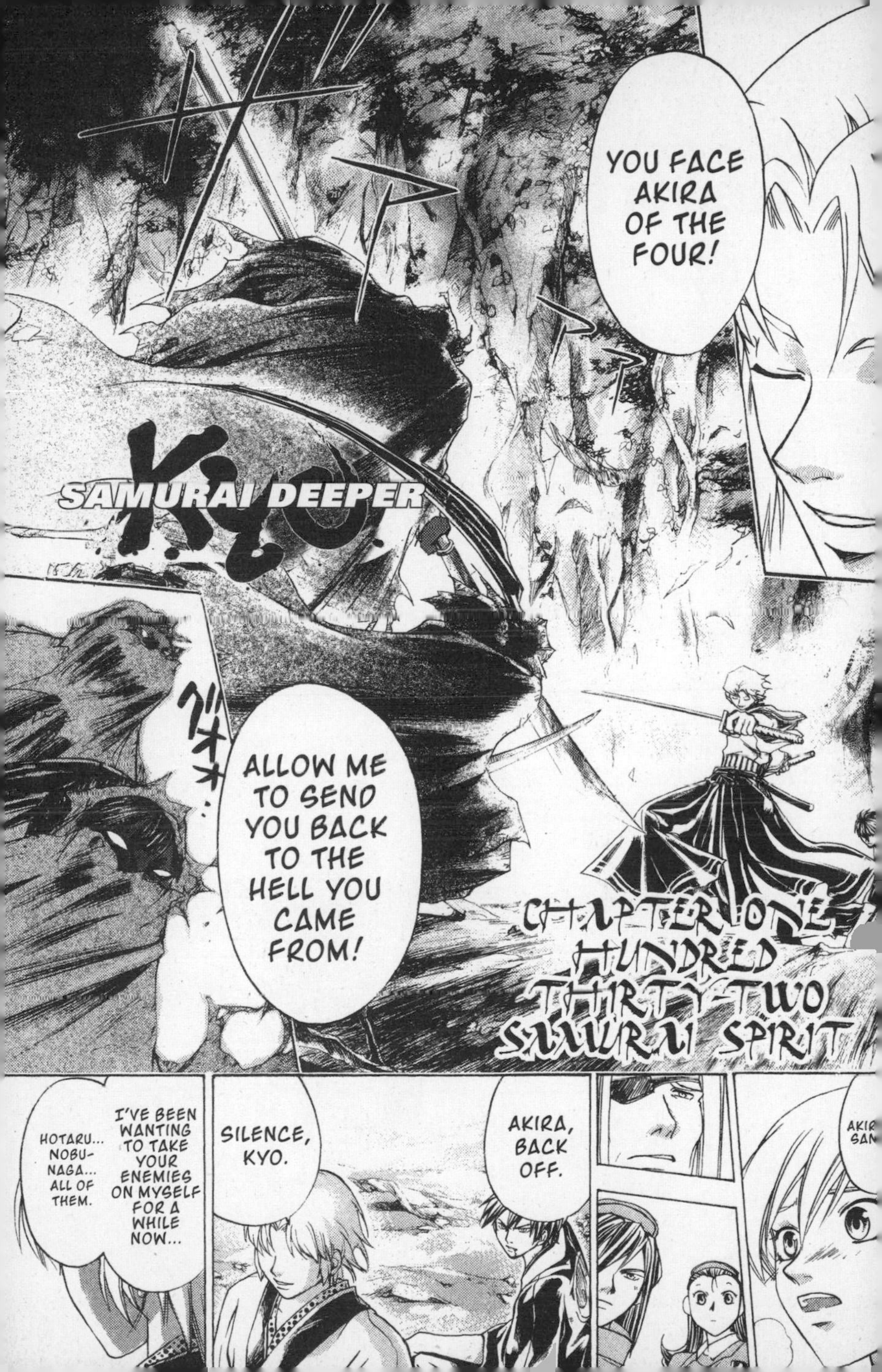
YOU FACE AKIRA OF THE FOUR!
SAMURAI DEEPER KYO
ALLOW ME TO SEND YOU BACK TO THE HELL YOU CAME FROM!
CHAPTER ONE HUNDRED THIRTY-TWO SAMURAI SPIRIT
AKIR SAN
AKIRA, BACK OFF.
SILENCE, KYO.
I'VE BEEN WANTING TO TAKE YOUR ENEMIES ON MYSELF FOR A WHILE NOW...
HOTARU... NOBU-NAGA... ALL OF THEM.

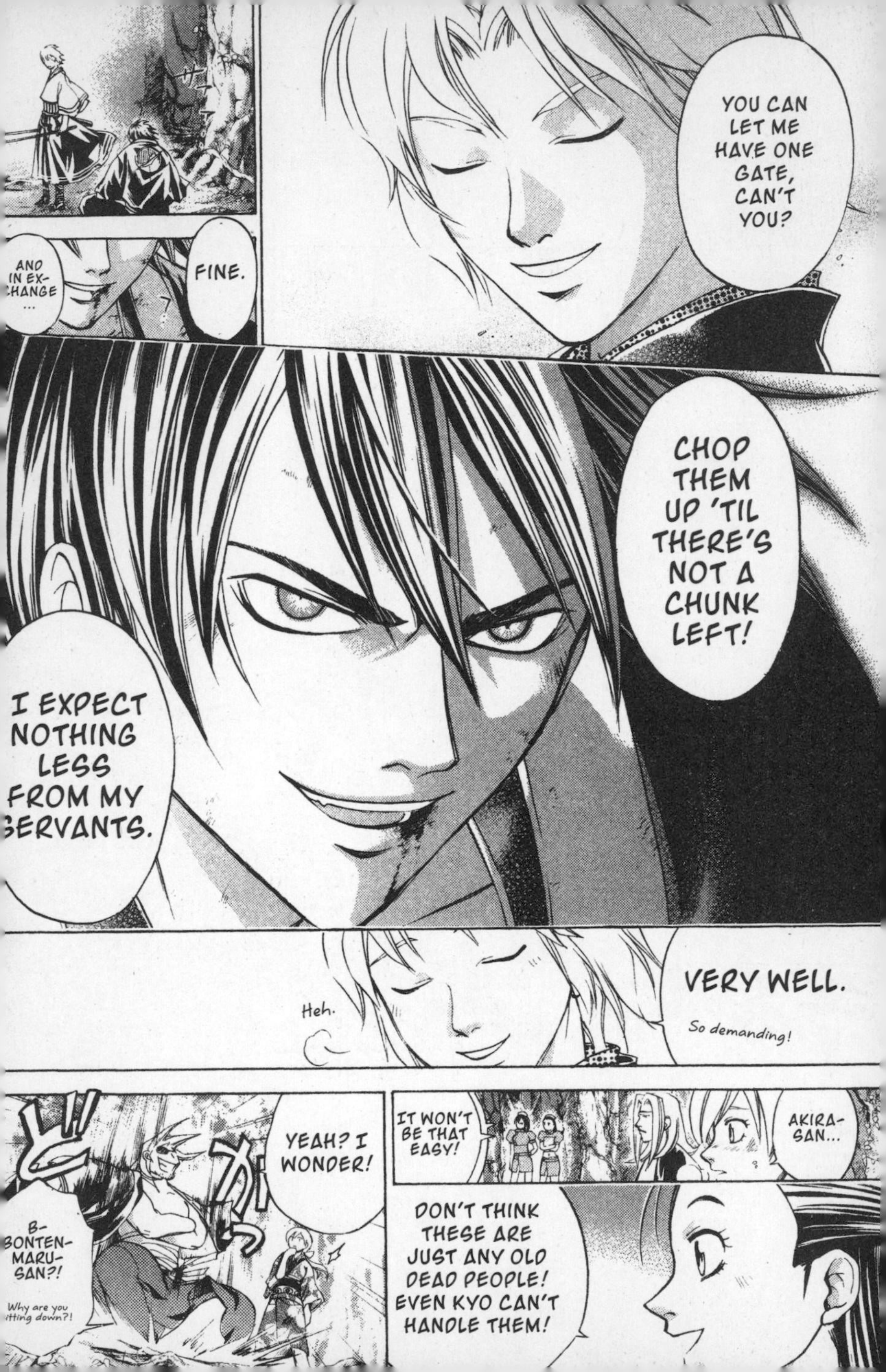
YOU CAN LET ME HAVE ONE GATE, CAN'T YOU?
FINE.
AND IN EX-CHANGE...
CHOP THEM UP 'TIL THERE'S NOT A CHUNK LEFT!
I EXPECT NOTHING LESS FROM MY SERVANTS.
VERY WELL.
So demanding!
Heh.
AKIRA-SAN...
IT WON'T BE THAT EASY!
DON'T THINK THESE ARE JUST ANY OLD DEAD PEOPLE! EVEN KYO CAN'T HANDLE THEM!
YEAH? I WONDER!
B-BONTEN-MARU-SAN?!
Why are you itting down?!

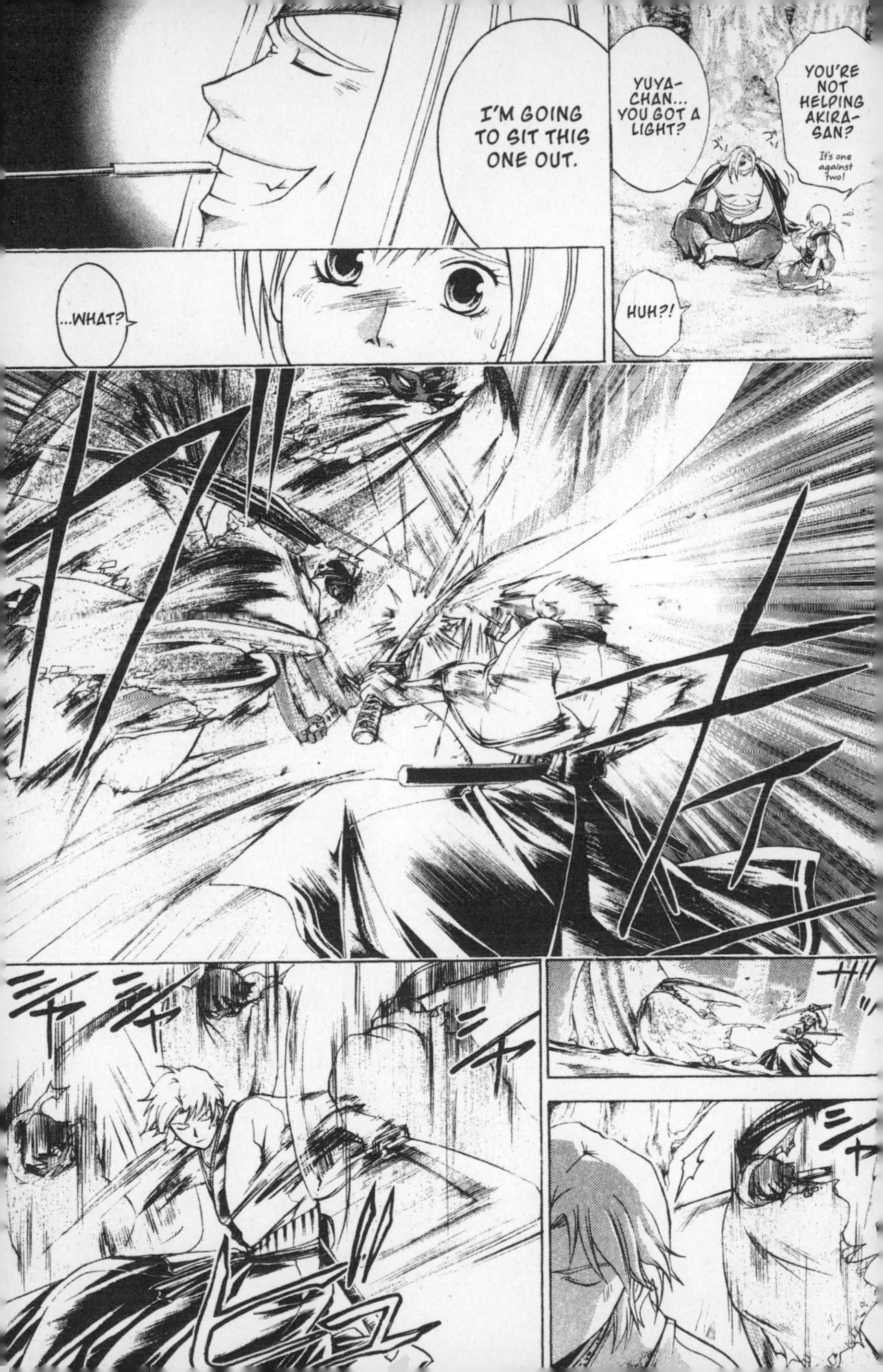
YOU'RE NOT HELPING AKIRA-SAN?
It's one against two!
YUYA-CHAN... YOU GOT A LIGHT?
HUH?!
I'M GOING TO SIT THIS ONE OUT.
...WHAT?

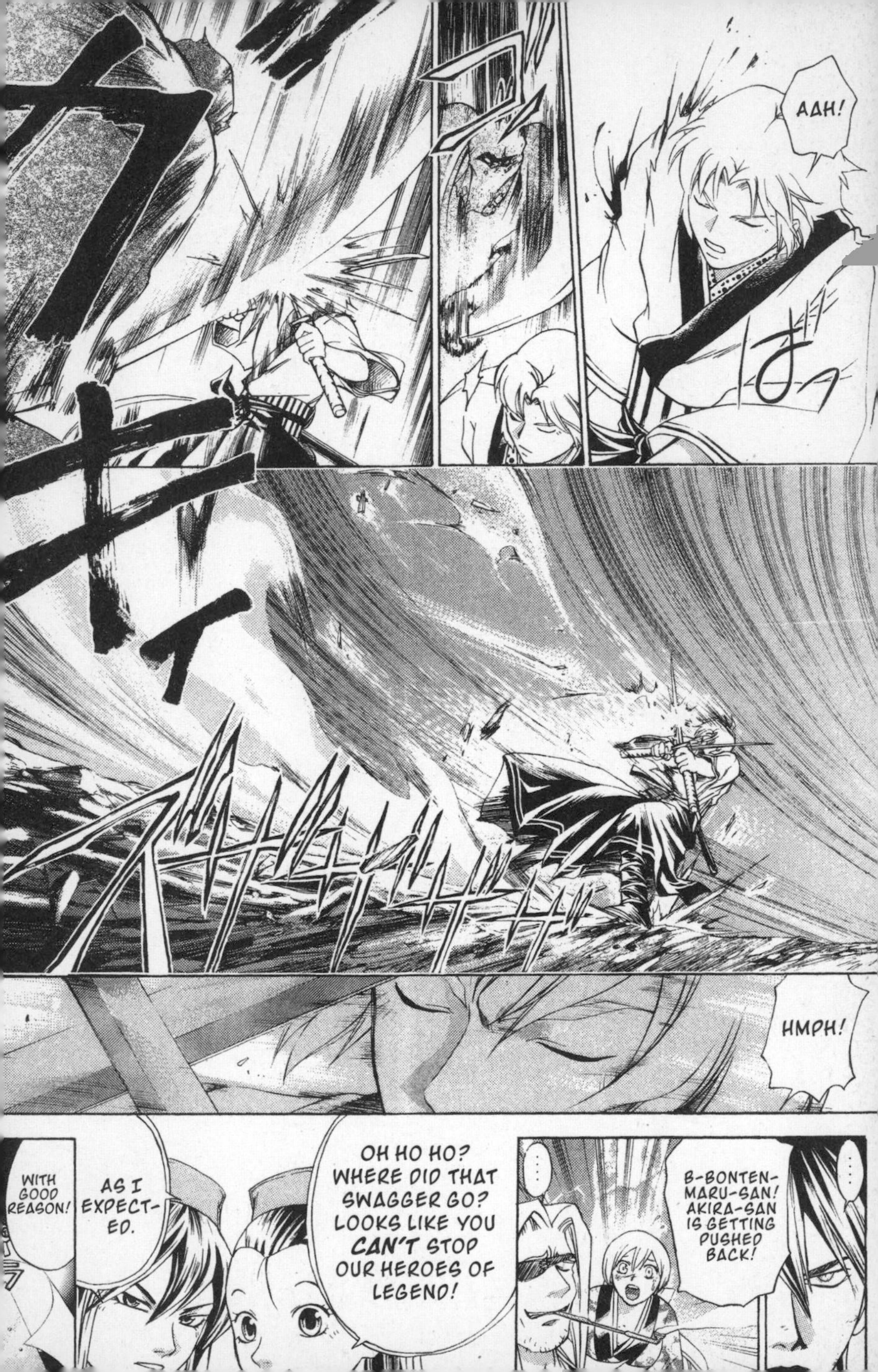
AAH!
ばっ
HMPH!
...
B-BONTEN-MARU-SAN! AKIRA-SAN IS GETTING PUSHED BACK!
...
OH HO HO? WHERE DID THAT SWAGGER GO? LOOKS LIKE YOU **CAN'T** STOP OUR HEROES OF LEGEND!
AS I EXPECT-ED.
WITH GOOD REASON!

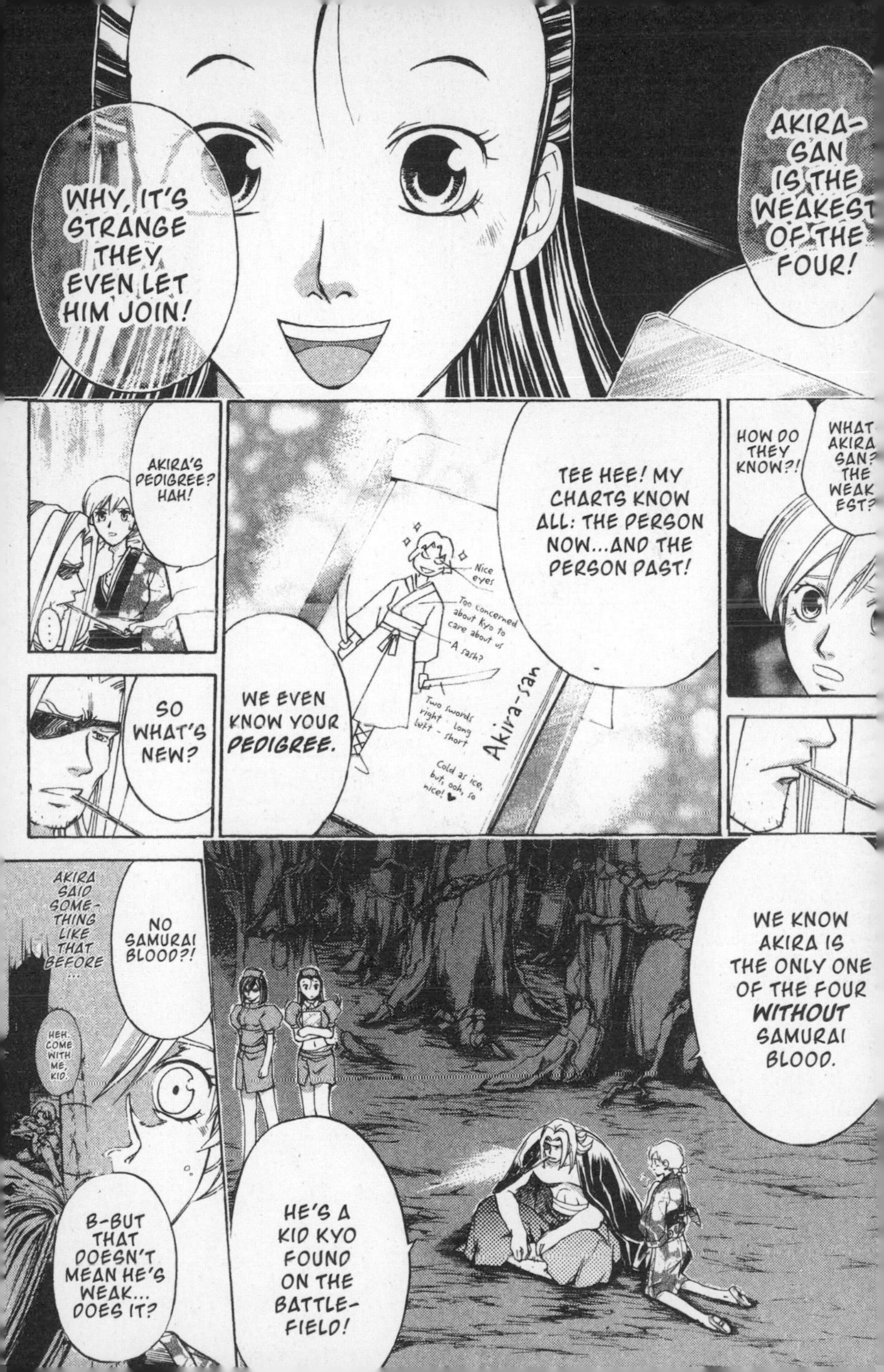
AKIRA-SAN IS THE WEAKEST OF THE FOUR!
WHY, IT'S STRANGE THEY EVEN LET HIM JOIN!
WHAT- AKIRA SAN? THE WEAKEST?
HOW DO THEY KNOW?!
TEE HEE! MY CHARTS KNOW ALL: THE PERSON NOW...AND THE PERSON PAST!
Nice eyes
Too concerned about Kyo to care about us
A sash?
Two swords right - long left - short
Cold as ice, but, ooh, so nice! ♥
Akira-san
WE EVEN KNOW YOUR PEDIGREE.
AKIRA'S PEDIGREE? HAH!
...
SO WHAT'S NEW?
WE KNOW AKIRA IS THE ONLY ONE OF THE FOUR WITHOUT SAMURAI BLOOD.
HE'S A KID KYO FOUND ON THE BATTLEFIELD!
NO SAMURAI BLOOD?!
AKIRA SAID SOMETHING LIKE THAT BEFORE...
HEH. COME WITH ME, KID.
B-BUT THAT DOESN'T MEAN HE'S WEAK... DOES IT?

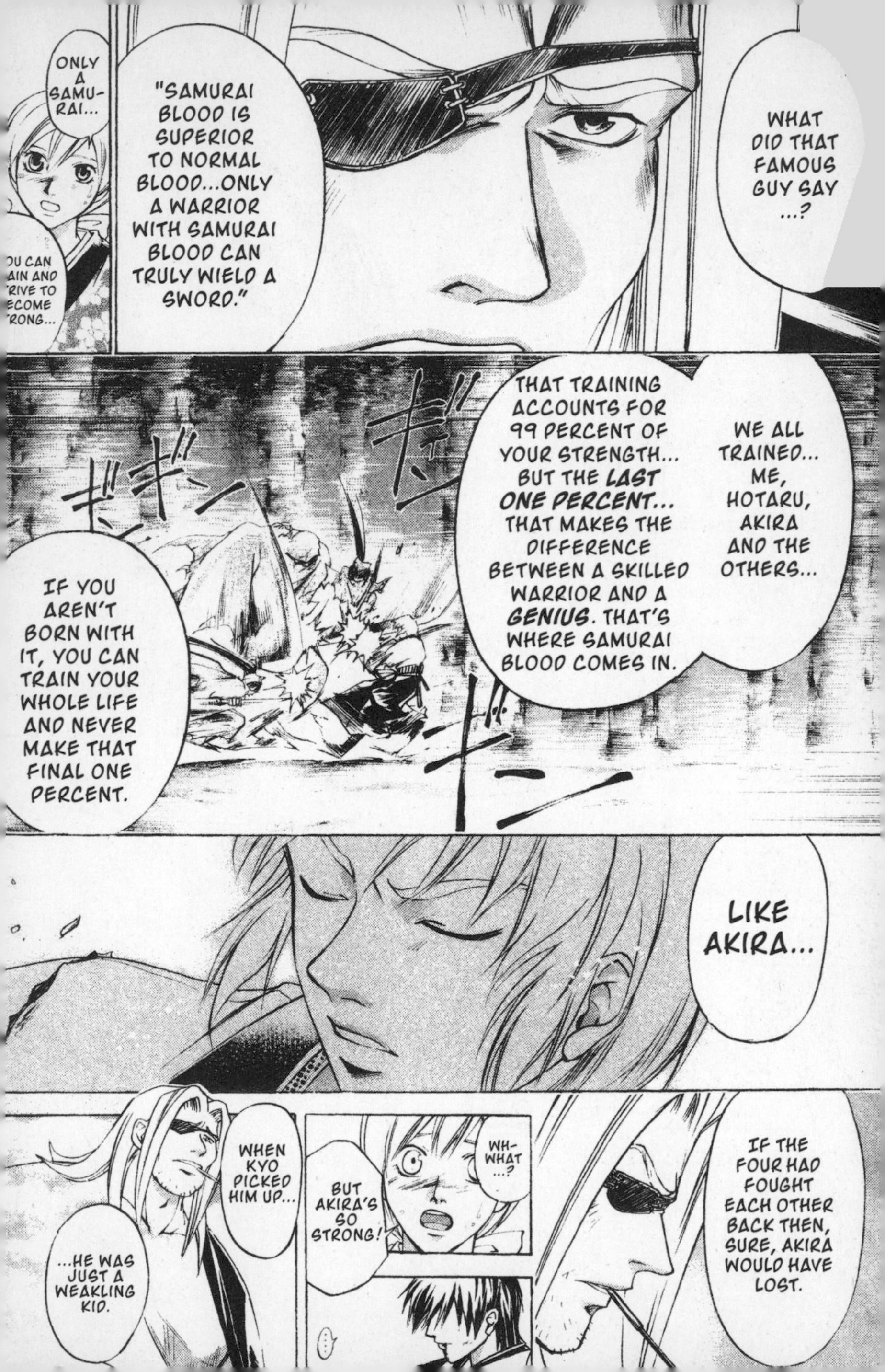
WHAT DID THAT FAMOUS GUY SAY ...?
"SAMURAI BLOOD IS SUPERIOR TO NORMAL BLOOD...ONLY A WARRIOR WITH SAMURAI BLOOD CAN TRULY WIELD A SWORD."
ONLY A SAMURAI...
OU CAN AIN AND TRIVE TO ECOME TRONG...
WE ALL TRAINED... ME, HOTARU, AKIRA AND THE OTHERS...
THAT TRAINING ACCOUNTS FOR 99 PERCENT OF YOUR STRENGTH... BUT THE LAST ONE PERCENT... THAT MAKES THE DIFFERENCE BETWEEN A SKILLED WARRIOR AND A GENIUS. THAT'S WHERE SAMURAI BLOOD COMES IN.
IF YOU AREN'T BORN WITH IT, YOU CAN TRAIN YOUR WHOLE LIFE AND NEVER MAKE THAT FINAL ONE PERCENT.
LIKE AKIRA...
IF THE FOUR HAD FOUGHT EACH OTHER BACK THEN, SURE, AKIRA WOULD HAVE LOST.
WH-WHAT ...?
BUT AKIRA'S SO STRONG!
...
WHEN KYO PICKED HIM UP...
...HE WAS JUST A WEAKLING KID.

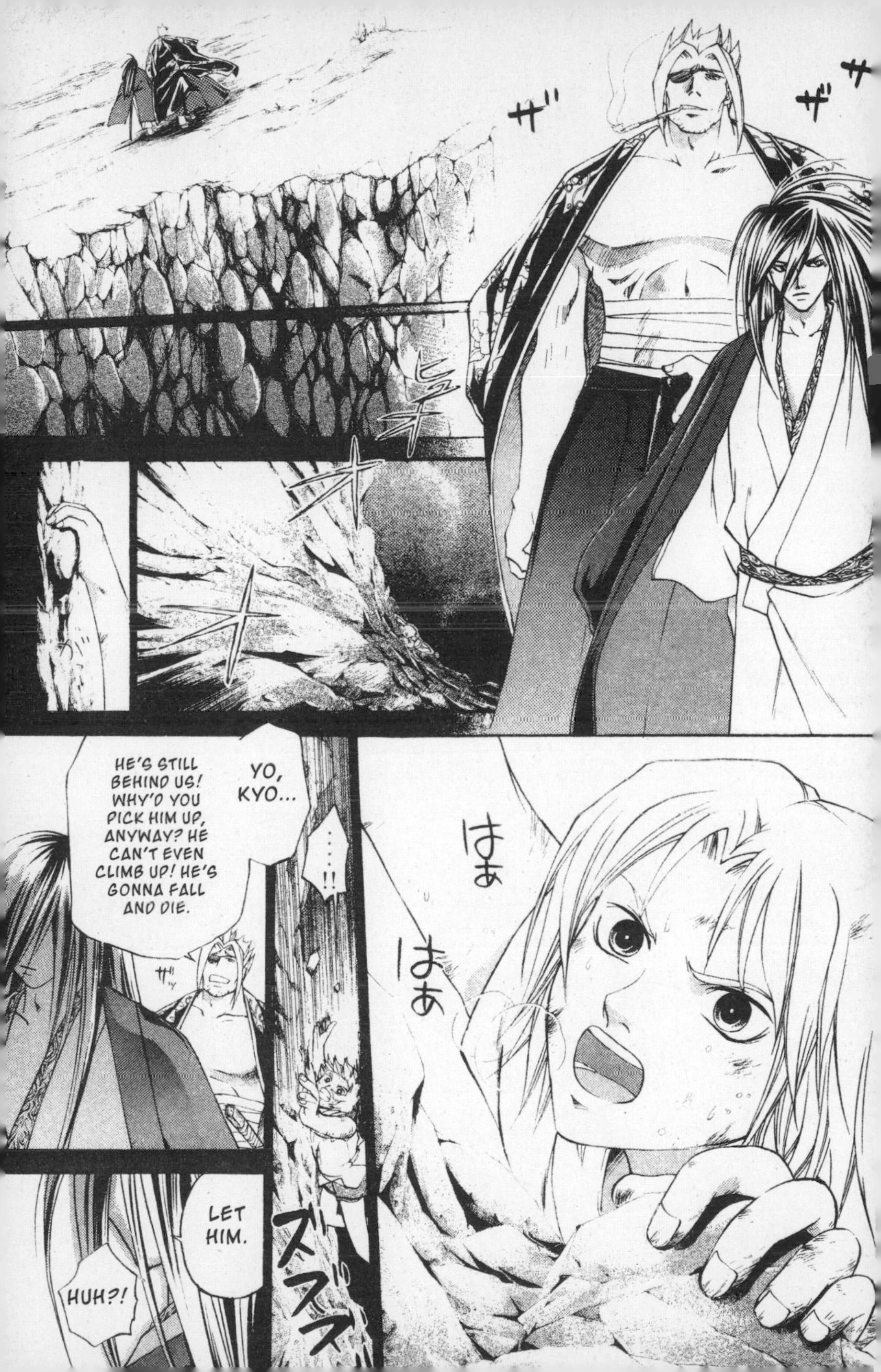
ザ
ザ
ザ
ヒュオオオ
はぁ
はぁ
YO, KYO...
HE'S STILL BEHIND US! WHY'D YOU PICK HIM UP, ANYWAY? HE CAN'T EVEN CLIMB UP! HE'S GONNA FALL AND DIE.
ザッ
...!!
LET HIM.
HUH?!
ズズズ

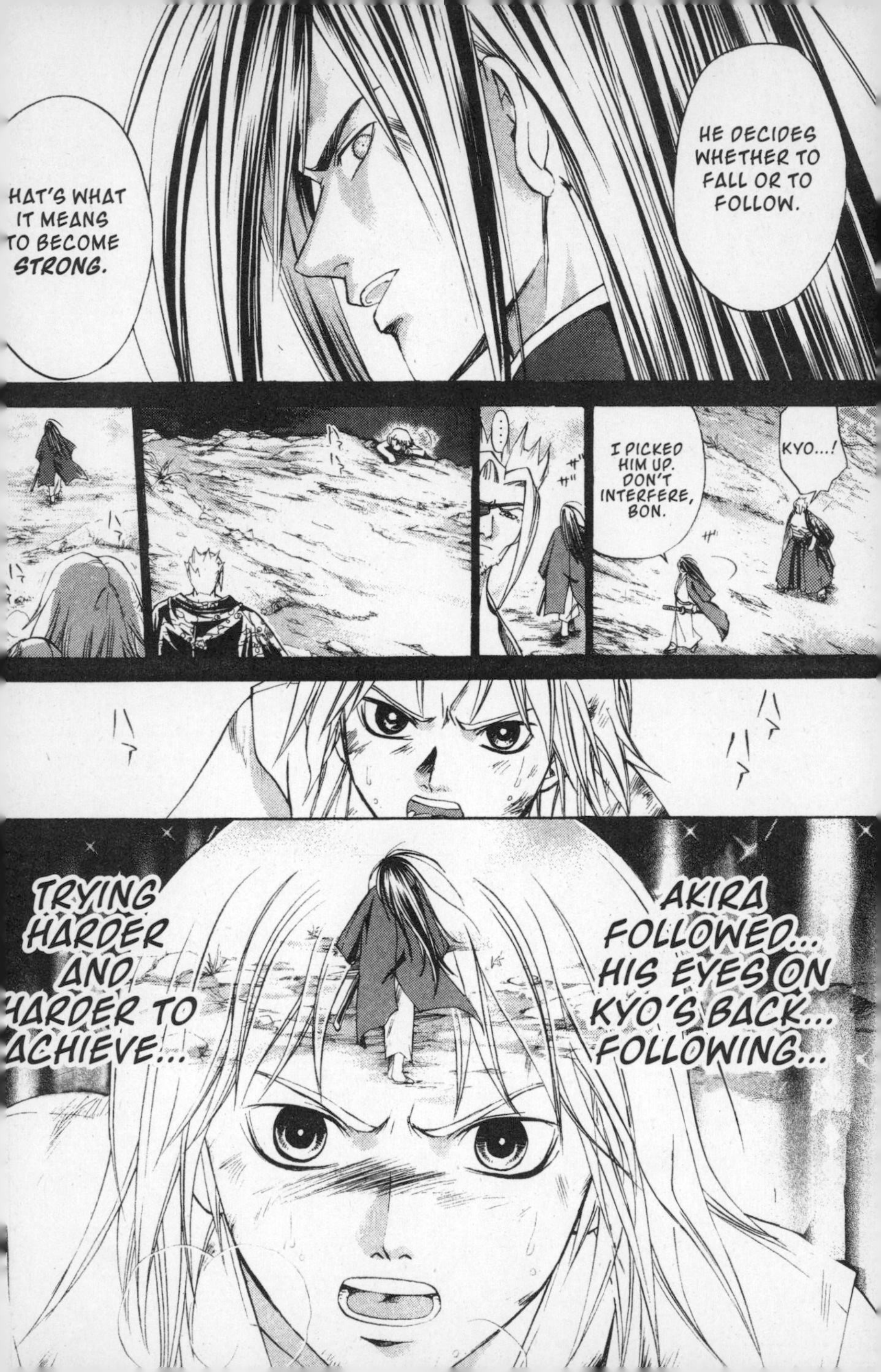
HE DECIDES WHETHER TO FALL OR TO FOLLOW.
HAT'S WHAT IT MEANS TO BECOME STRONG.
KYO...!
I PICKED HIM UP. DON'T INTERFERE, BON.
...
AKIRA FOLLOWED... HIS EYES ON KYO'S BACK... FOLLOWING...
TRYING HARDER AND HARDER TO ACHIEVE...

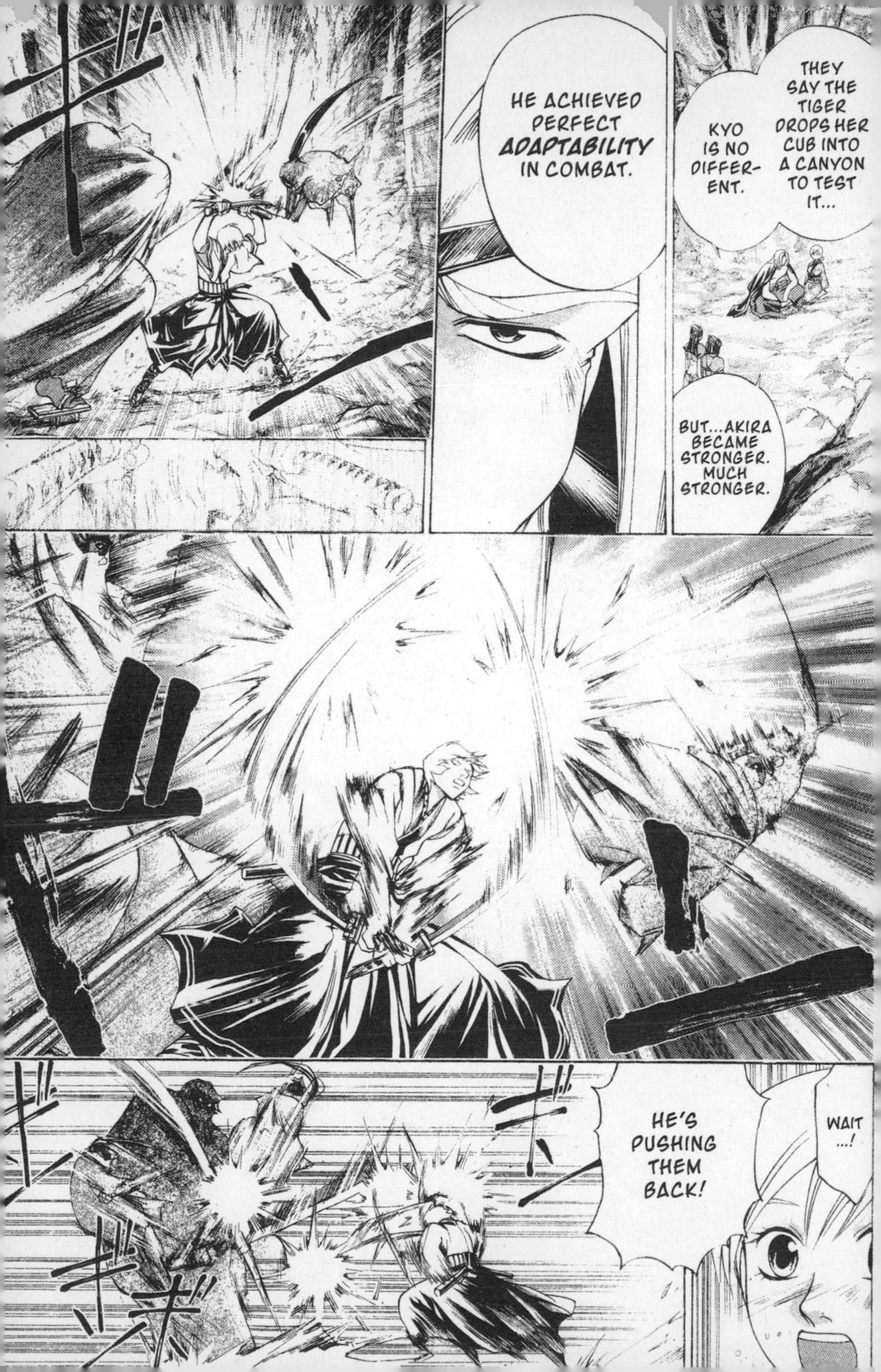
THEY SAY THE TIGER DROPS HER CUB INTO A CANYON TO TEST IT...
KYO IS NO DIFFER-ENT.
BUT...AKIRA BECAME STRONGER. MUCH STRONGER.
HE ACHIEVED PERFECT ADAPTABILITY IN COMBAT.
WAIT ...!
HE'S PUSHING THEM BACK!

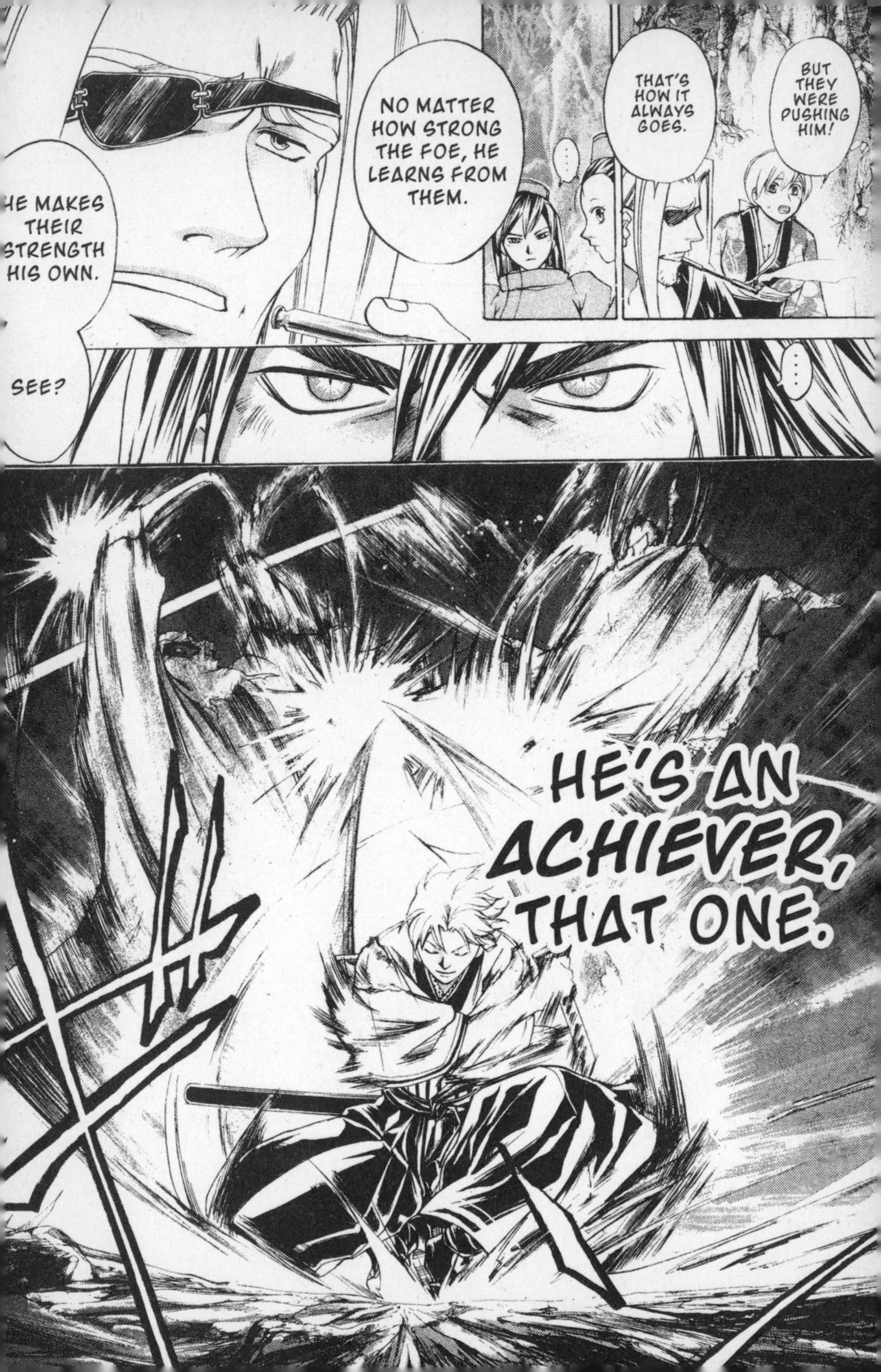

BUT THEY WERE PUSHING HIM!
THAT'S HOW IT ALWAYS GOES.
...
NO MATTER HOW STRONG THE FOE, HE LEARNS FROM THEM.
HE MAKES THEIR STRENGTH HIS OWN.
...
SEE?
HE'S AN ACHIEVER, THAT ONE.

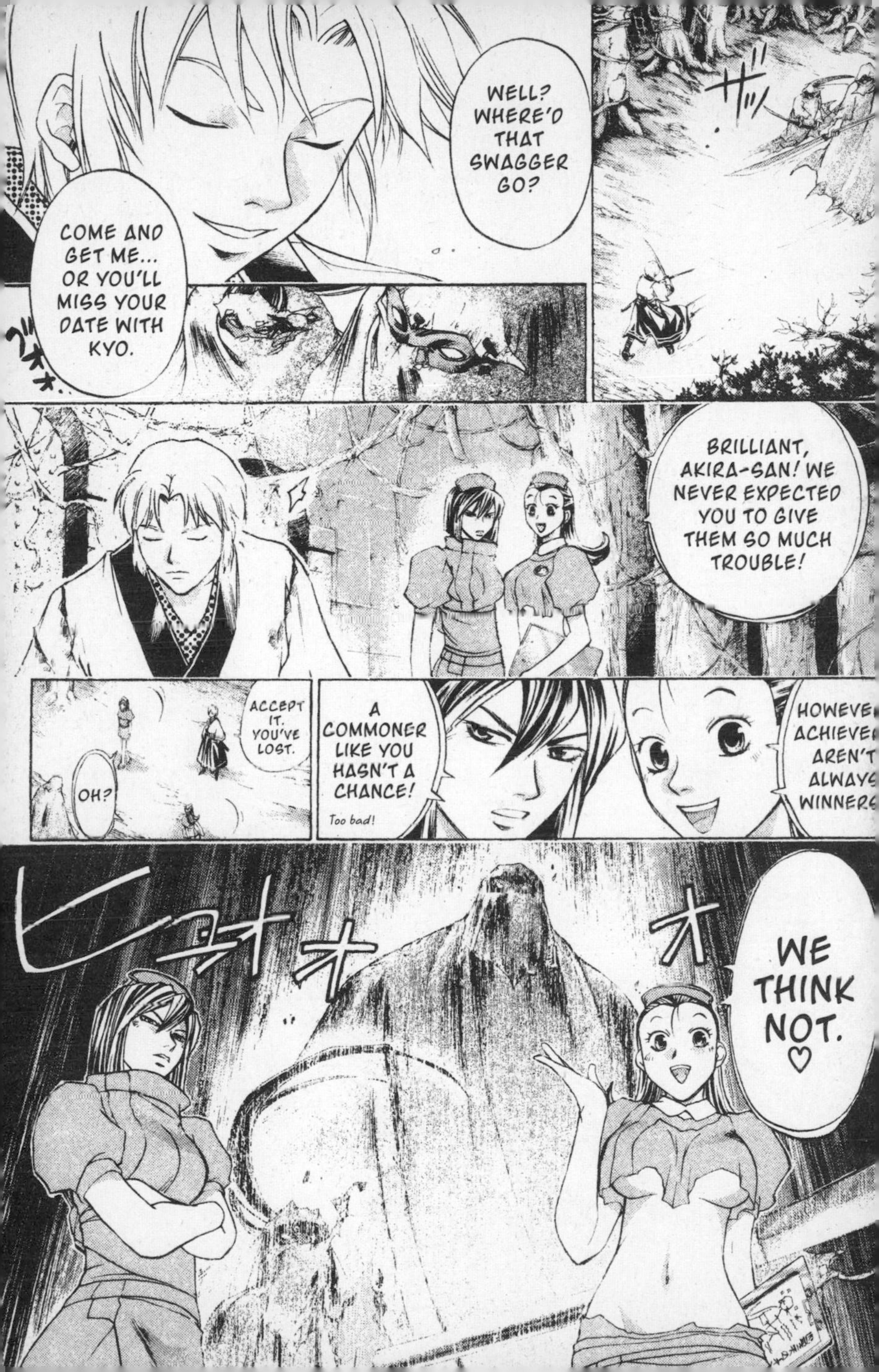
WELL? WHERE'D THAT SWAGGER GO?
COME AND GET ME... OR YOU'LL MISS YOUR DATE WITH KYO.
BRILLIANT, AKIRA-SAN! WE NEVER EXPECTED YOU TO GIVE THEM SO MUCH TROUBLE!
HOWEVE ACHIEVE AREN'T ALWAYS WINNERS
A COMMONER LIKE YOU HASN'T A CHANCE!
Too bad!
ACCEPT IT. YOU'VE LOST.
OH?
WE THINK NOT. ♥

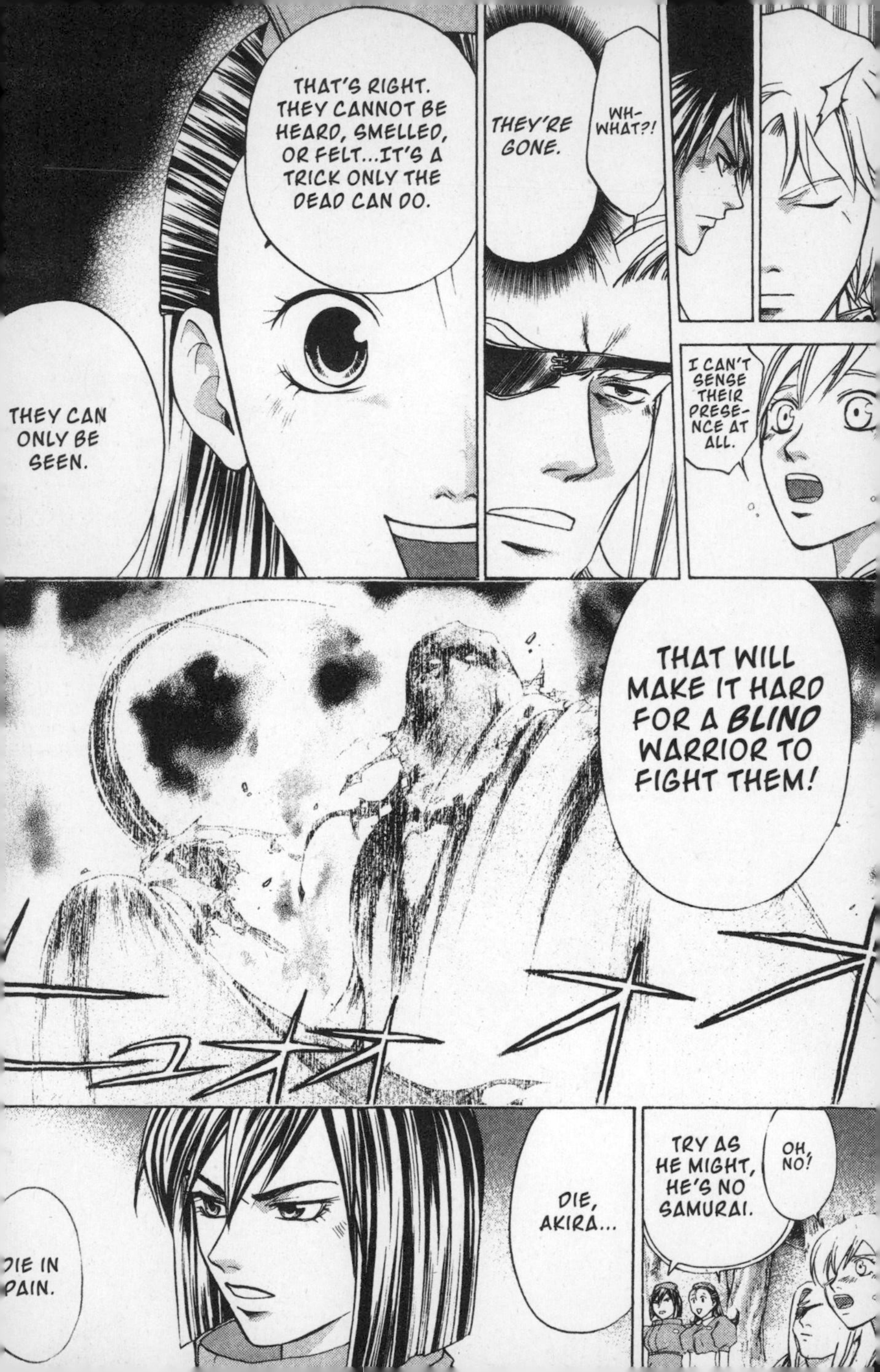
WH-WHAT?!
I CAN'T SENSE THEIR PRESENCE AT ALL.
THEY'RE GONE.
THAT'S RIGHT. THEY CANNOT BE HEARD, SMELLED, OR FELT...IT'S A TRICK ONLY THE DEAD CAN DO.
THEY CAN ONLY BE SEEN.
THAT WILL MAKE IT HARD FOR A *BLIND* WARRIOR TO FIGHT THEM!
OH, NO!
TRY AS HE MIGHT, HE'S NO SAMURAI.
DIE, AKIRA...
DIE IN PAIN.

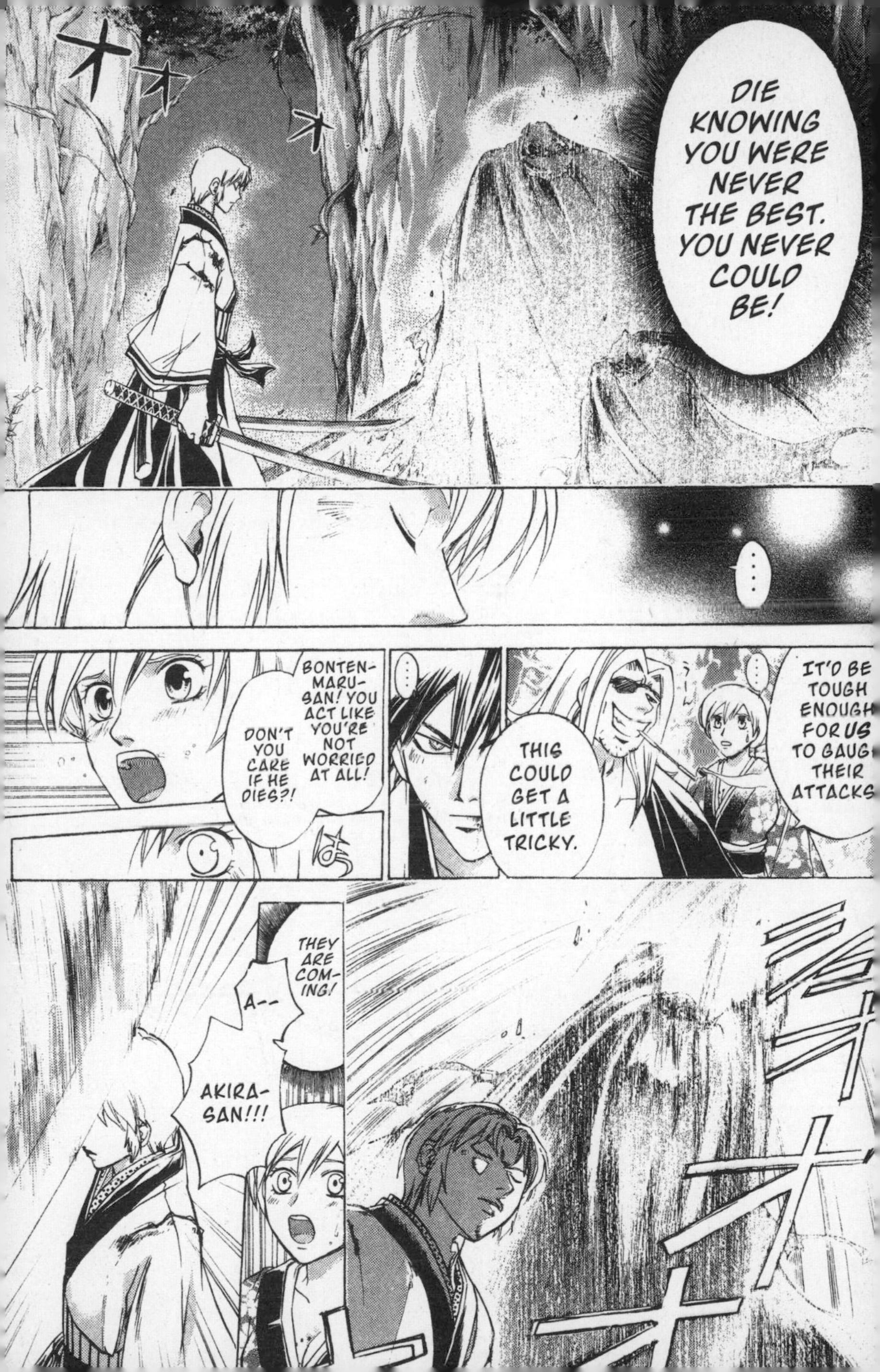
DIE KNOWING YOU WERE NEVER THE BEST. YOU NEVER COULD BE!
....
IT'D BE TOUGH ENOUGH FOR US TO GAUG THEIR ATTACKS
...
...
THIS COULD GET A LITTLE TRICKY.
BONTEN-MARU-SAN! YOU ACT LIKE YOU'RE NOT WORRIED AT ALL!
DON'T YOU CARE IF HE DIES?!
THEY ARE COMING!
A--
AKIRA-SAN!!!

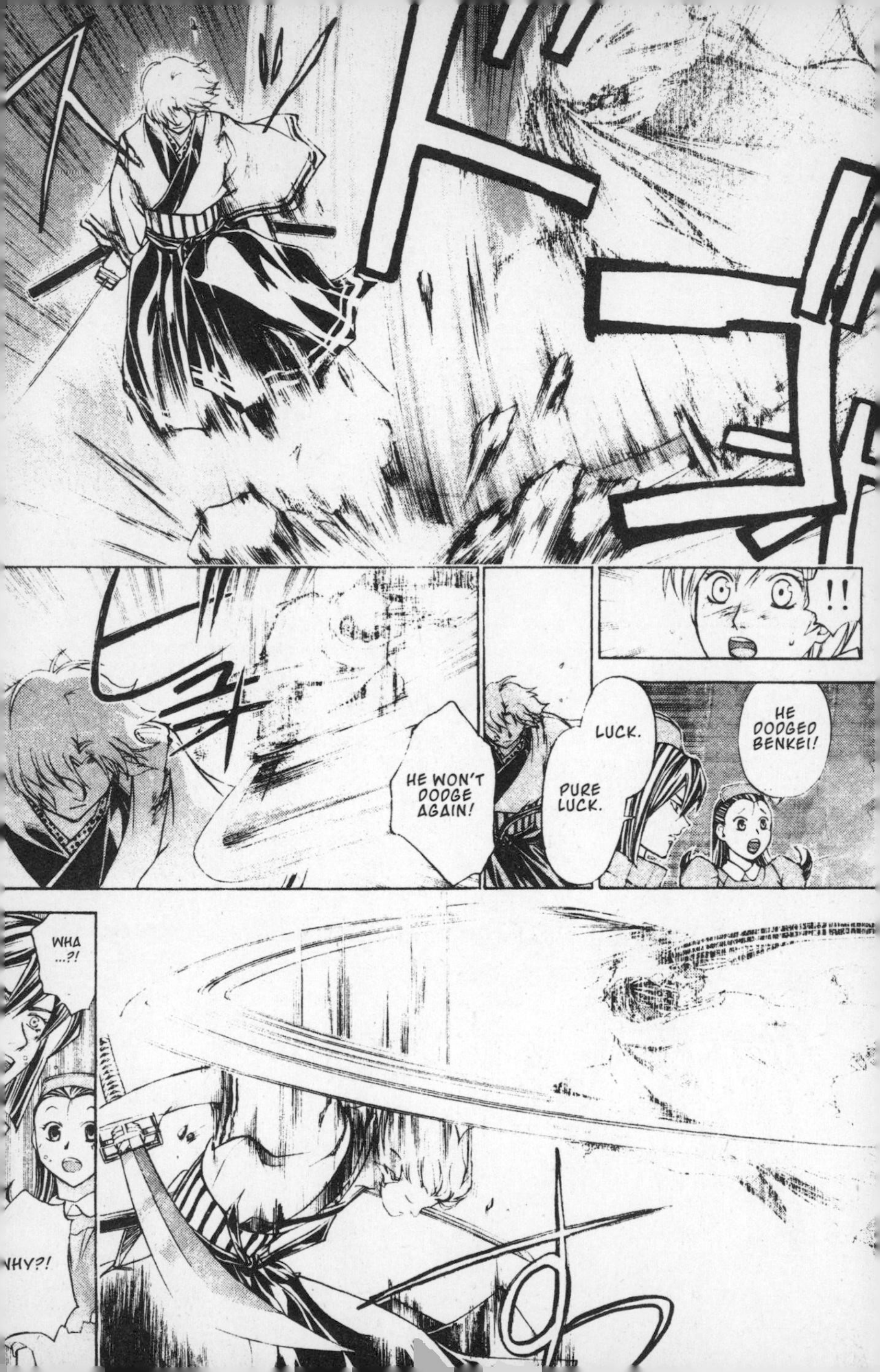
!!
HE DODGED BENKEI!
LUCK.
PURE LUCK.
HE WON'T DODGE AGAIN!
WHA ...?!
WHY?!

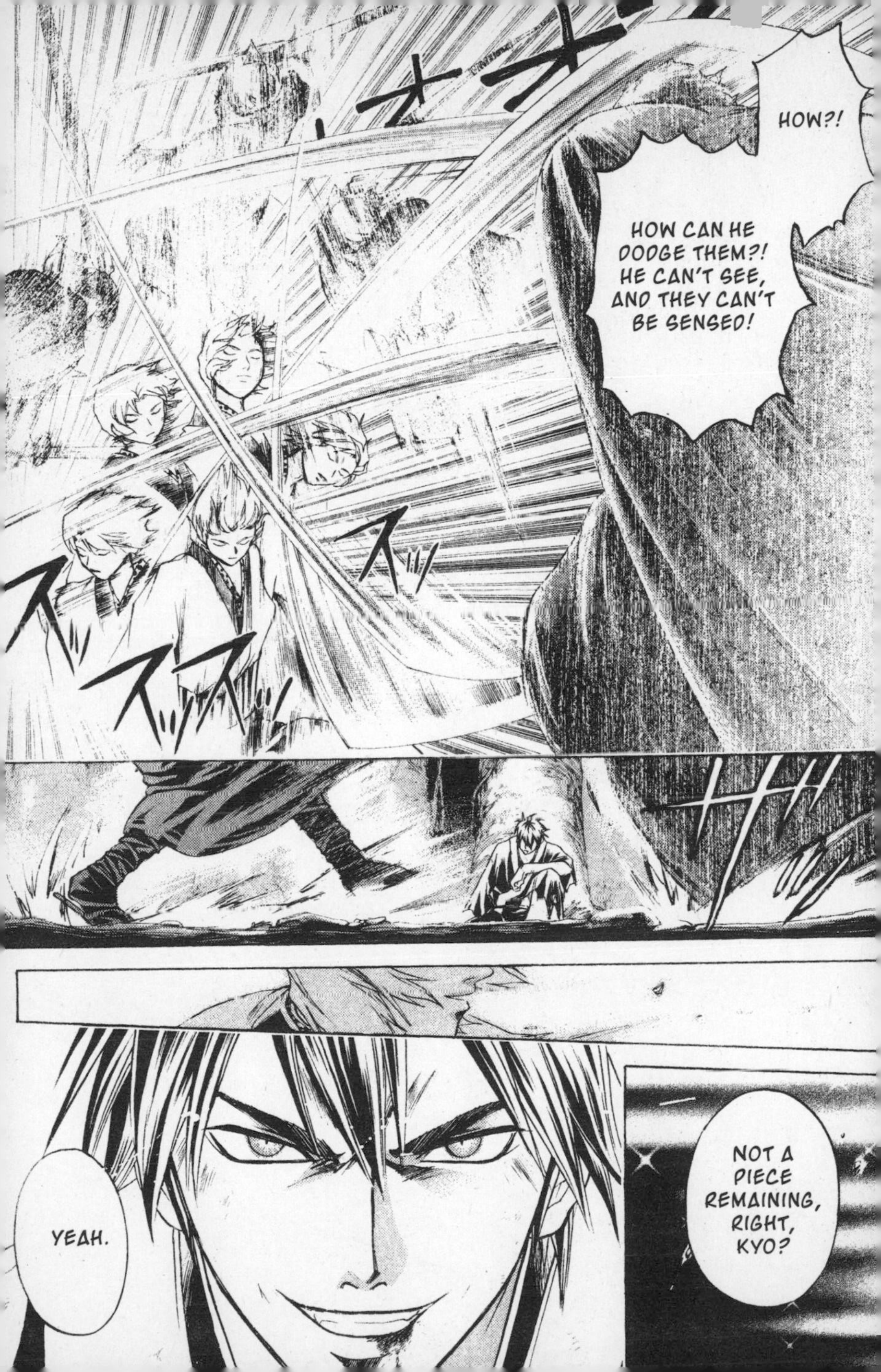
HOW?!
HOW CAN HE DODGE THEM?! HE CAN'T SEE, AND THEY CAN'T BE SENSED!
NOT A PIECE REMAINING, RIGHT, KYO?
YEAH.

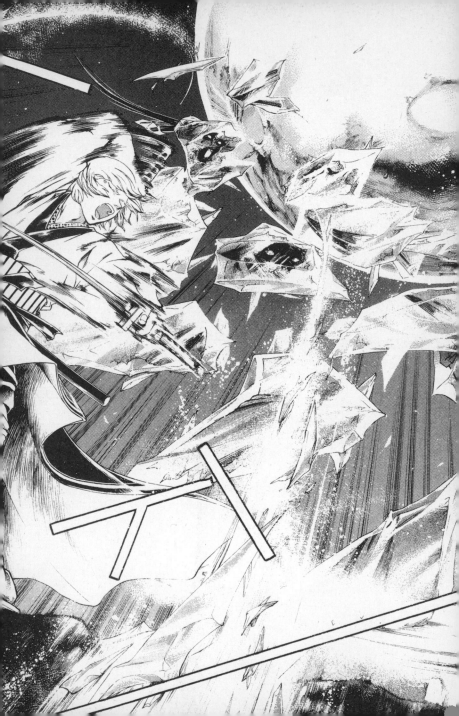

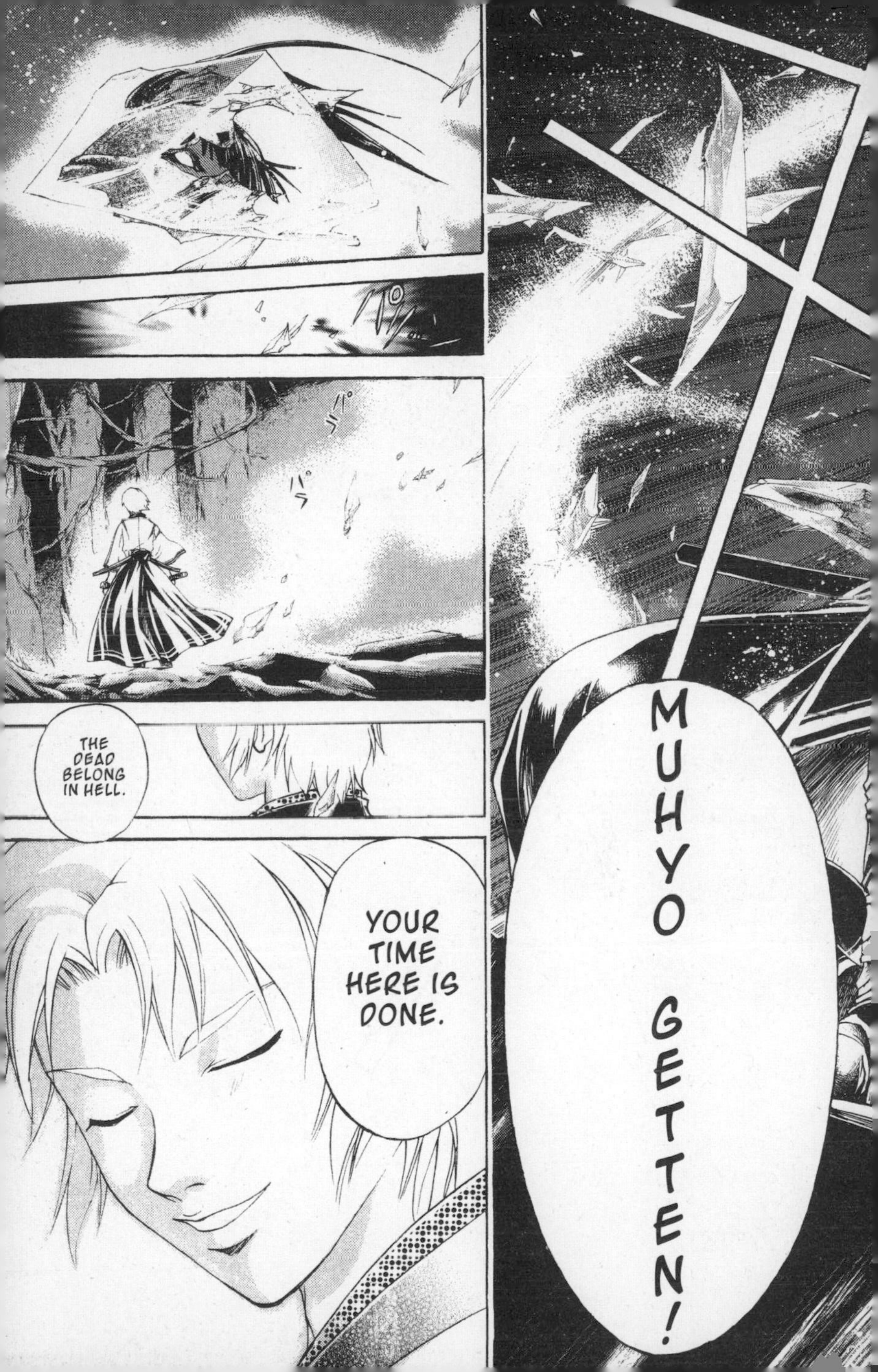
MUHYO GETTEN!
THE DEAD BELONG IN HELL.
YOUR TIME HERE IS DONE.

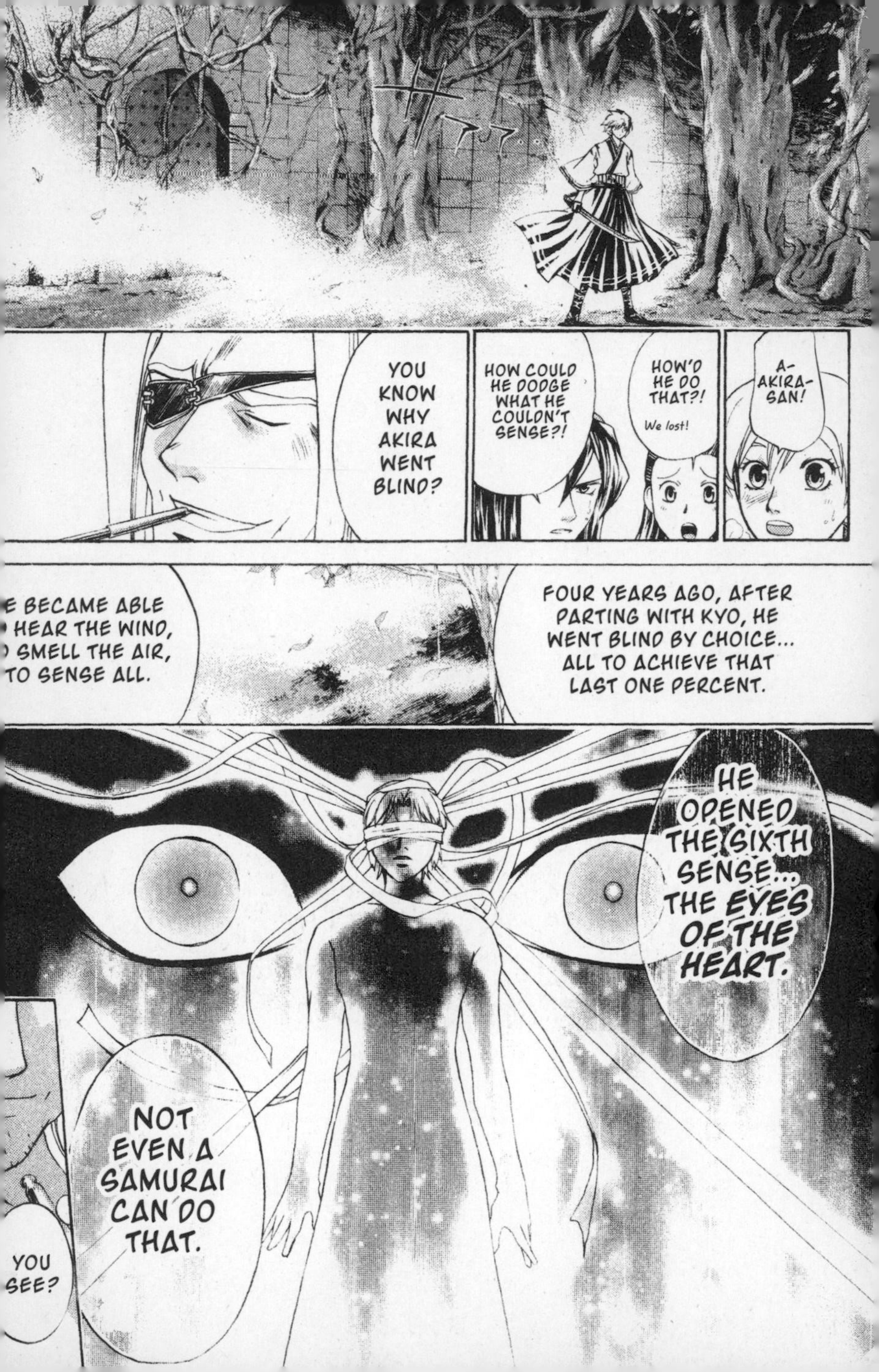
A- AKIRA-SAN!
HOW'D HE DO THAT?!
We lost!
HOW COULD HE DODGE WHAT HE COULDN'T SENSE?!
YOU KNOW WHY AKIRA WENT BLIND?
FOUR YEARS AGO, AFTER PARTING WITH KYO, HE WENT BLIND BY CHOICE... ALL TO ACHIEVE THAT LAST ONE PERCENT.
E BECAME ABLE HEAR THE WIND, SMELL THE AIR, TO SENSE ALL.
HE OPENED THE SIXTH SENSE... THE *EYES OF THE HEART*.
NOT EVEN A SAMURAI CAN DO THAT.
YOU SEE?

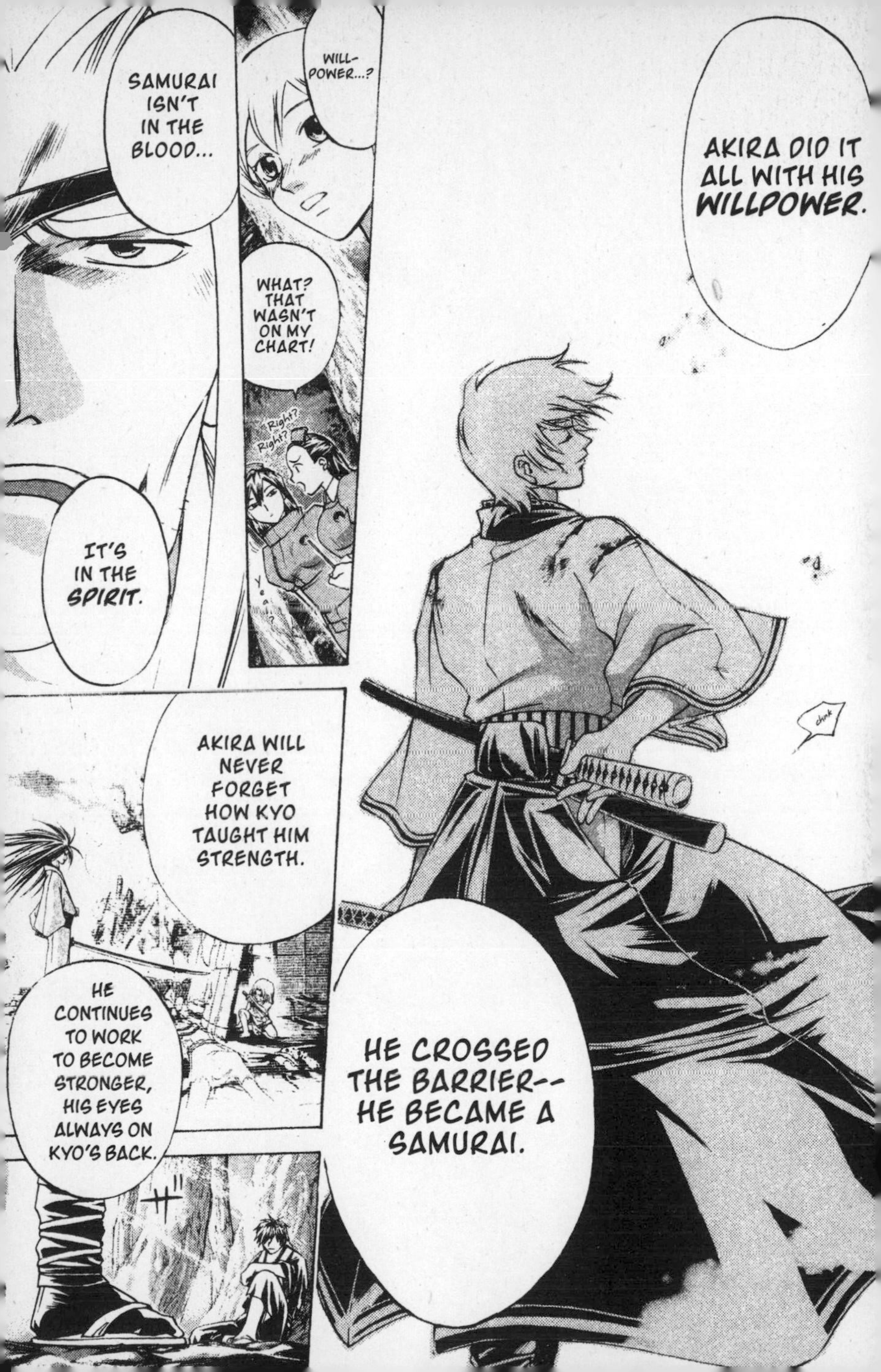

AKIRA DID IT ALL WITH HIS WILLPOWER.
chink
HE CROSSED THE BARRIER-- HE BECAME A SAMURAI.
WILL-POWER...?
WHAT? THAT WASN'T ON MY CHART!
Right? Right?
Yeah...?
SAMURAI ISN'T IN THE BLOOD...
IT'S IN THE SPIRIT.
AKIRA WILL NEVER FORGET HOW KYO TAUGHT HIM STRENGTH.
HE CONTINUES TO WORK TO BECOME STRONGER, HIS EYES ALWAYS ON KYO'S BACK.

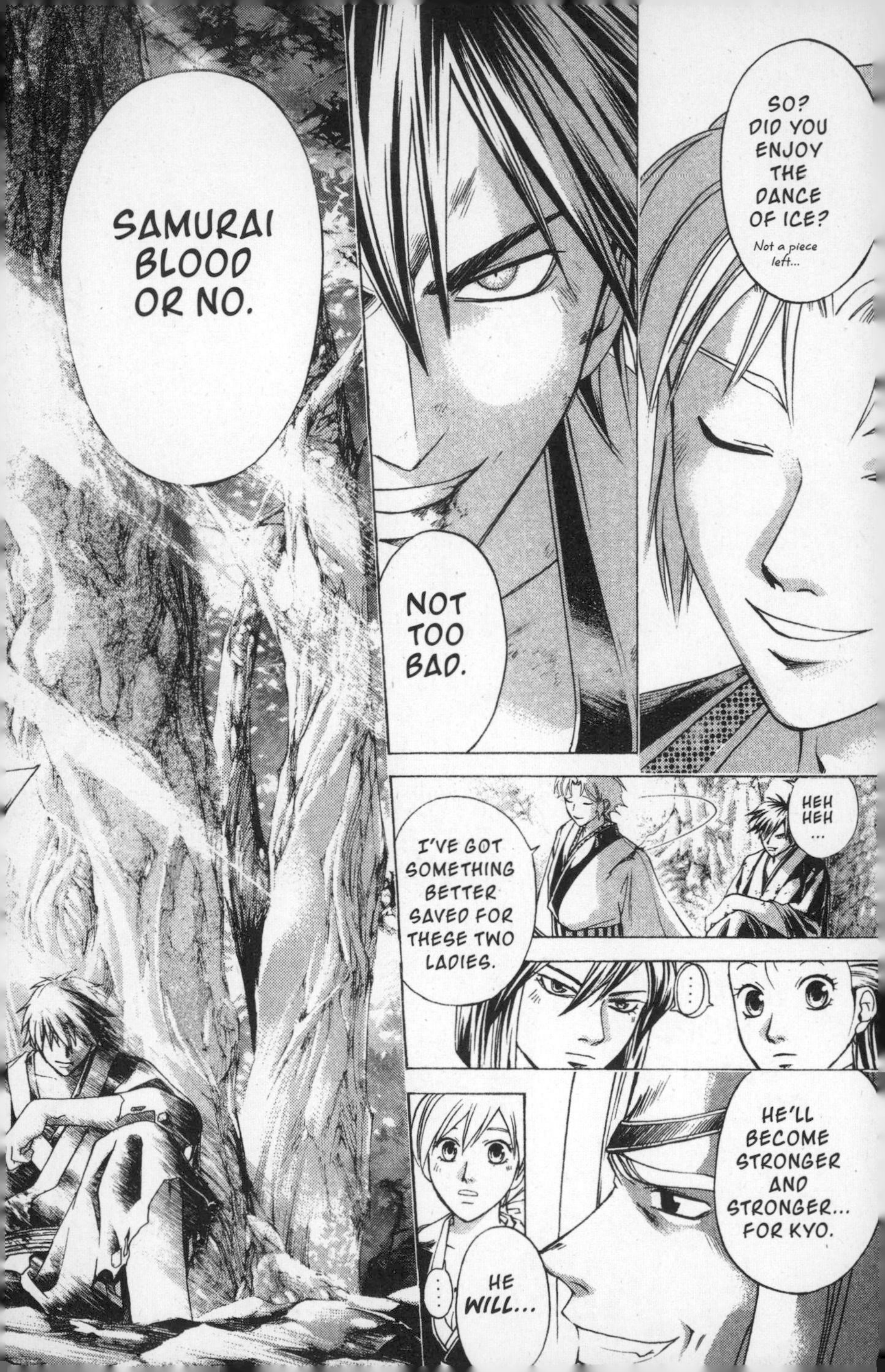
SO? DID YOU ENJOY THE DANCE OF ICE?
Not a piece left...
NOT TOO BAD.
HEH HEH ...
I'VE GOT SOMETHING BETTER SAVED FOR THESE TWO LADIES.
....
HE'LL BECOME STRONGER AND STRONGER... FOR KYO.
....
HE WILL...
SAMURAI BLOOD OR NO.

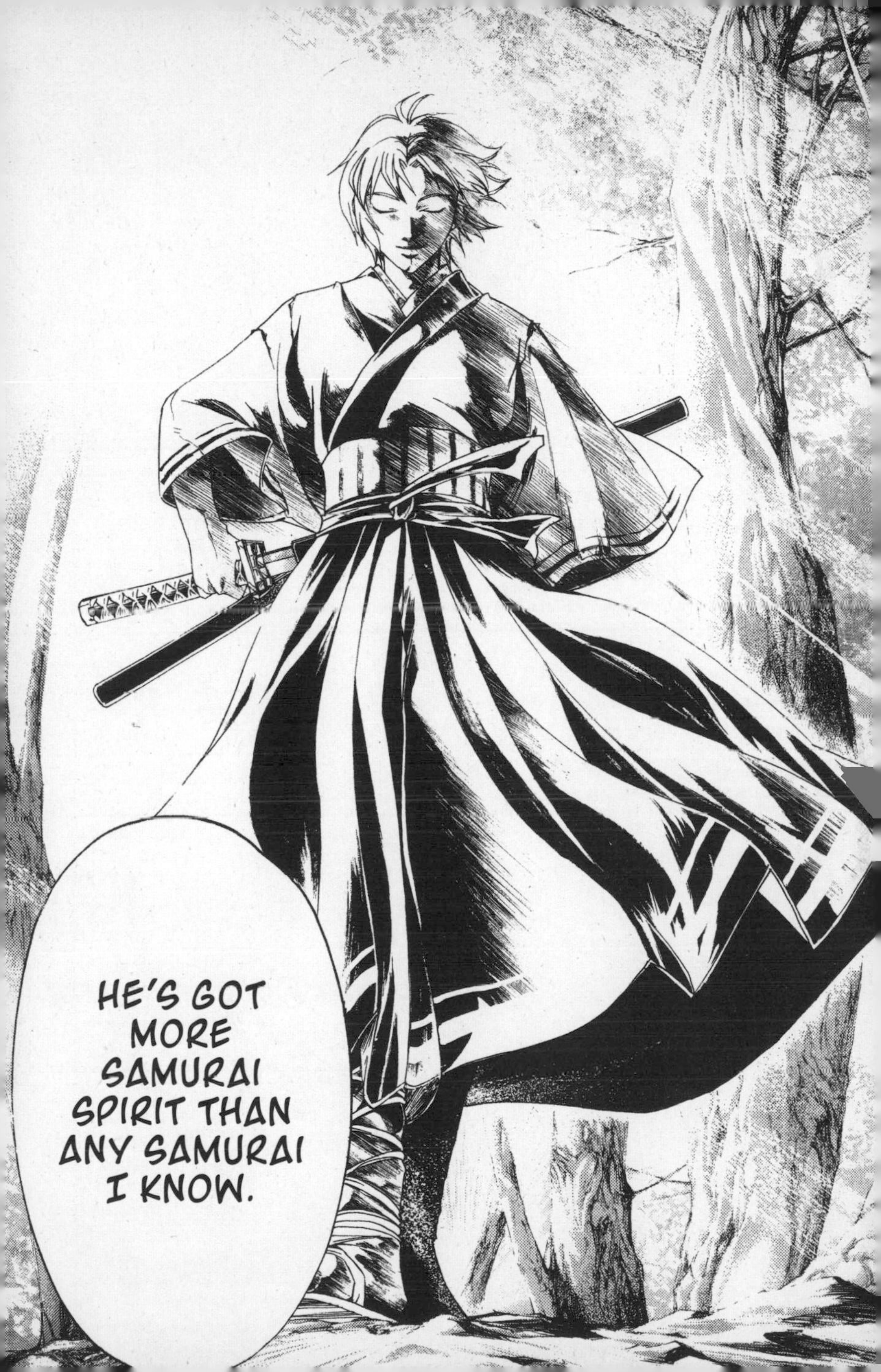
HE'S GOT MORE SAMURAI SPIRIT THAN ANY SAMURAI I KNOW.

The Kamijyo Report

MY HOUSE
ONE DAY, A FAX CAME.
HEY, A FAX! WHO'S IT FROM?
GAH!
I-IT'S FROM OSHIMA-SENSEI! THE GUY WHO DRAWS "SHOOT!"!!!
SHOOT!
IT'S SO AMAZING, I CAN'T DRAW IT.
B-BUT WHY ME?
HUH?!
OH, YOU GOT OSHIMA'S FAX? SORRY ABOUT THAT--SEE, I GOTTA GO TO YOUR PLACE ANYHOW, SO I HAD HIM SEND IT THERE FOR ME.
WHAT DO I LOOK LIKE? KINKO'S?
Could you put it in order?
MR. H
HE'S ONLY NICE WHEN HE WANTS SOMETHING...
MR. H EDITS "SHOOT!"

Lately, me and SDK have been overwhelmed by the anime and the game...things are hopping! And everyone seems to be enjoying themselves, too! I'm counting my blessings.

That said, things really haven't changed that much day-to-day for me. I make each title page, and I draw each frame, just like before. For some reason, drawing manga makes it hard to just enjoy drawing. But having people enjoy reading it is amazing, so I'll keep on keepin' on!

It's all thanks to you, the readers. Thanks!

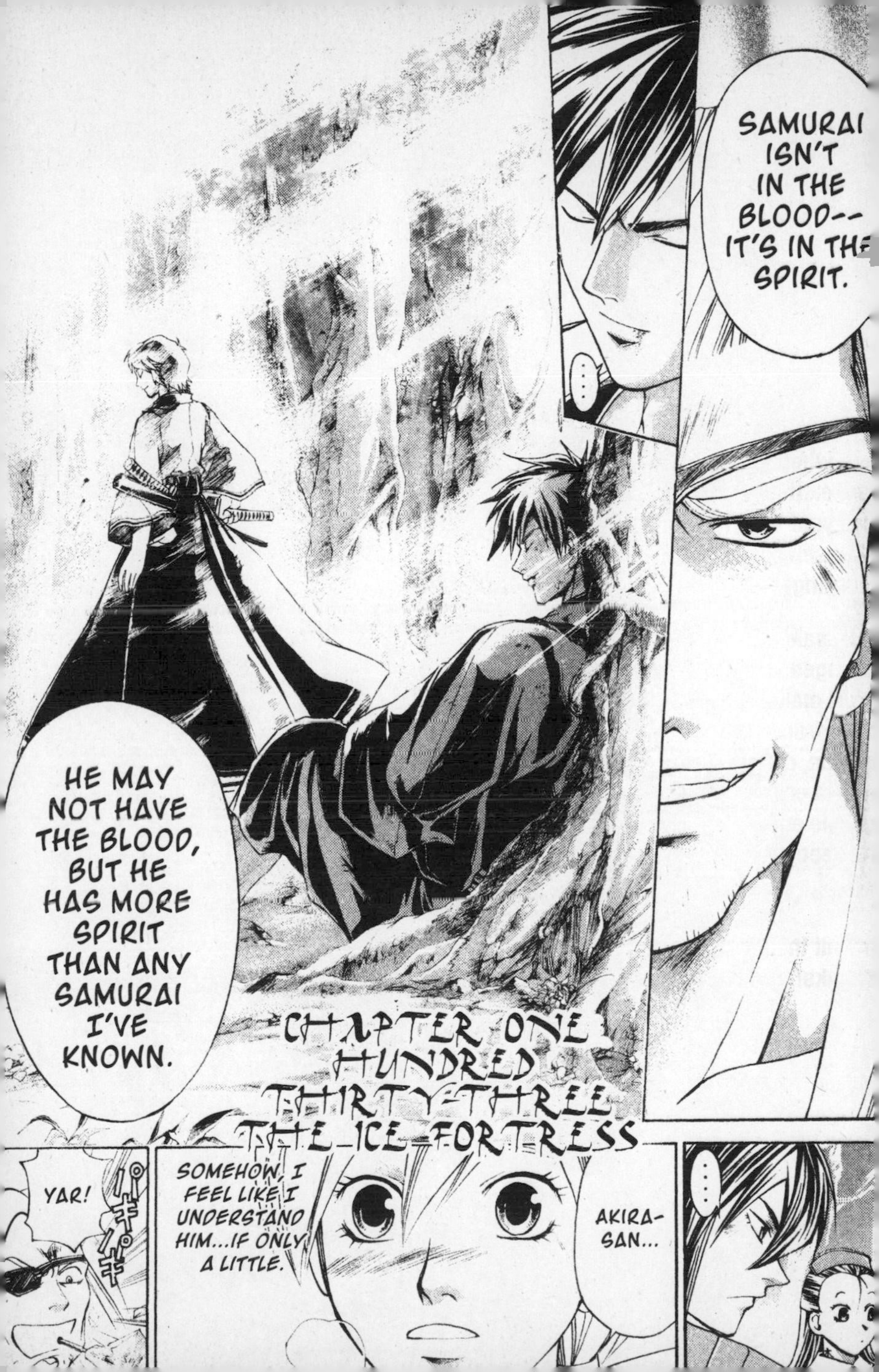
SAMURAI ISN'T IN THE BLOOD--IT'S IN THE SPIRIT.
...
HE MAY NOT HAVE THE BLOOD, BUT HE HAS MORE SPIRIT THAN ANY SAMURAI I'VE KNOWN.
CHAPTER ONE HUNDRED THIRTY-THREE
THE ICE FORTRESS
...
AKIRA-SAN...
SOMEHOW, I FEEL LIKE I UNDERSTAND HIM...IF ONLY A LITTLE.
YAR!

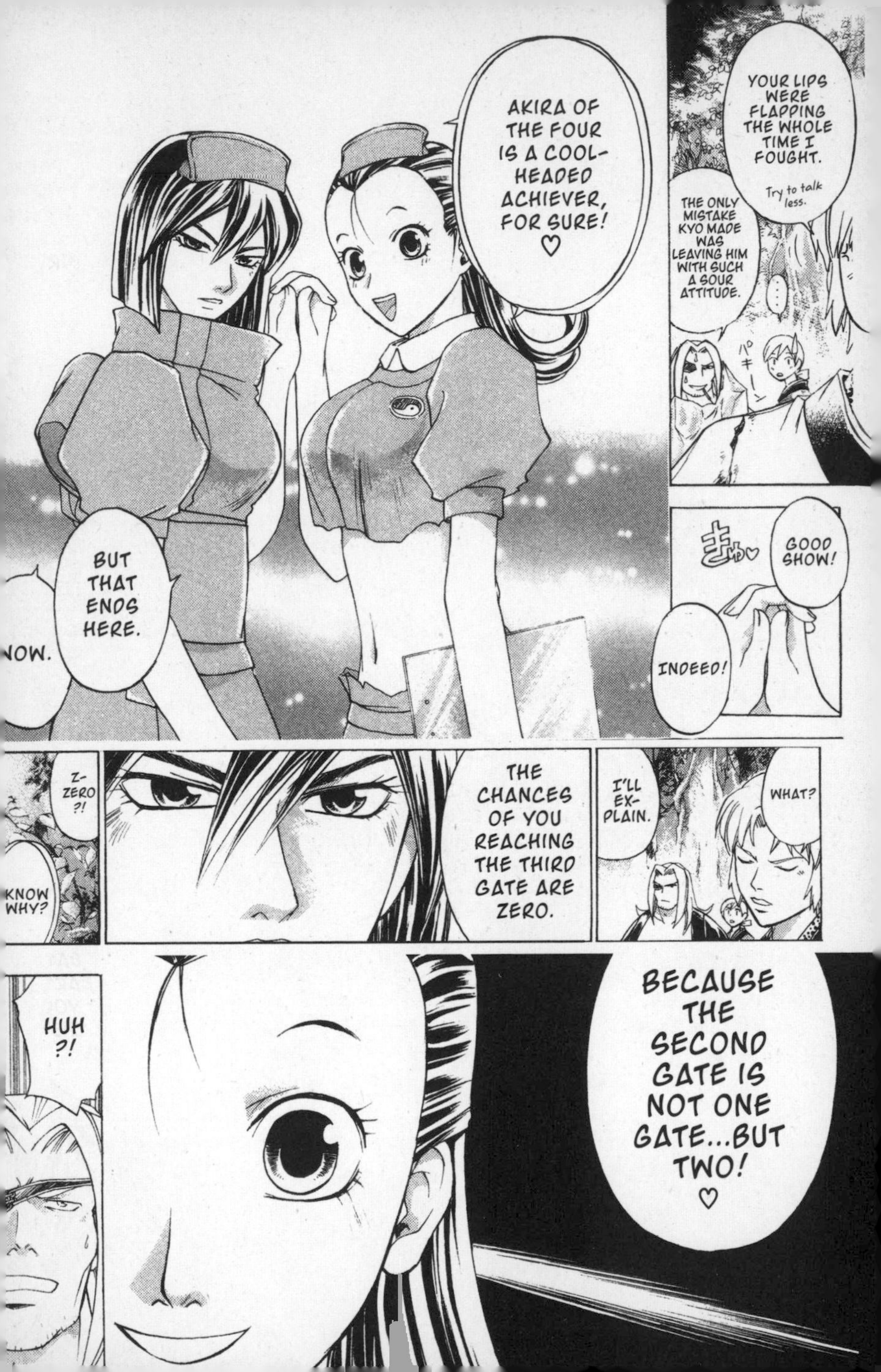
YOUR LIPS WERE FLAPPING THE WHOLE TIME I FOUGHT.
Try to talk less.
THE ONLY MISTAKE KYO MADE WAS LEAVING HIM WITH SUCH A SOUR ATTITUDE.
...
パキーン
GOOD SHOW!
きゅ♡
INDEED!
AKIRA OF THE FOUR IS A COOL-HEADED ACHIEVER, FOR SURE! ♡
BUT THAT ENDS HERE.
NOW.
WHAT?
I'LL EX-PLAIN.
THE CHANCES OF YOU REACHING THE THIRD GATE ARE ZERO.
Z-ZERO ?!
KNOW WHY?
BECAUSE THE SECOND GATE IS NOT ONE GATE...BUT TWO! ♡
HUH ?!

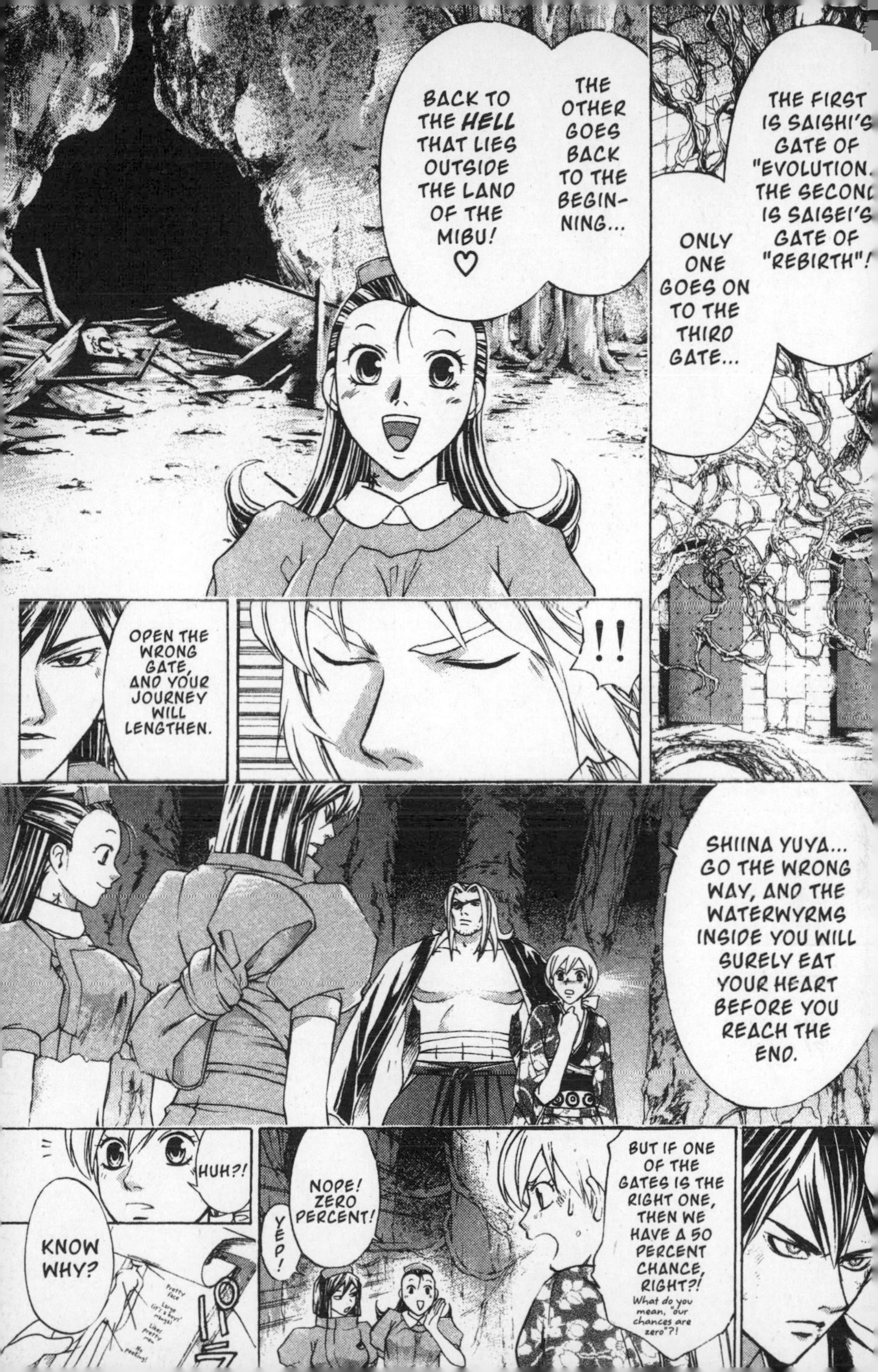
THE FIRST IS SAISHI'S GATE OF "EVOLUTION." THE SECOND IS SAISEI'S GATE OF "REBIRTH"!
ONLY ONE GOES ON TO THE THIRD GATE...
THE OTHER GOES BACK TO THE BEGINNING...
BACK TO THE HELL THAT LIES OUTSIDE THE LAND OF THE MIBU! ♡
!!
OPEN THE WRONG GATE, AND YOUR JOURNEY WILL LENGTHEN.
SHIINA YUYA... GO THE WRONG WAY, AND THE WATERWYRMS INSIDE YOU WILL SURELY EAT YOUR HEART BEFORE YOU REACH THE END.
BUT IF ONE OF THE GATES IS THE RIGHT ONE, THEN WE HAVE A 50 PERCENT CHANCE, RIGHT?!
What do you mean, "our chances are zero"?!
NOPE! ZERO PERCENT!
YEP!
HUH?!
KNOW WHY?
Pretty face
Large (it's a boys' manga)
Likes pretty men
No peeking!

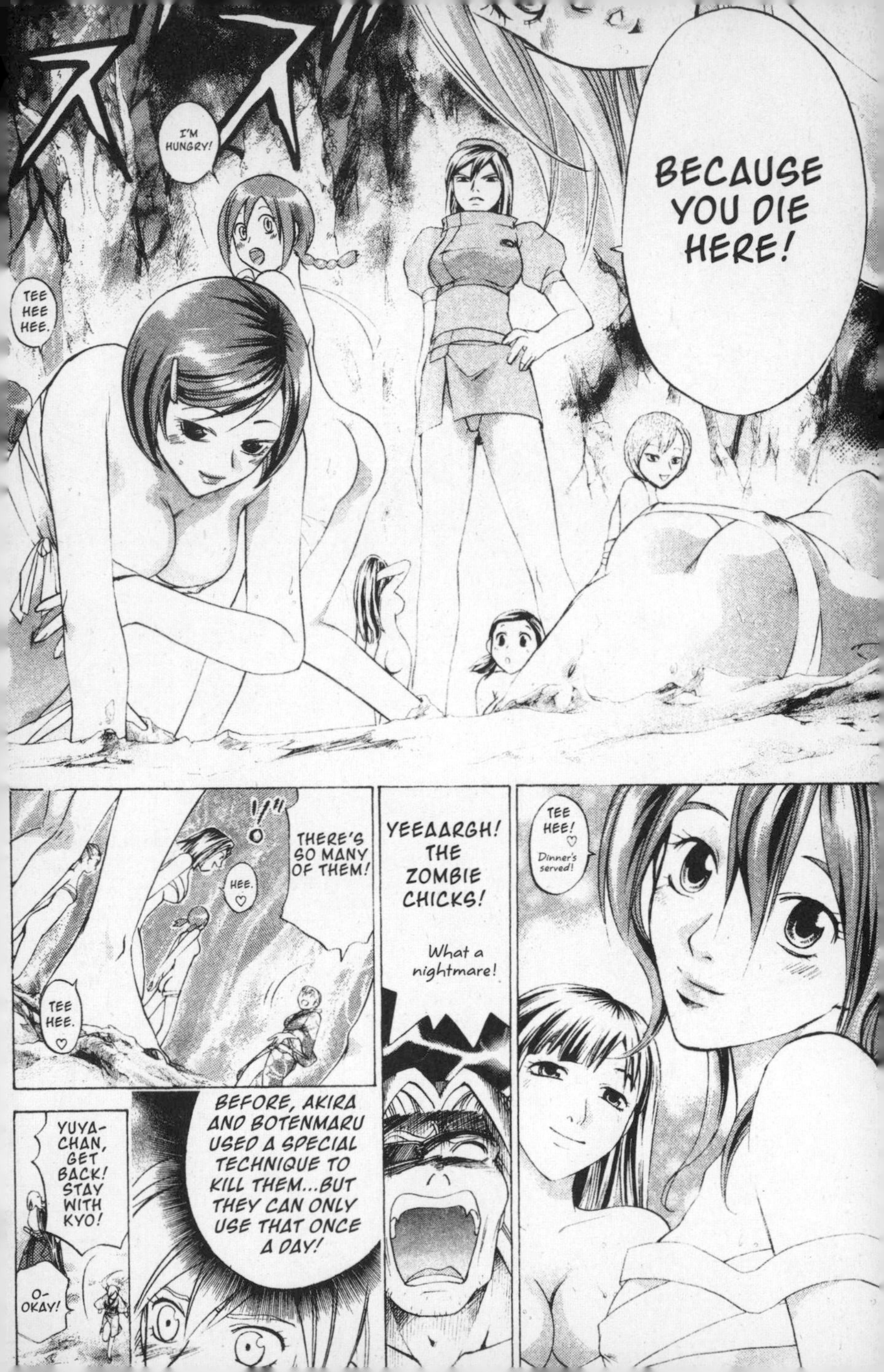
BECAUSE YOU DIE HERE!
I'M HUNGRY!
TEE HEE HEE.
TEE HEE! ♡
Dinner's served!
YEEAARGH! THE ZOMBIE CHICKS!
What a nightmare!
THERE'S SO MANY OF THEM!
HEE. ♡
TEE HEE. ♡
BEFORE, AKIRA AND BOTENMARU USED A SPECIAL TECHNIQUE TO KILL THEM...BUT THEY CAN ONLY USE THAT ONCE A DAY!
YUYA-CHAN, GET BACK! STAY WITH KYO!
O-OKAY!

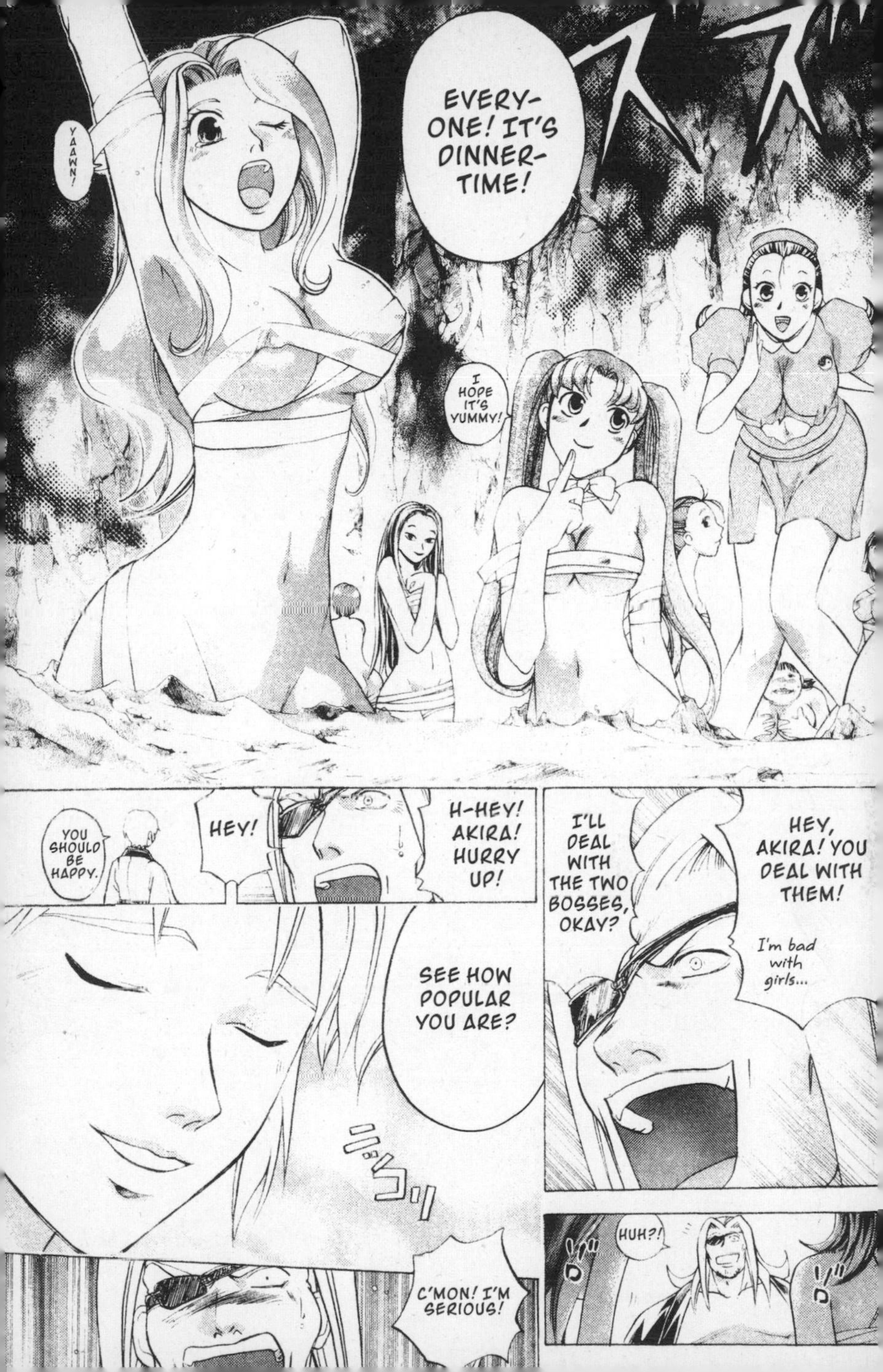
EVERY-ONE! IT'S DINNER-TIME!
YAAWN!
I HOPE IT'S YUMMY!
HEY, AKIRA! YOU DEAL WITH THEM!
I'LL DEAL WITH THE TWO BOSSES, OKAY?
I'm bad with girls...
H-HEY! AKIRA! HURRY UP!
HEY!
YOU SHOULD BE HAPPY.
SEE HOW POPULAR YOU ARE?
HUH?!
C'MON! I'M SERIOUS!

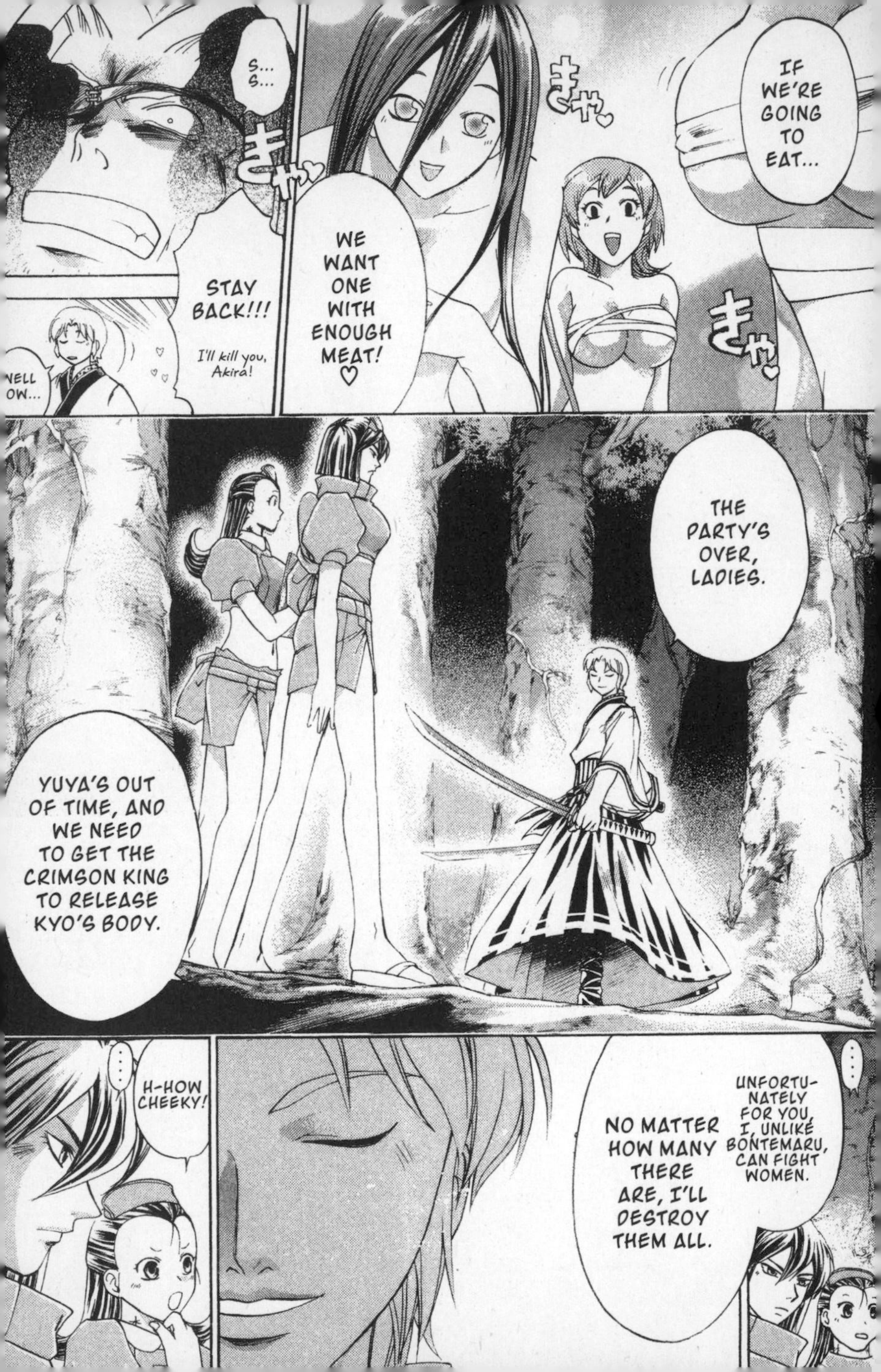
IF WE'RE GOING TO EAT...
きゃ♡
きゃ♡
WE WANT ONE WITH ENOUGH MEAT! ♡
きゃ♡
S... S...
STAY BACK!!!
I'll kill you, Akira!
NELL OW...
THE PARTY'S OVER, LADIES.
YUYA'S OUT OF TIME, AND WE NEED TO GET THE CRIMSON KING TO RELEASE KYO'S BODY.
...
UNFORTU-NATELY FOR YOU, I, UNLIKE BONTEMARU, CAN FIGHT WOMEN.
NO MATTER HOW MANY THERE ARE, I'LL DESTROY THEM ALL.
...
H-HOW CHEEKY!

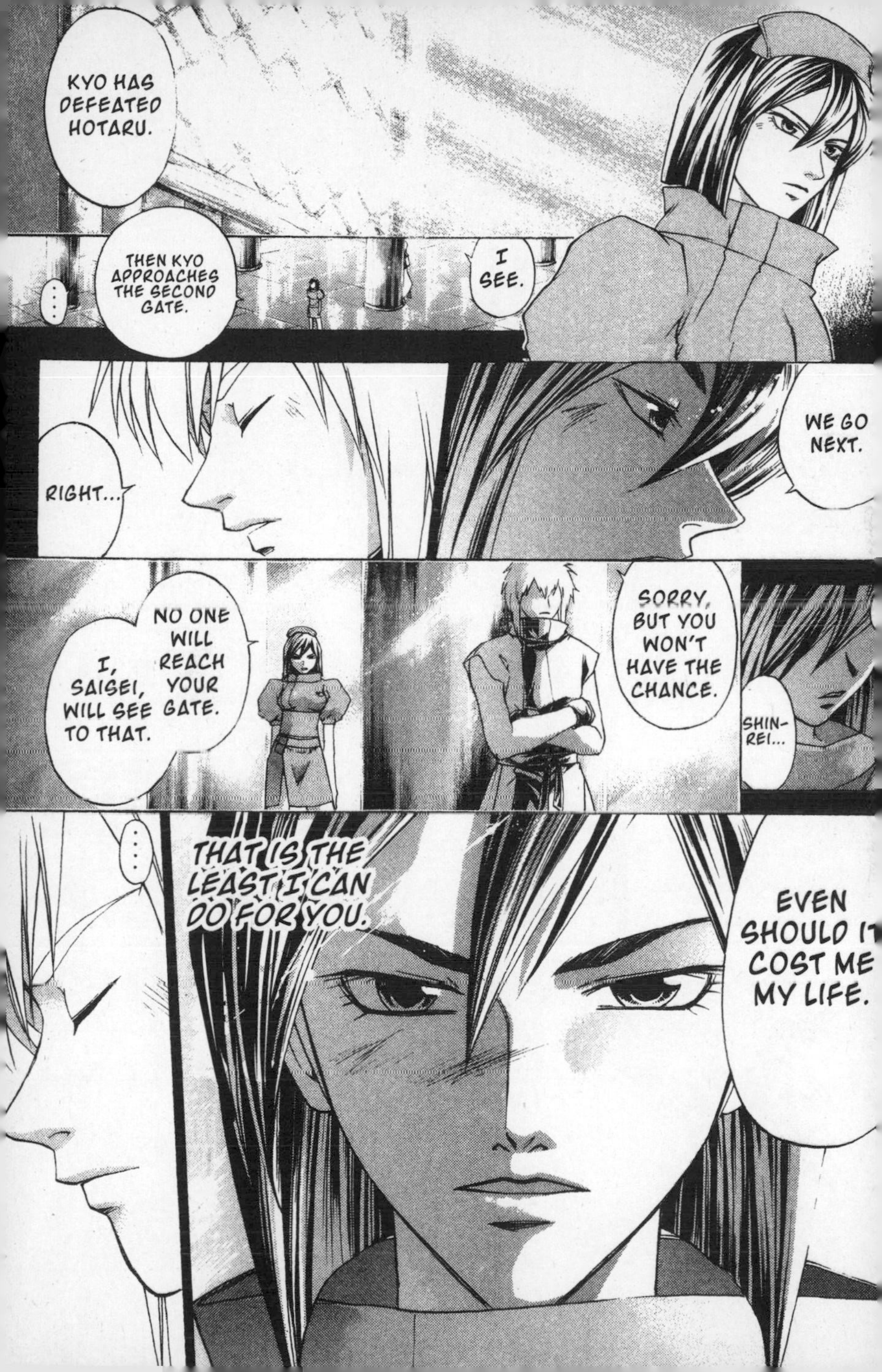
KYO HAS DEFEATED HOTARU.
I SEE.
THEN KYO APPROACHES THE SECOND GATE.
...
WE GO NEXT.
RIGHT...
SHIN-REI...
SORRY, BUT YOU WON'T HAVE THE CHANCE.
NO ONE WILL REACH YOUR GATE.
I, SAISEI, WILL SEE TO THAT.
EVEN SHOULD IT COST ME MY LIFE.
THAT IS THE LEAST I CAN DO FOR YOU.
...

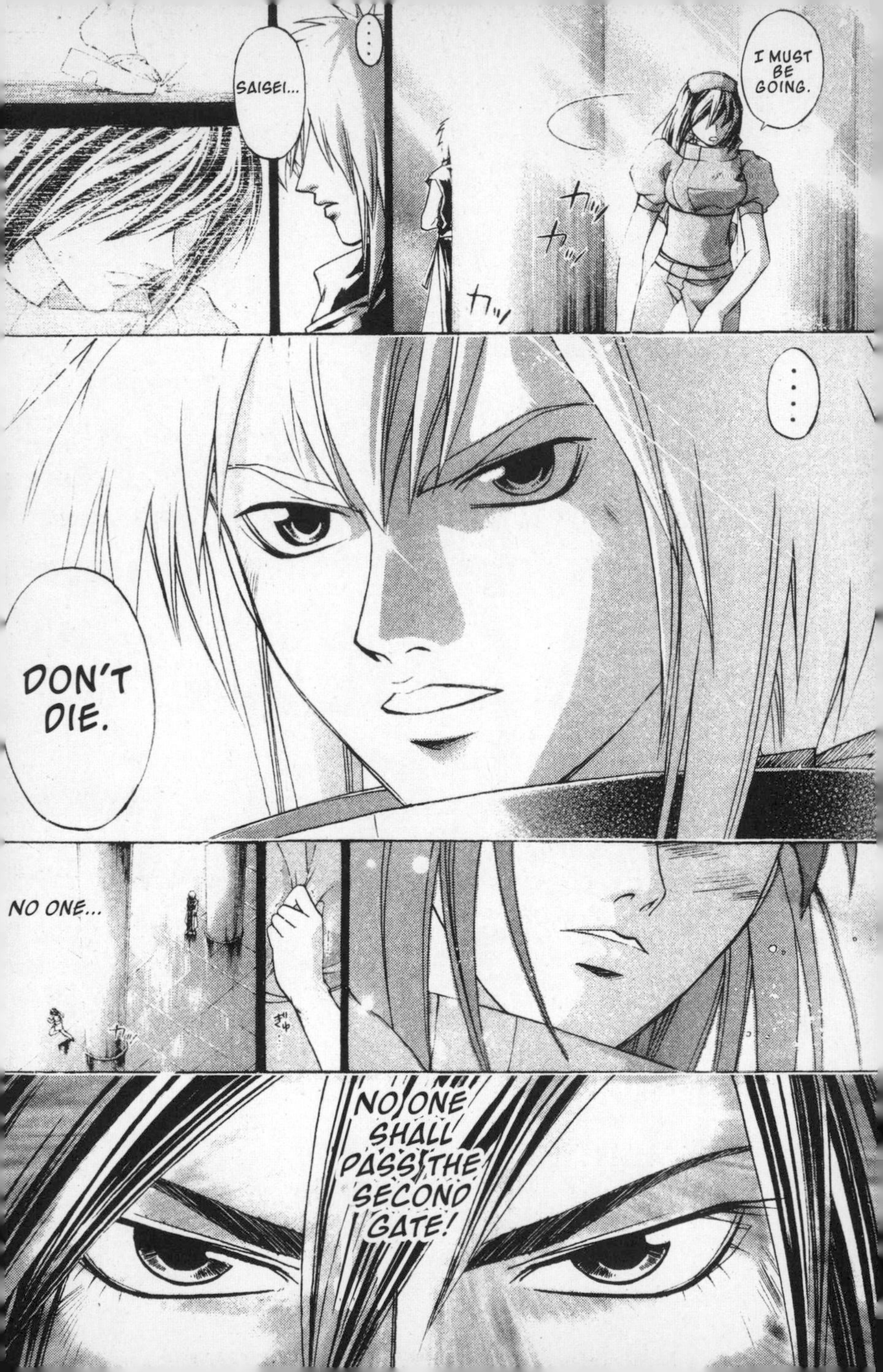
I MUST BE GOING.
カッ
カッ
カッ
...
SAISEI...
...
DON'T DIE.
NO ONE...
NO ONE SHALL PASS THE SECOND GATE!

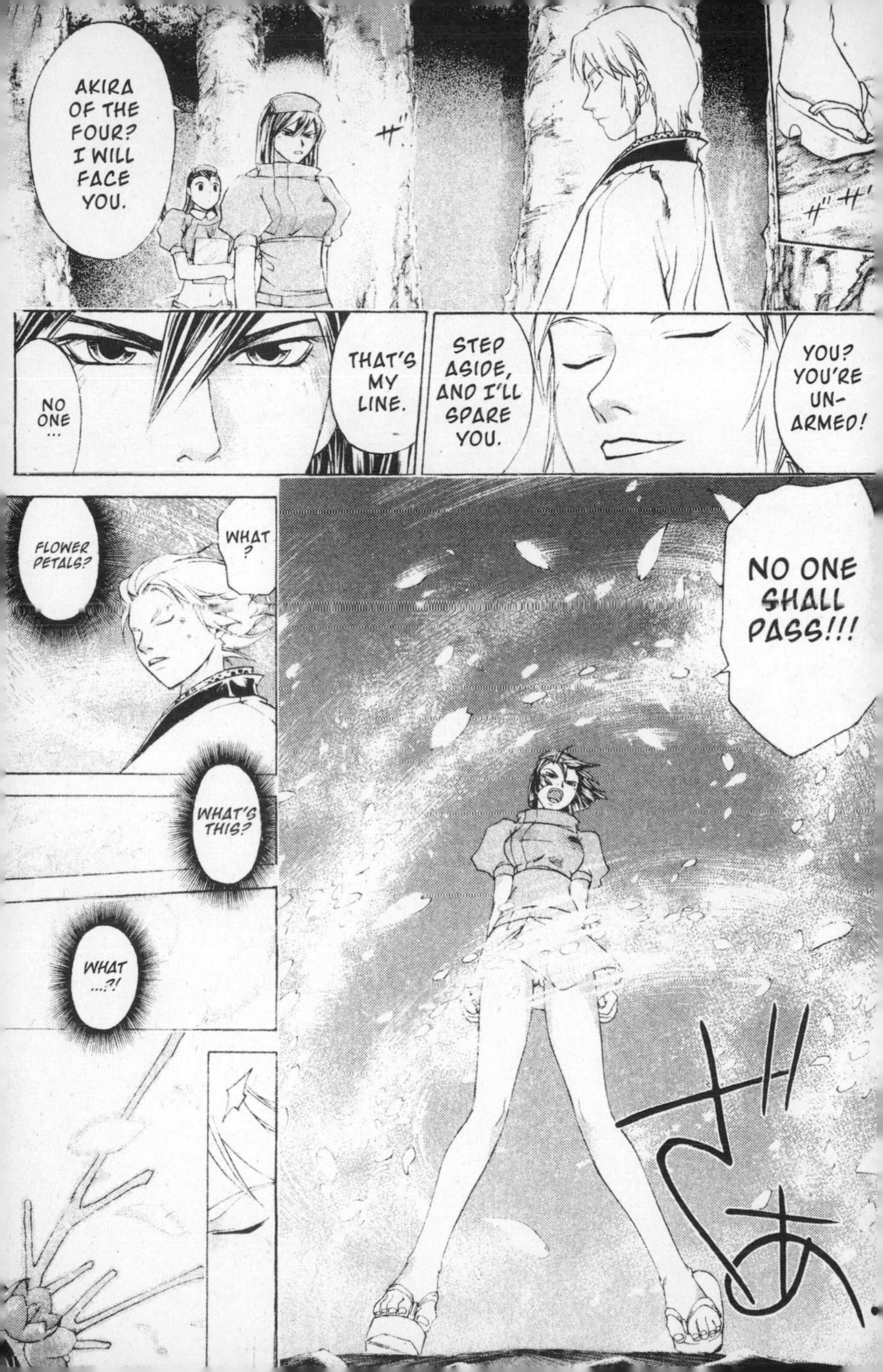
AKIRA OF THE FOUR? I WILL FACE YOU.
YOU? YOU'RE UN-ARMED!
STEP ASIDE, AND I'LL SPARE YOU.
THAT'S MY LINE.
NO ONE ...
NO ONE SHALL PASS!!!
WHAT ?
FLOWER PETALS?
WHAT'S THIS?
WHAT ...?!

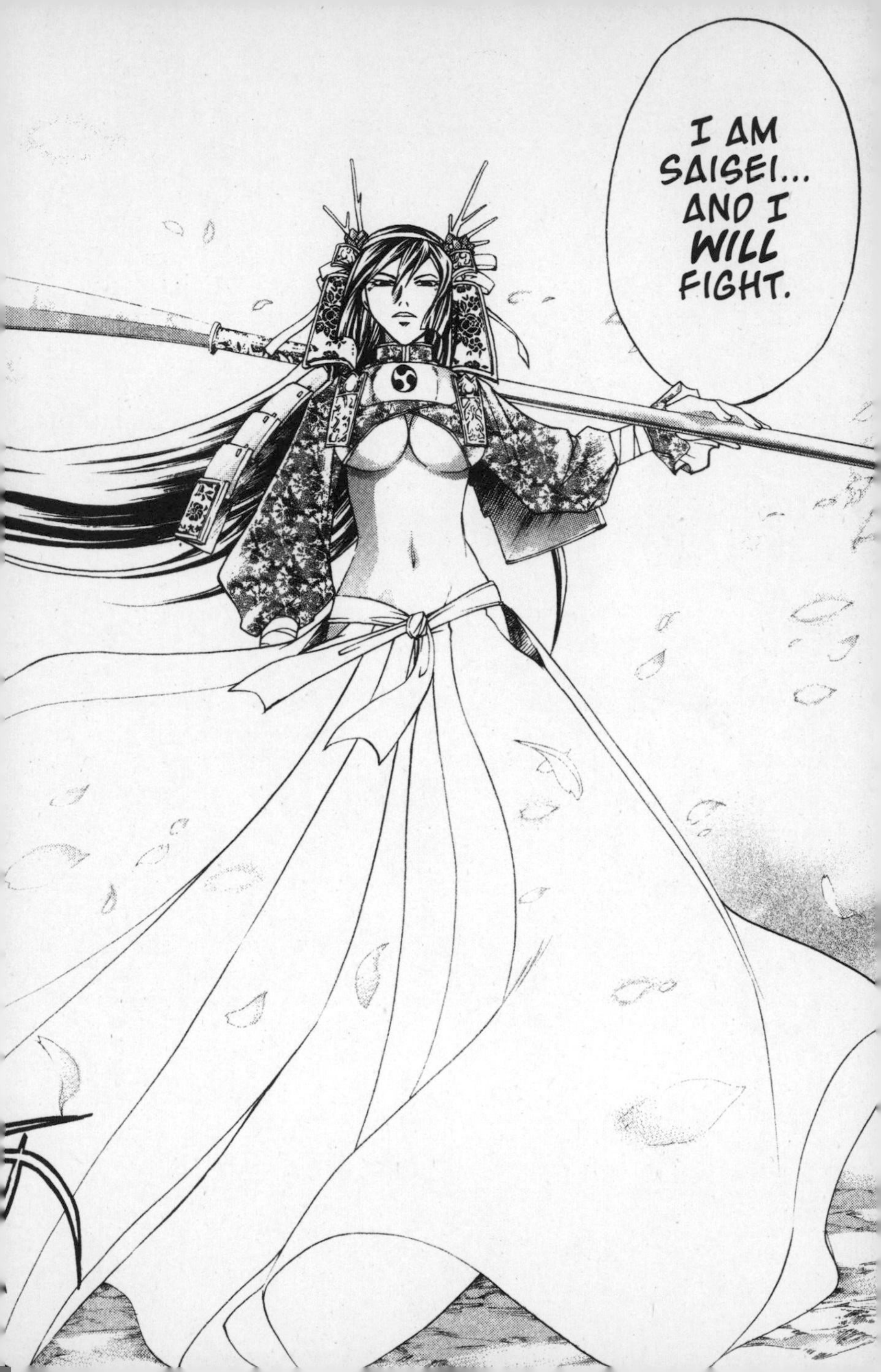
I AM SAISEI... AND I WILL FIGHT.

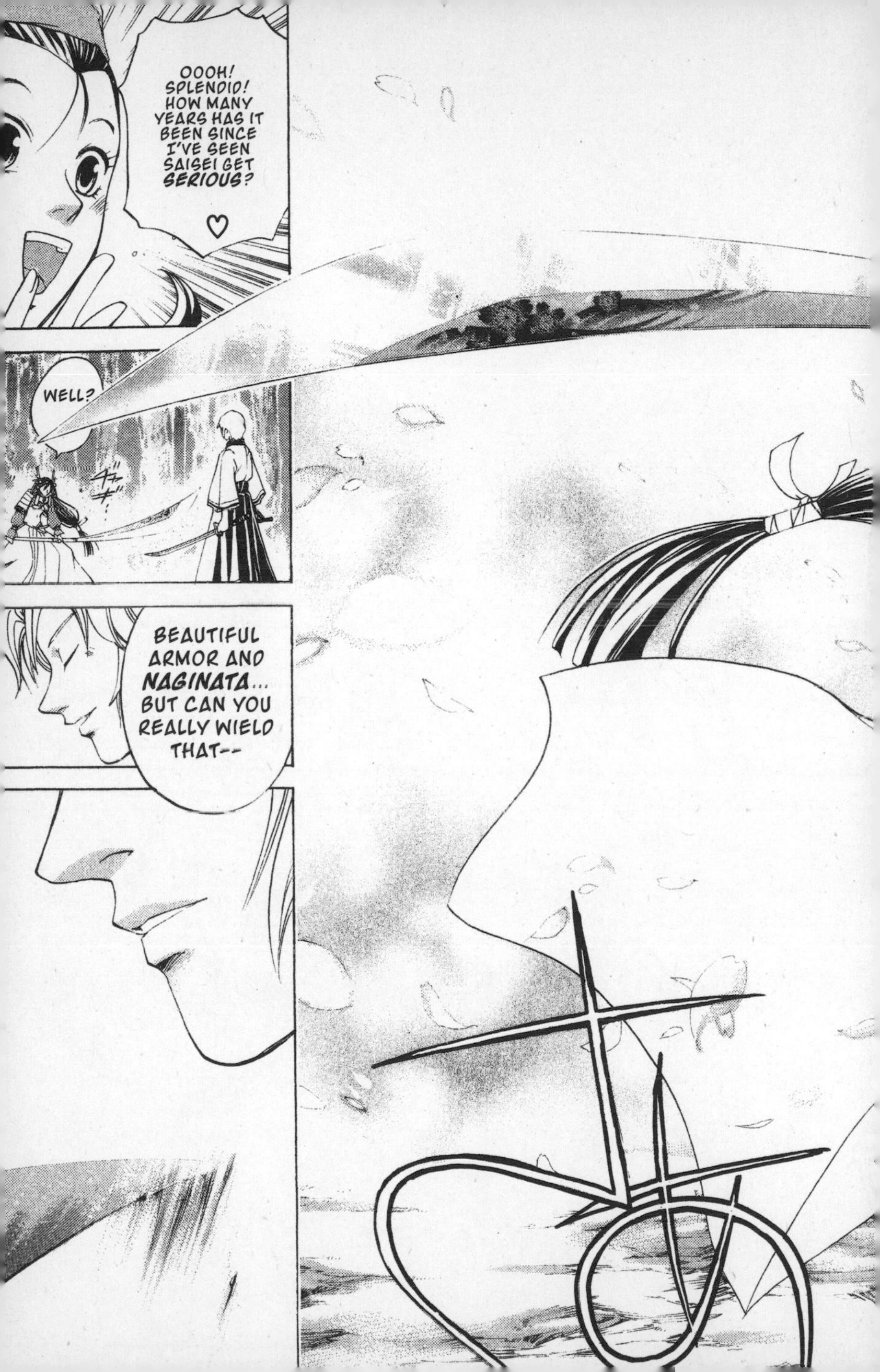
OOOH! SPLENDID! HOW MANY YEARS HAS IT BEEN SINCE I'VE SEEN SAISEI GET SERIOUS? ♡
WELL?
BEAUTIFUL ARMOR AND NAGINATA... BUT CAN YOU REALLY WIELD THAT--

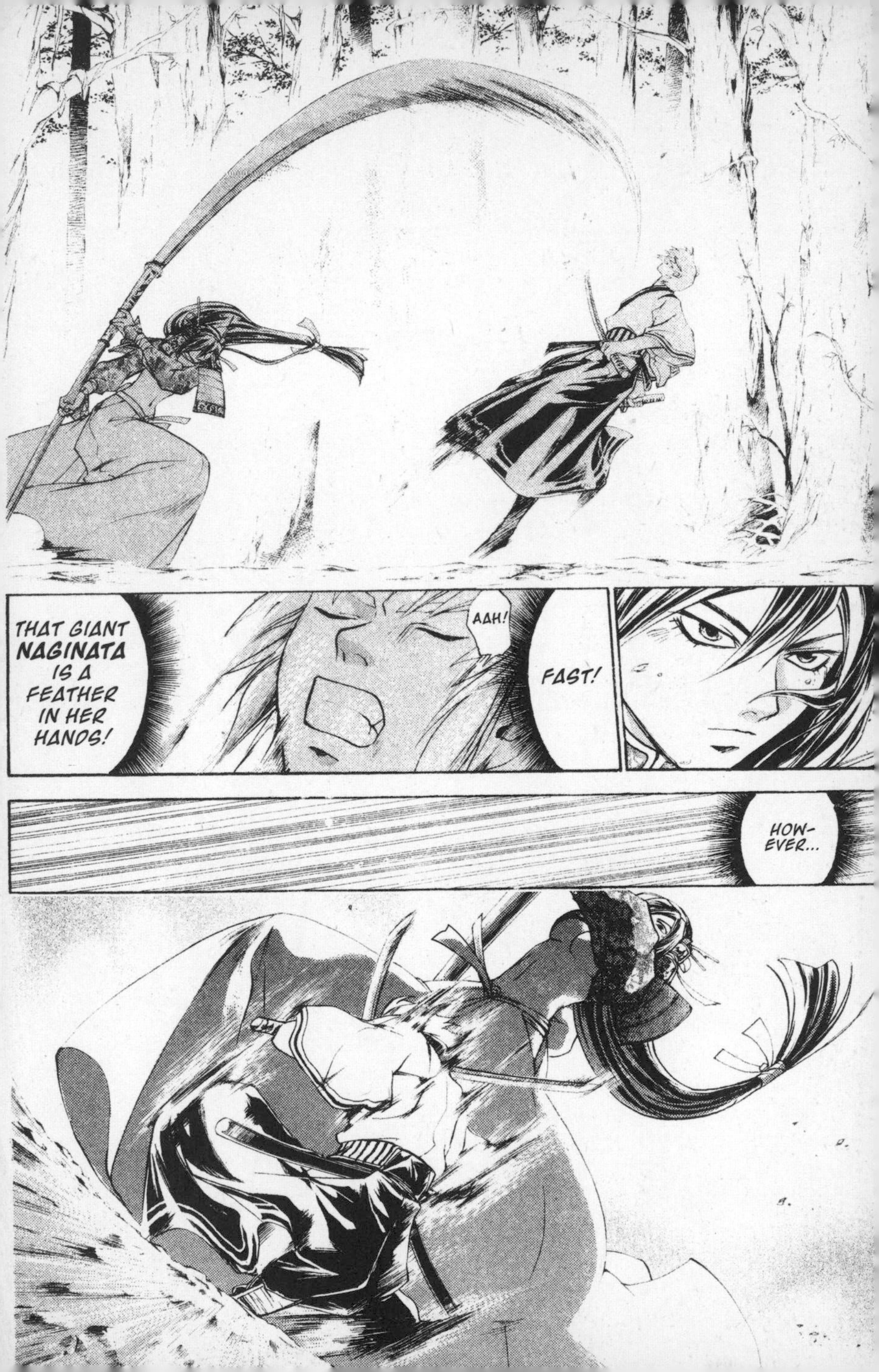
FAST!
AAH!
THAT GIANT NAGINATA IS A FEATHER IN HER HANDS!
HOW-EVER...

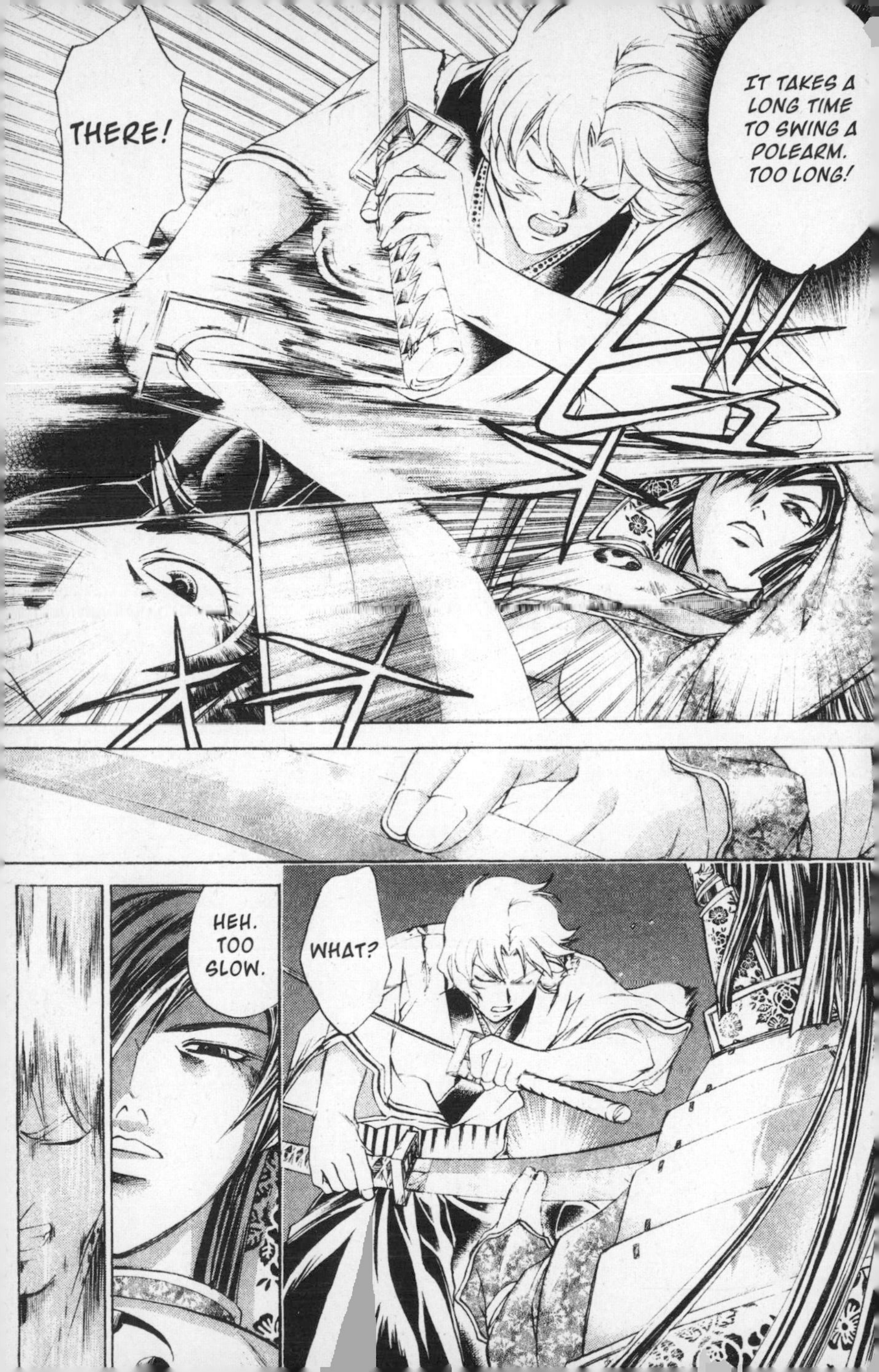
IT TAKES A LONG TIME TO SWING A POLEARM. TOO LONG!
THERE!
WHAT?
HEH. TOO SLOW.

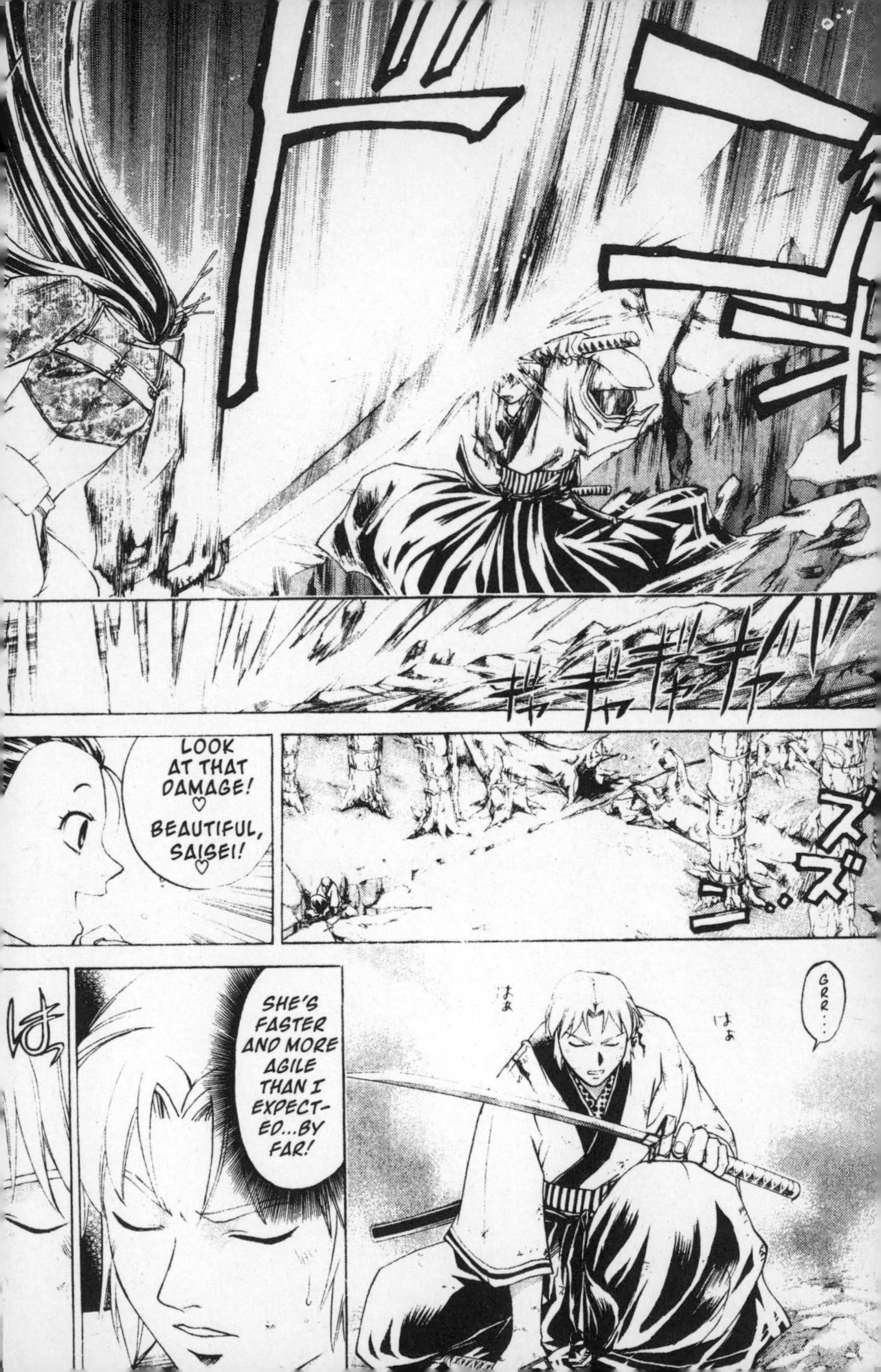
LOOK AT THAT DAMAGE! ♡
BEAUTIFUL, SAISEI! ♡
GRR...
SHE'S FASTER AND MORE AGILE THAN I EXPECTED...BY FAR!

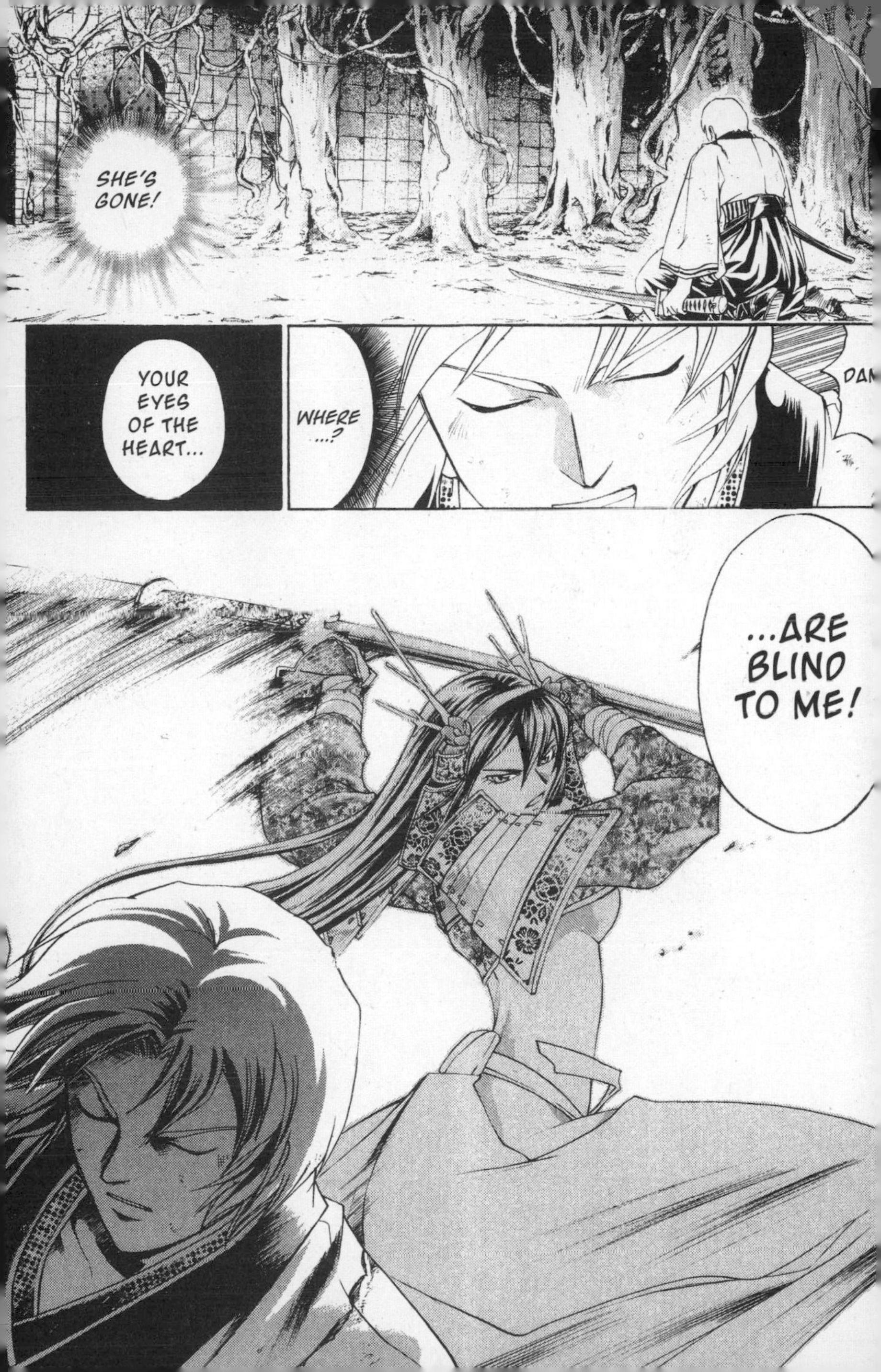
SHE'S GONE!
DAM
WHERE ...?
YOUR EYES OF THE HEART...
...ARE BLIND TO ME!

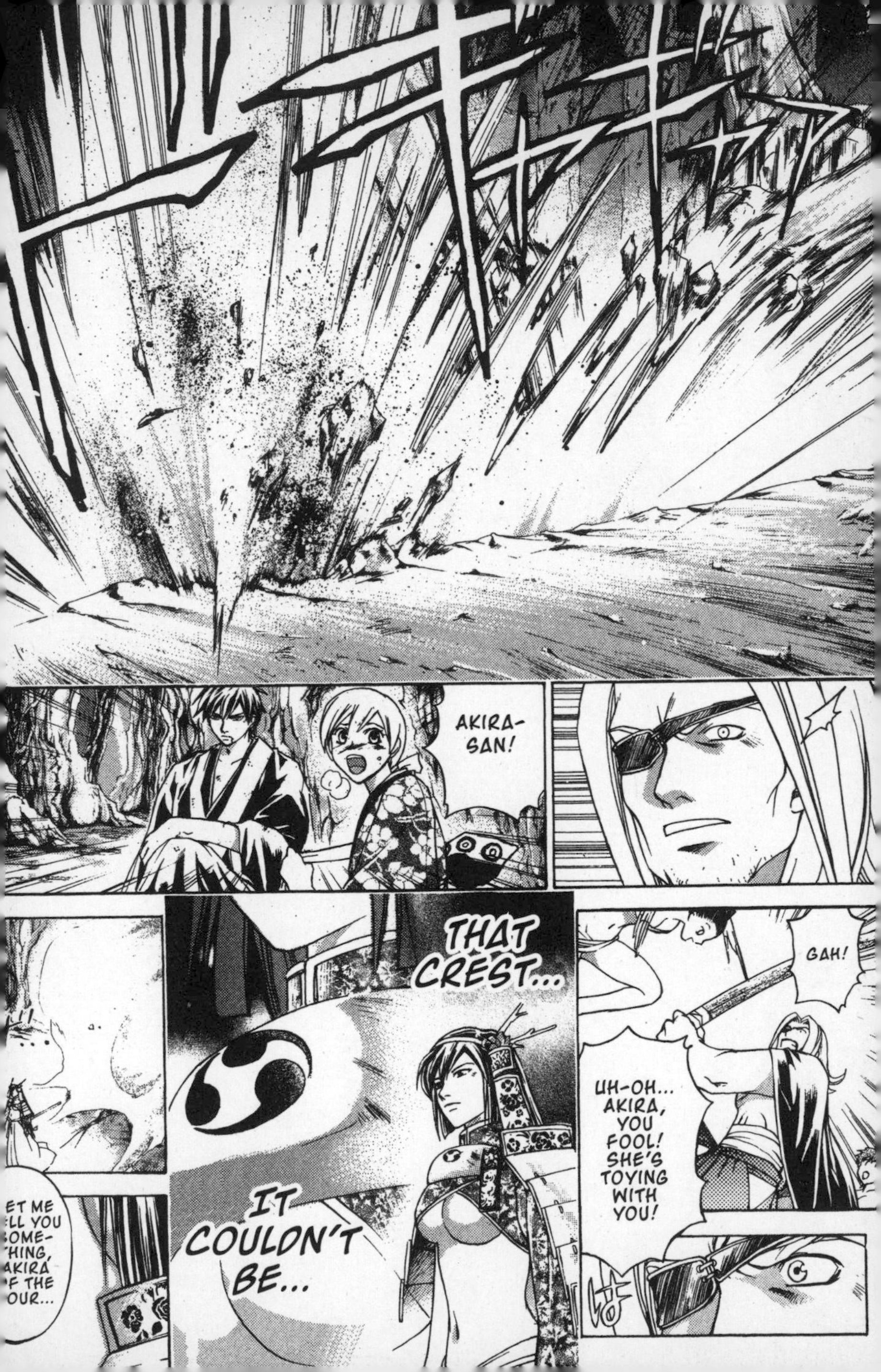
AKIRA-SAN!
GAH!
UH-OH... AKIRA, YOU FOOL! SHE'S TOYING WITH YOU!
THAT CREST...
IT COULDN'T BE...
ET ME ELL YOU OME-HING, AKIRA F THE OUR...

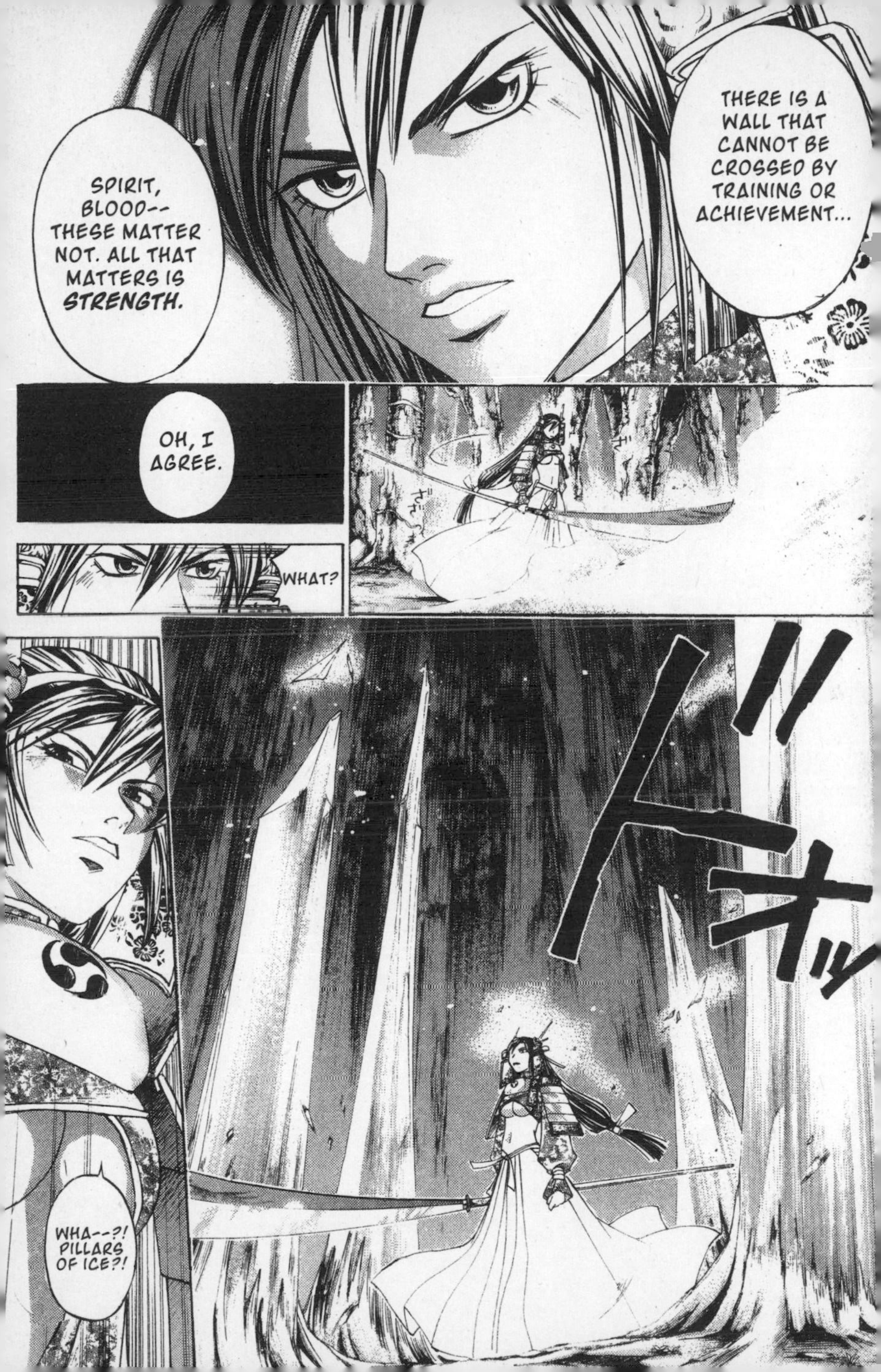
THERE IS A WALL THAT CANNOT BE CROSSED BY TRAINING OR ACHIEVEMENT...
SPIRIT, BLOOD-- THESE MATTER NOT. ALL THAT MATTERS IS STRENGTH.
OH, I AGREE.
WHAT?
WHA--?! PILLARS OF ICE?!

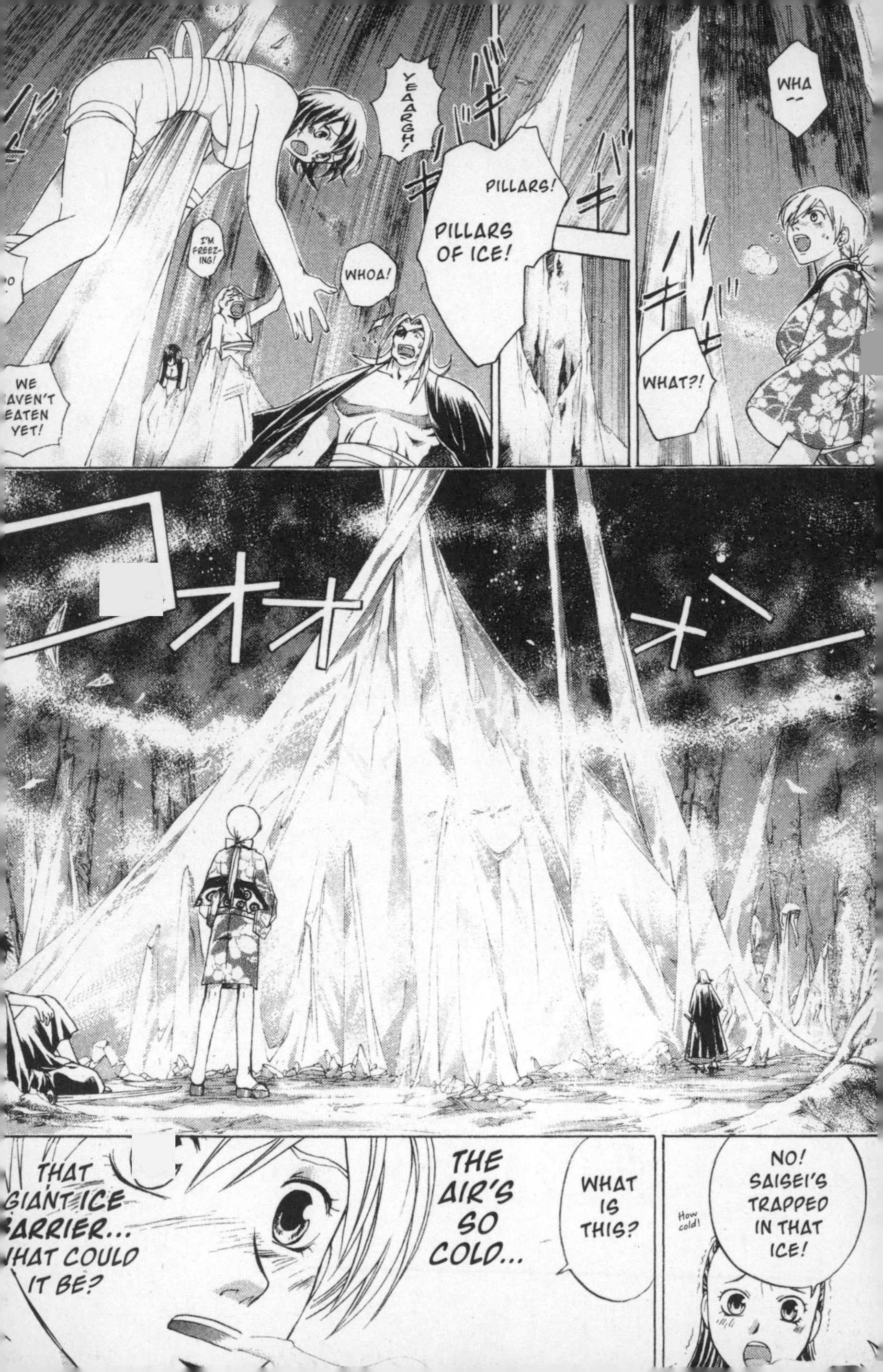
WHA --
WHAT?!
PILLARS! PILLARS OF ICE!
YEAAARGH!
WHOA!
I'M FREEZING!
WE AVEN'T EATEN YET!
NO! SAISEI'S TRAPPED IN THAT ICE!
How cold!
WHAT IS THIS?
THE AIR'S SO COLD...
THAT GIANT ICE ARRIER... HAT COULD IT BE?

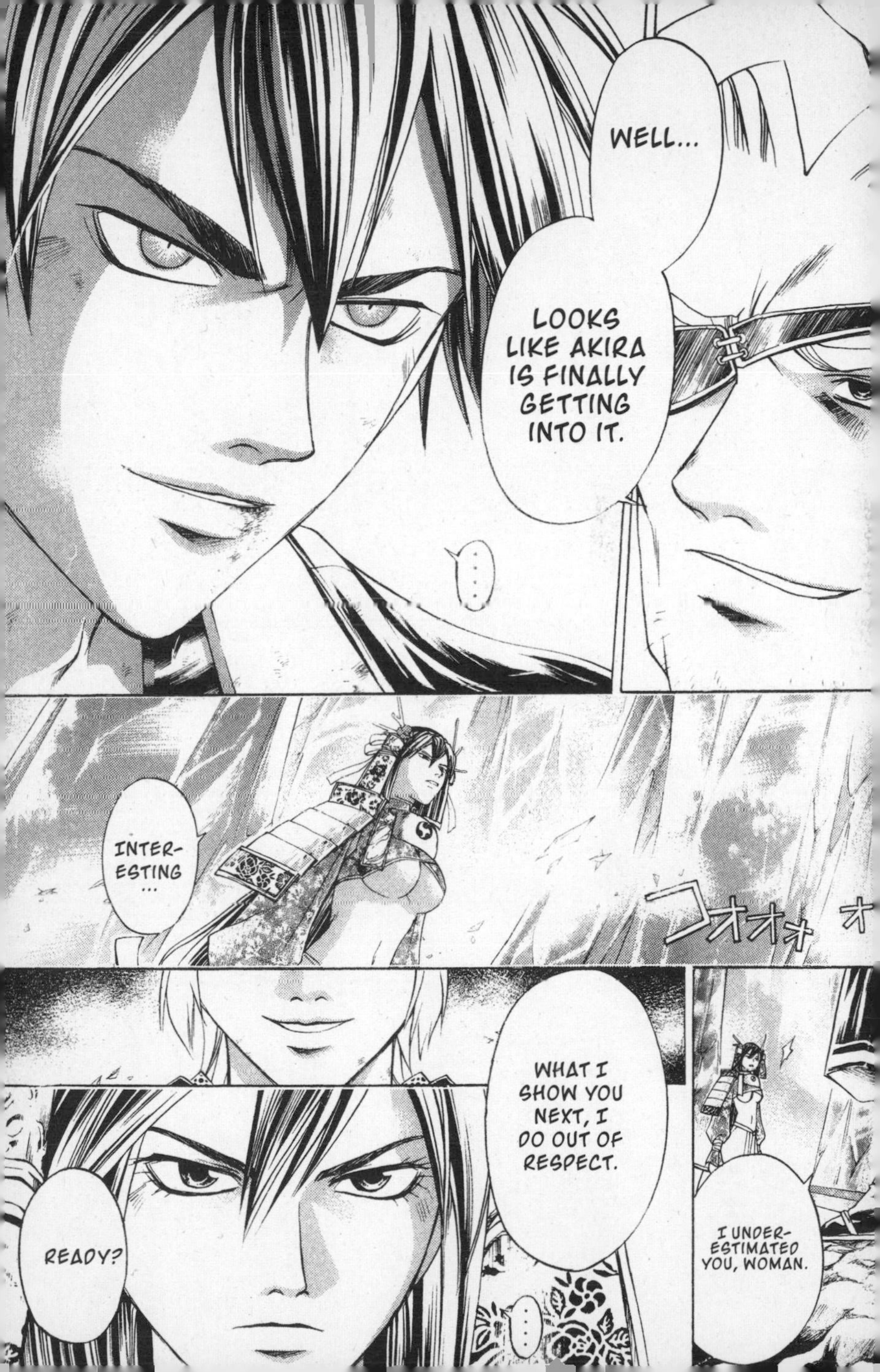
WELL...
LOOKS LIKE AKIRA IS FINALLY GETTING INTO IT.
...
コオオォ オ
INTER-ESTING ...
I UNDER-ESTIMATED YOU, WOMAN.
WHAT I SHOW YOU NEXT, I DO OUT OF RESPECT.
...
READY?

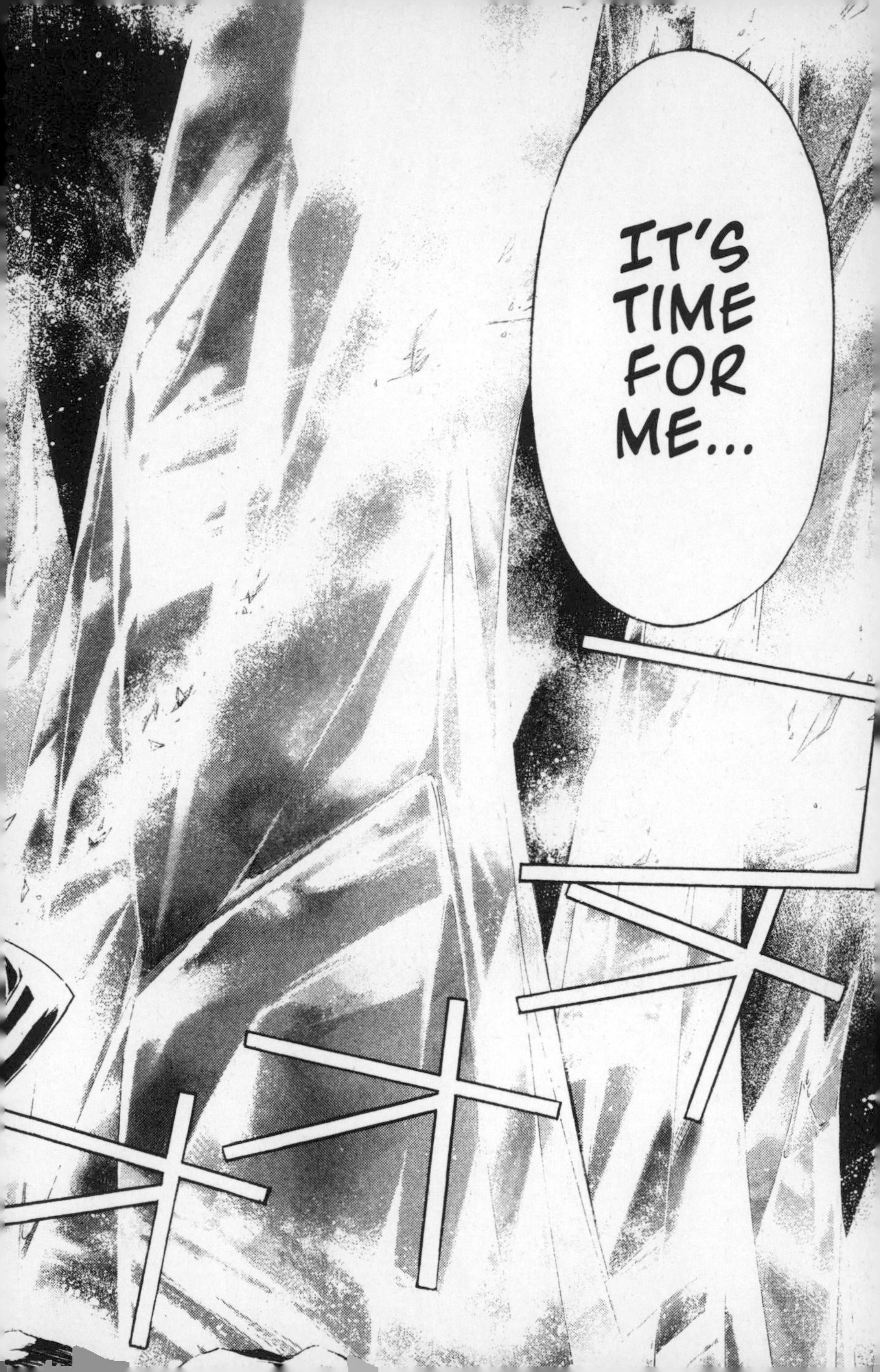
IT'S TIME FOR ME...

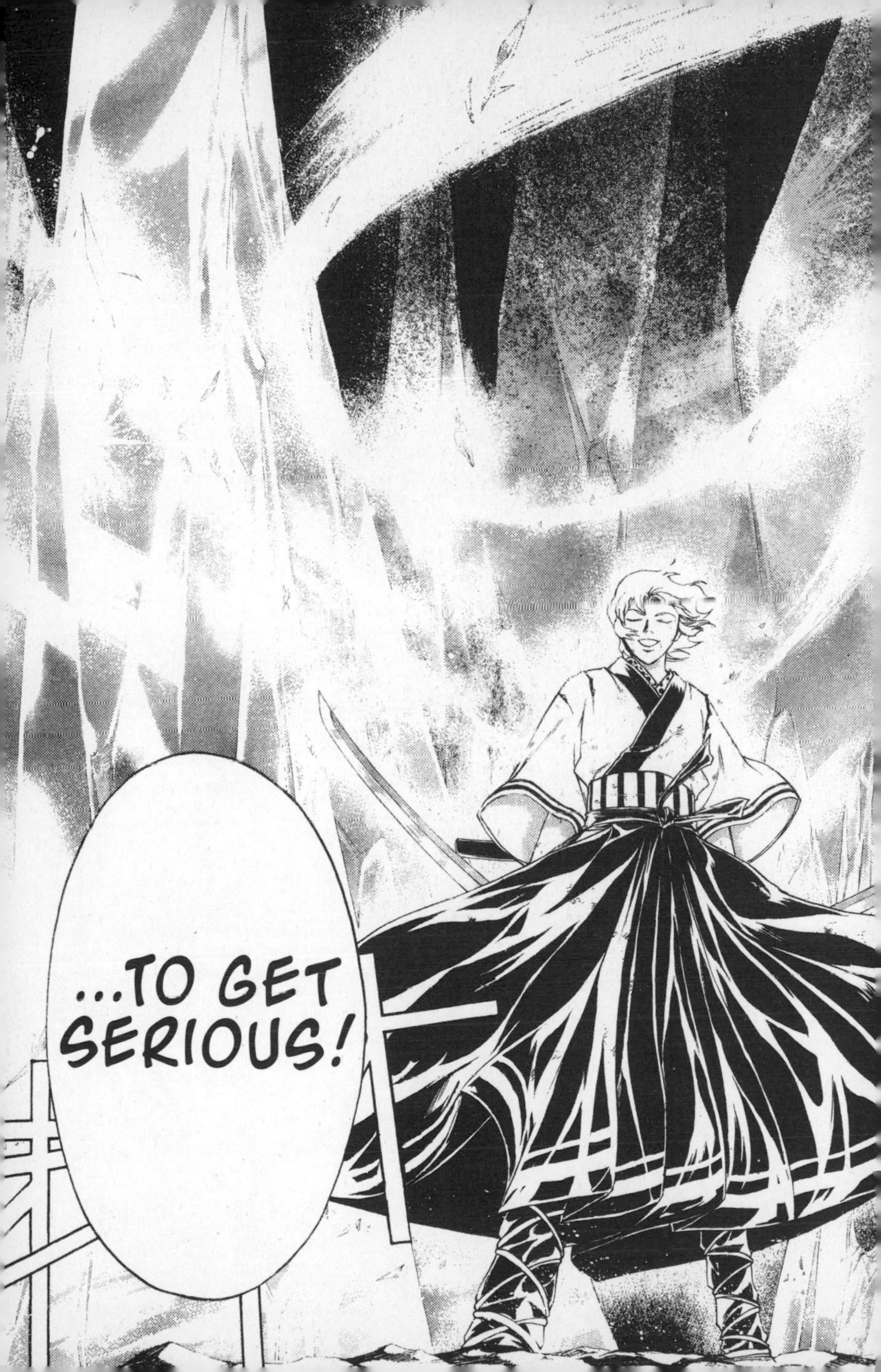
...TO GET SERIOUS!

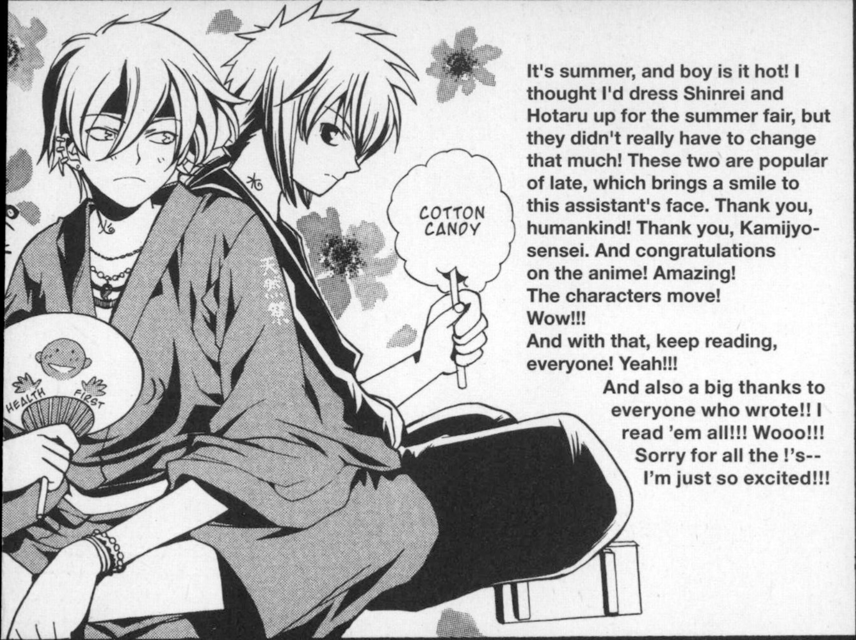
COTTON CANDY
HEALTH FIRST

It's summer, and boy is it hot! I thought I'd dress Shinrei and Hotaru up for the summer fair, but they didn't really have to change that much! These two are popular of late, which brings a smile to this assistant's face. Thank you, humankind! Thank you, Kamijyo-sensei. And congratulations on the anime! Amazing!
The characters move!
Wow!!!
And with that, keep reading, everyone! Yeah!!!

And also a big thanks to everyone who wrote!! I read 'em all!!! Wooo!!! Sorry for all the !'s-- I'm just so excited!!!

Kamijyo: Thanks, humankind! Thanks Mr. Asami! Anime! Anime!

Hazuki Asami (The Chief)

Soma Akatsuki (The Sub-Chief)

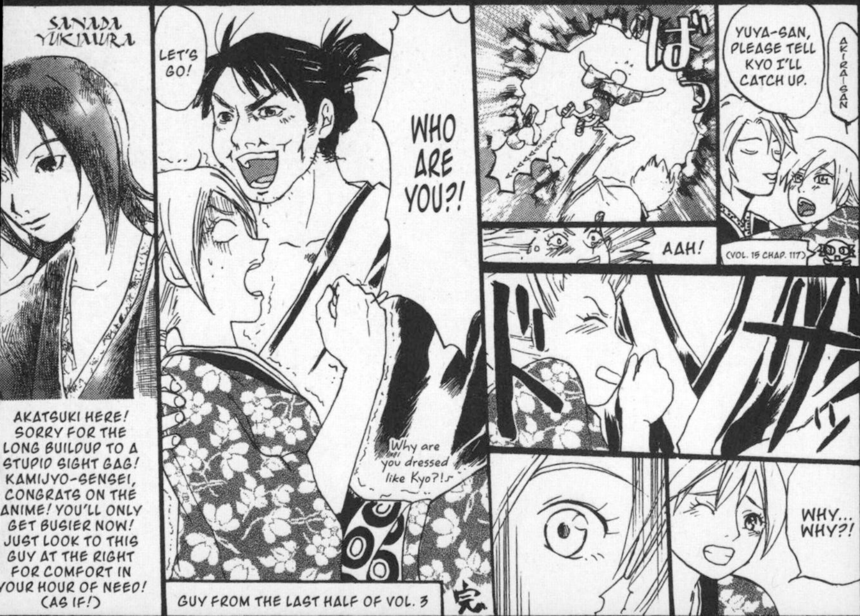
YUYA-SAN, PLEASE TELL KYO I'LL CATCH UP.
AKIRA-SAN
ばっ
AAH!
(VOL. 15 CHAP. 117)
ドサッ
WHY... WHY?!
LET'S GO!
WHO ARE YOU?!
Why are you dressed like Kyo?!
GUY FROM THE LAST HALF OF VOL. 3
完
SANADA YUKIMURA
AKATSUKI HERE! SORRY FOR THE LONG BUILDUP TO A STUPID SIGHT GAG! KAMIJYO-SENSEI, CONGRATS ON THE ANIME! YOU'LL ONLY GET BUSIER NOW! JUST LOOK TO THIS GUY AT THE RIGHT FOR COMFORT IN YOUR HOUR OF NEED! (AS IF!)

Kamijyo: Who was that guy?! :-)

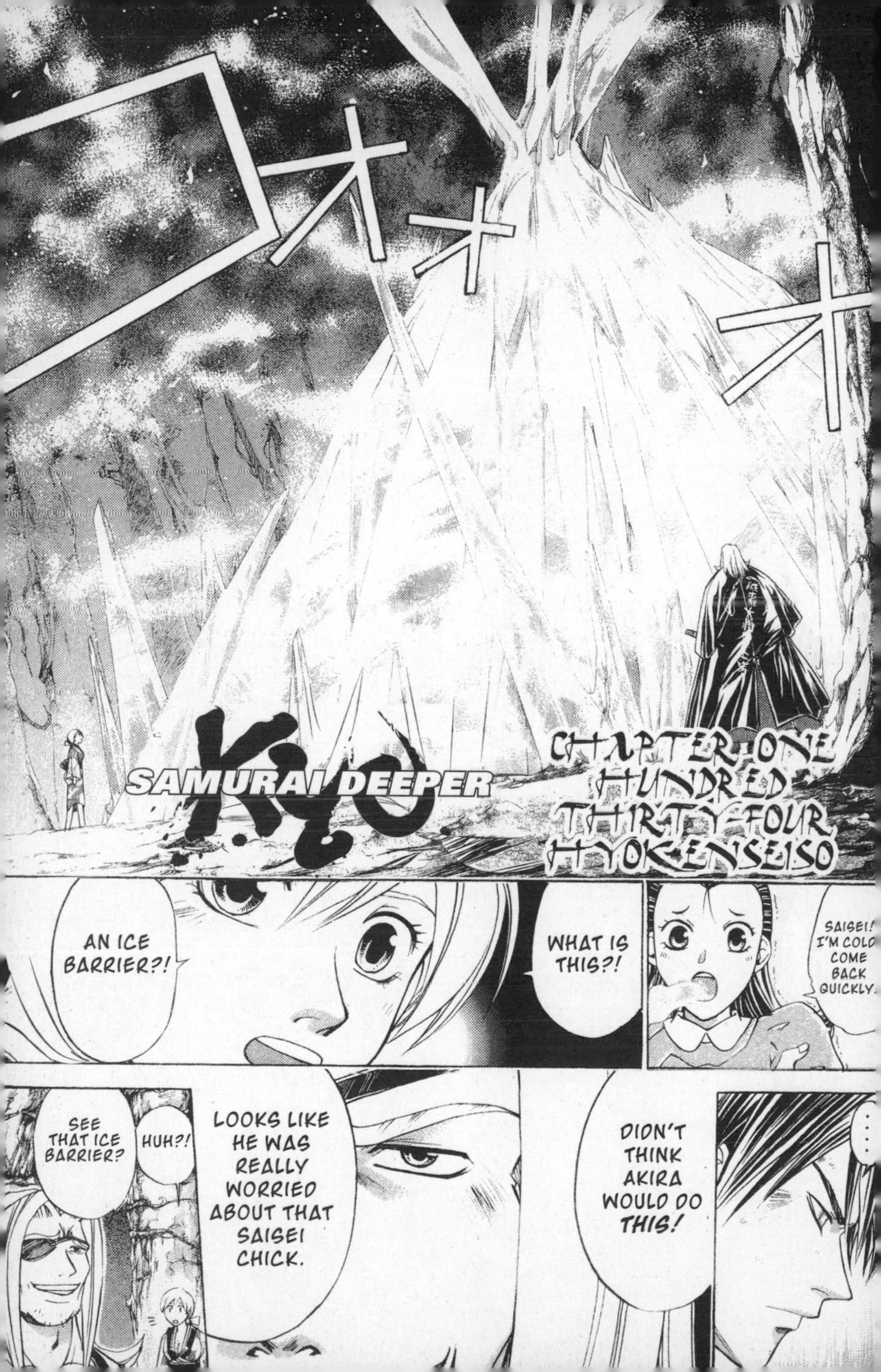
CHAPTER ONE HUNDRED THIRTY-FOUR HYOKENSEISO
SAMURAI DEEPER KYO
SAISEI! I'M COLD COME BACK QUICKLY.
WHAT IS THIS?!
AN ICE BARRIER?!
...
DIDN'T THINK AKIRA WOULD DO THIS!
LOOKS LIKE HE WAS REALLY WORRIED ABOUT THAT SAISEI CHICK.
HUH?!
SEE THAT ICE BARRIER?

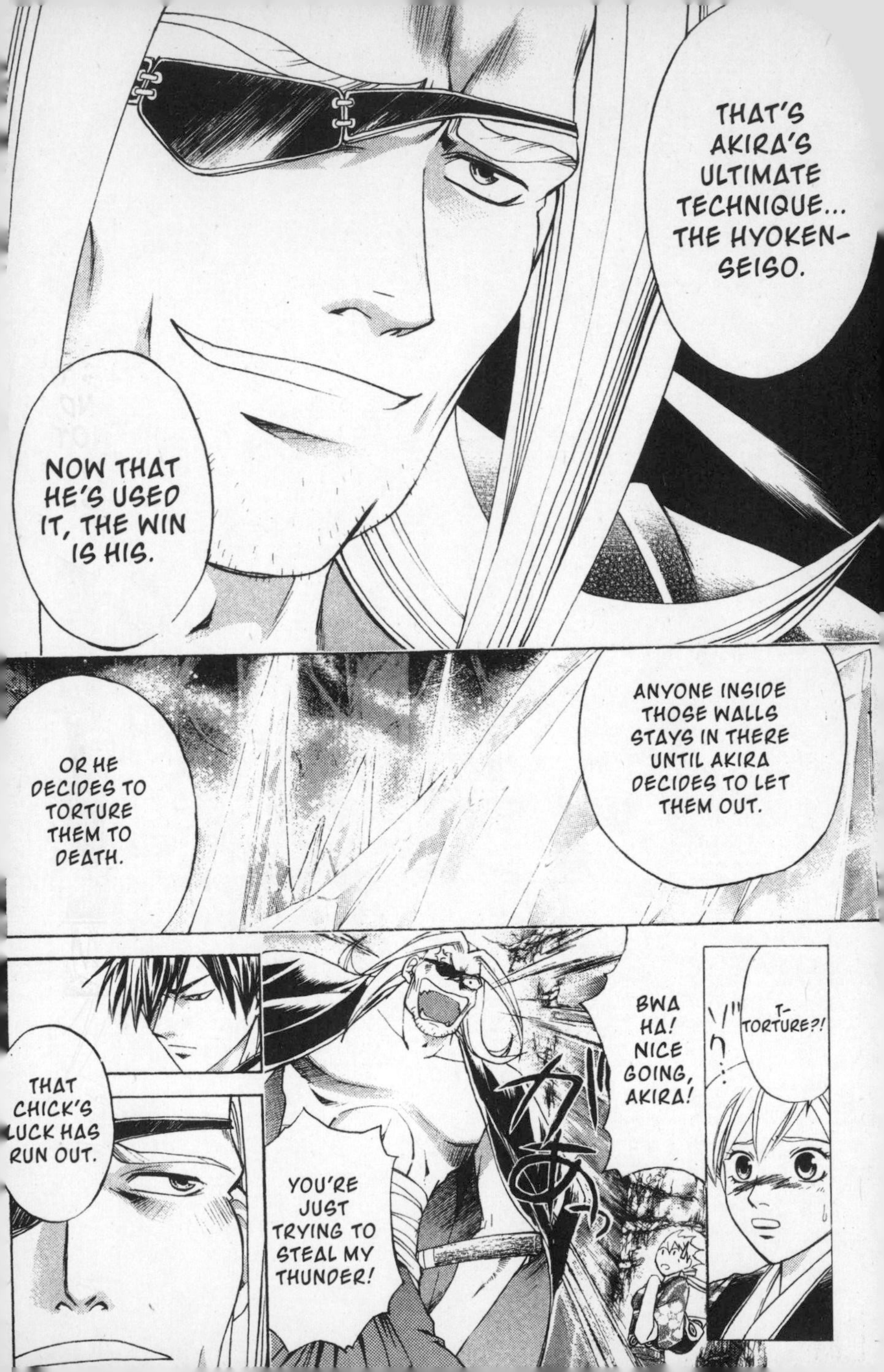
THAT'S AKIRA'S ULTIMATE TECHNIQUE... THE HYOKEN-SEISO.
NOW THAT HE'S USED IT, THE WIN IS HIS.
ANYONE INSIDE THOSE WALLS STAYS IN THERE UNTIL AKIRA DECIDES TO LET THEM OUT.
OR HE DECIDES TO TORTURE THEM TO DEATH.
T-TORTURE?!
BWA HA! NICE GOING, AKIRA!
YOU'RE JUST TRYING TO STEAL MY THUNDER!
THAT CHICK'S LUCK HAS RUN OUT.

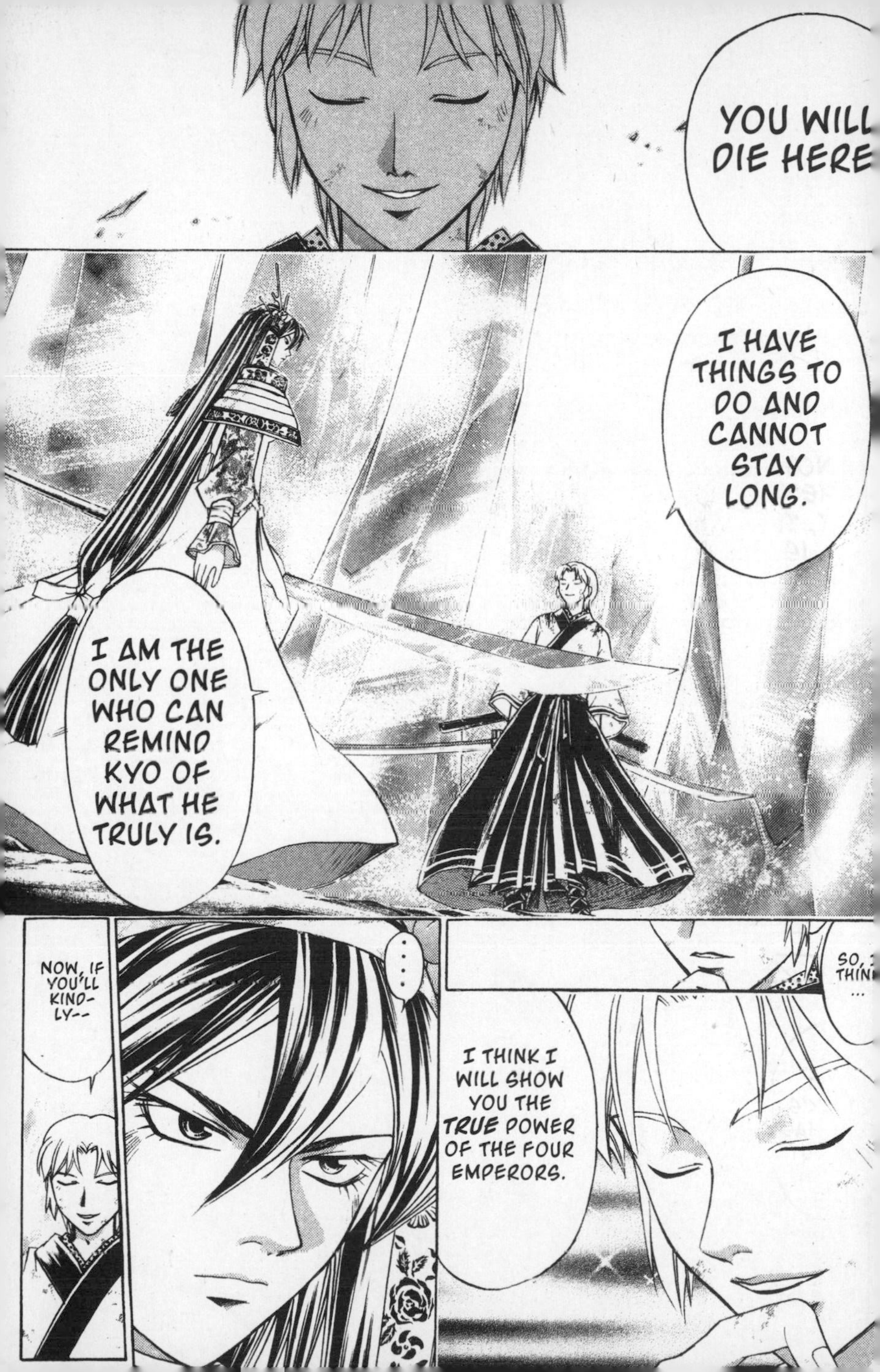
YOU WILL DIE HERE
I HAVE THINGS TO DO AND CANNOT STAY LONG.
I AM THE ONLY ONE WHO CAN REMIND KYO OF WHAT HE TRULY IS.
SO, THIN ...
I THINK I WILL SHOW YOU THE *TRUE* POWER OF THE FOUR EMPERORS.
....
NOW, IF YOU'LL KINDLY--

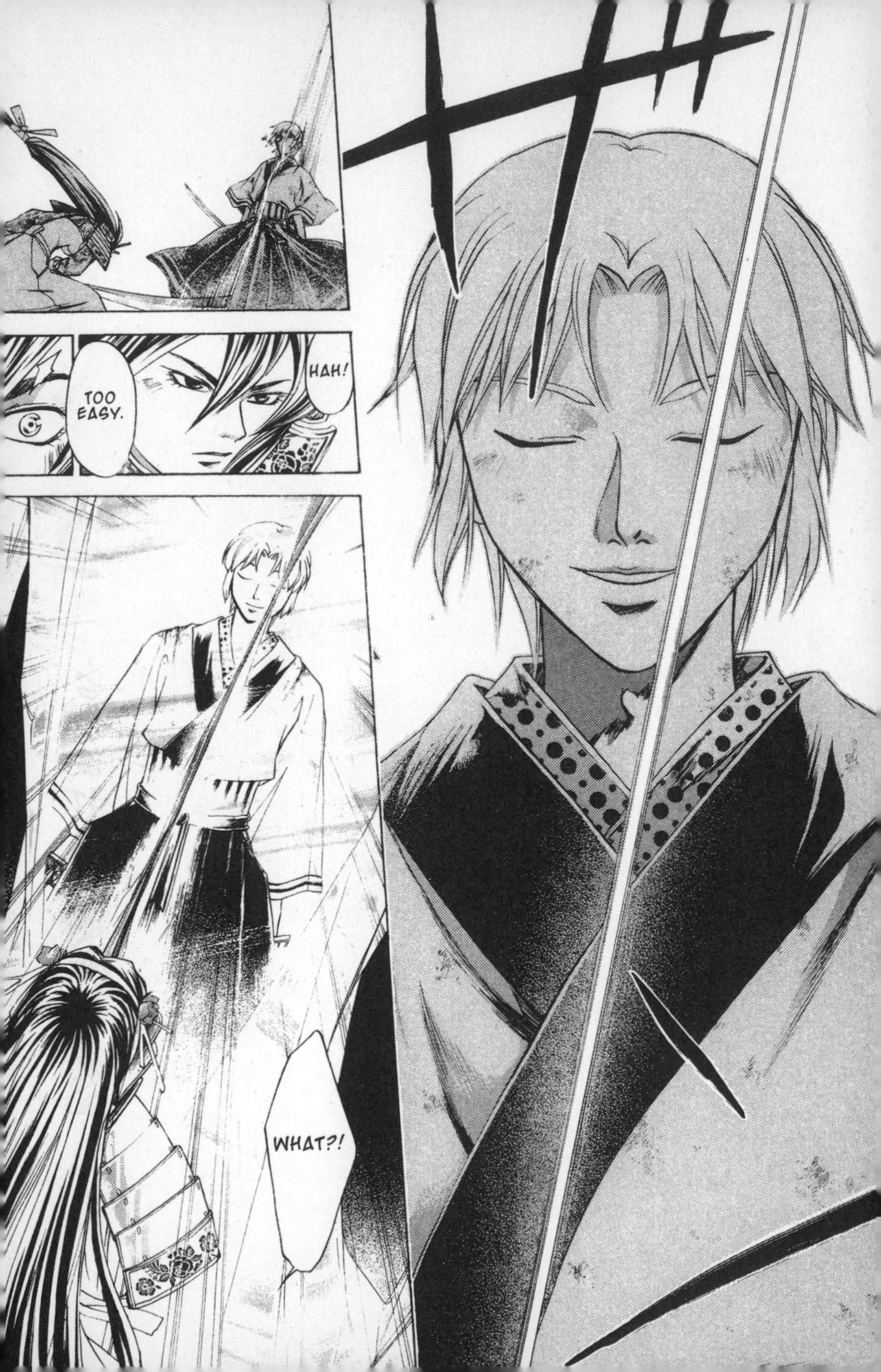
HAH!
TOO EASY.
WHAT?!

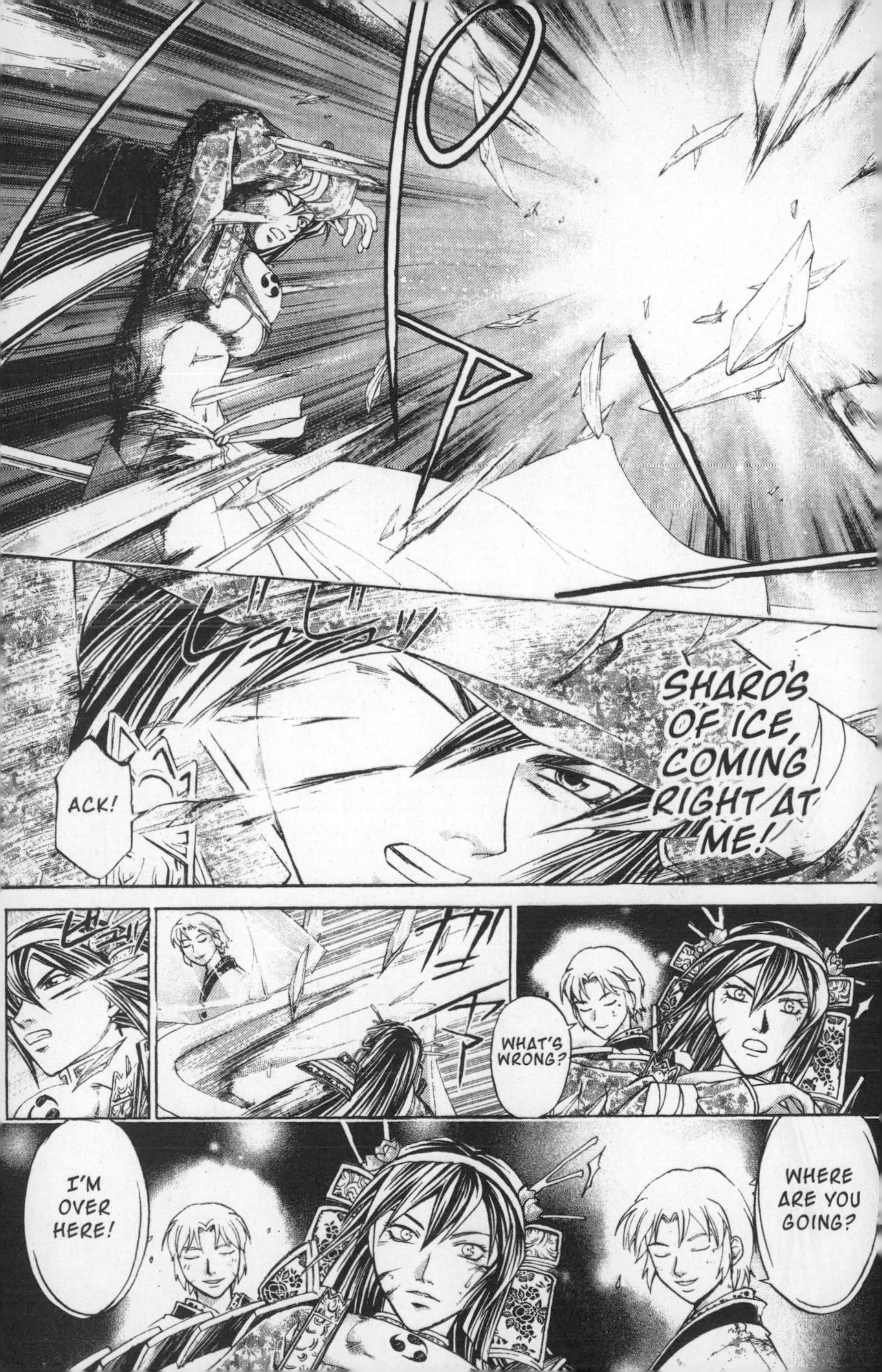
SHARDS OF ICE, COMING RIGHT AT ME!
ACK!
WHAT'S WRONG?
WHERE ARE YOU GOING?
I'M OVER HERE!

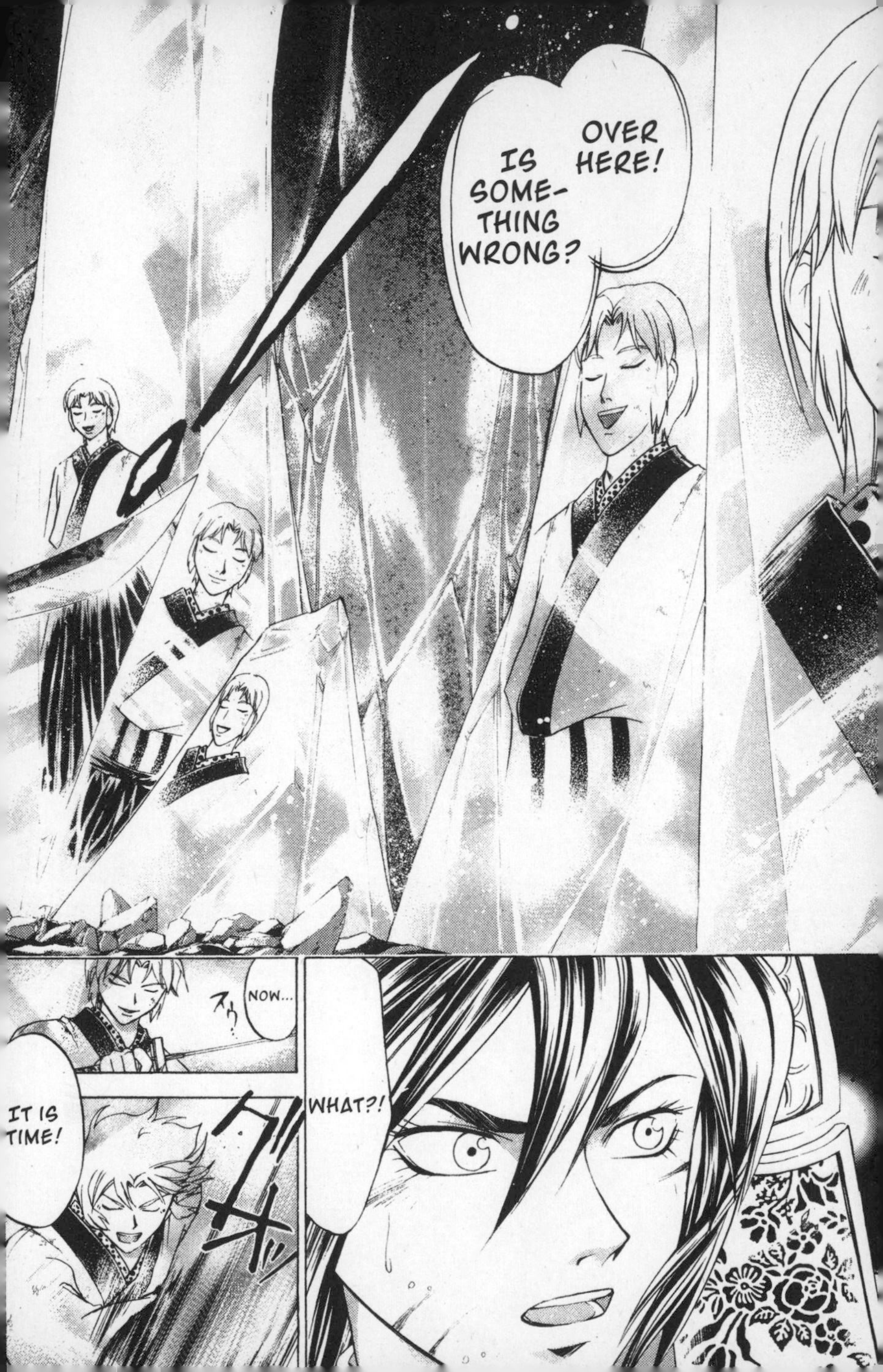
OVER HERE!
IS SOMETHING WRONG?
NOW...
IT IS TIME!
WHAT?!

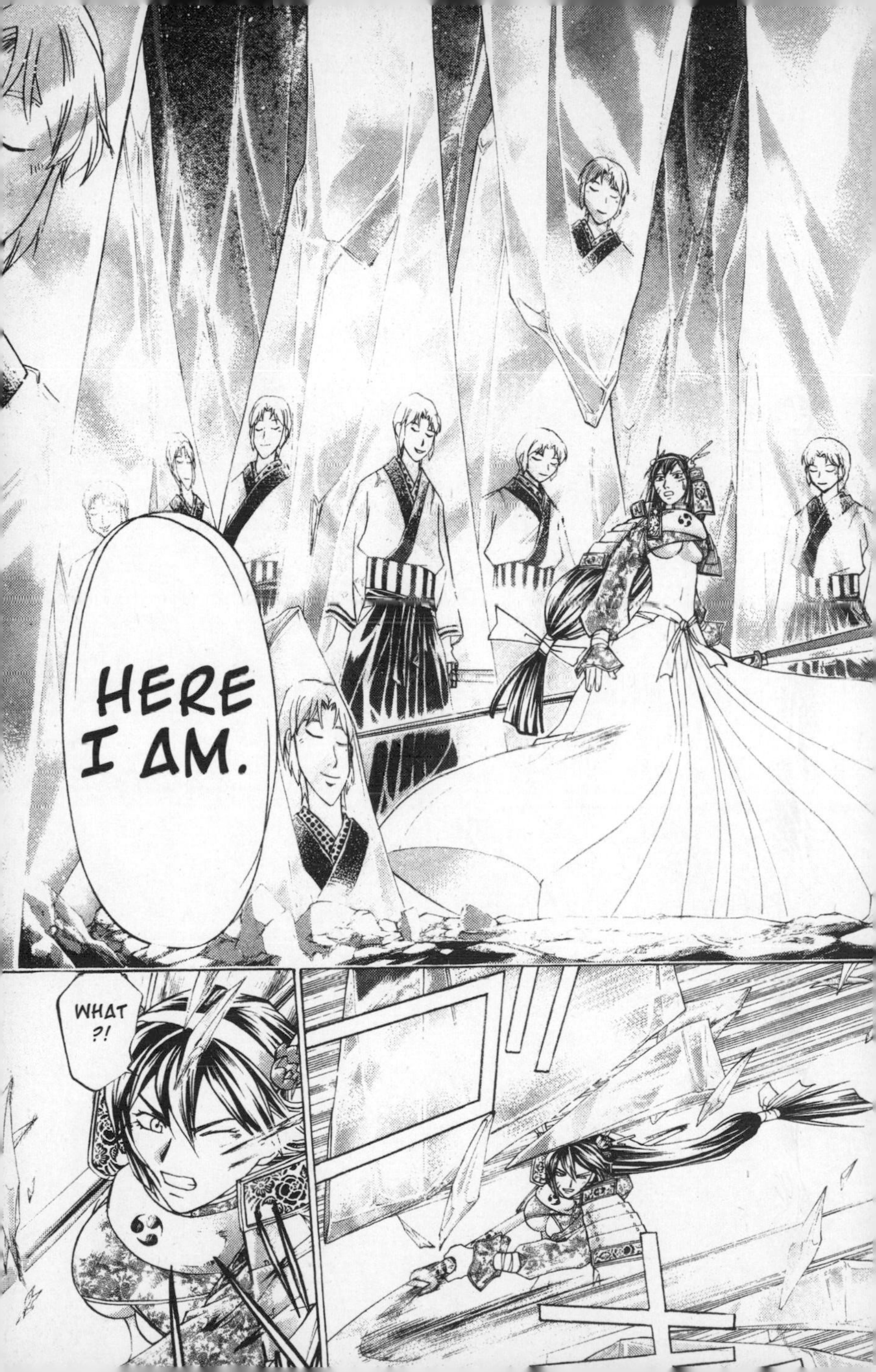
HERE I AM.
WHAT ?!

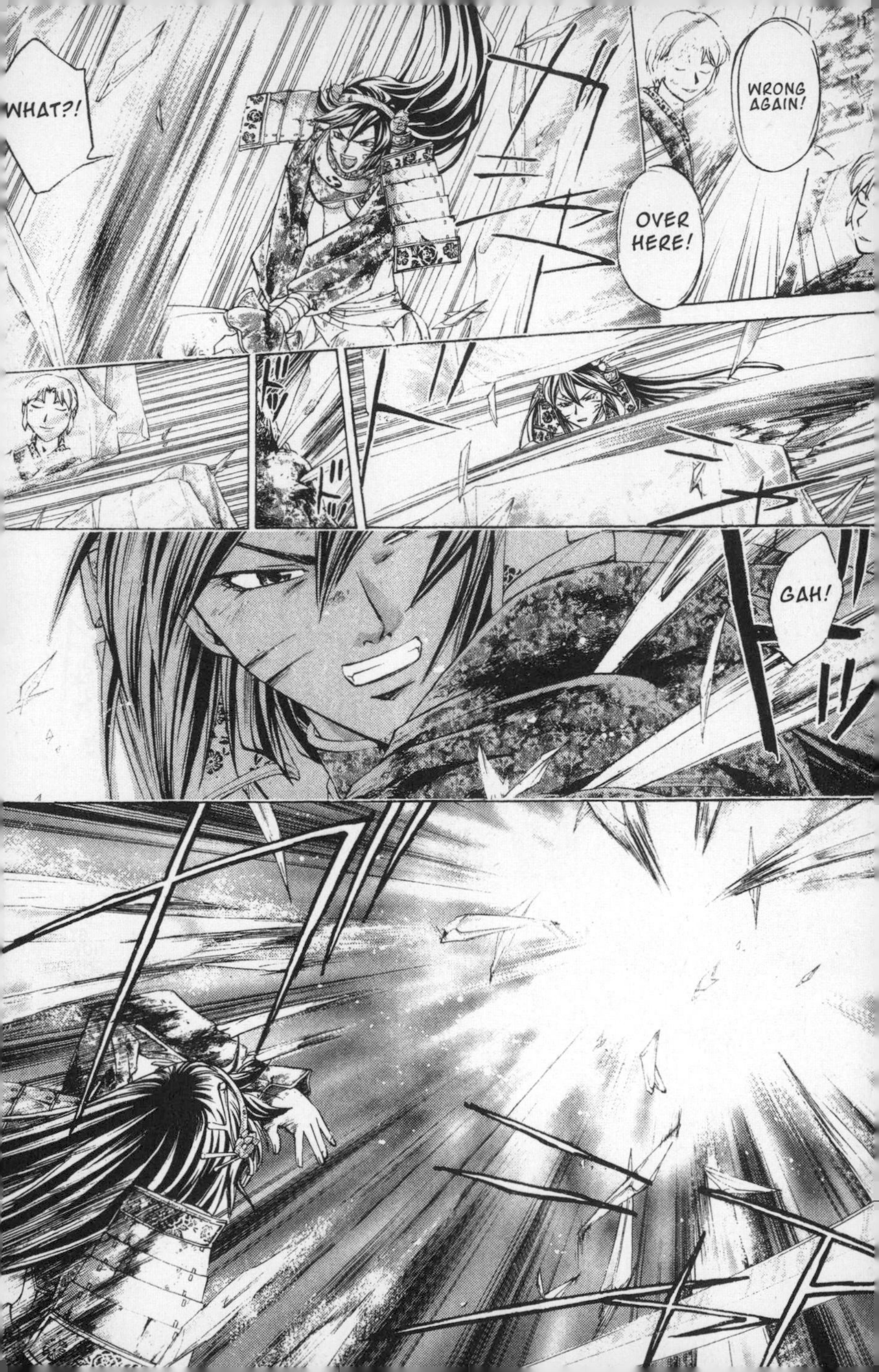
WRONG AGAIN!
OVER HERE!
WHAT?!
GAH!

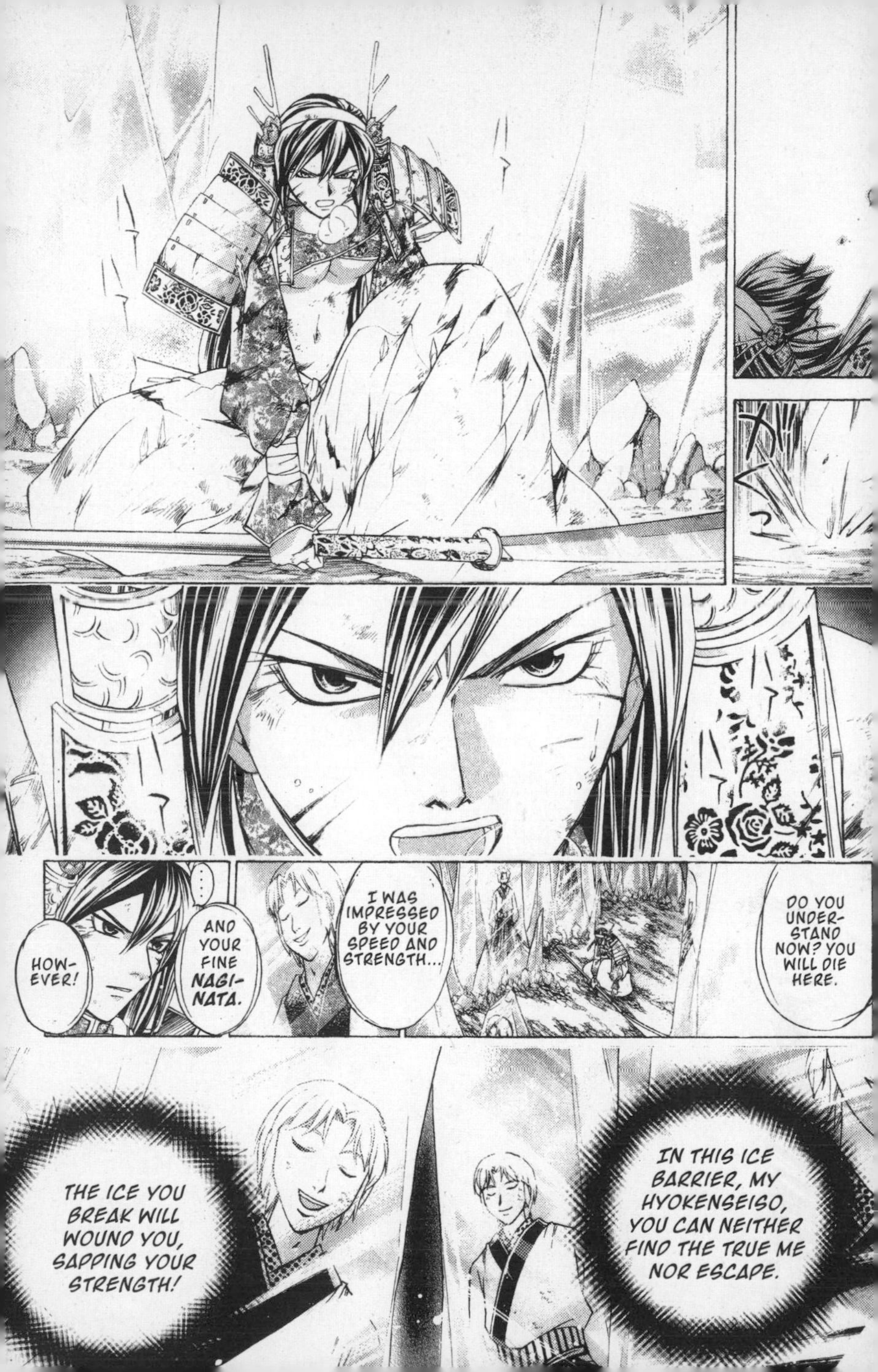
DO YOU UNDER-STAND NOW? YOU WILL DIE HERE.
I WAS IMPRESSED BY YOUR SPEED AND STRENGTH...
...
AND YOUR FINE *NAGI-NATA*.
HOW-EVER!
IN THIS ICE BARRIER, MY HYOKENSEISO, YOU CAN NEITHER FIND THE TRUE ME NOR ESCAPE.
THE ICE YOU BREAK WILL WOUND YOU, SAPPING YOUR STRENGTH!

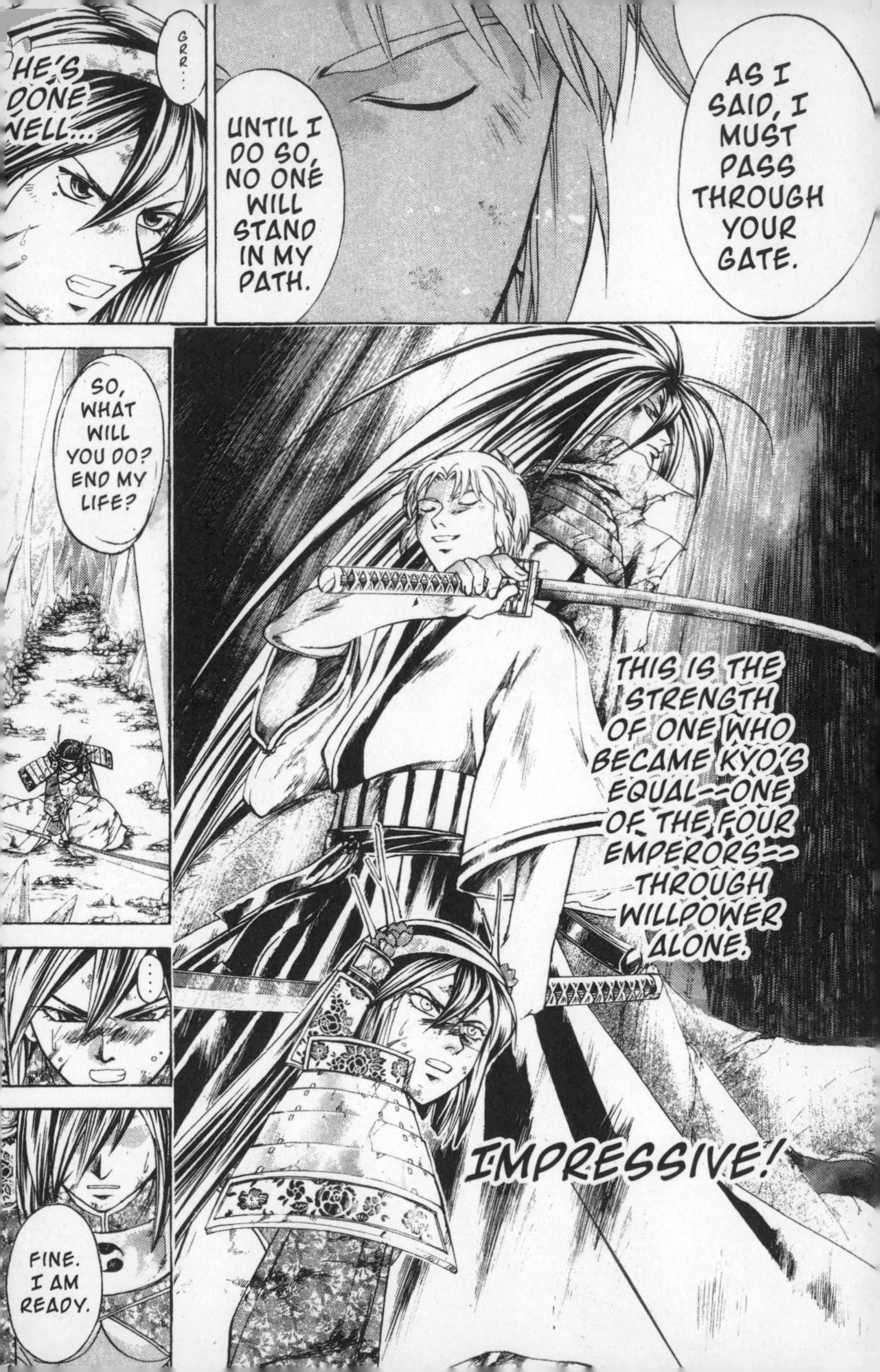
AS I SAID, I MUST PASS THROUGH YOUR GATE.
UNTIL I DO SO, NO ONE WILL STAND IN MY PATH.
GRR...
HE'S DONE WELL...
THIS IS THE STRENGTH OF ONE WHO BECAME KYO'S EQUAL--ONE OF THE FOUR EMPERORS--THROUGH WILLPOWER ALONE.
IMPRESSIVE!
SO, WHAT WILL YOU DO? END MY LIFE?
....
FINE. I AM READY.

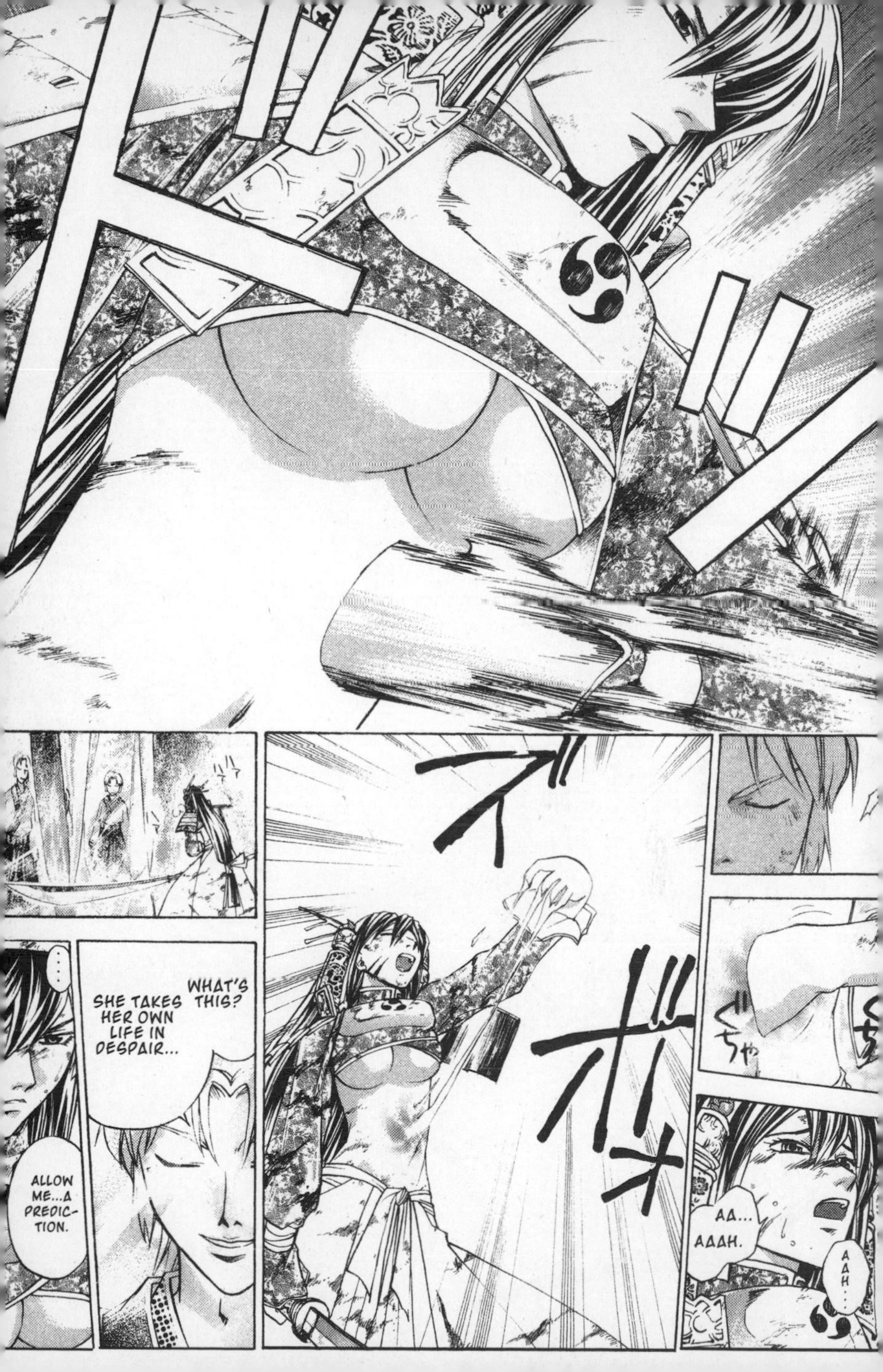
ぐちゃ
AA...
AAAH.
AAH...
WHAT'S THIS?
SHE TAKES HER OWN LIFE IN DESPAIR...
ALLOW ME...A PREDICTION.
....

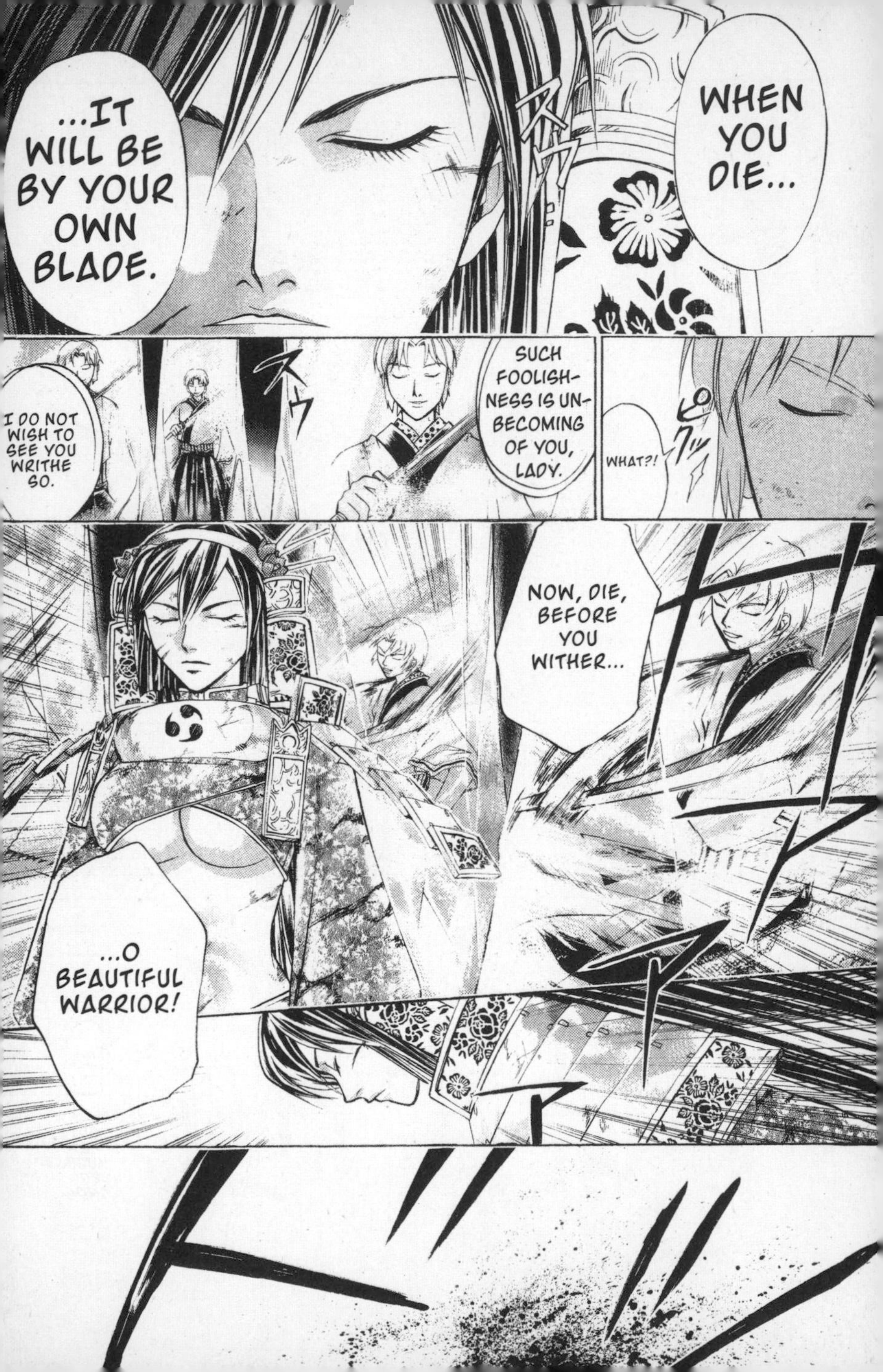
WHEN YOU DIE...
...IT WILL BE BY YOUR OWN BLADE.
WHAT?!
SUCH FOOLISH-NESS IS UN-BECOMING OF YOU, LADY.
I DO NOT WISH TO SEE YOU WRITHE SO.
NOW, DIE, BEFORE YOU WITHER...
...O BEAUTIFUL WARRIOR!

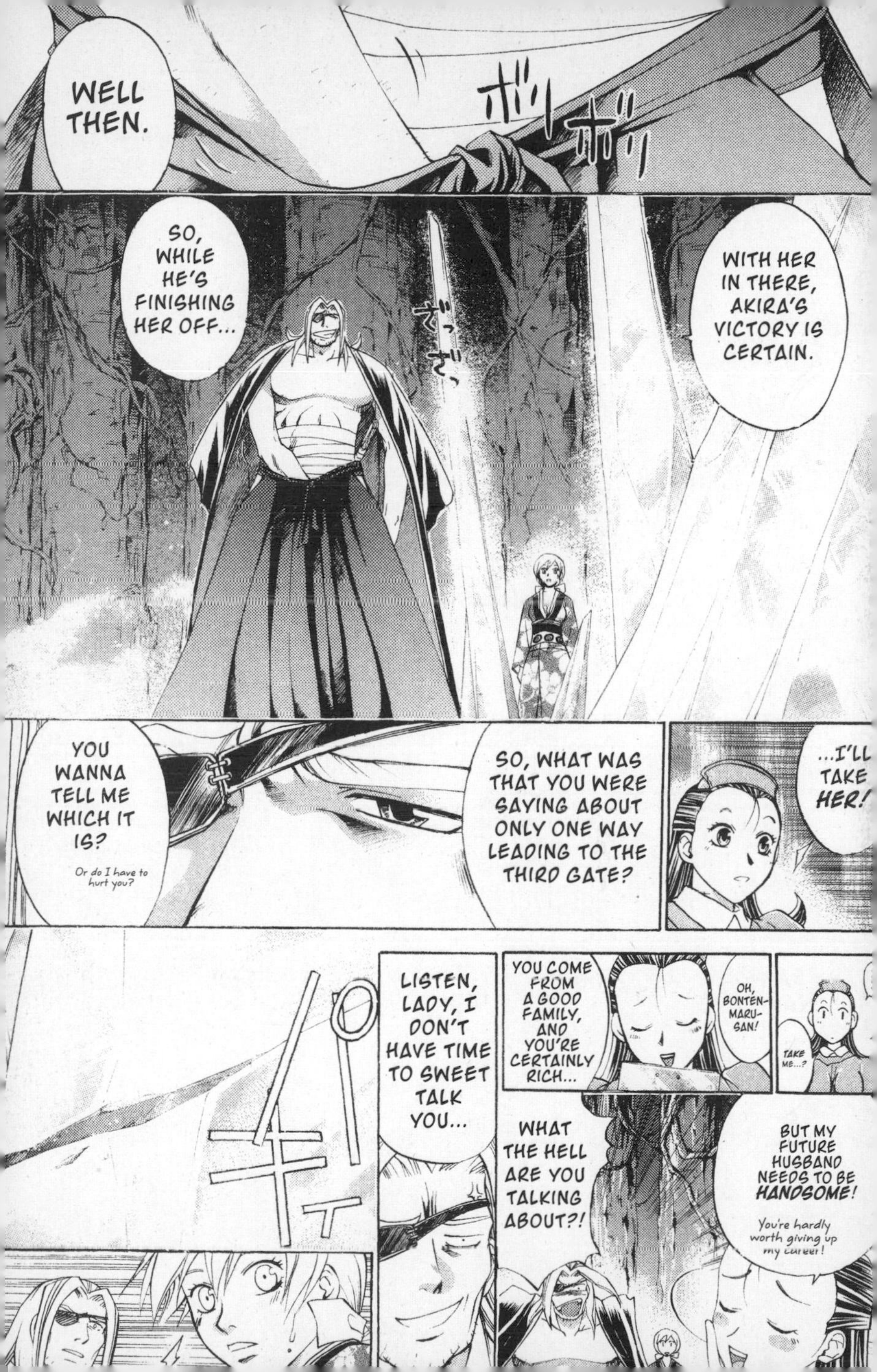
WELL THEN.
ボリ ボリ
WITH HER IN THERE, AKIRA'S VICTORY IS CERTAIN.
ざっ ざっ
SO, WHILE HE'S FINISHING HER OFF...
...I'LL TAKE HER!
SO, WHAT WAS THAT YOU WERE SAYING ABOUT ONLY ONE WAY LEADING TO THE THIRD GATE?
YOU WANNA TELL ME WHICH IT IS?
Or do I have to hurt you?
TAKE ME...?
OH, BONTEN-MARU-SAN!
YOU COME FROM A GOOD FAMILY, AND YOU'RE CERTAINLY RICH...
BUT MY FUTURE HUSBAND NEEDS TO BE HANDSOME!
You're hardly worth giving up my career!
WHAT THE HELL ARE YOU TALKING ABOUT?!
LISTEN, LADY, I DON'T HAVE TIME TO SWEET TALK YOU...

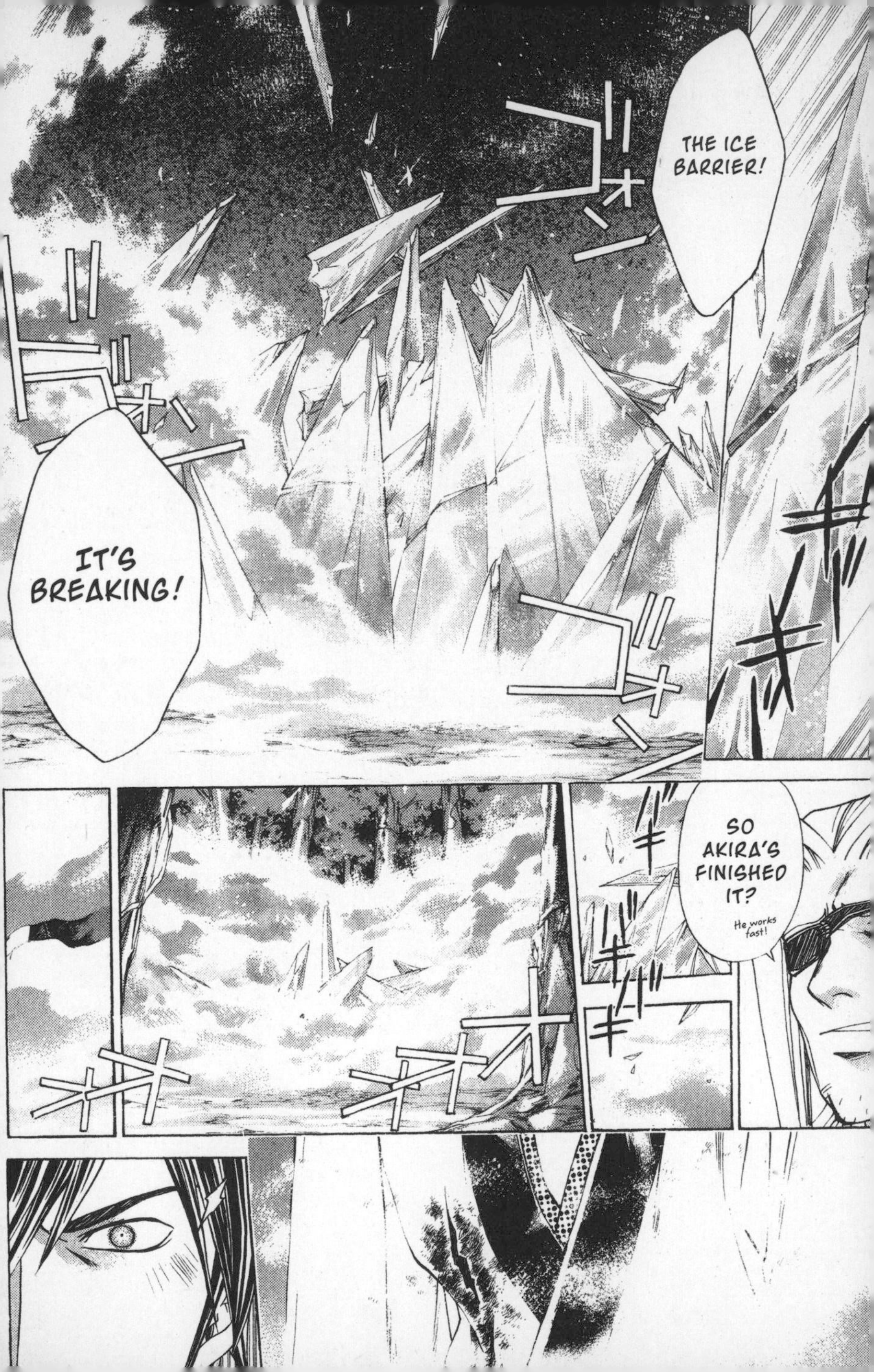
THE ICE BARRIER!
IT'S BREAKING!
SO AKIRA'S FINISHED IT?
He works fast!

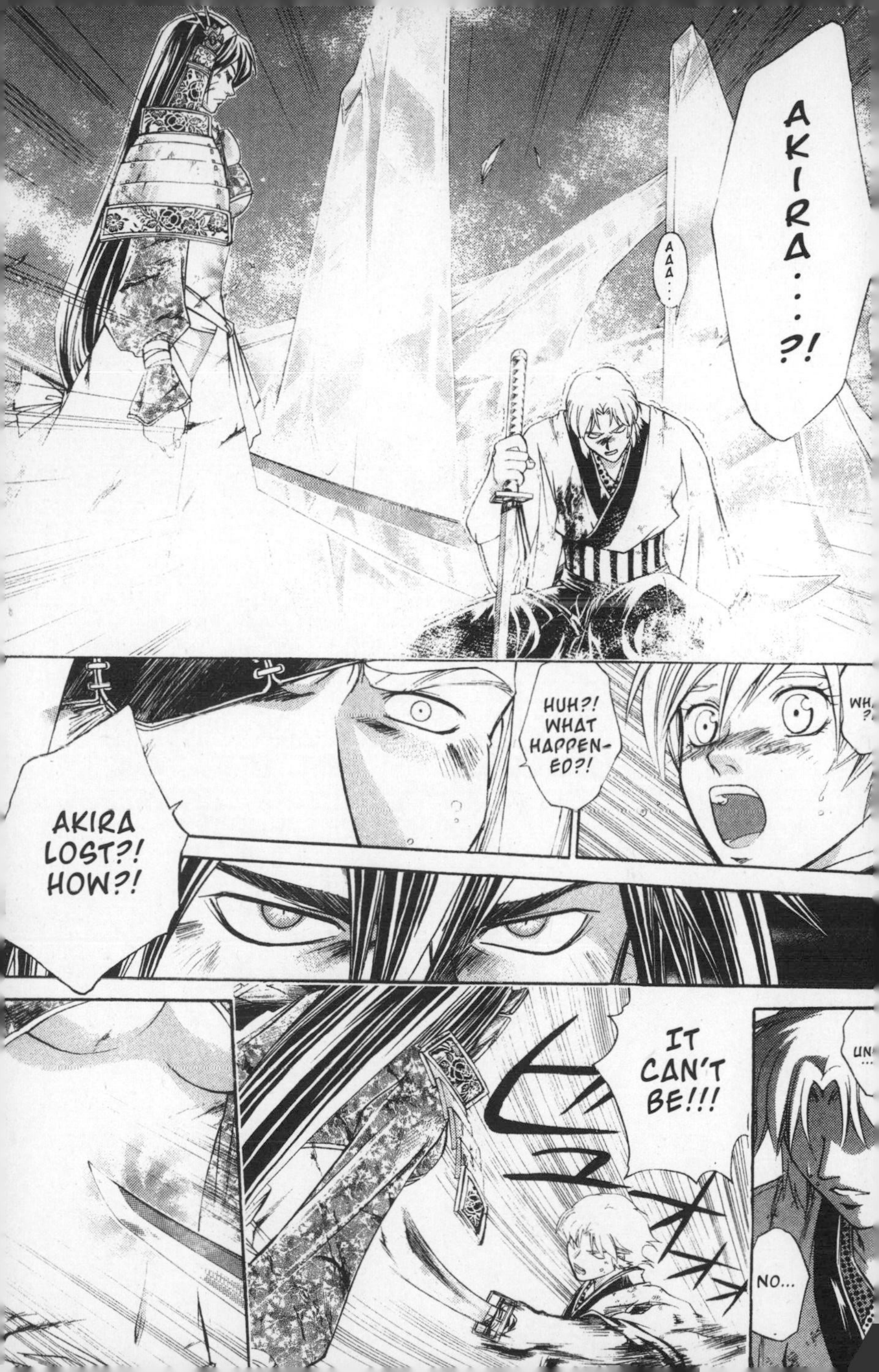
AKIRA... ?!
AAA...
WHA ?
HUH?! WHAT HAPPENED?!
AKIRA LOST?! HOW?!
UN...
NO...
IT CAN'T BE!!!

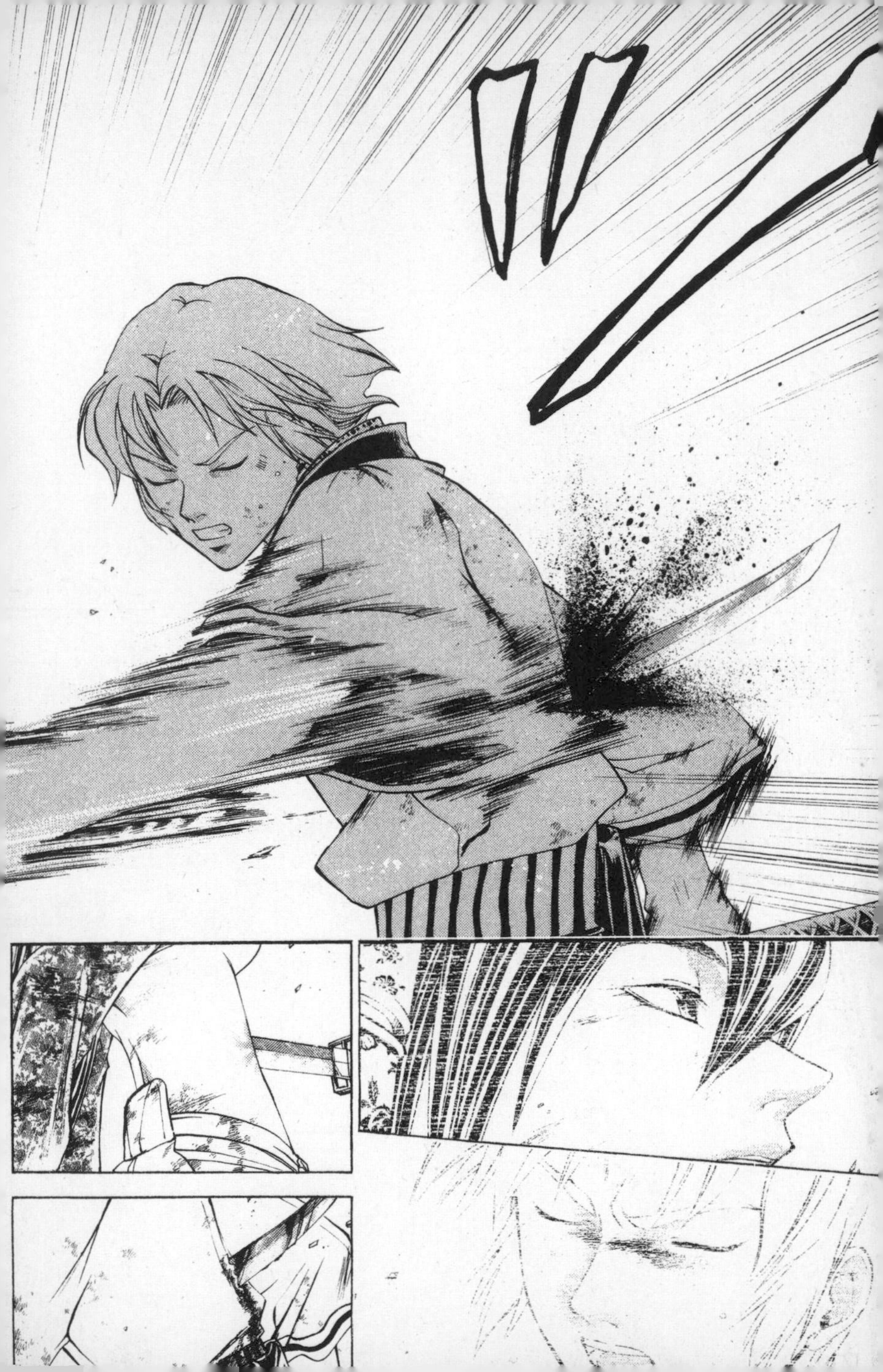

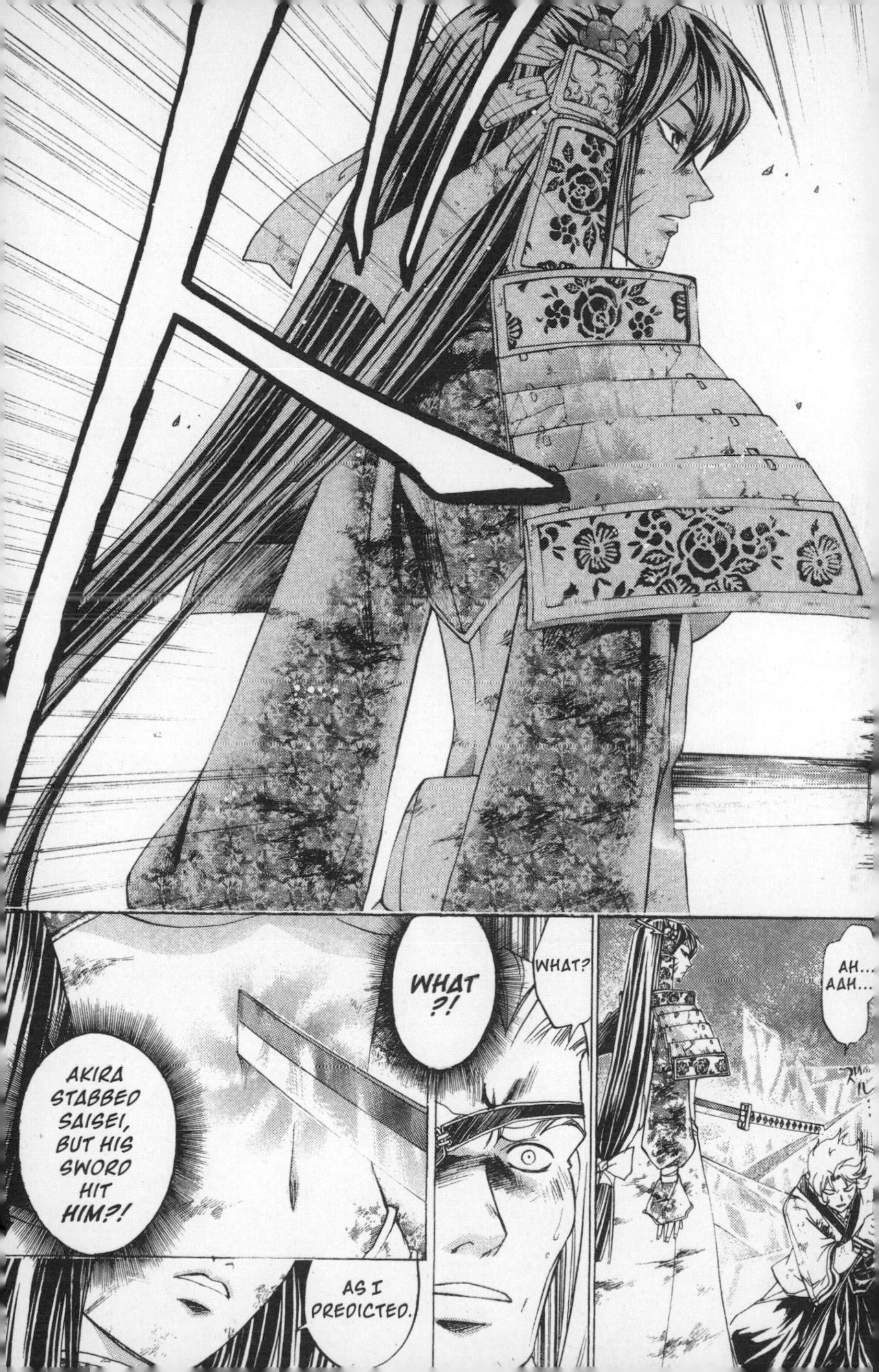
AH... AAH...
WHAT?
WHAT ?!
AKIRA STABBED SAISEI, BUT HIS SWORD HIT HIM?!
AS I PREDICTED.

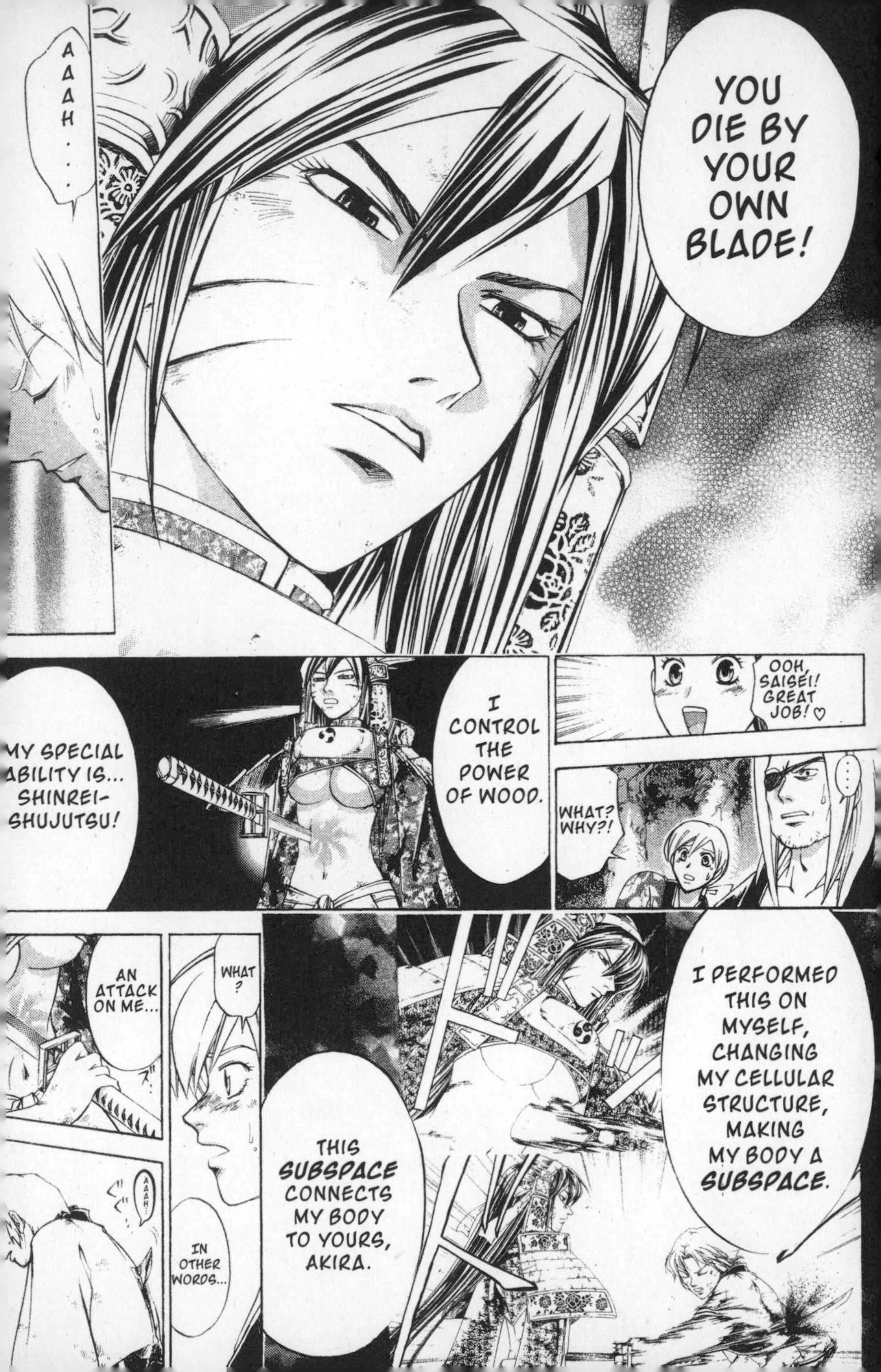
YOU DIE BY YOUR OWN BLADE!
AAAH...
OOH, SAISEI! GREAT JOB! ♡
...
WHAT? WHY?!
I CONTROL THE POWER OF WOOD.
MY SPECIAL ABILITY IS... SHINREI-SHUJUTSU!
I PERFORMED THIS ON MYSELF, CHANGING MY CELLULAR STRUCTURE, MAKING MY BODY A SUBSPACE.
THIS SUBSPACE CONNECTS MY BODY TO YOURS, AKIRA.
WHAT?
AN ATTACK ON ME...
AAAH...
IN OTHER WORDS...

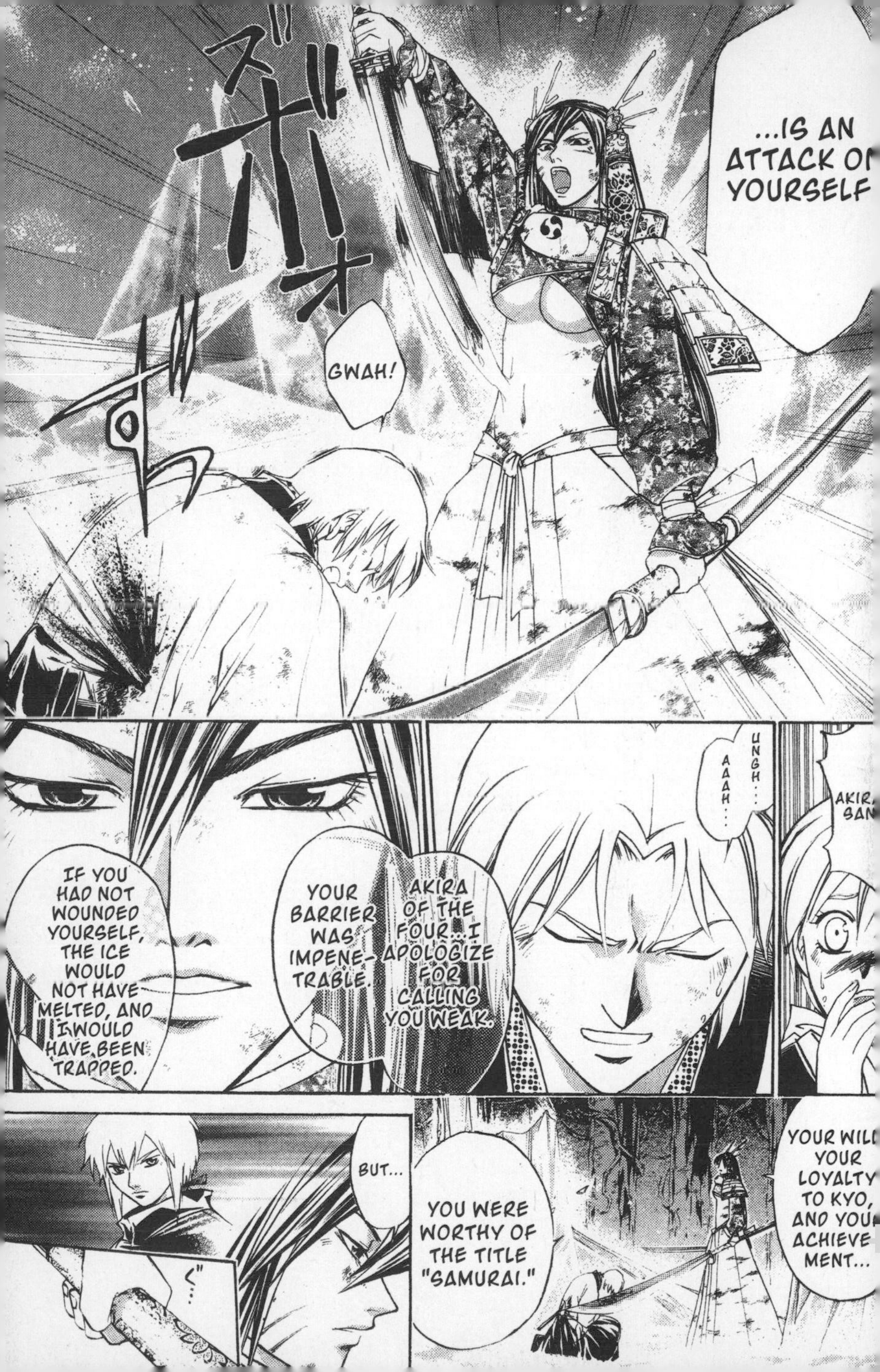
...IS AN ATTACK ON YOURSELF
GWAH!
AKIRA SAN
UNGH... AAAH...
AKIRA OF THE FOUR... I APOLOGIZE FOR CALLING YOU WEAK.
YOUR BARRIER WAS IMPENE-TRABLE.
IF YOU HAD NOT WOUNDED YOURSELF, THE ICE WOULD NOT HAVE MELTED, AND I WOULD HAVE BEEN TRAPPED.
YOUR WILL YOUR LOYALTY TO KYO, AND YOUR ACHIEVE MENT...
YOU WERE WORTHY OF THE TITLE "SAMURAI."
BUT...
ぐ…

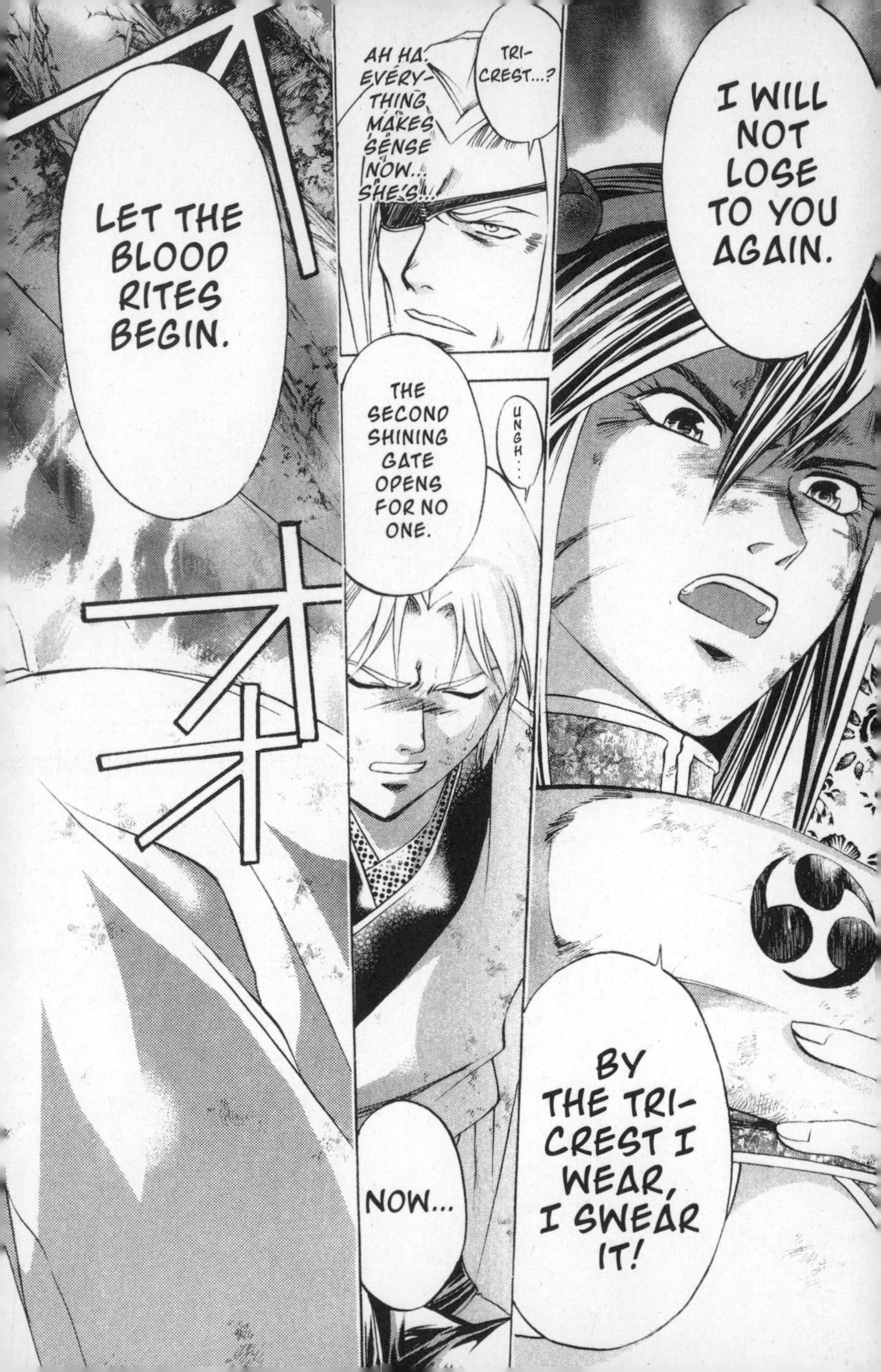
I WILL NOT LOSE TO YOU AGAIN.
BY THE TRI-CREST I WEAR, I SWEAR IT!
TRI-CREST...?
AH HA. EVERY-THING MAKES SENSE NOW... SHE'S...
UNGH...
THE SECOND SHINING GATE OPENS FOR NO ONE.
NOW...
LET THE BLOOD RITES BEGIN.

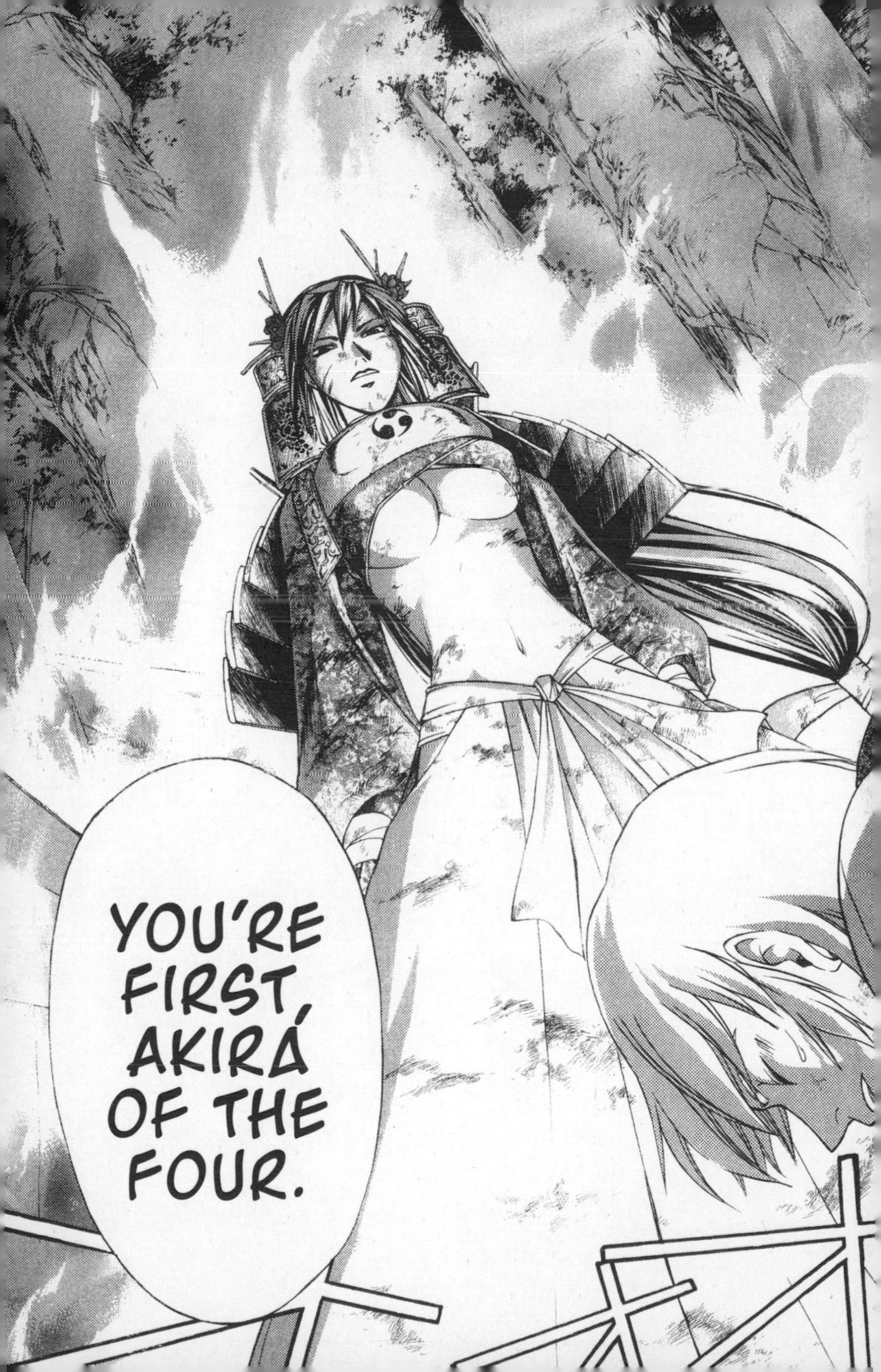
YOU'RE FIRST, AKIRA OF THE FOUR.

Kamijyo: Go, Ruri-chan!

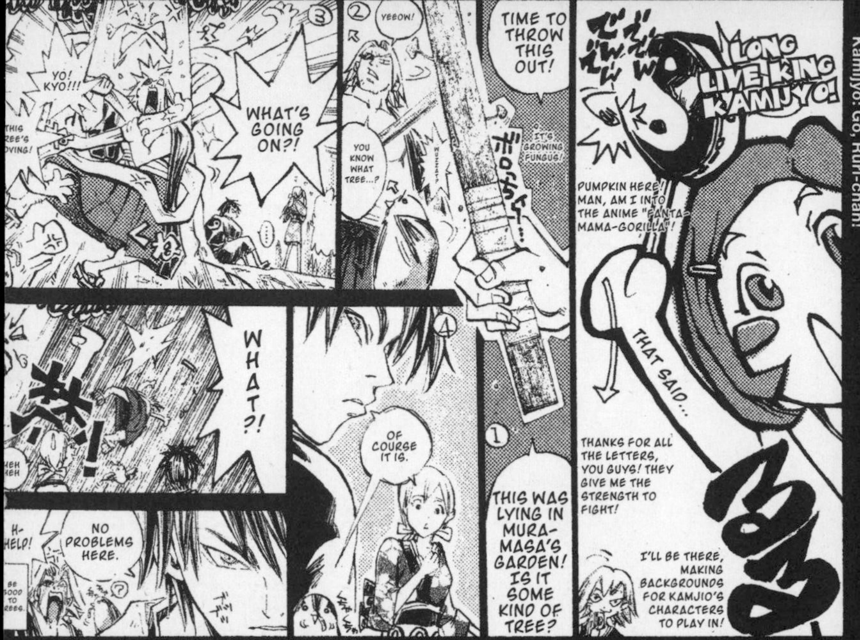
LONG LIVE KING KAMIJYO!
PUMPKIN HERE! MAN, AM I INTO THE ANIME "FANTA-MAMA-GORILLA"!
THAT SAID...
THANKS FOR ALL THE LETTERS, YOU GUYS! THEY GIVE ME THE STRENGTH TO FIGHT!
I'LL BE THERE, MAKING BACKGROUNDS FOR KAMJIO'S CHARACTERS TO PLAY IN!
TIME TO THROW THIS OUT!
IT'S GROWING FUNGUS!
THIS WAS LYING IN MURA-MASA'S GARDEN! IS IT SOME KIND OF TREE?
YEEOW!
YOU KNOW WHAT TREE...?
YO! KYO!!!
WHAT'S GOING ON?!
...
OF COURSE IT IS.
WHAT?!
NO PROBLEMS HERE.
H-HELP!

The Gentleman Pumpkin

Shiba Tateoka

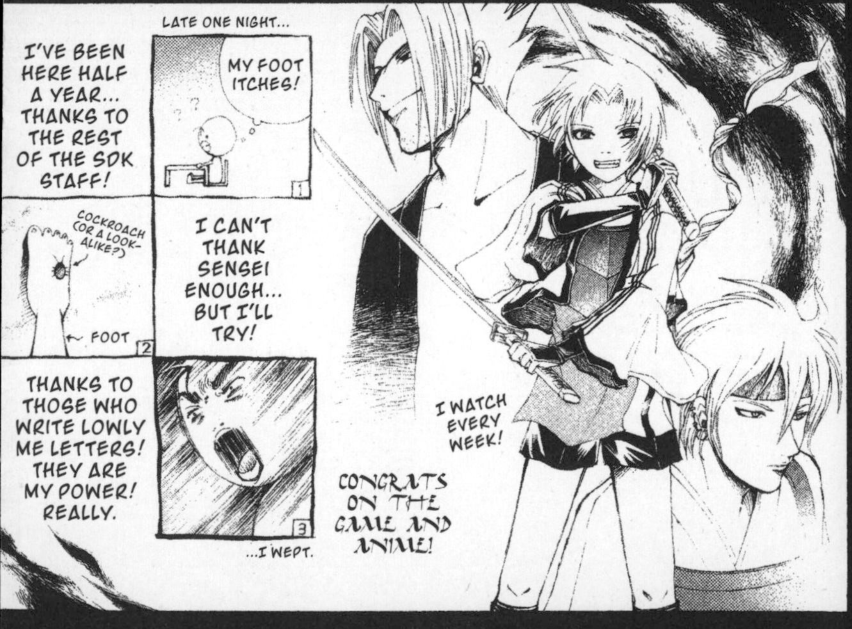
I WATCH EVERY WEEK!
CONGRATS ON THE GAME AND ANIME!
LATE ONE NIGHT...
MY FOOT ITCHES!
I'VE BEEN HERE HALF A YEAR... THANKS TO THE REST OF THE SDK STAFF!
COCKROACH (OR A LOOK-ALIKE?)
FOOT
I CAN'T THANK SENSEI ENOUGH... BUT I'LL TRY!
...I WEPT.
THANKS TO THOSE WHO WRITE LOWLY ME LETTERS! THEY ARE MY POWER! REALLY.

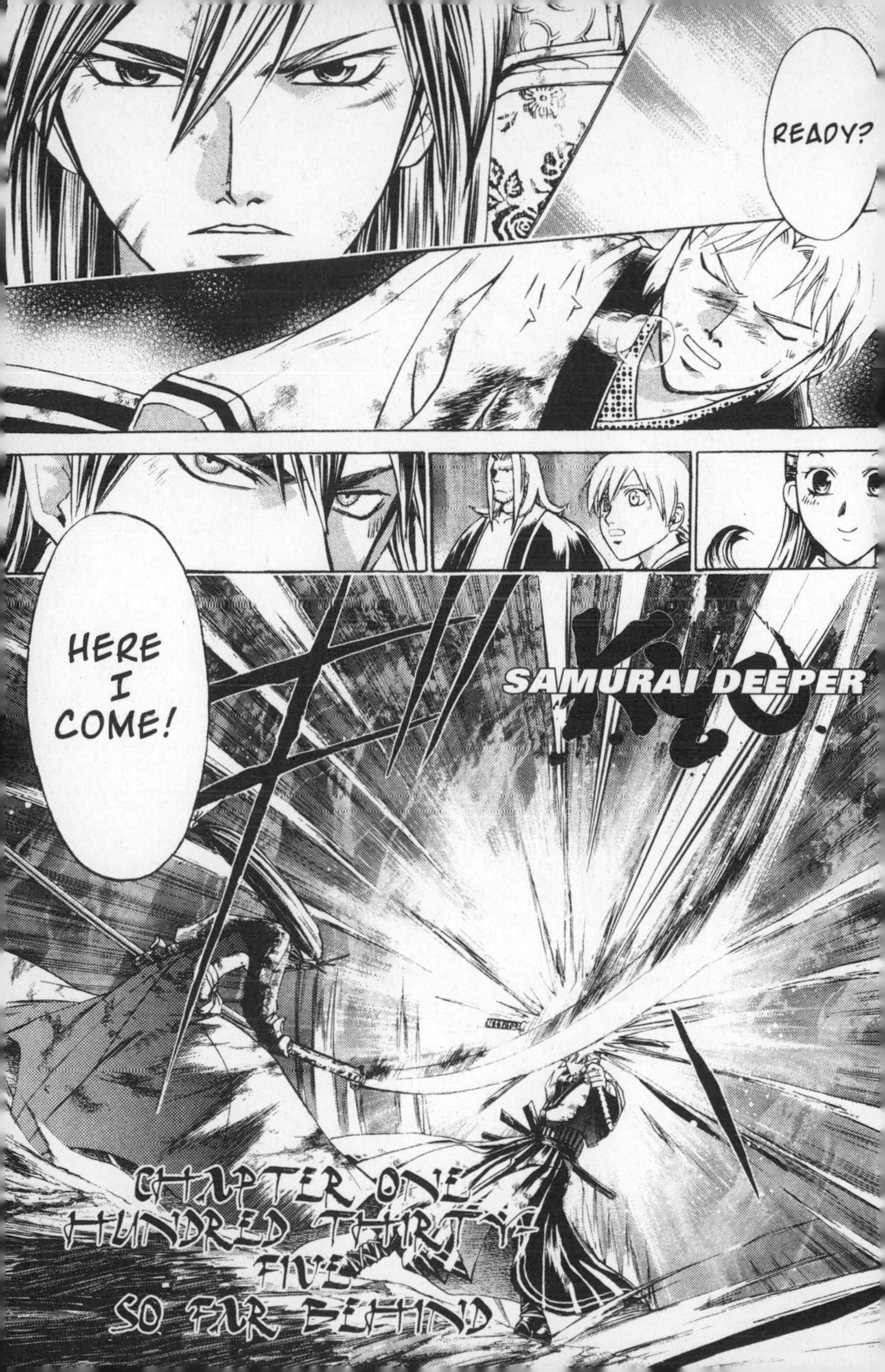
READY?
HERE I COME!
SAMURAI DEEPER KYO
CHAPTER ONE HUNDRED THIRTY-FIVE
SO FAR BEHIND

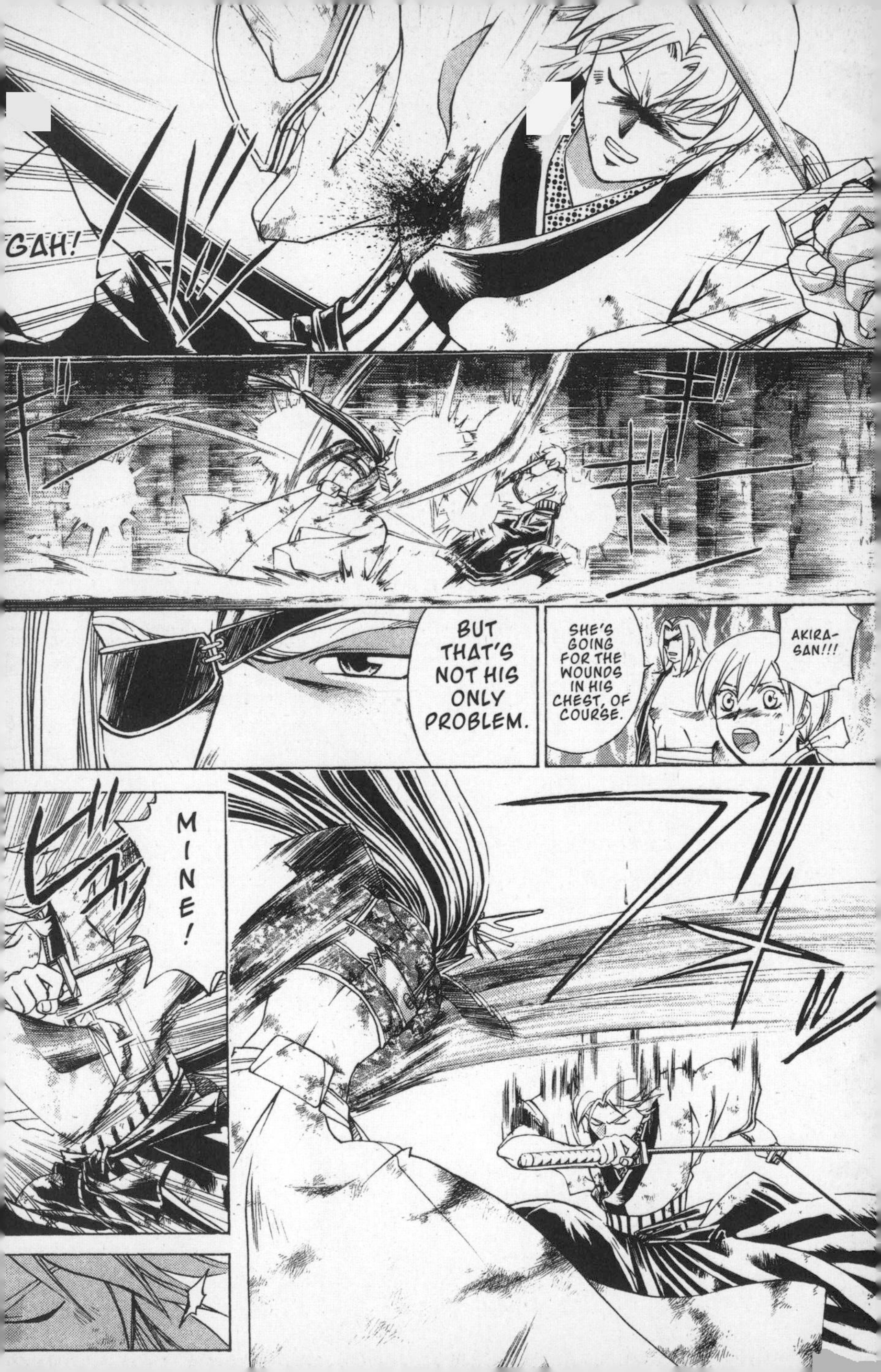
GAH!
AKIRA-SAN!!!
SHE'S GOING FOR THE WOUNDS IN HIS CHEST, OF COURSE.
BUT THAT'S NOT HIS ONLY PROBLEM.
MINE!

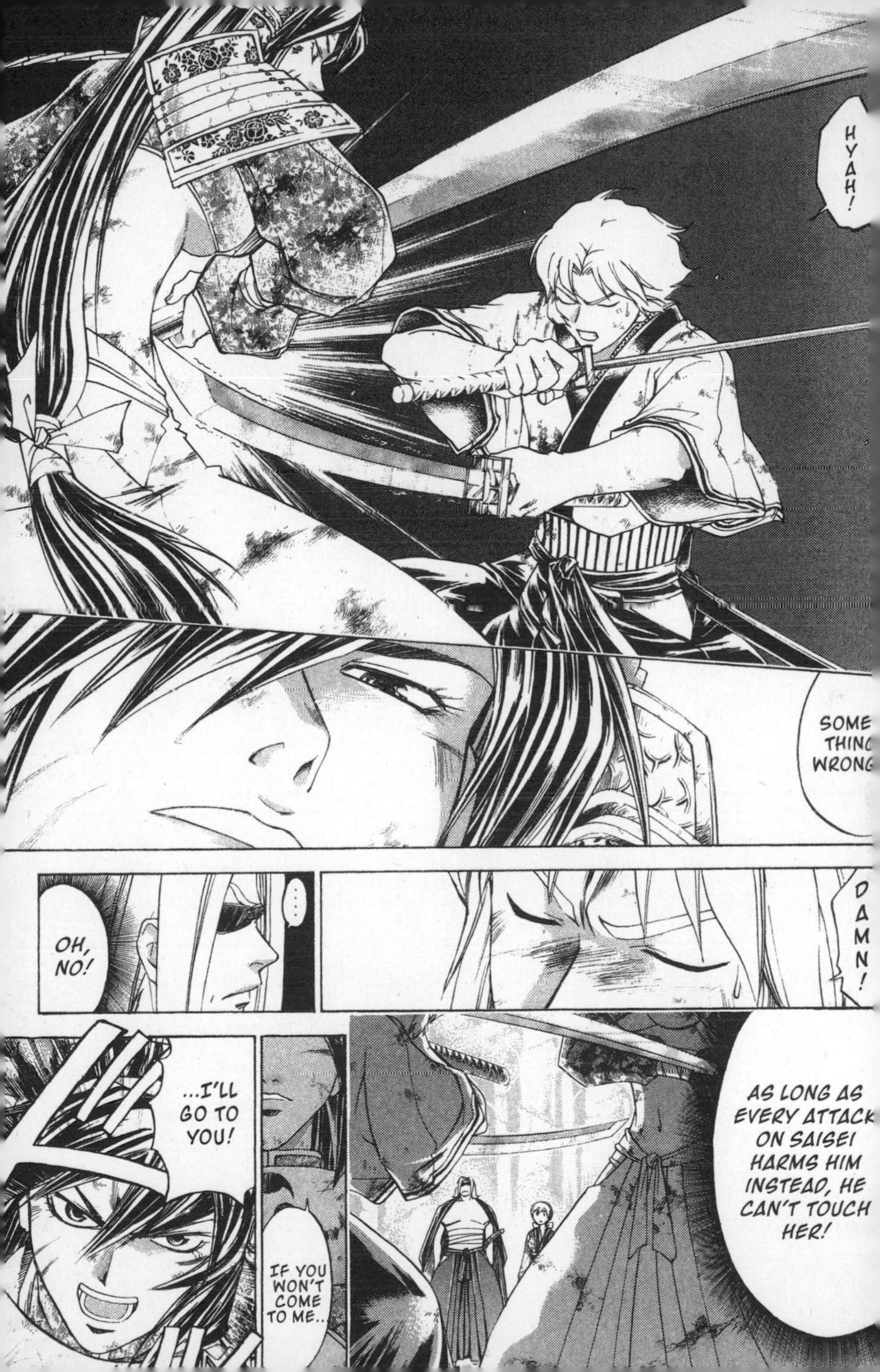
HYAH!
SOMETHING WRONG
DAMN!
....
OH, NO!
AS LONG AS EVERY ATTACK ON SAISEI HARMS HIM INSTEAD, HE CAN'T TOUCH HER!
IF YOU WON'T COME TO ME..
...I'LL GO TO YOU!

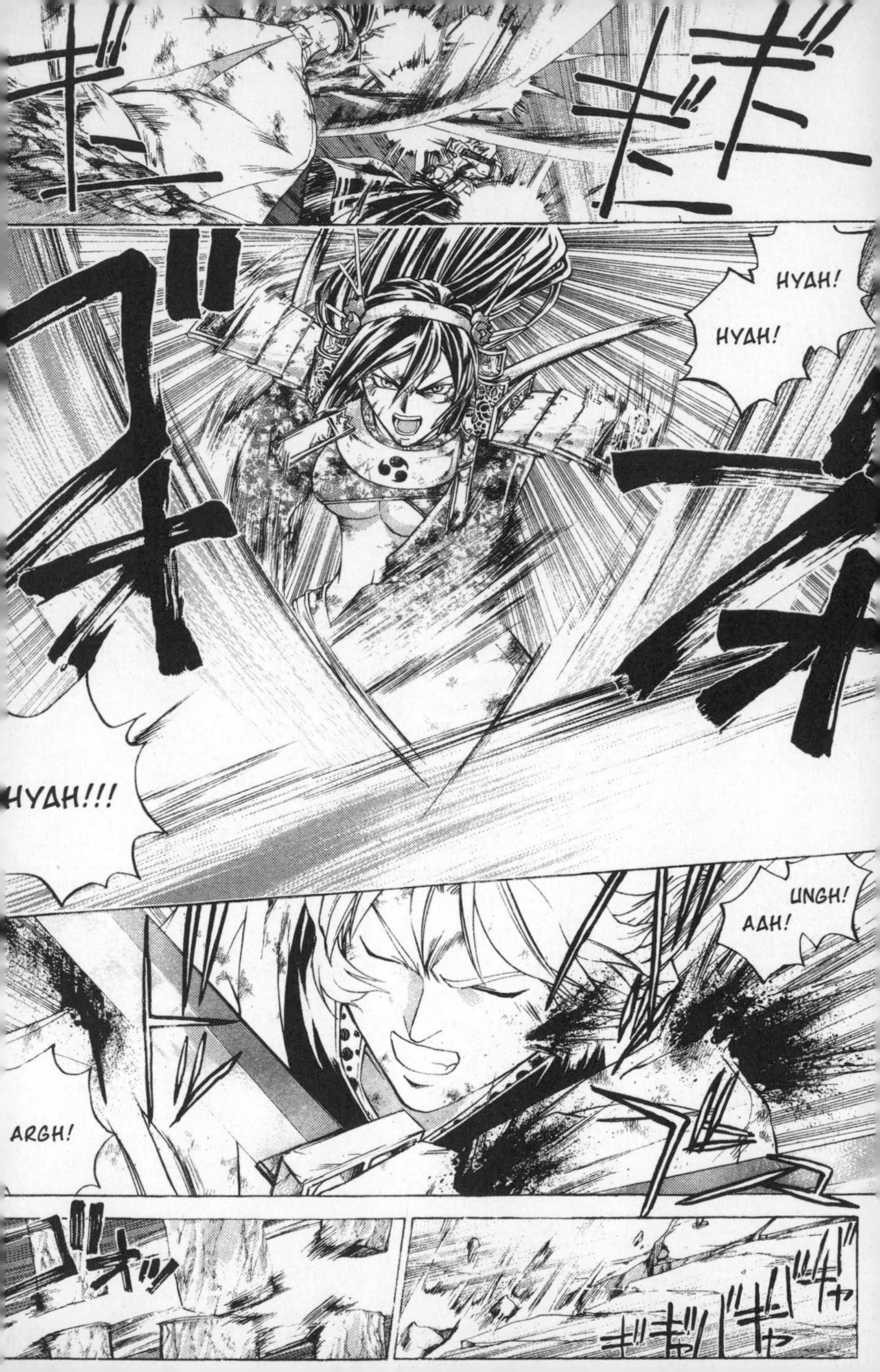
HYAH!
HYAH!
HYAH!!!
UNGH!
AAH!
ARGH!

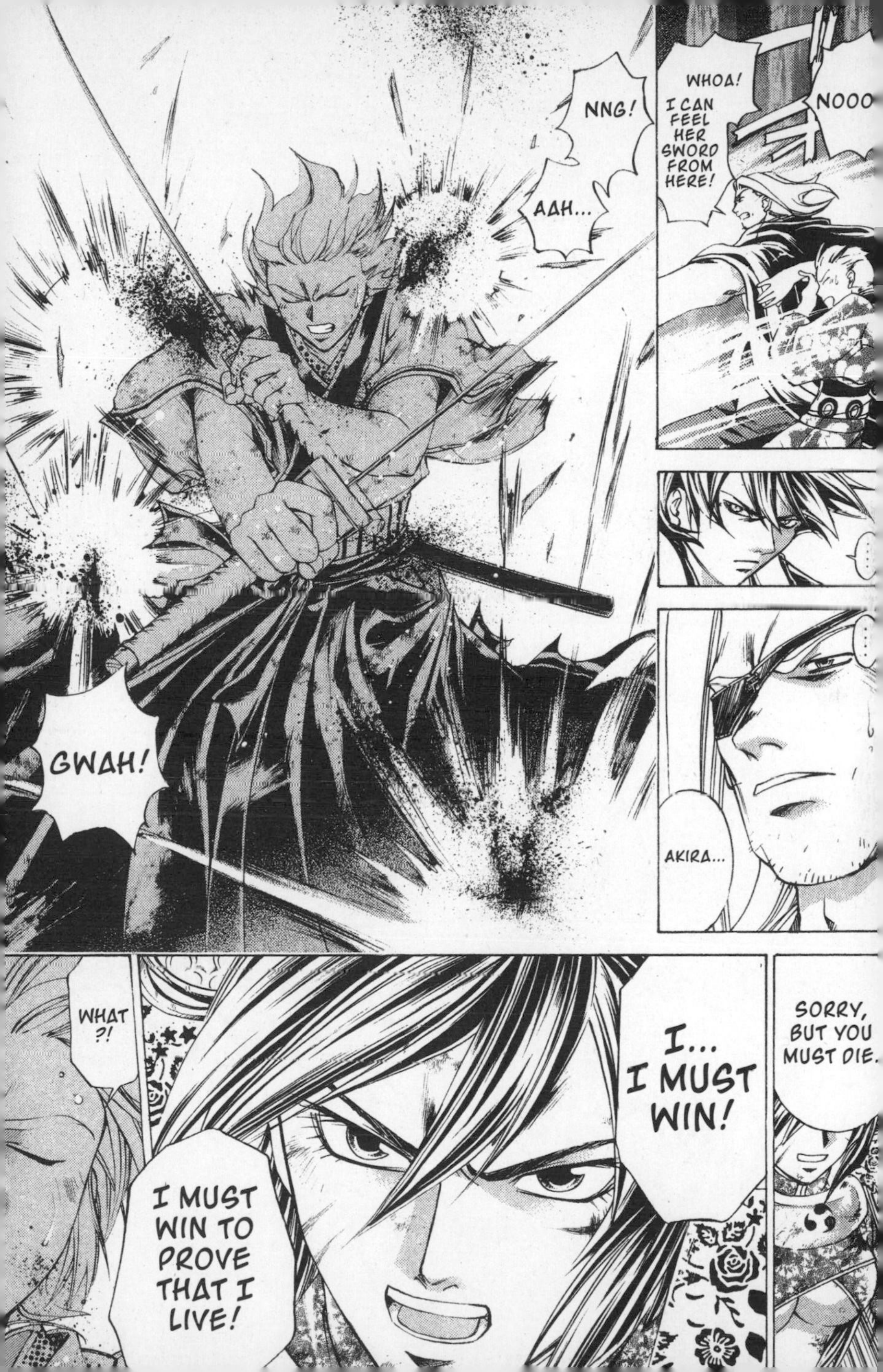
NOOO
WHOA! I CAN FEEL HER SWORD FROM HERE!
AKIRA...
NNG!
AAH...
GWAH!
SORRY, BUT YOU MUST DIE.
I... I MUST WIN!
I MUST WIN TO PROVE THAT I LIVE!
WHAT ?!

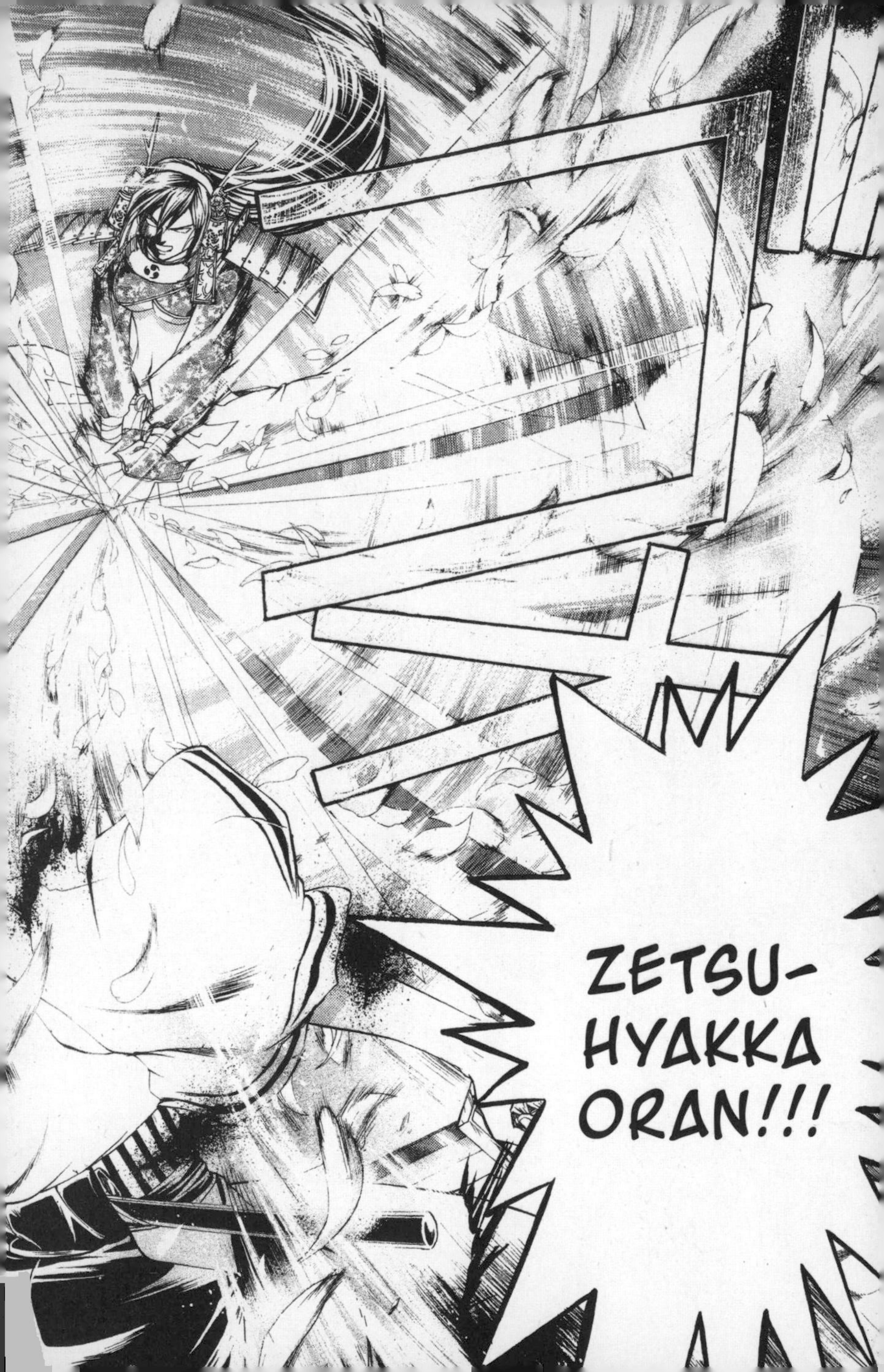
ZETSU-
HYAKKA
ORAN!!!

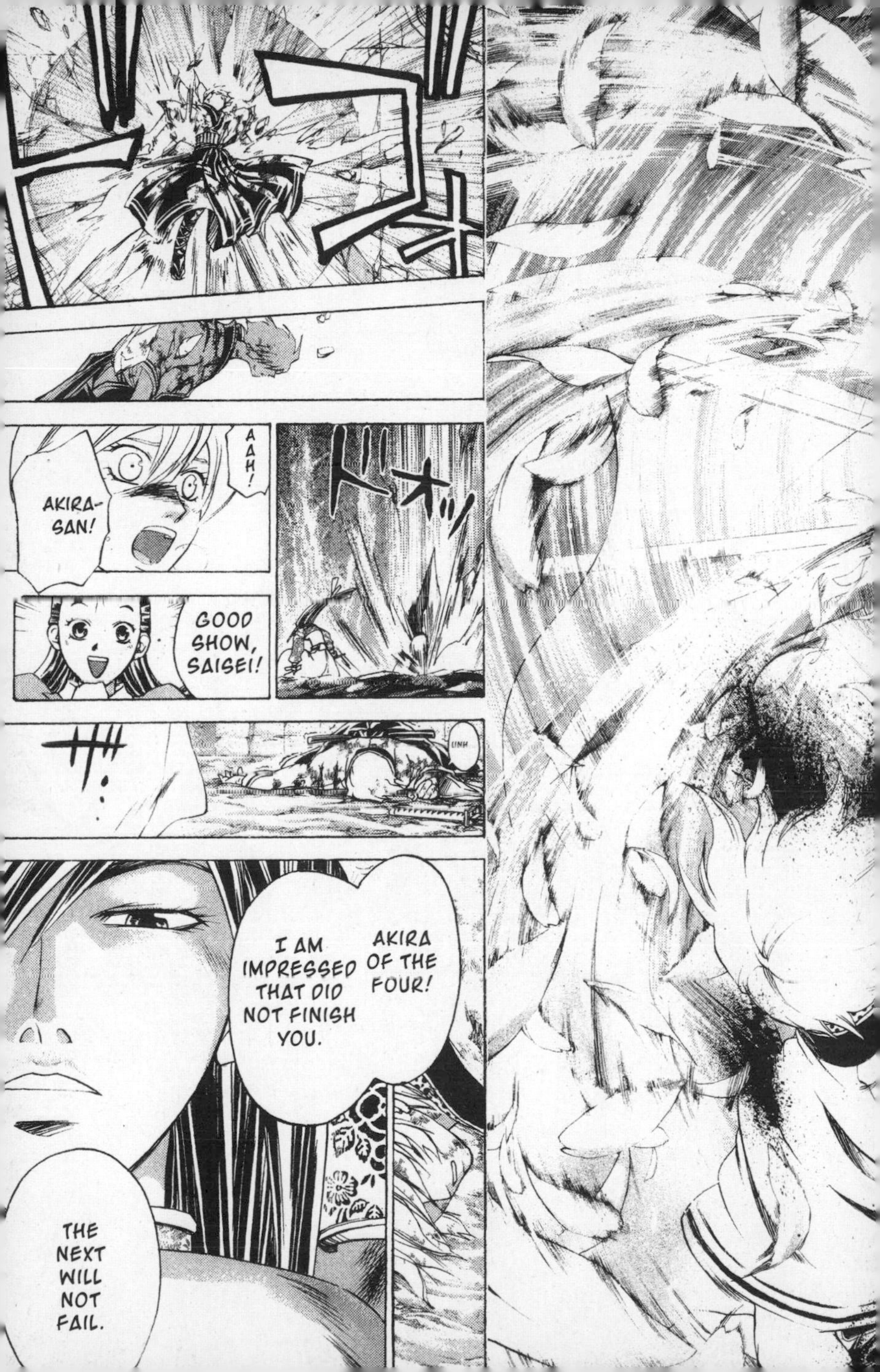
AAH!
AKIRA-SAN!
GOOD SHOW, SAISEI!
UNH...
AKIRA OF THE FOUR!
I AM IMPRESSED THAT DID NOT FINISH YOU.
THE NEXT WILL NOT FAIL.

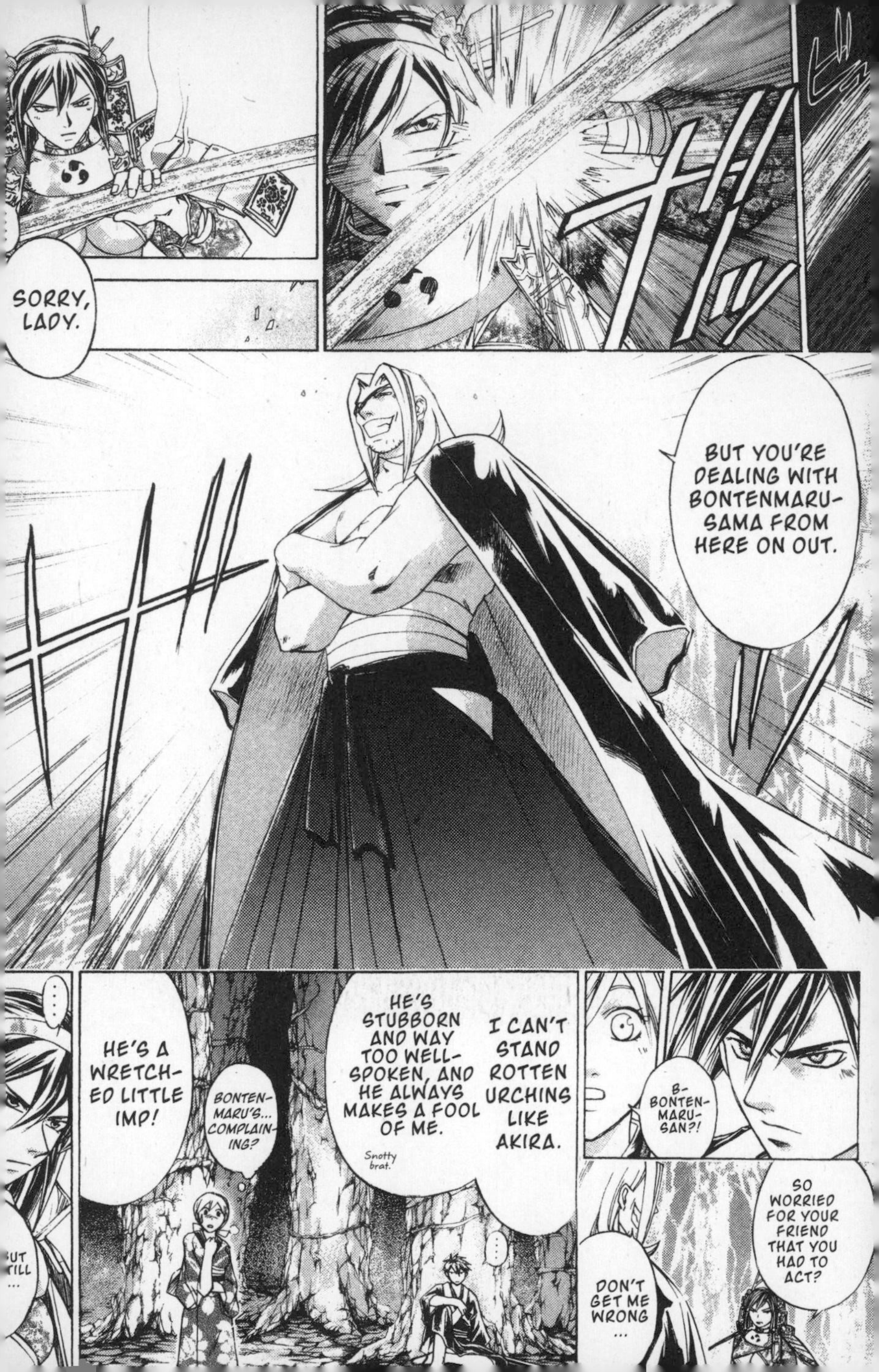
SORRY, LADY.
BUT YOU'RE DEALING WITH BONTENMARU-SAMA FROM HERE ON OUT.
B-BONTEN-MARU-SAN?!
SO WORRIED FOR YOUR FRIEND THAT YOU HAD TO ACT?
DON'T GET ME WRONG ...
I CAN'T STAND ROTTEN URCHINS LIKE AKIRA.
HE'S STUBBORN AND WAY TOO WELL-SPOKEN, AND HE ALWAYS MAKES A FOOL OF ME.
Snotty brat.
...
BONTEN-MARU'S... COMPLAINING?
HE'S A WRETCHED LITTLE IMP!
...

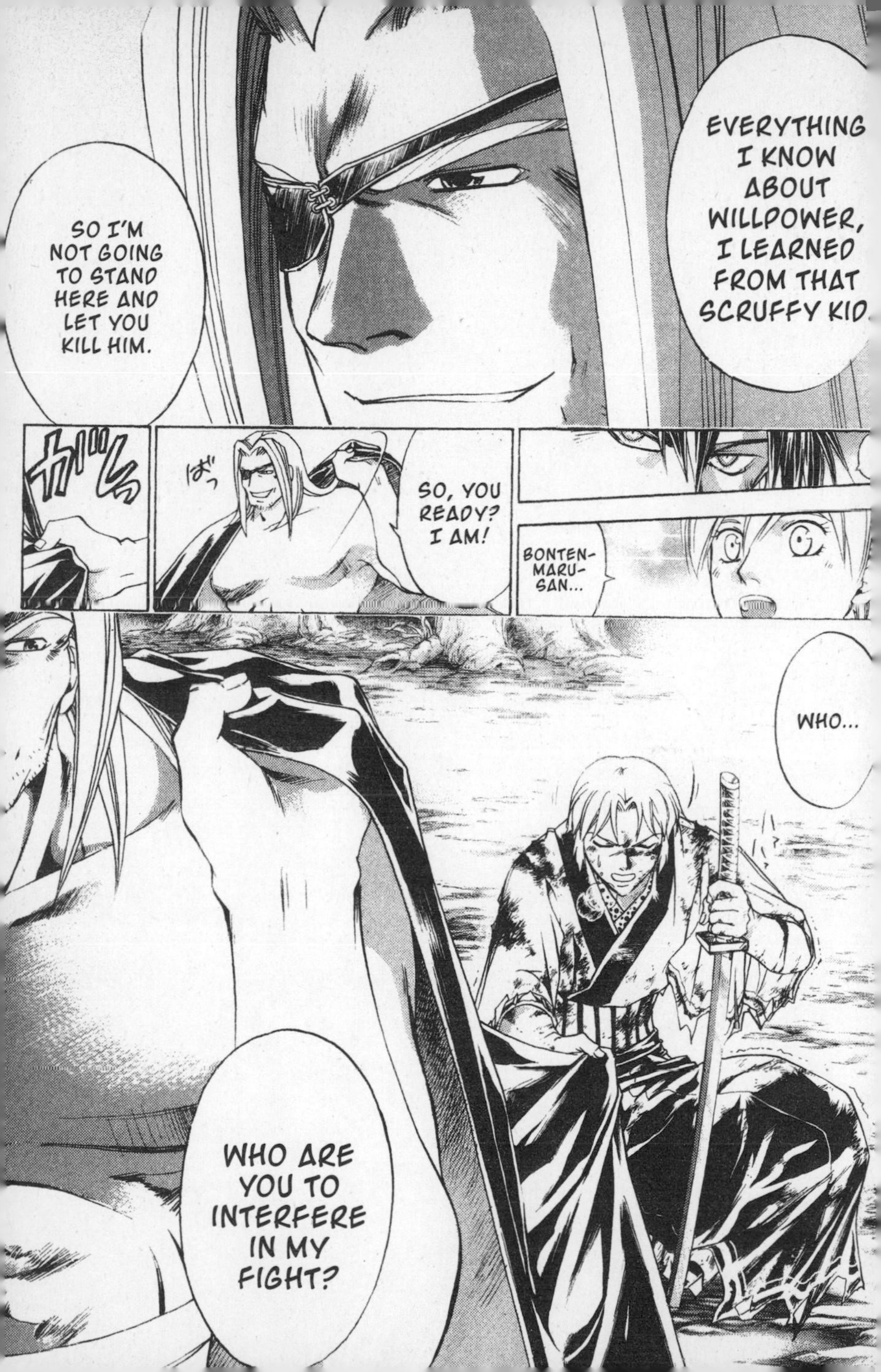
EVERYTHING I KNOW ABOUT WILLPOWER, I LEARNED FROM THAT SCRUFFY KID.
SO I'M NOT GOING TO STAND HERE AND LET YOU KILL HIM.
BONTEN-MARU-SAN...
SO, YOU READY? I AM!
ぱっ
WHO...
WHO ARE YOU TO INTERFERE IN MY FIGHT?

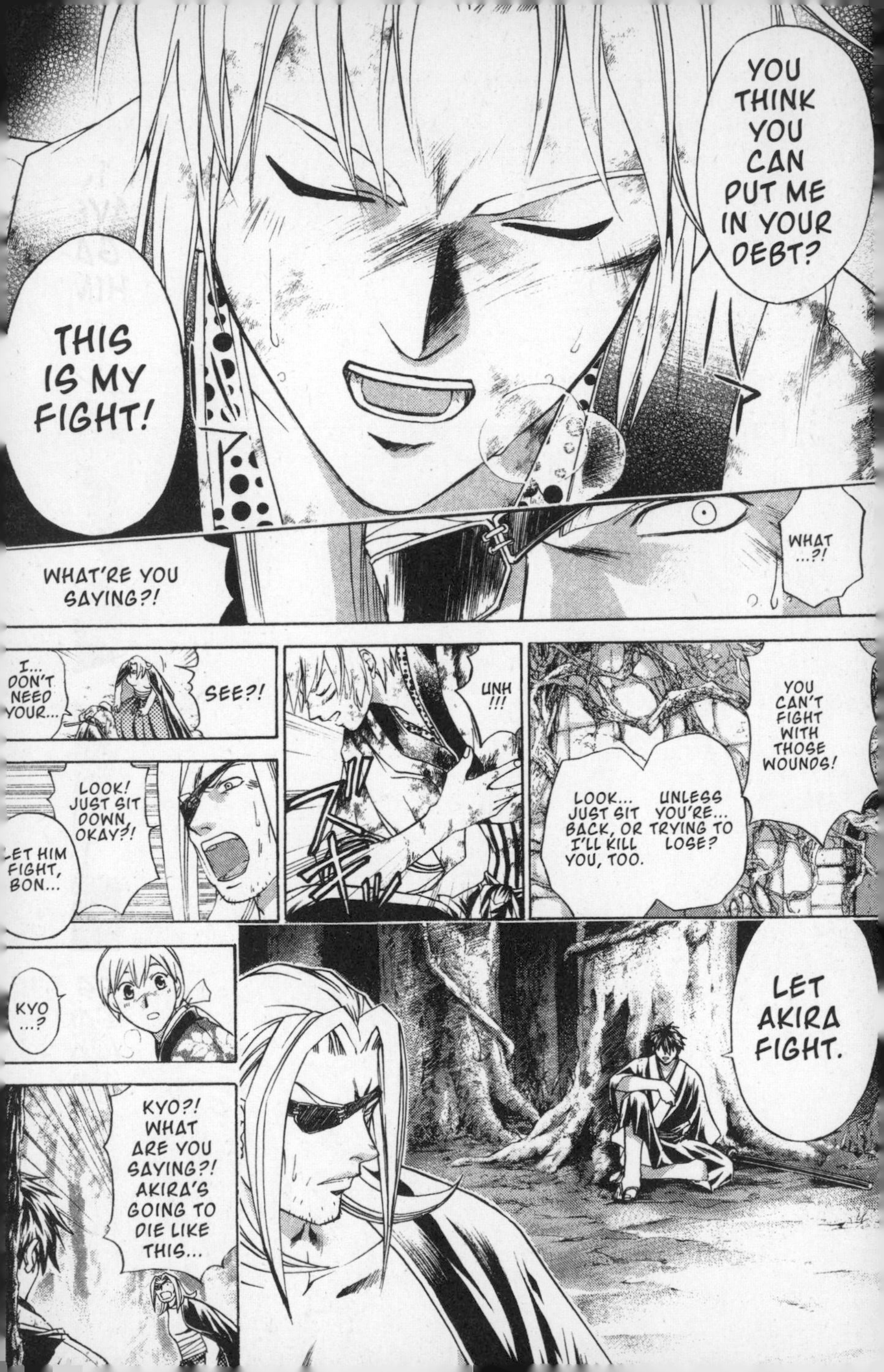
YOU THINK YOU CAN PUT ME IN YOUR DEBT?
THIS IS MY FIGHT!
WHAT ...?!
WHAT'RE YOU SAYING?!
YOU CAN'T FIGHT WITH THOSE WOUNDS!
UNLESS YOU'RE... TRYING TO LOSE?
LOOK... JUST SIT BACK, OR I'LL KILL YOU, TOO.
UNH !!!
SEE?!
I... DON'T NEED YOUR...
LOOK! JUST SIT DOWN, OKAY?!
LET HIM FIGHT, BON...
LET AKIRA FIGHT.
KYO ...?
KYO?! WHAT ARE YOU SAYING?! AKIRA'S GOING TO DIE LIKE THIS...

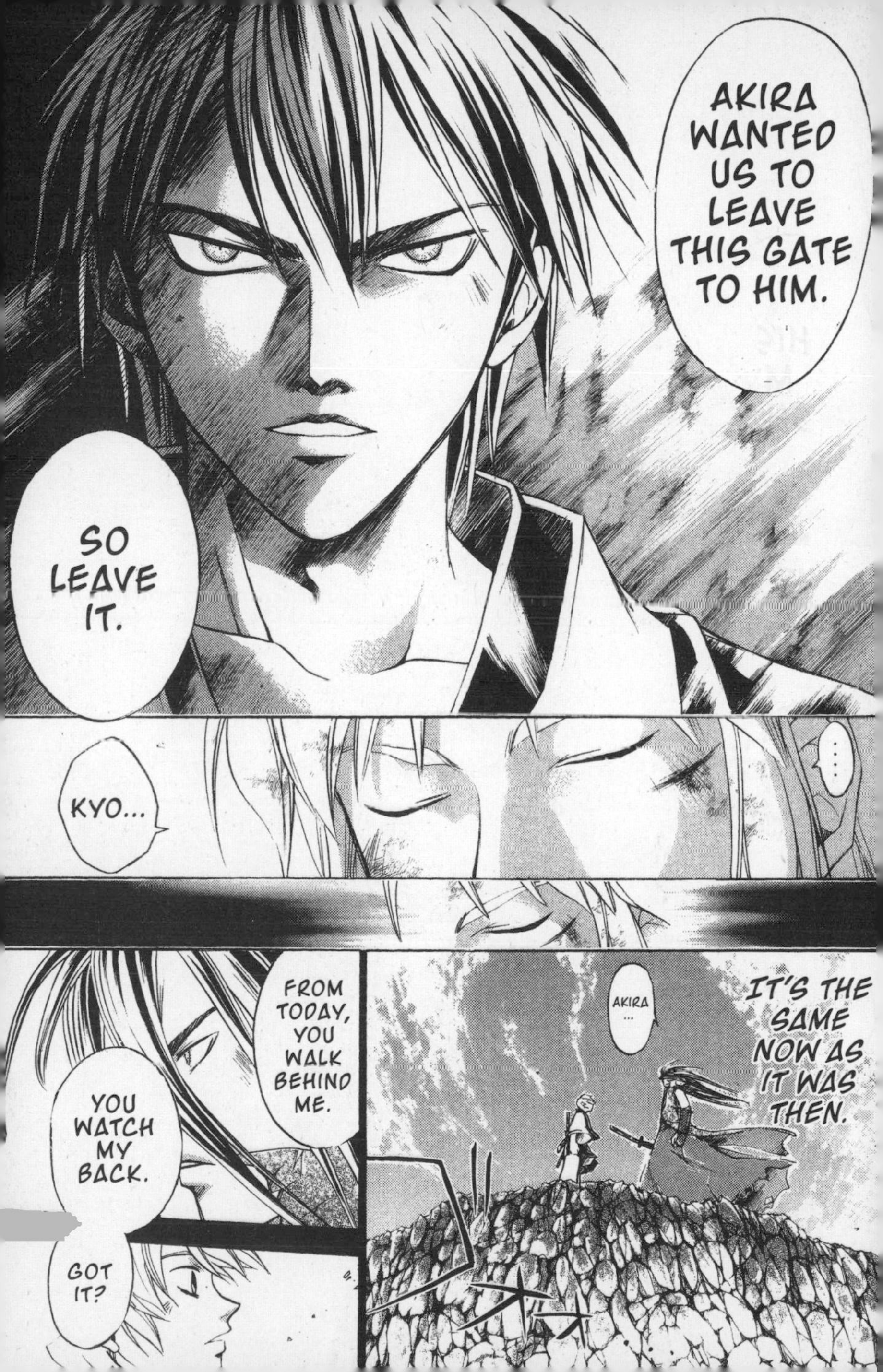
AKIRA WANTED US TO LEAVE THIS GATE TO HIM.
SO LEAVE IT.
....
KYO...
IT'S THE SAME NOW AS IT WAS THEN.
AKIRA ...
FROM TODAY, YOU WALK BEHIND ME.
YOU WATCH MY BACK.
GOT IT?

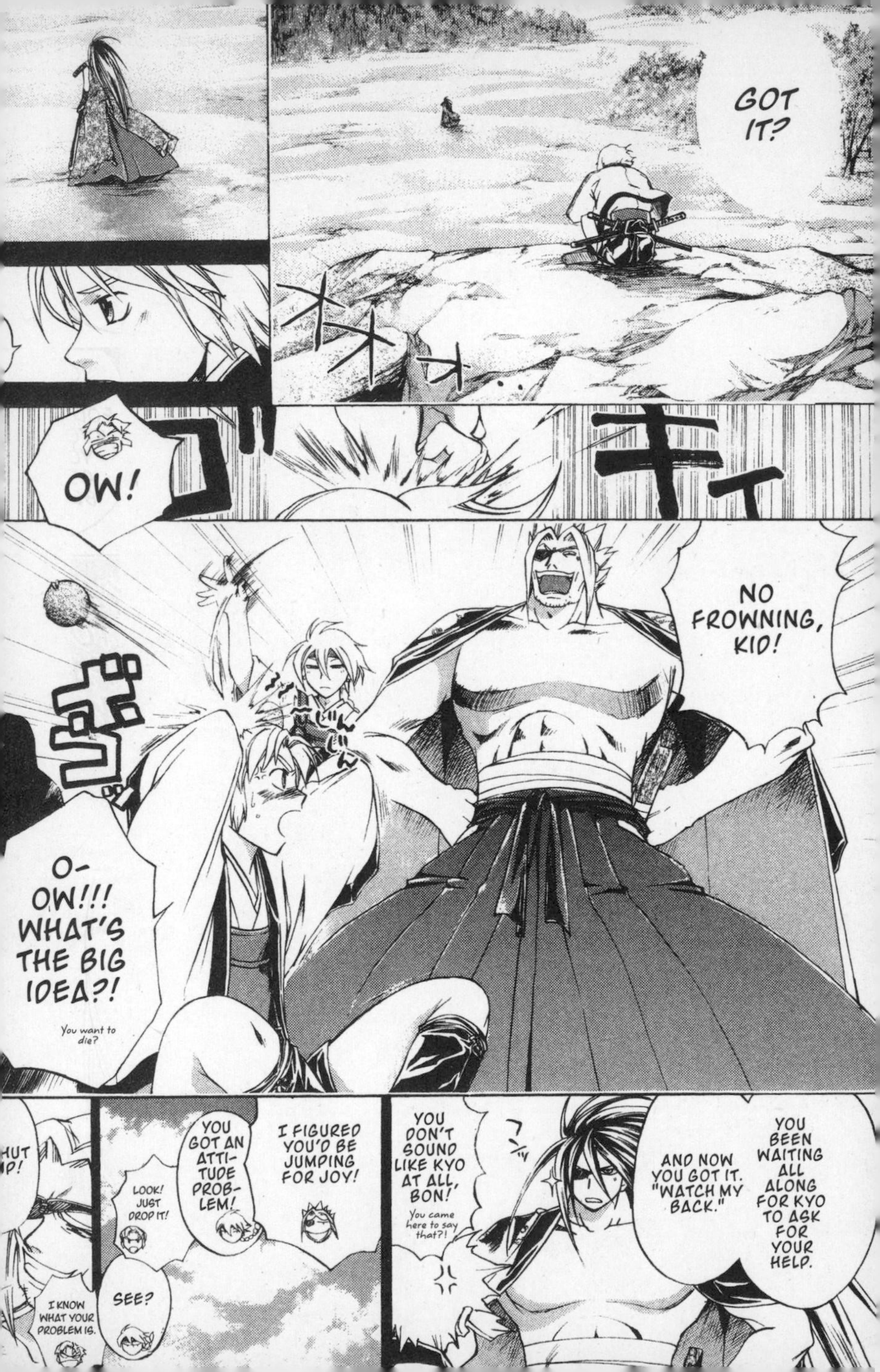
GOT IT?
OW!
NO FROWNING, KID!
O-OW!!! WHAT'S THE BIG IDEA?!
You want to die?
YOU BEEN WAITING ALL ALONG FOR KYO TO ASK FOR YOUR HELP.
AND NOW YOU GOT IT. "WATCH MY BACK."
YOU DON'T SOUND LIKE KYO AT ALL, BON!
You came here to say that?!
I FIGURED YOU'D BE JUMPING FOR JOY!
YOU GOT AN ATTITUDE PROBLEM!
LOOK! JUST DROP IT!
SEE?
I KNOW WHAT YOUR PROBLEM IS.

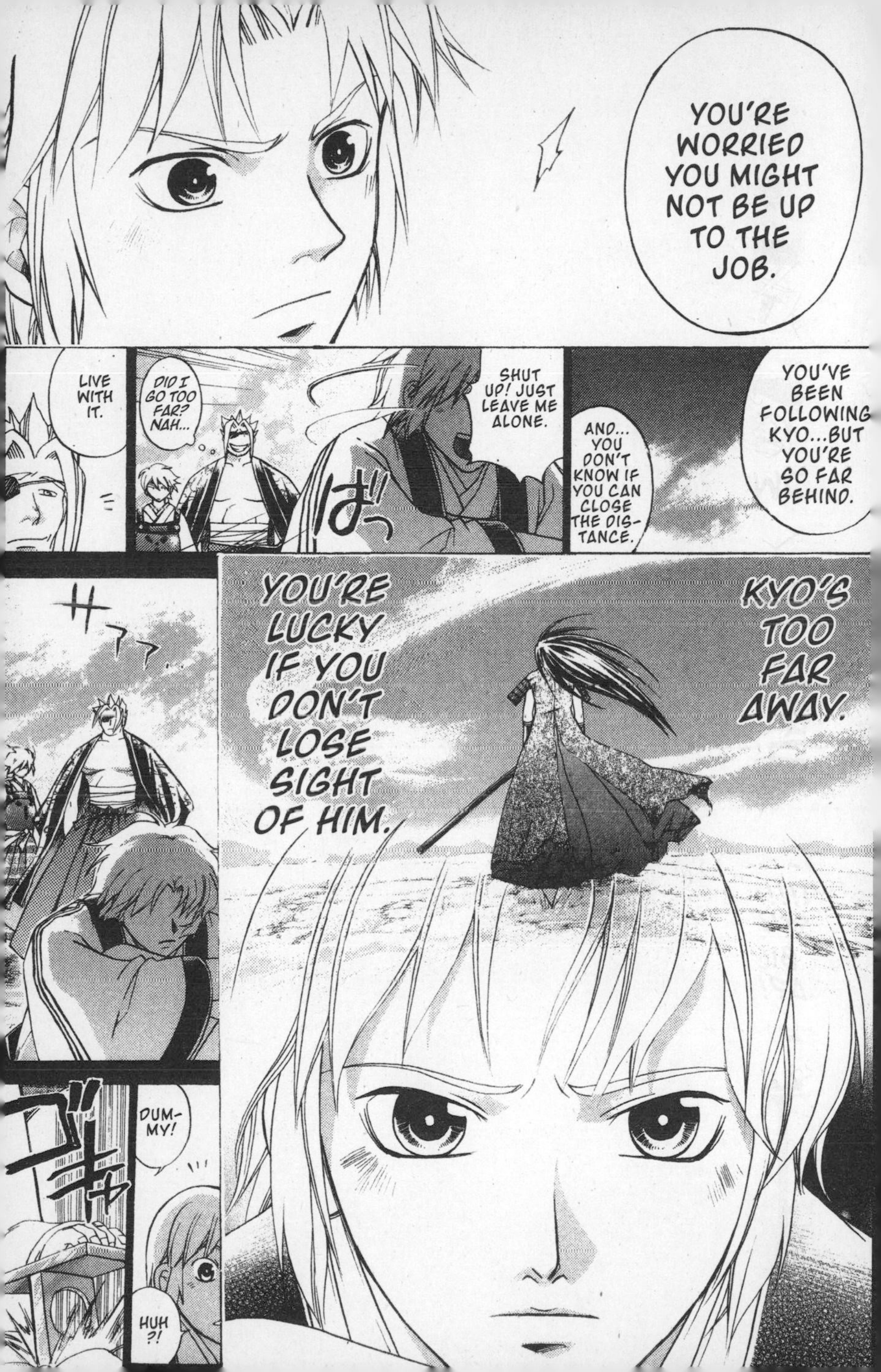
YOU'RE WORRIED YOU MIGHT NOT BE UP TO THE JOB.
YOU'VE BEEN FOLLOWING KYO...BUT YOU'RE SO FAR BEHIND.
AND... YOU DON'T KNOW IF YOU CAN CLOSE THE DIS-TANCE.
SHUT UP! JUST LEAVE ME ALONE.
ばっ
DID I GO TOO FAR? NAH...
LIVE WITH IT.
KYO'S TOO FAR AWAY.
YOU'RE LUCKY IF YOU DON'T LOSE SIGHT OF HIM.
サァァ
ゴキャ
DUM-MY!
HUH?!

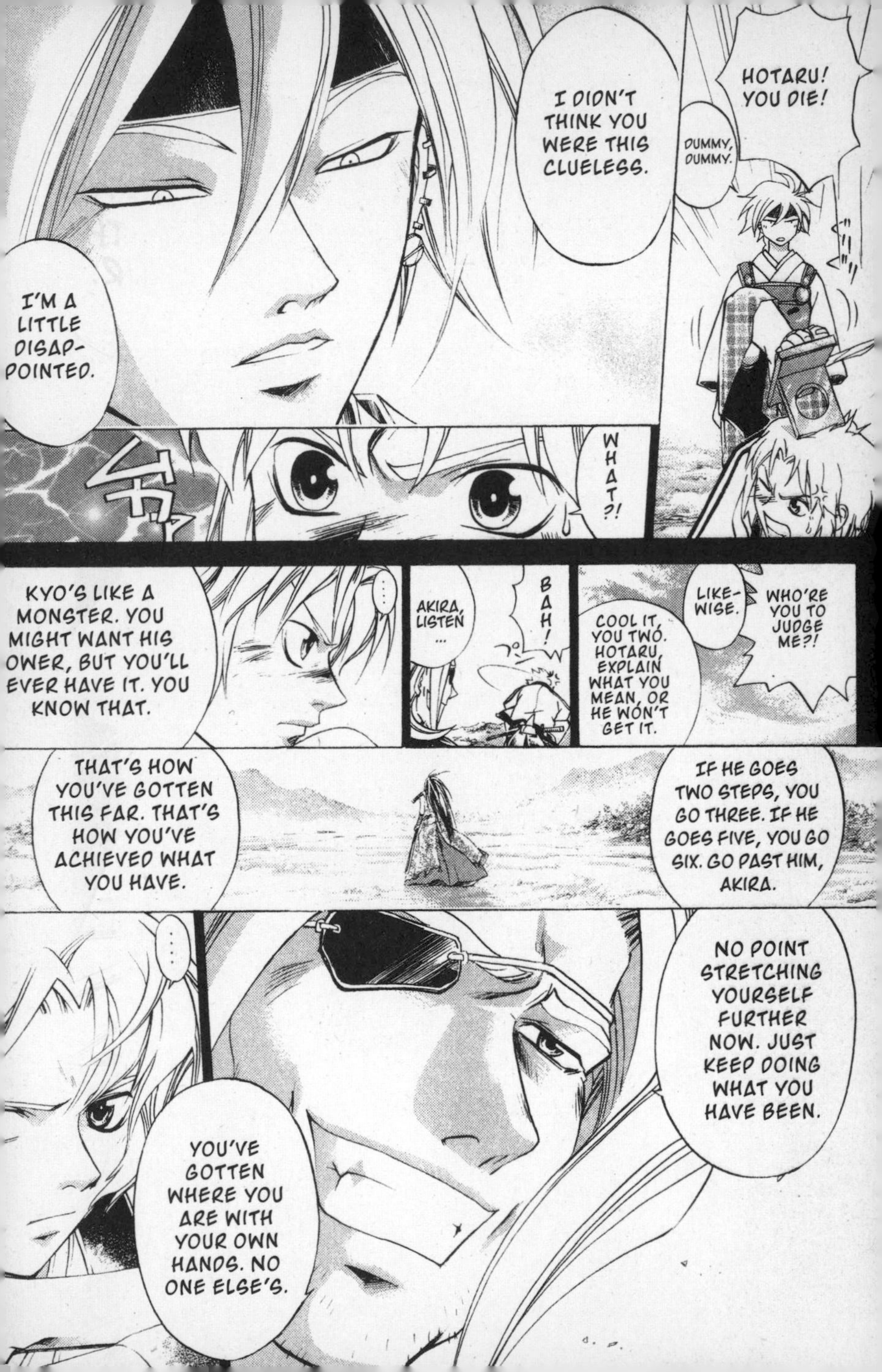
HOTARU! YOU DIE!
DUMMY, DUMMY.
I DIDN'T THINK YOU WERE THIS CLUELESS.
I'M A LITTLE DISAP-POINTED.
WHAT?!
WHO'RE YOU TO JUDGE ME?!
LIKE-WISE.
COOL IT, YOU TWO. HOTARU, EXPLAIN WHAT YOU MEAN, OR HE WON'T GET IT.
BAH!
AKIRA, LISTEN ...
...
KYO'S LIKE A MONSTER. YOU MIGHT WANT HIS OWER, BUT YOU'LL EVER HAVE IT. YOU KNOW THAT.
IF HE GOES TWO STEPS, YOU GO THREE. IF HE GOES FIVE, YOU GO SIX. GO PAST HIM, AKIRA.
THAT'S HOW YOU'VE GOTTEN THIS FAR. THAT'S HOW YOU'VE ACHIEVED WHAT YOU HAVE.
NO POINT STRETCHING YOURSELF FURTHER NOW. JUST KEEP DOING WHAT YOU HAVE BEEN.
YOU'VE GOTTEN WHERE YOU ARE WITH YOUR OWN HANDS. NO ONE ELSE'S.
......

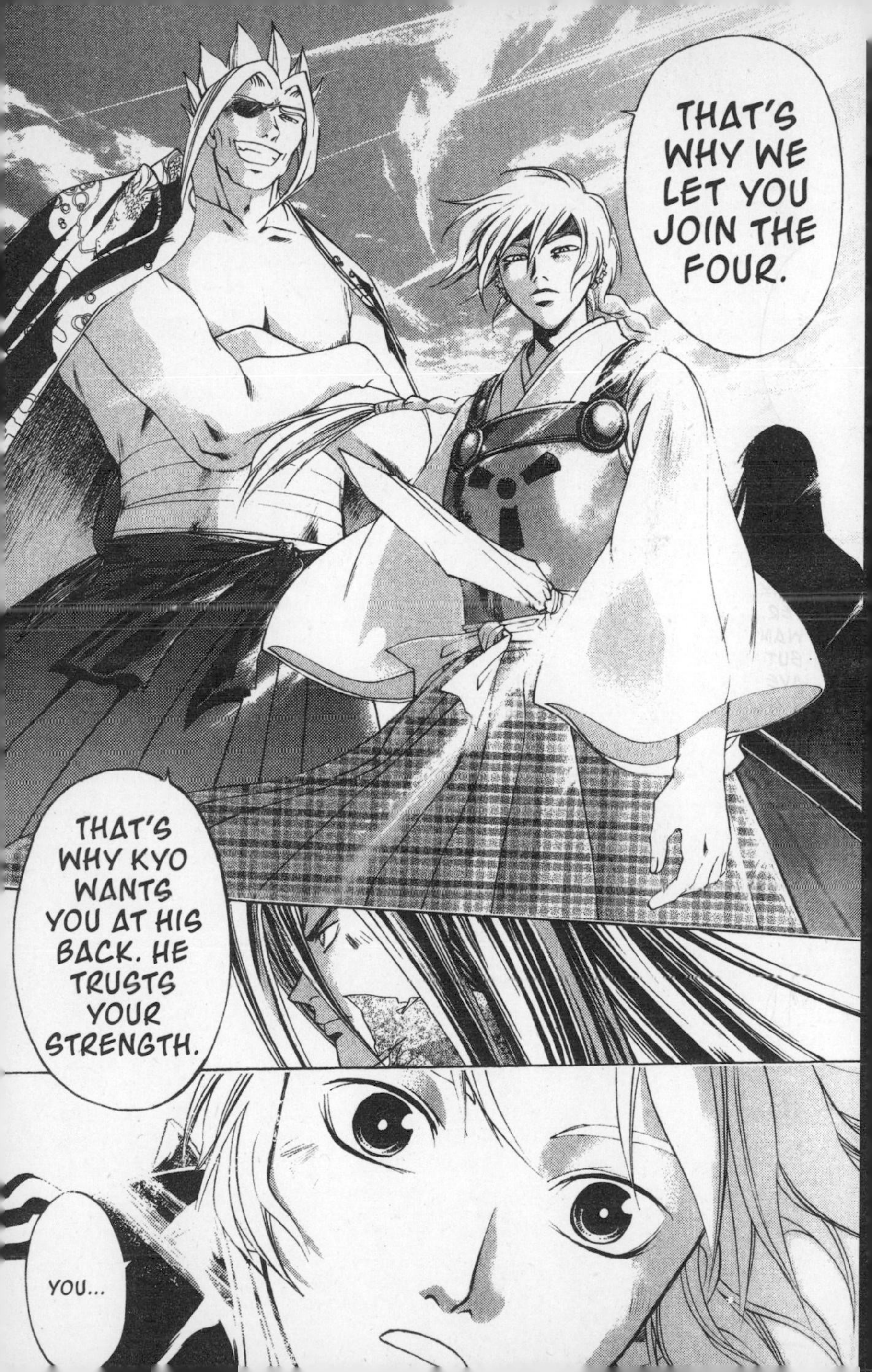
THAT'S WHY WE LET YOU JOIN THE FOUR.
THAT'S WHY KYO WANTS YOU AT HIS BACK. HE TRUSTS YOUR STRENGTH.
YOU...

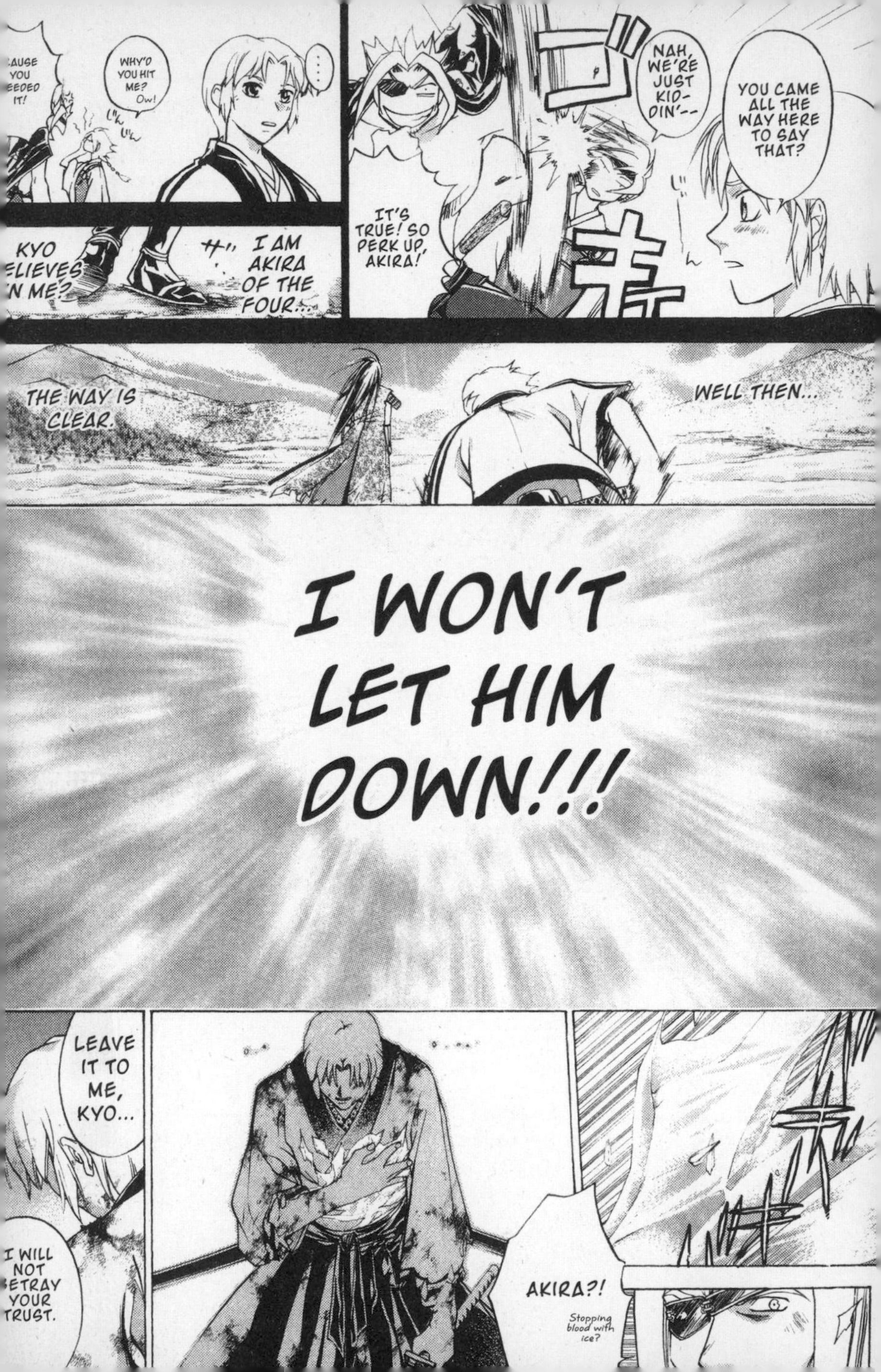
YOU CAME ALL THE WAY HERE TO SAY THAT?
NAH, WE'RE JUST KID-DIN'--
IT'S TRUE! SO PERK UP, AKIRA!
. . .
WHY'D YOU HIT ME? Ow!
AUSE YOU EEDED IT!
I AM AKIRA OF THE FOUR...
KYO ELIEVES N ME?
WELL THEN...
THE WAY IS CLEAR.
I WON'T LET HIM DOWN!!!
AKIRA?!
Stopping blood with ice?
LEAVE IT TO ME, KYO...
I WILL NOT ETRAY YOUR RUST.

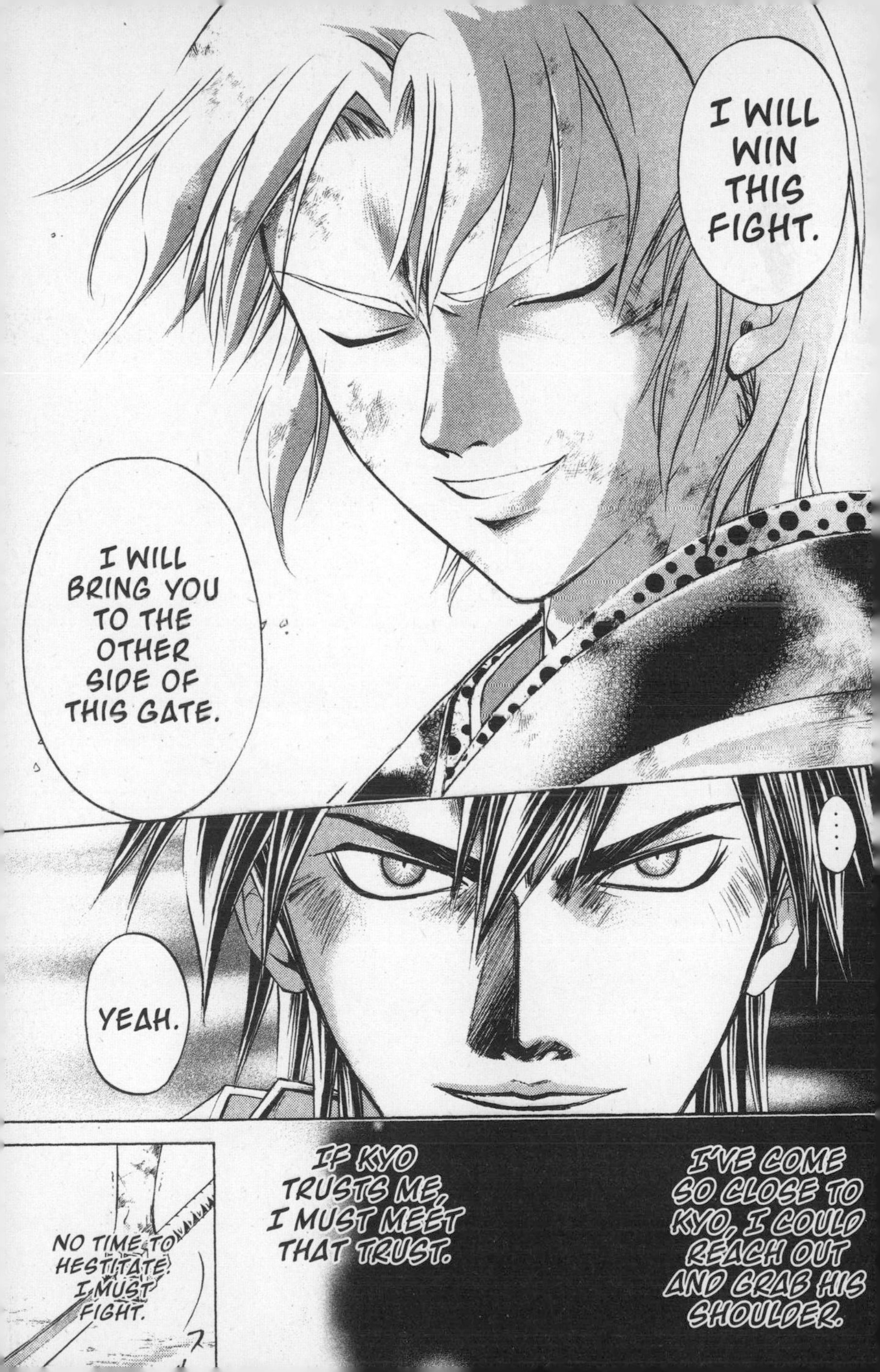
I WILL WIN THIS FIGHT.
I WILL BRING YOU TO THE OTHER SIDE OF THIS GATE.
....
YEAH.
I'VE COME SO CLOSE TO KYO, I COULD REACH OUT AND GRAB HIS SHOULDER.
IF KYO TRUSTS ME, I MUST MEET THAT TRUST.
NO TIME TO HESTITATE. I MUST FIGHT.

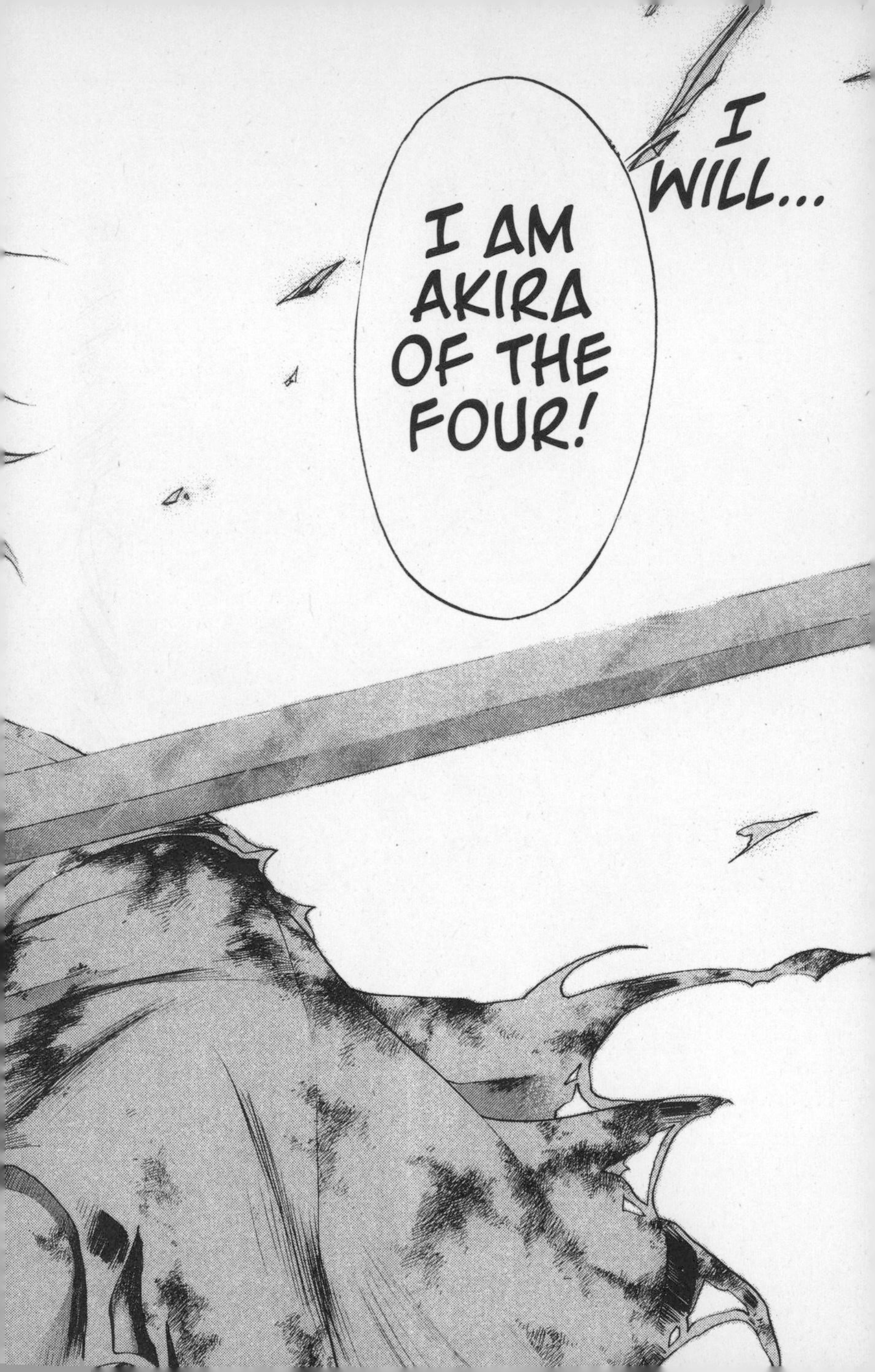
I WILL...
I AM AKIRA OF THE FOUR!

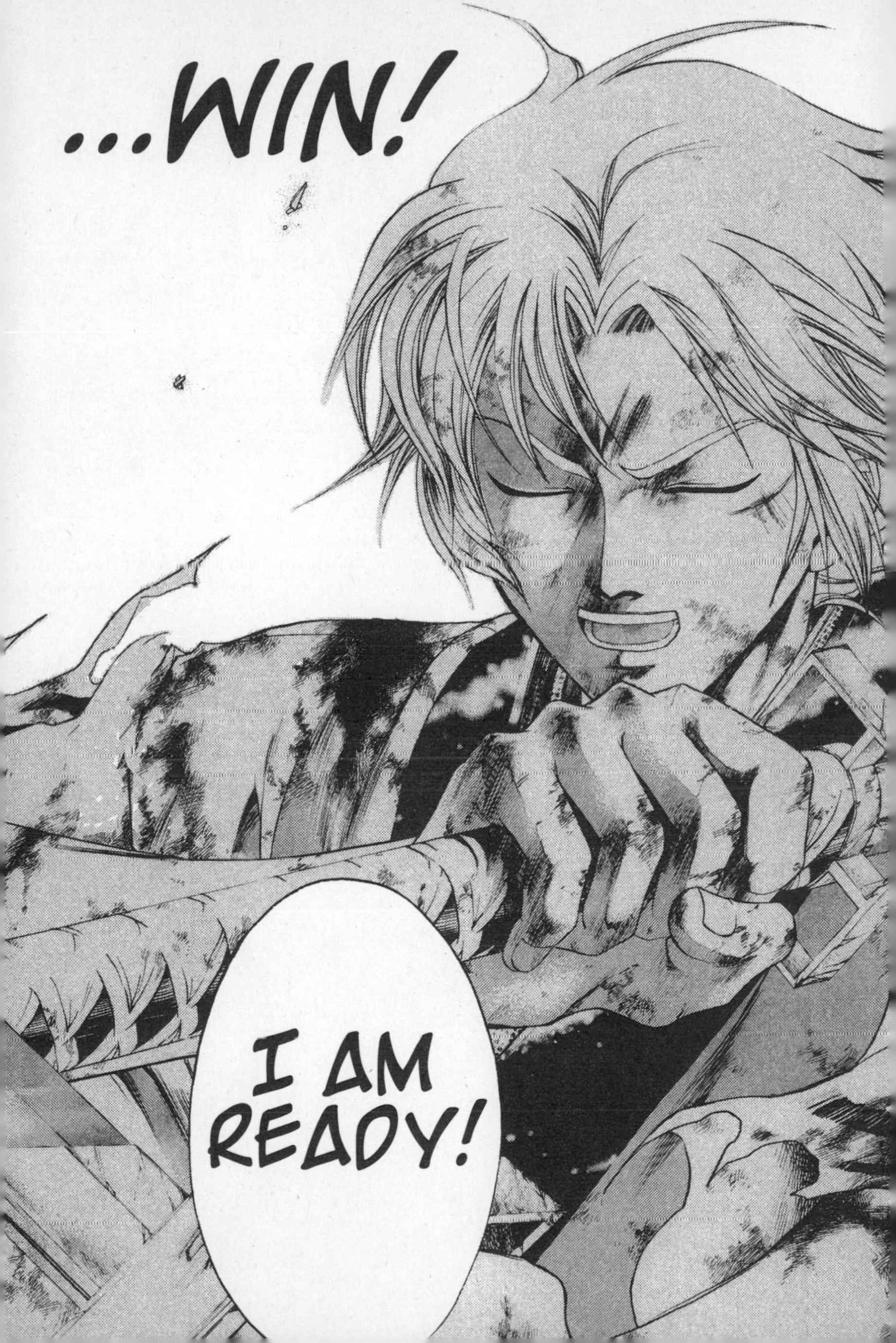
...WIN!
I AM READY!

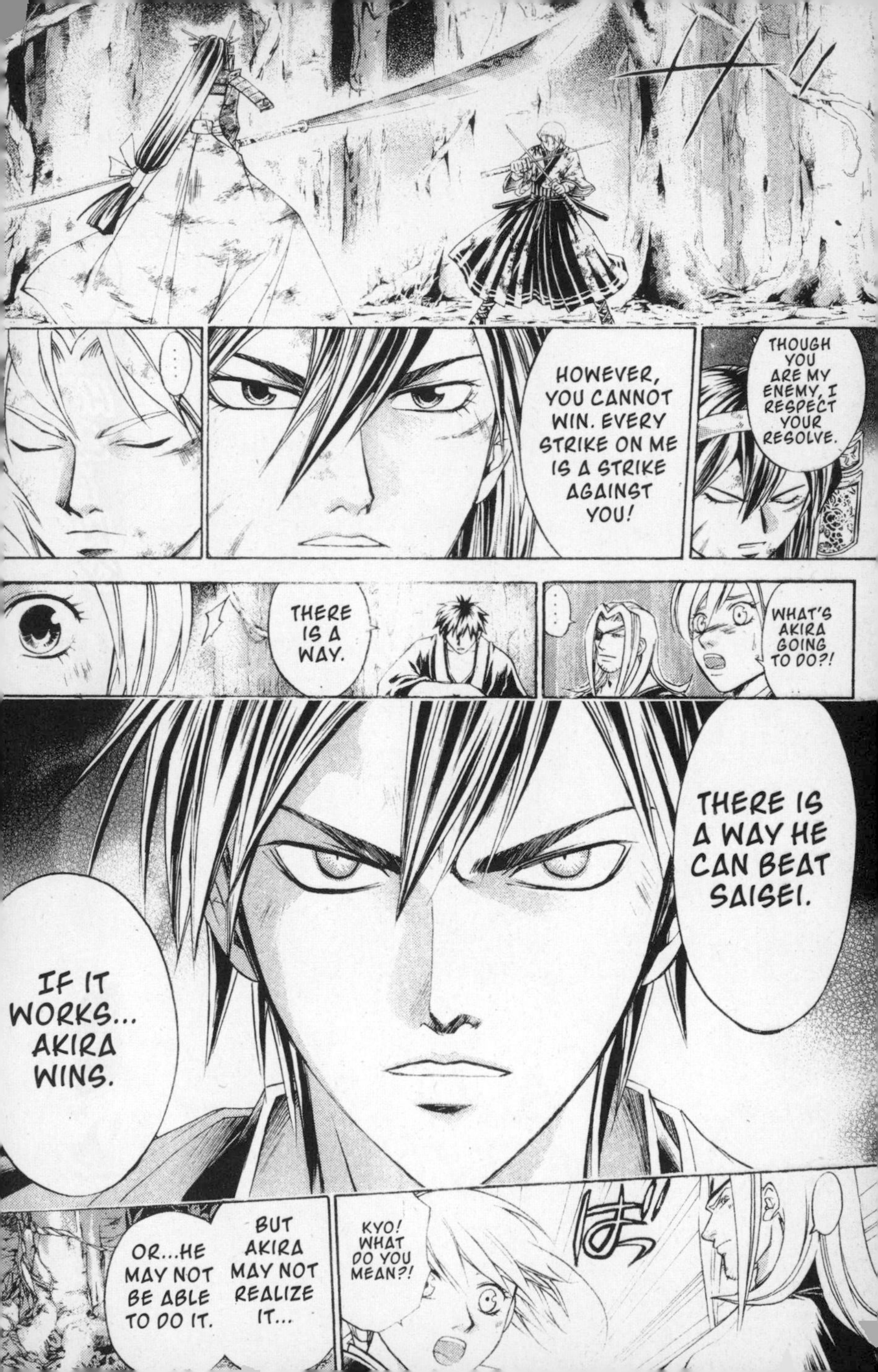
THOUGH YOU ARE MY ENEMY, I RESPECT YOUR RESOLVE.
HOWEVER, YOU CANNOT WIN. EVERY STRIKE ON ME IS A STRIKE AGAINST YOU!
....
WHAT'S AKIRA GOING TO DO?!
....
THERE IS A WAY.
THERE IS A WAY HE CAN BEAT SAISEI.
IF IT WORKS... AKIRA WINS.
KYO! WHAT DO YOU MEAN?!
BUT AKIRA MAY NOT REALIZE IT...
OR...HE MAY NOT BE ABLE TO DO IT.

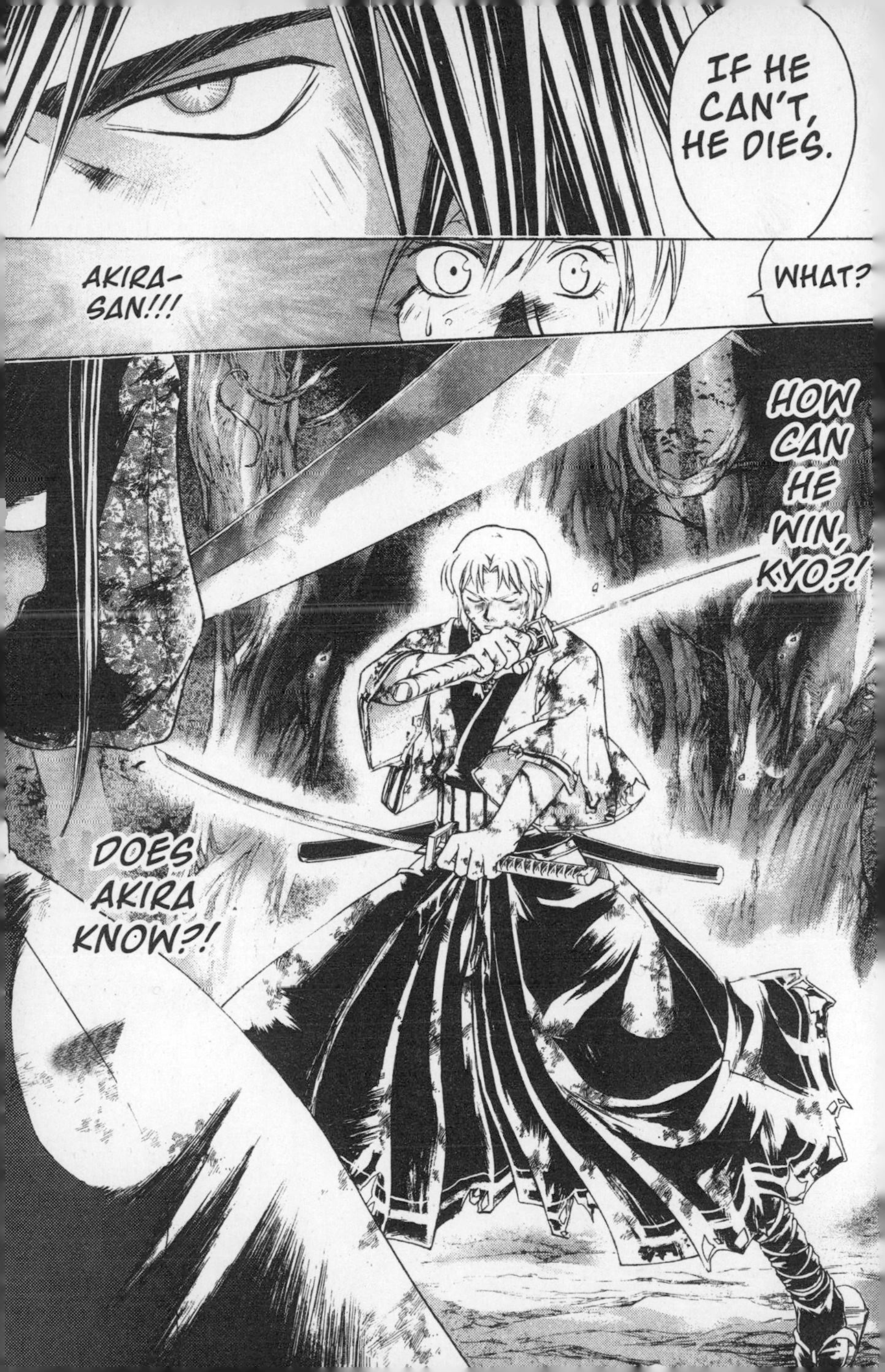
IF HE CAN'T, HE DIES.
WHAT?
AKIRA-SAN!!!
HOW CAN HE WIN, KYO?!
DOES AKIRA KNOW?!

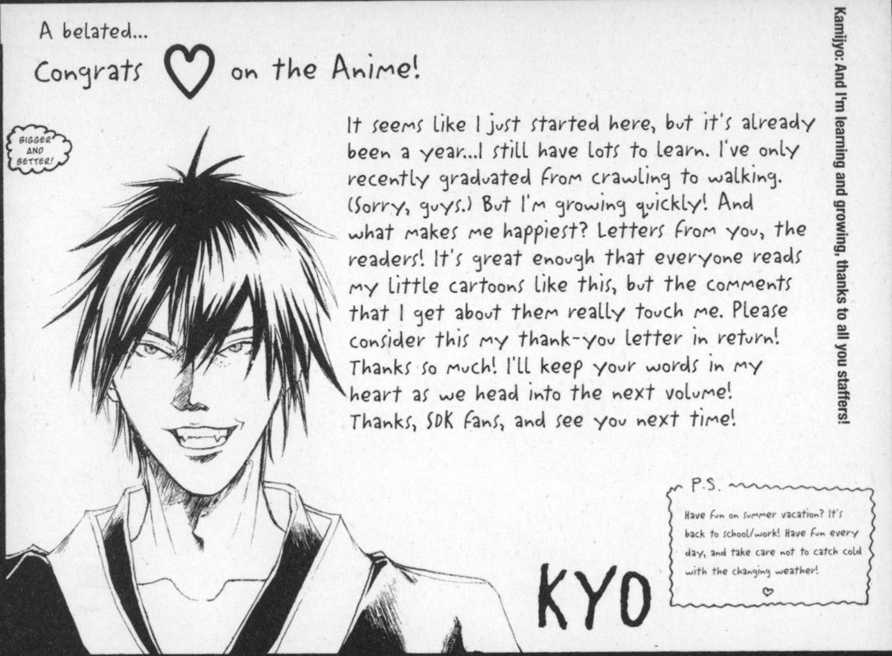
A belated...
Congrats ♡ on the Anime!
BIGGER AND BETTER!
It seems like I just started here, but it's already been a year...I still have lots to learn. I've only recently graduated from crawling to walking. (Sorry, guys.) But I'm growing quickly! And what makes me happiest? Letters from you, the readers! It's great enough that everyone reads my little cartoons like this, but the comments that I get about them really touch me. Please consider this my thank-you letter in return! Thanks so much! I'll keep your words in my heart as we head into the next volume! Thanks, SDK fans, and see you next time!
P.S.
Have fun on summer vacation? It's back to school/work! Have fun every day, and take care not to catch cold with the changing weather! ♡
KYO

Kamijyo: And I'm learning and growing, thanks to all you staffers!

RISO

Kiyoshi Kamimura

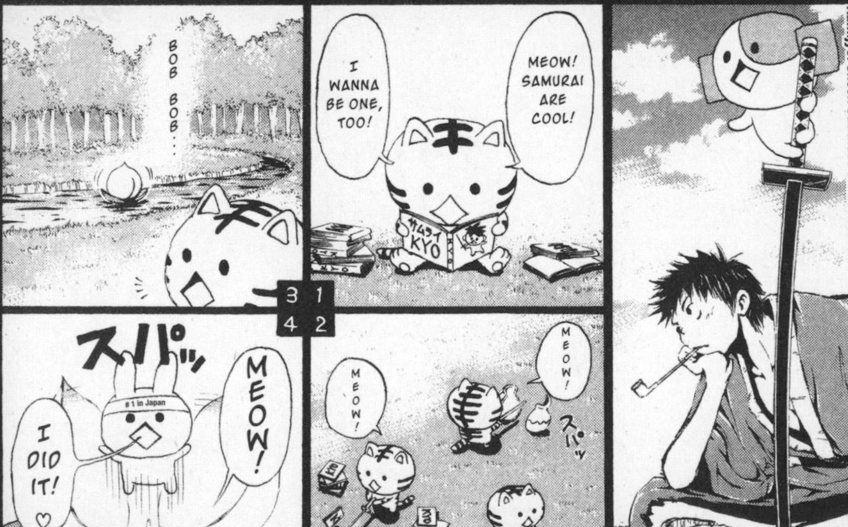
MEOW! SAMURAI ARE COOL!
I WANNA BE ONE, TOO!
サムライ KYO
1
MEOW!
MEOW!
スパッ
MEOW!
スパッ
スパッ
2
BOB BOB...
3
4
スパッ
#1 in Japan
MEOW!
I DID IT! ♡

Kamijyo: Check out those samurai skills!

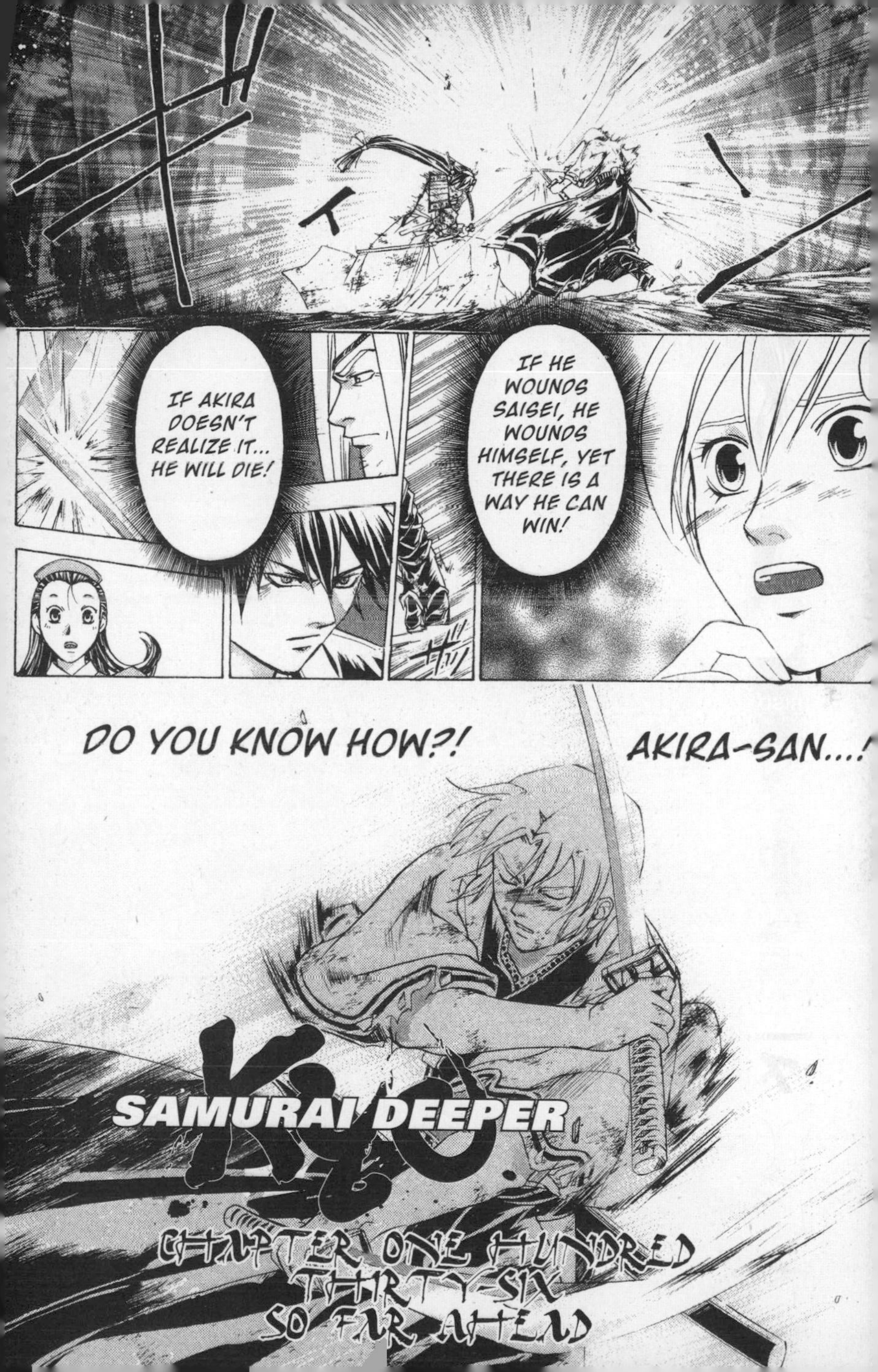
IF HE WOUNDS SAISEI, HE WOUNDS HIMSELF, YET THERE IS A WAY HE CAN WIN!
IF AKIRA DOESN'T REALIZE IT... HE WILL DIE!
AKIRA-SAN...!
DO YOU KNOW HOW?!
SAMURAI DEEPER KYO
CHAPTER ONE HUNDRED THIRTY-SIX
SO FAR AHEAD

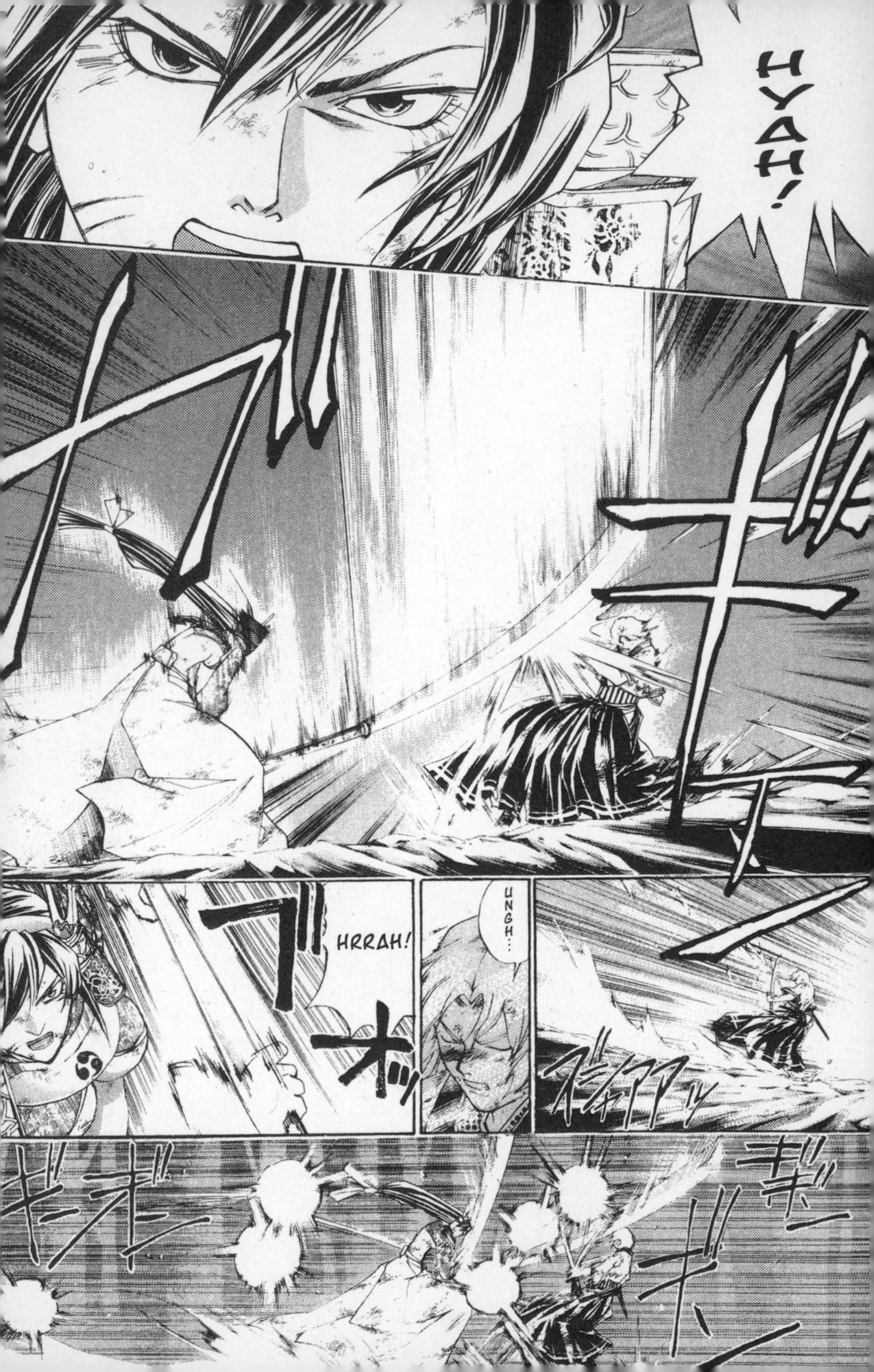
HYAH!
UNGH...
HRRAH!

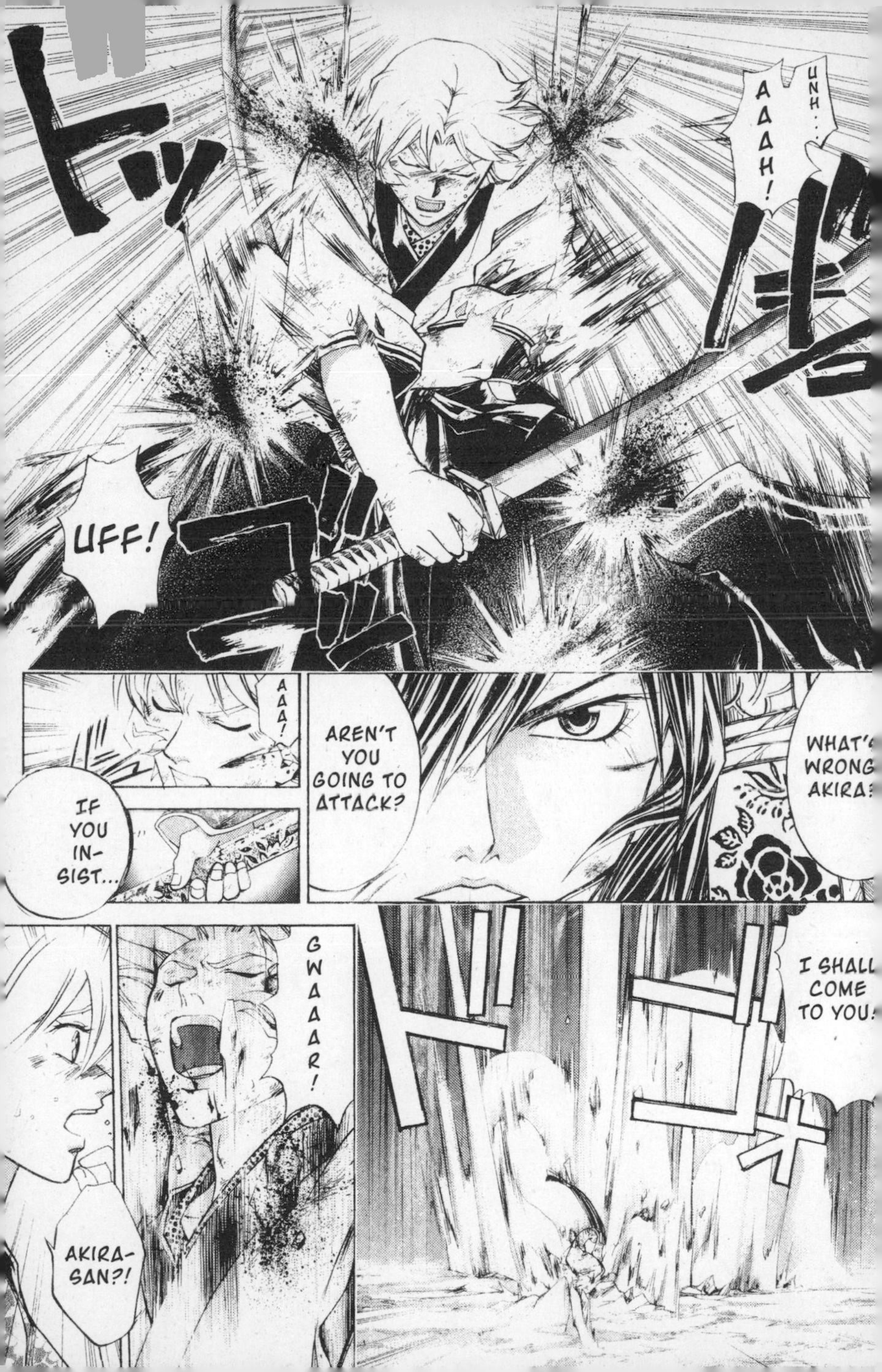
UNH... AAAH!
UFF!
WHAT'S WRONG AKIRA?
AREN'T YOU GOING TO ATTACK?
AAA!
IF YOU IN-SIST...
I SHALL COME TO YOU!
GWAAAAR!
AKIRA-SAN?!

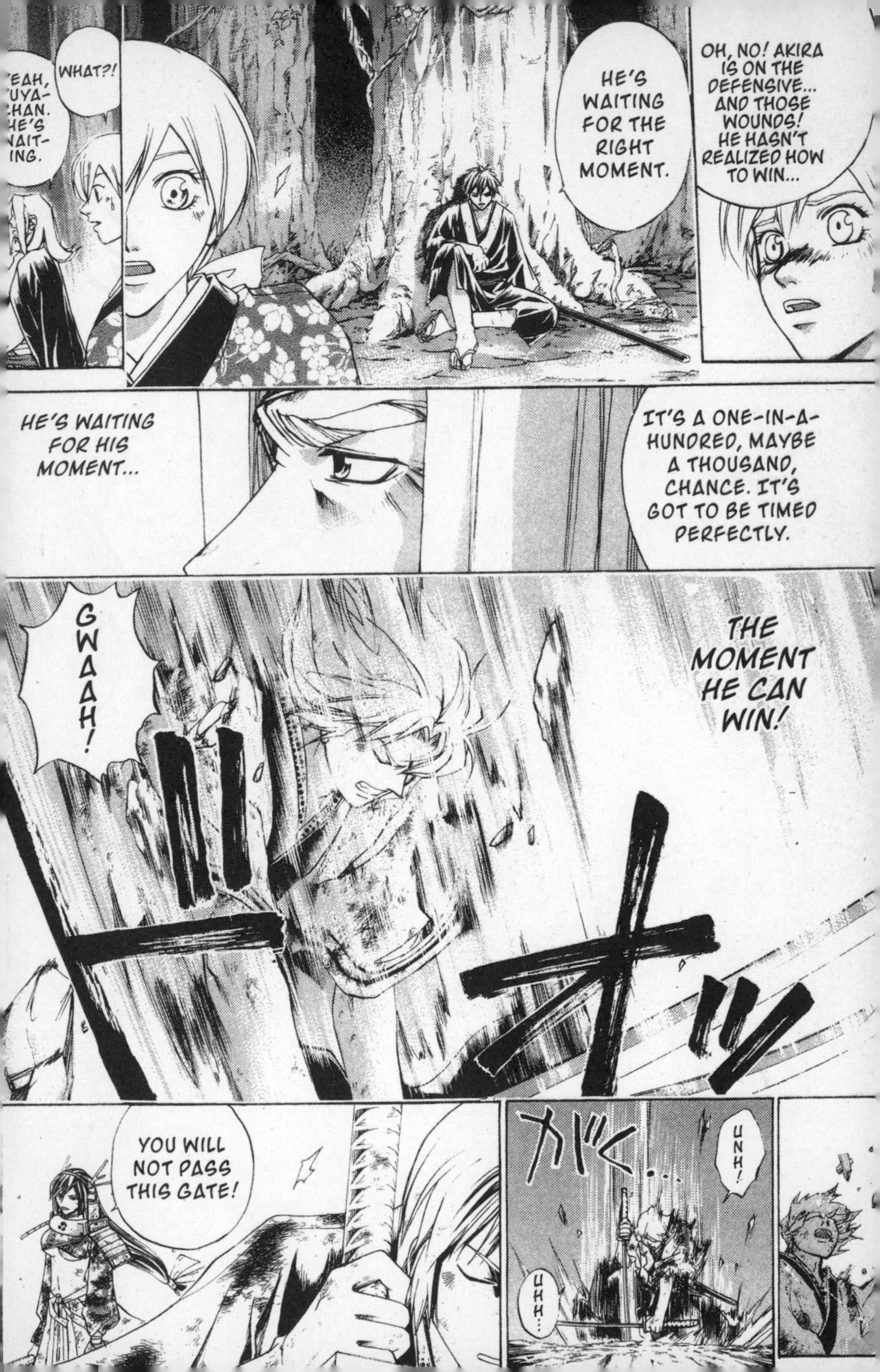
OH, NO! AKIRA IS ON THE DEFENSIVE... AND THOSE WOUNDS! HE HASN'T REALIZED HOW TO WIN...
HE'S WAITING FOR THE RIGHT MOMENT.
WHAT?!
EAH, UYA-HAN. HE'S AIT-ING.
IT'S A ONE-IN-A-HUNDRED, MAYBE A THOUSAND, CHANCE. IT'S GOT TO BE TIMED PERFECTLY.
HE'S WAITING FOR HIS MOMENT...
THE MOMENT HE CAN WIN!
GWAAAH!
UNH!
UHH...
YOU WILL NOT PASS THIS GATE!

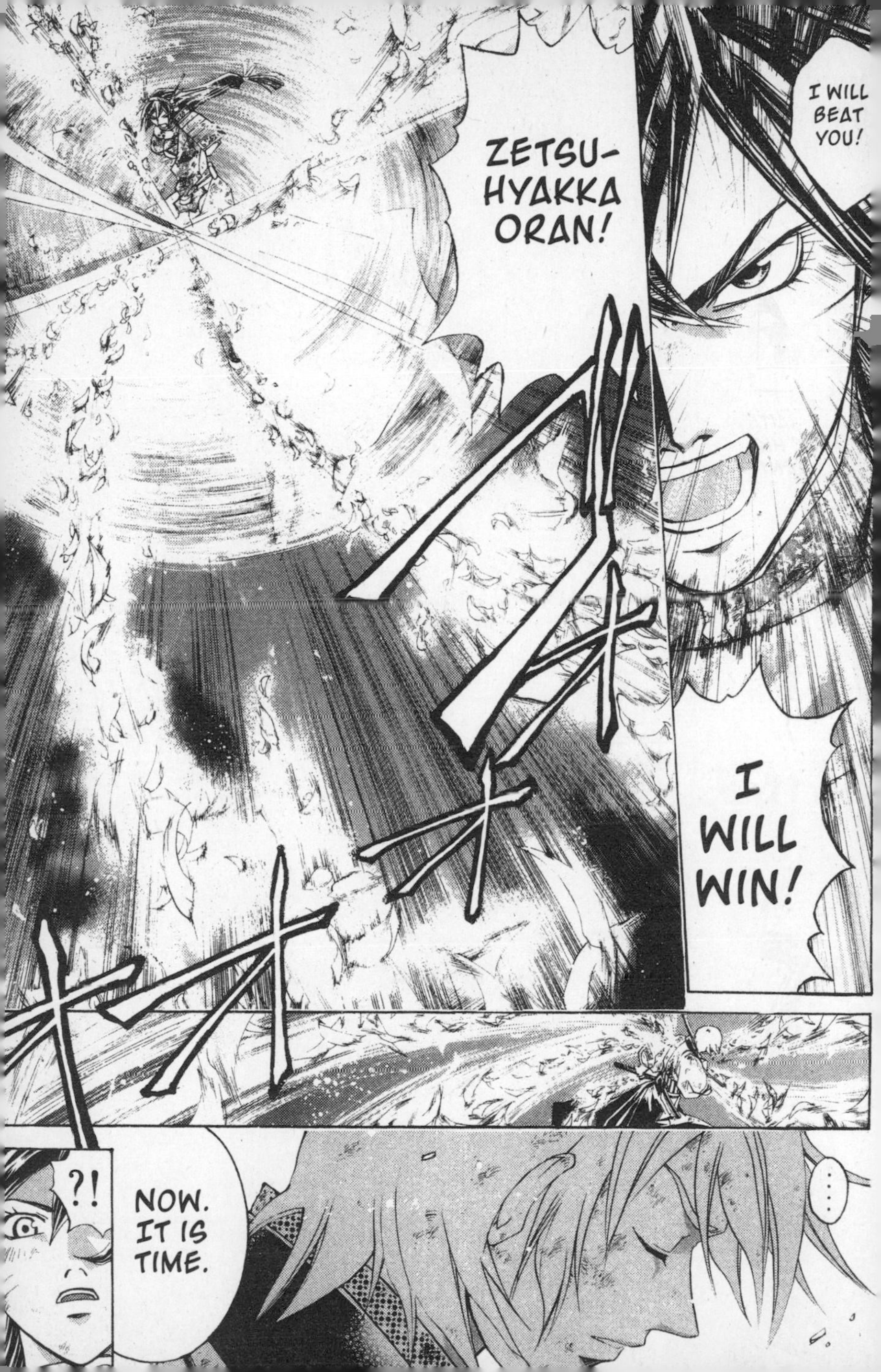

I WILL BEAT YOU!
I WILL WIN!
ZETSU-HYAKKA ORAN!
...
NOW. IT IS TIME.
?!

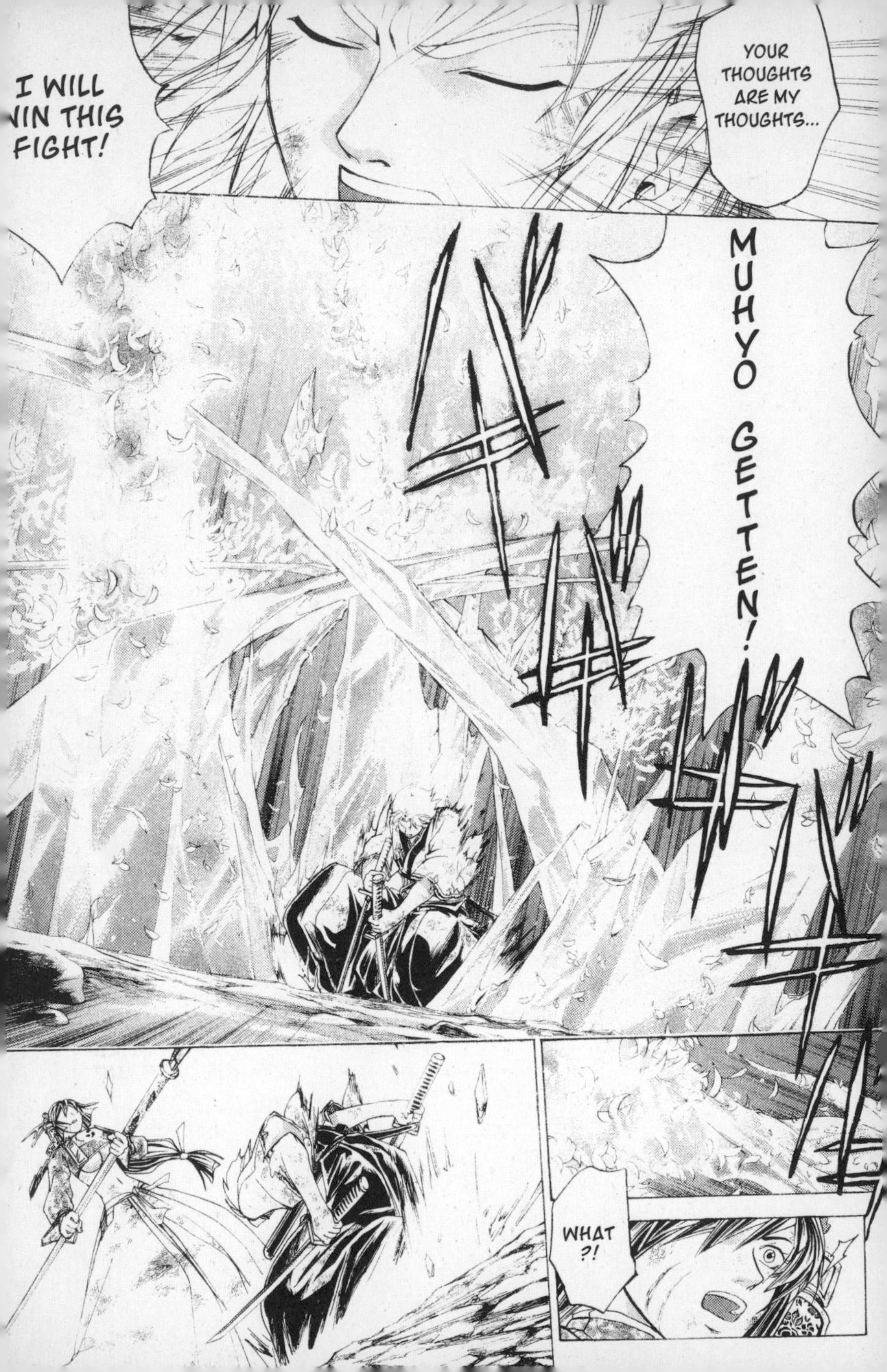
YOUR THOUGHTS ARE MY THOUGHTS...
I WILL WIN THIS FIGHT!
MUHYO GETTEN!
WHAT?!

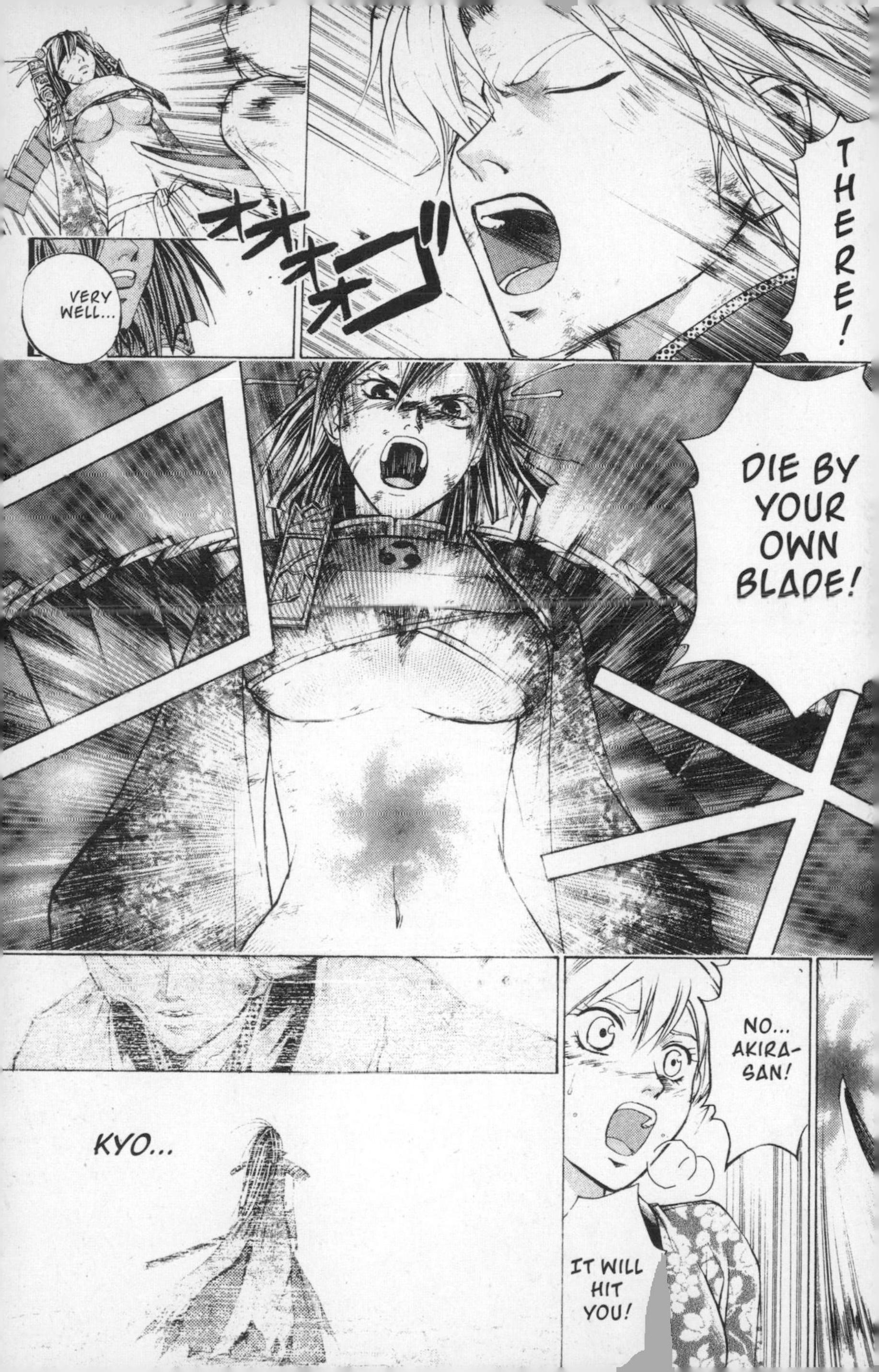
THERE!
ゴオオオ
VERY WELL...
DIE BY YOUR OWN BLADE!
NO... AKIRA-SAN!
IT WILL HIT YOU!
KYO...

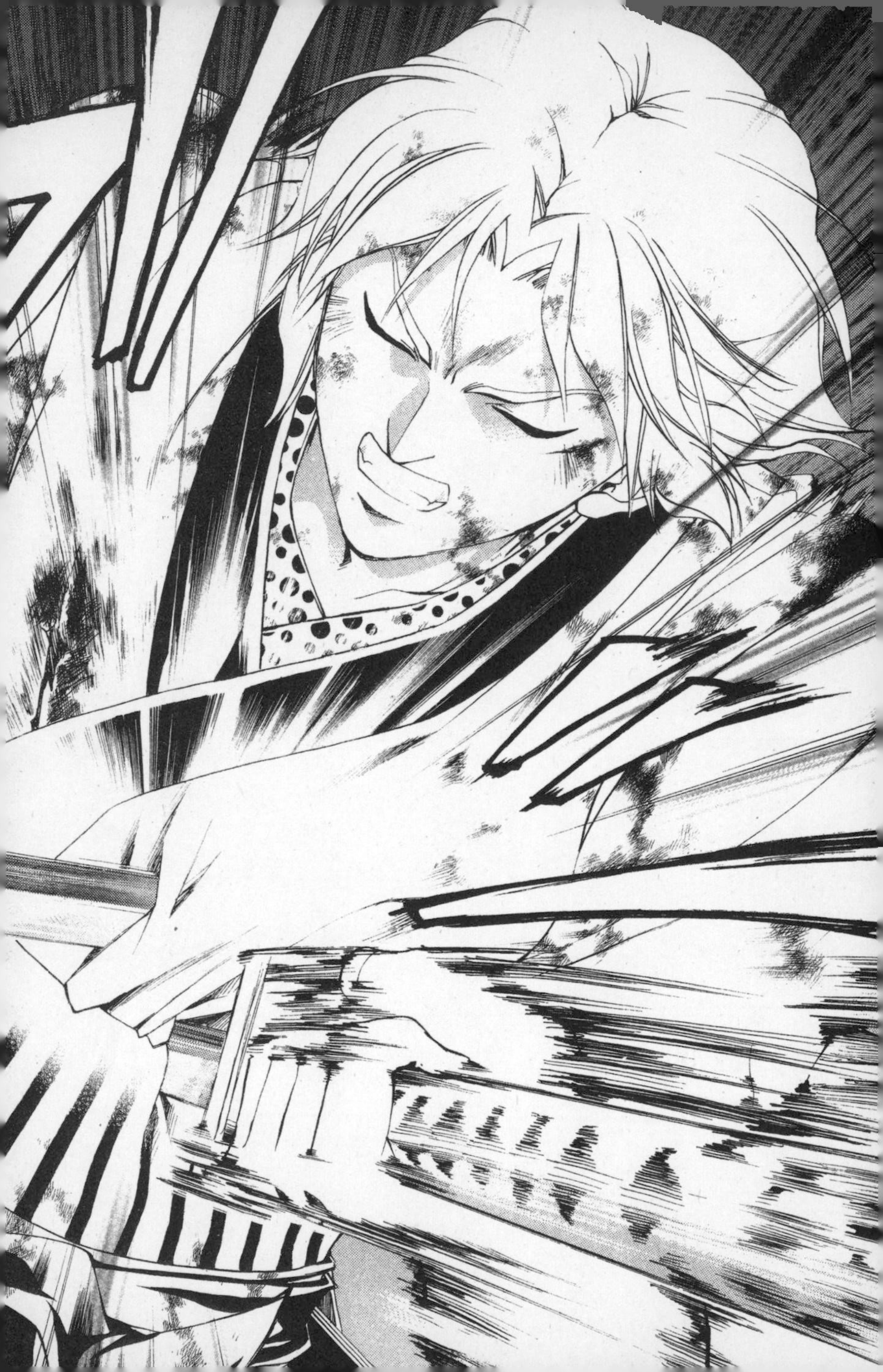

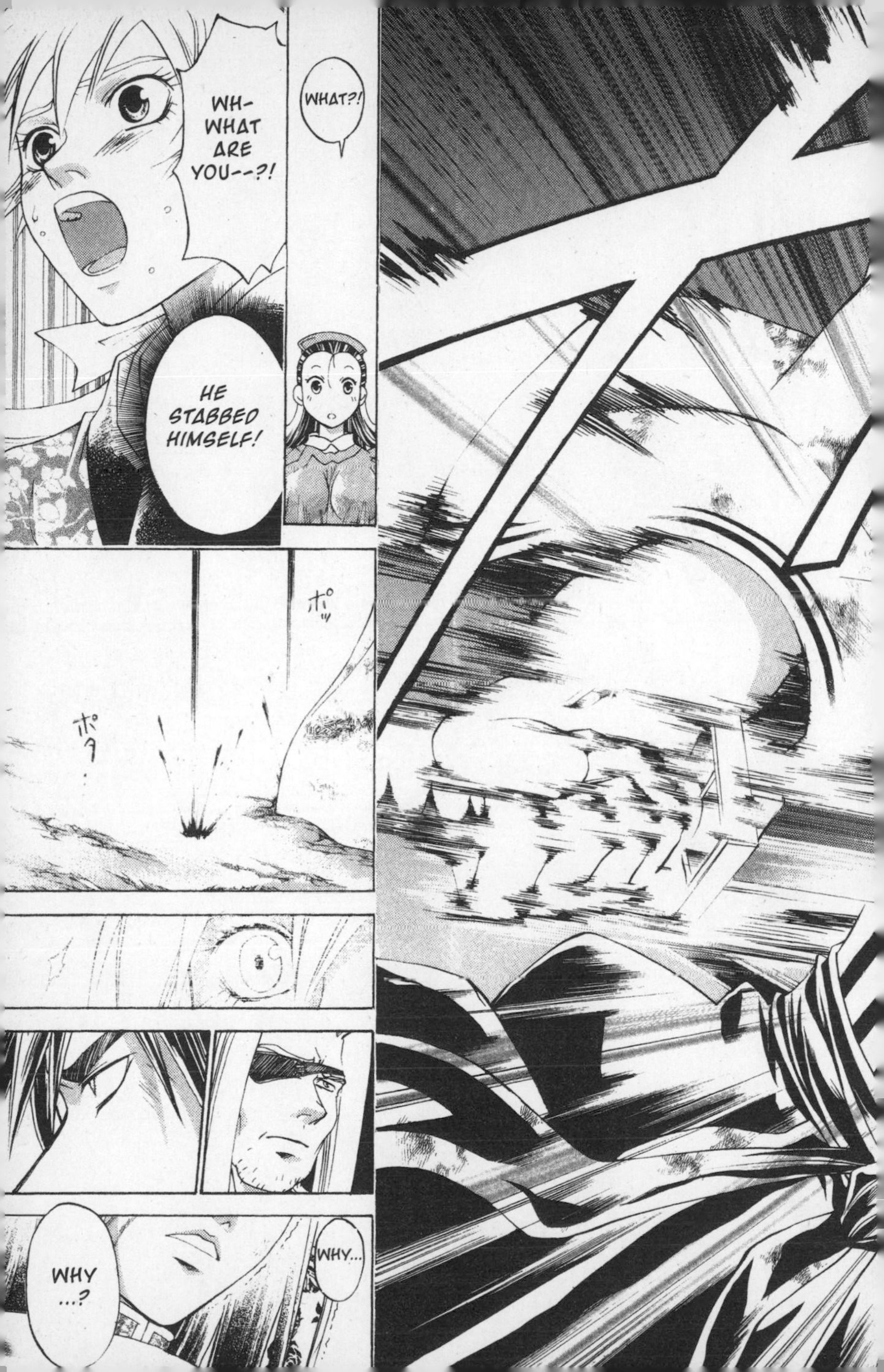
WHAT?!
WH- WHAT ARE YOU--?!
HE STABBED HIMSELF!
ポツ
ポタ
WHY...
WHY ...?

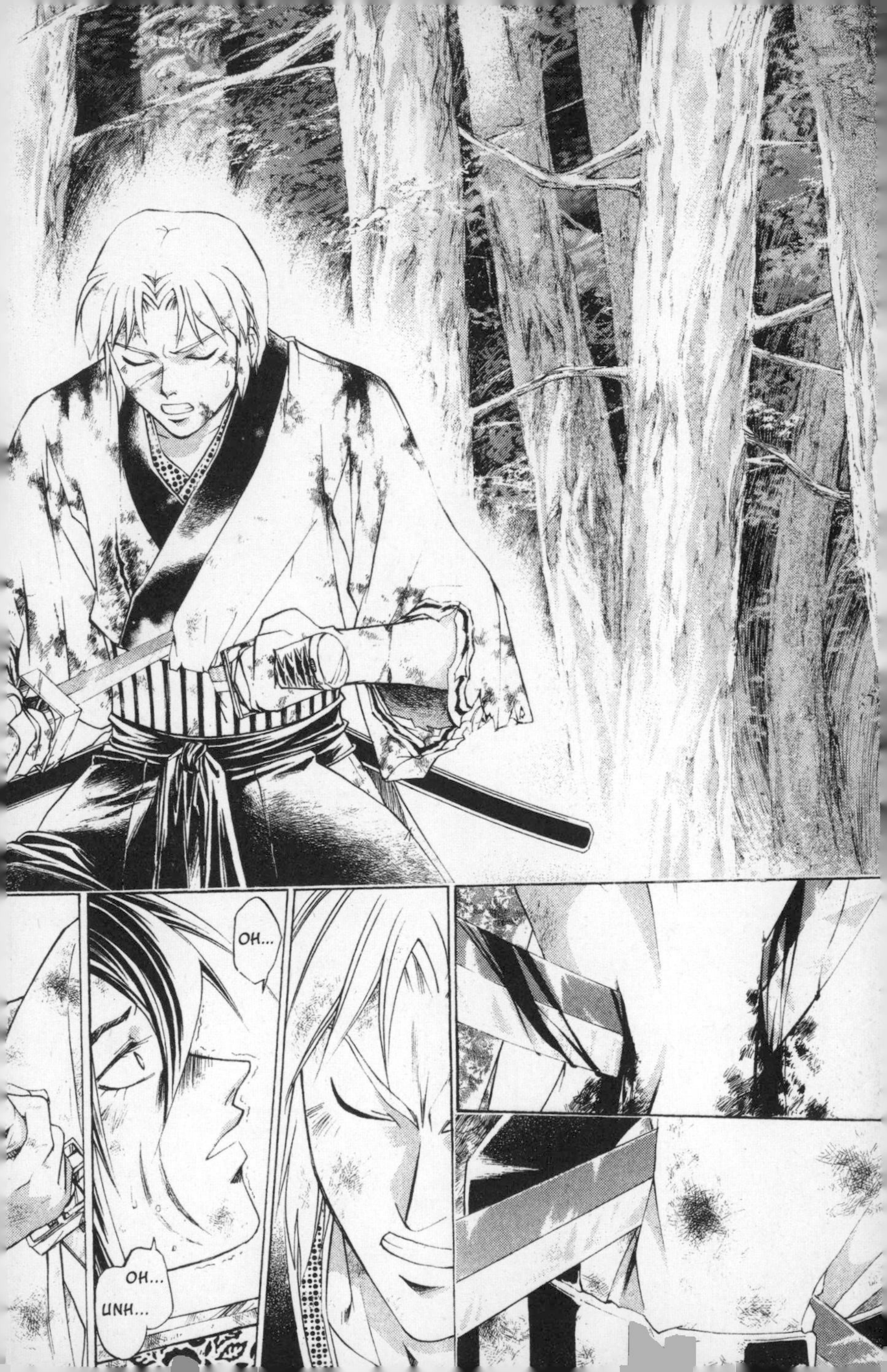
OH...
OH... UNH...

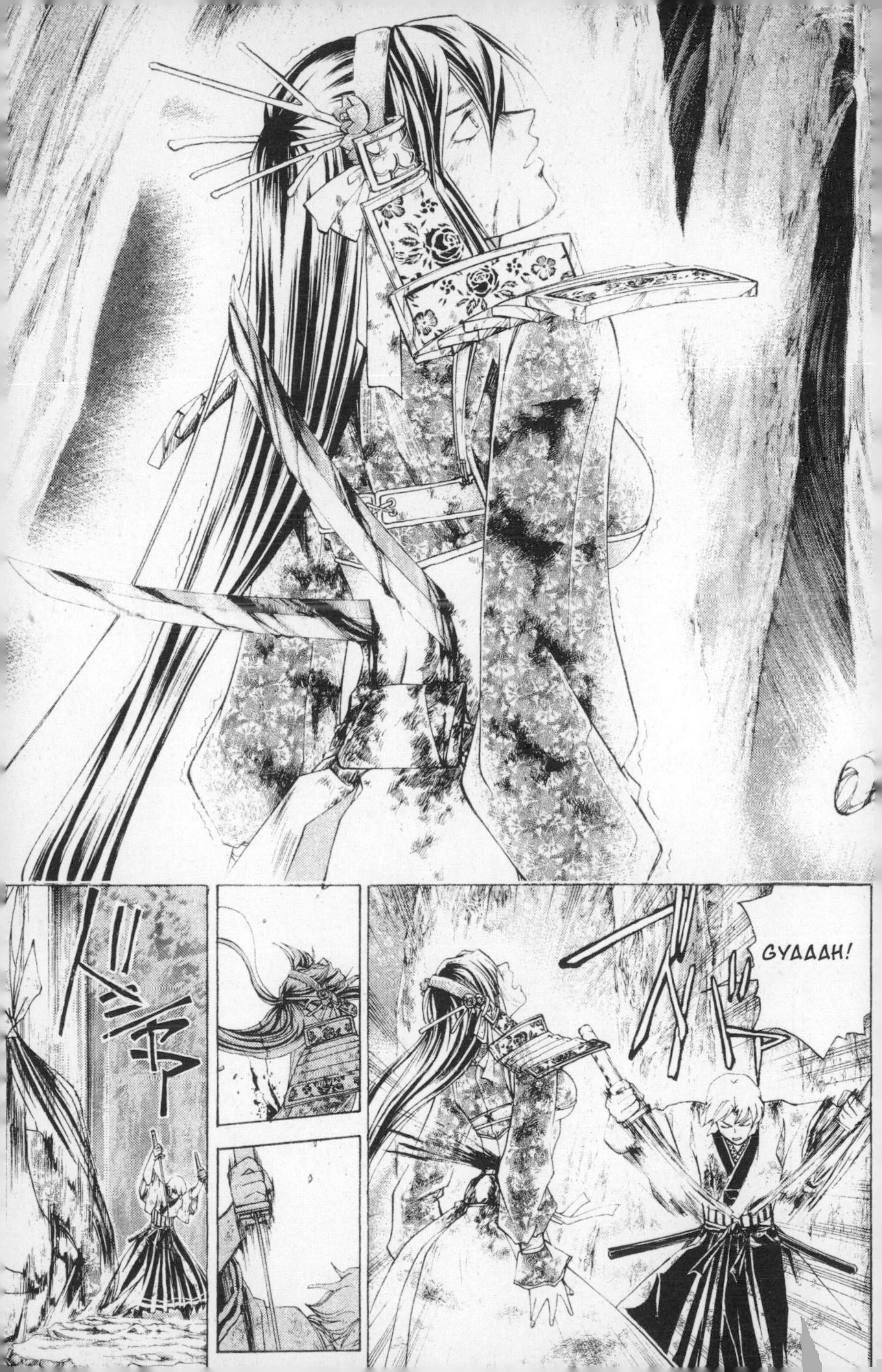
GYAAAH!
ドシャアー

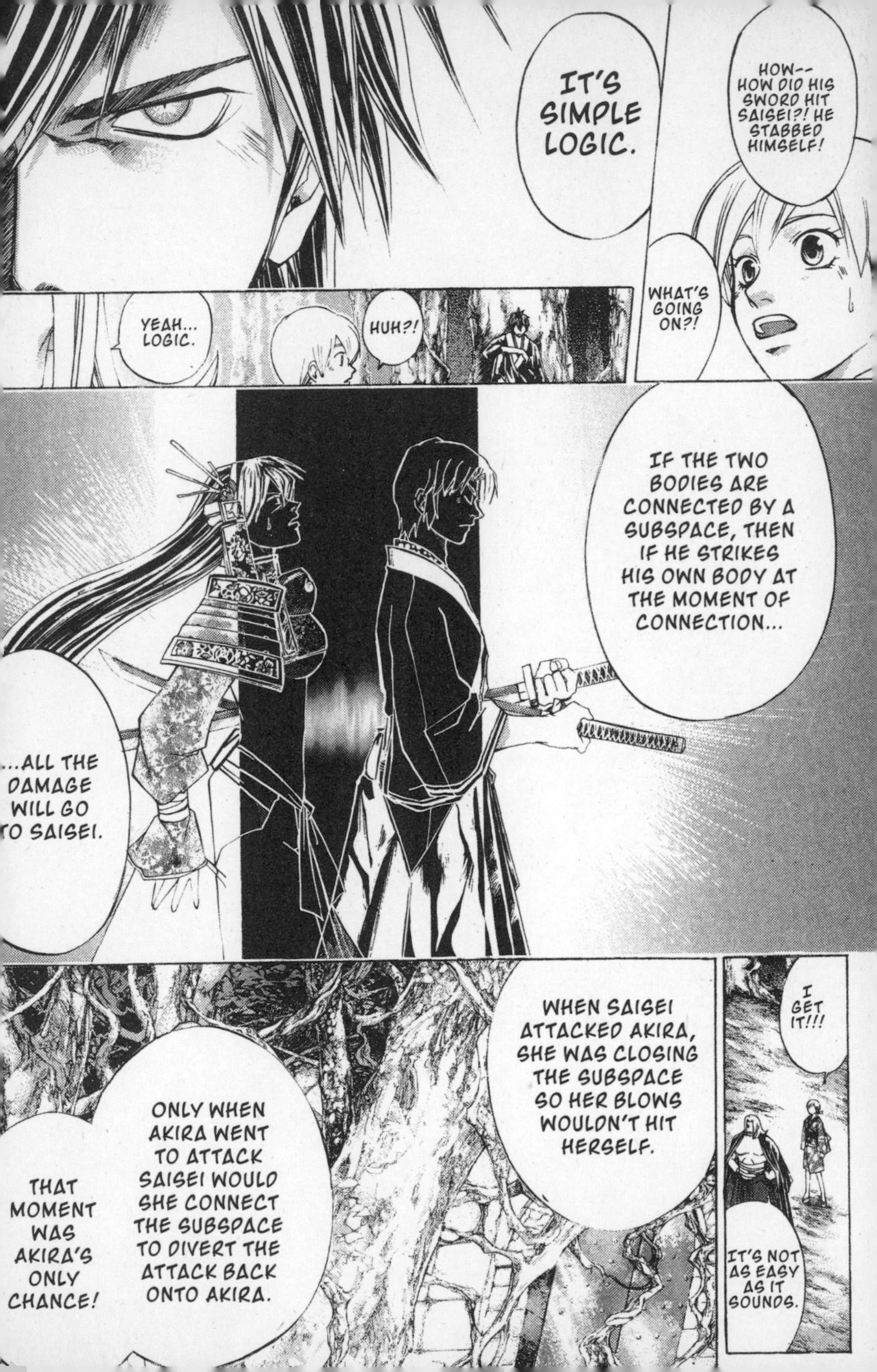
HOW-- HOW DID HIS SWORD HIT SAISEI?! HE STABBED HIMSELF!
WHAT'S GOING ON?!
IT'S SIMPLE LOGIC.
HUH?!
YEAH... LOGIC.
IF THE TWO BODIES ARE CONNECTED BY A SUBSPACE, THEN IF HE STRIKES HIS OWN BODY AT THE MOMENT OF CONNECTION...
...ALL THE DAMAGE WILL GO TO SAISEI.
I GET IT!!!
IT'S NOT AS EASY AS IT SOUNDS.
WHEN SAISEI ATTACKED AKIRA, SHE WAS CLOSING THE SUBSPACE SO HER BLOWS WOULDN'T HIT HERSELF.
ONLY WHEN AKIRA WENT TO ATTACK SAISEI WOULD SHE CONNECT THE SUBSPACE TO DIVERT THE ATTACK BACK ONTO AKIRA.
THAT MOMENT WAS AKIRA'S ONLY CHANCE!

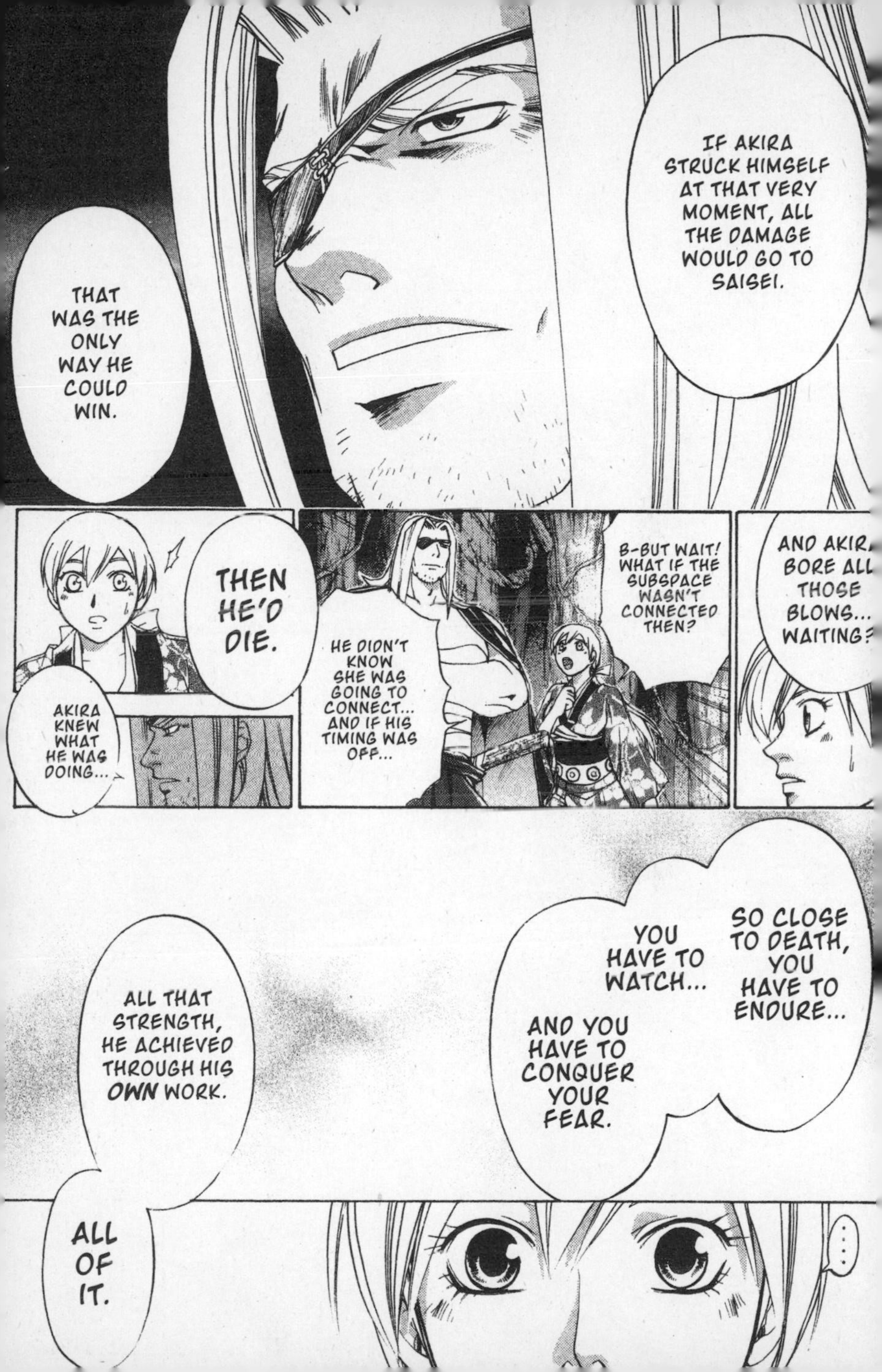
IF AKIRA STRUCK HIMSELF AT THAT VERY MOMENT, ALL THE DAMAGE WOULD GO TO SAISEI.
THAT WAS THE ONLY WAY HE COULD WIN.
AND AKIRA BORE ALL THOSE BLOWS... WAITING?
B-BUT WAIT! WHAT IF THE SUBSPACE WASN'T CONNECTED THEN?
HE DIDN'T KNOW SHE WAS GOING TO CONNECT... AND IF HIS TIMING WAS OFF...
THEN HE'D DIE.
AKIRA KNEW WHAT HE WAS DOING...
SO CLOSE TO DEATH, YOU HAVE TO ENDURE...
YOU HAVE TO WATCH...
AND YOU HAVE TO CONQUER YOUR FEAR.
ALL THAT STRENGTH, HE ACHIEVED THROUGH HIS OWN WORK.
...
ALL OF IT.

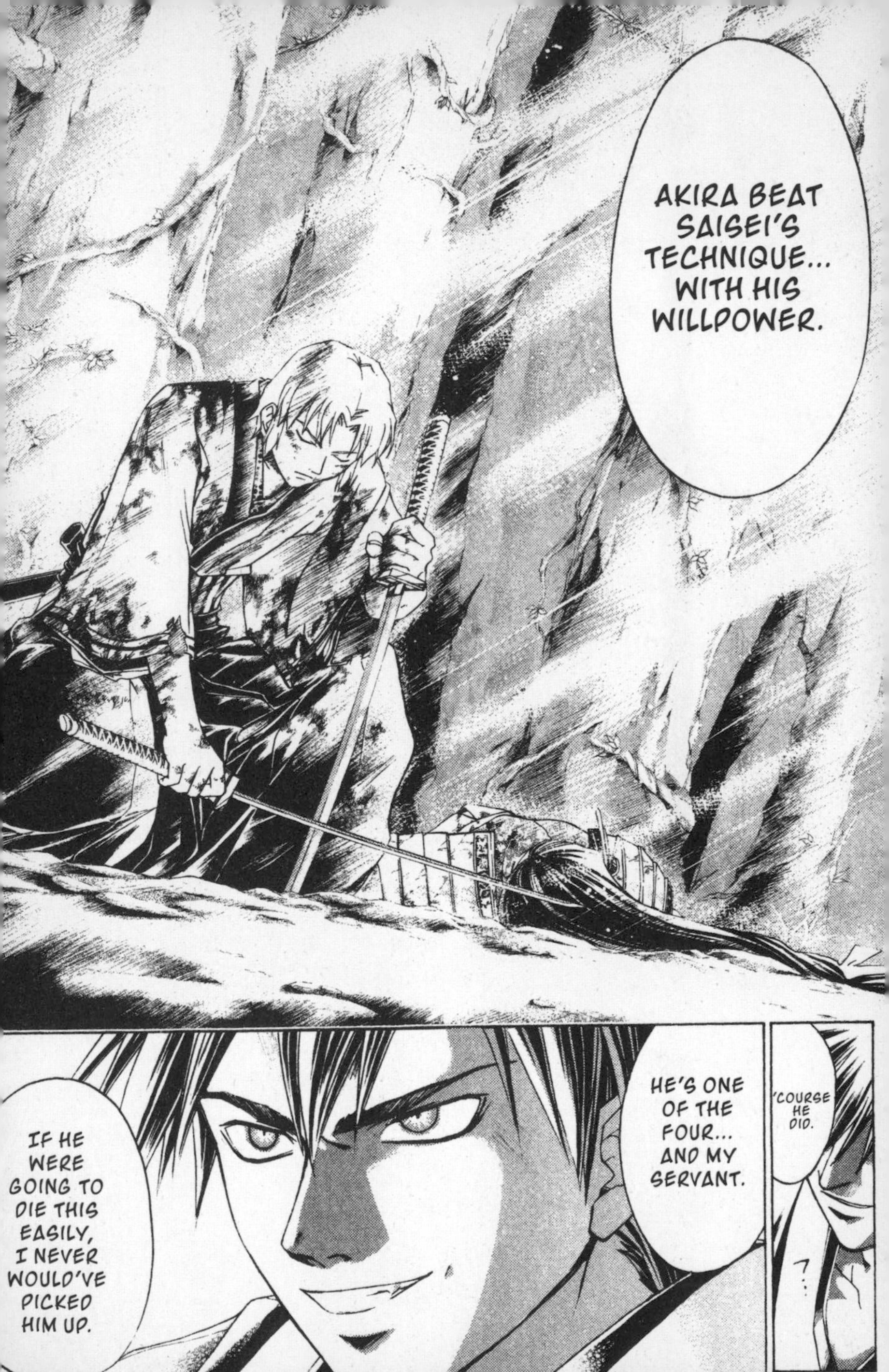
AKIRA BEAT SAISEI'S TECHNIQUE... WITH HIS WILLPOWER.
'COURSE HE DID.
HE'S ONE OF THE FOUR... AND MY SERVANT.
IF HE WERE GOING TO DIE THIS EASILY, I NEVER WOULD'VE PICKED HIM UP.

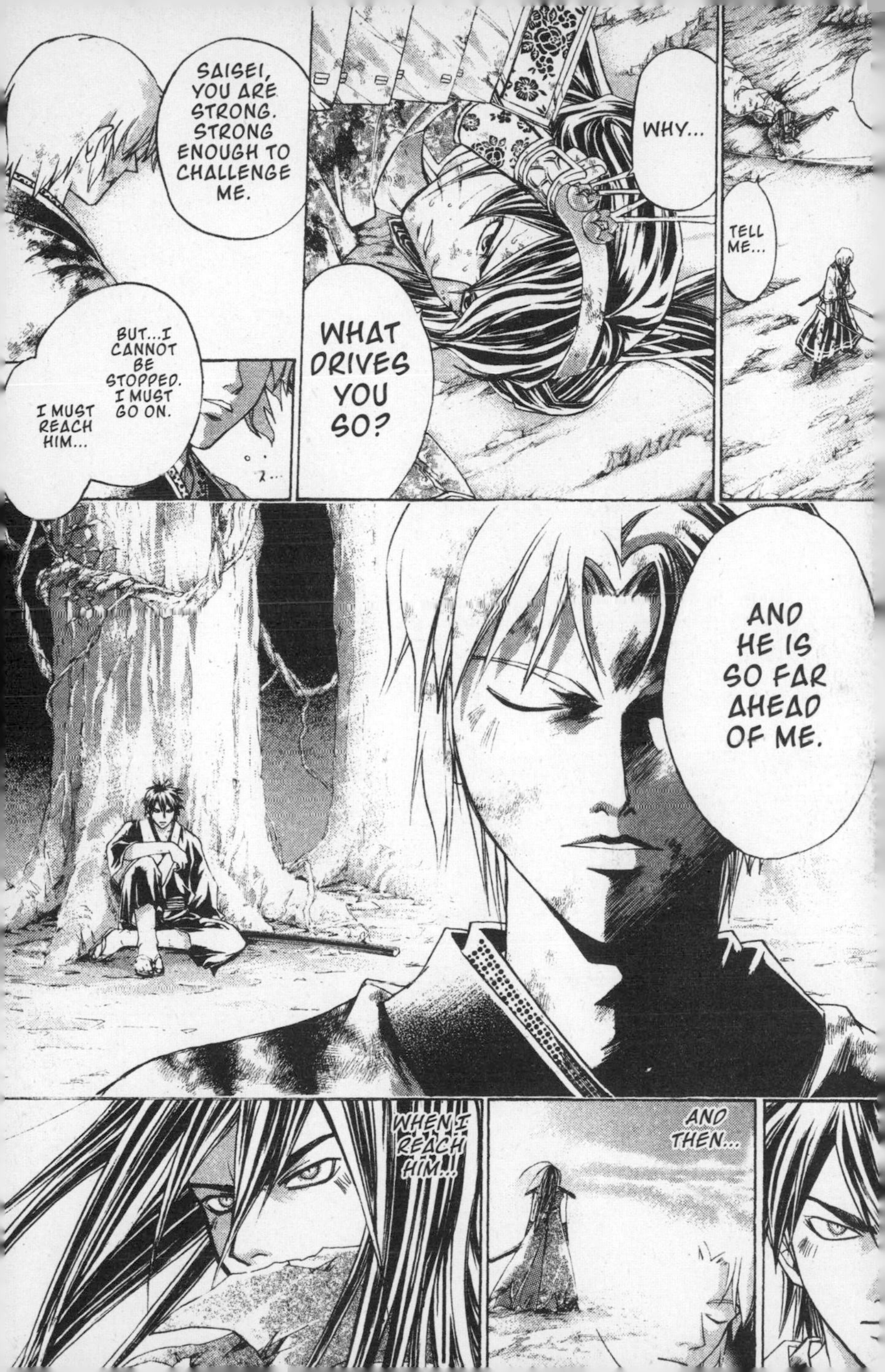
WHY...
TELL ME...
WHAT DRIVES YOU SO?
SAISEI, YOU ARE STRONG. STRONG ENOUGH TO CHALLENGE ME.
BUT...I CANNOT BE STOPPED. I MUST GO ON.
I MUST REACH HIM...
AND HE IS SO FAR AHEAD OF ME.
AND THEN...
WHEN I REACH HIM...

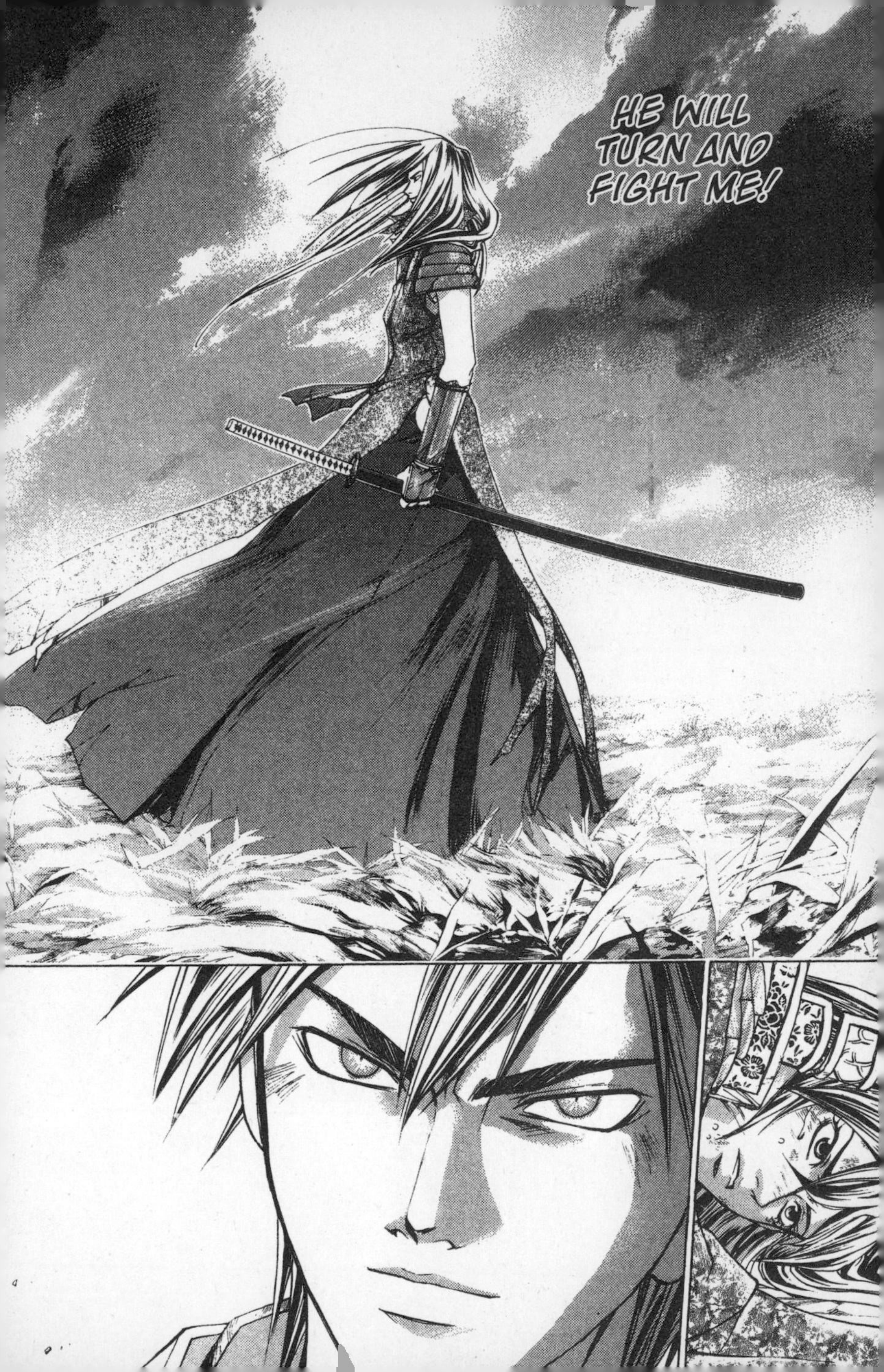
HE WILL TURN AND FIGHT ME!

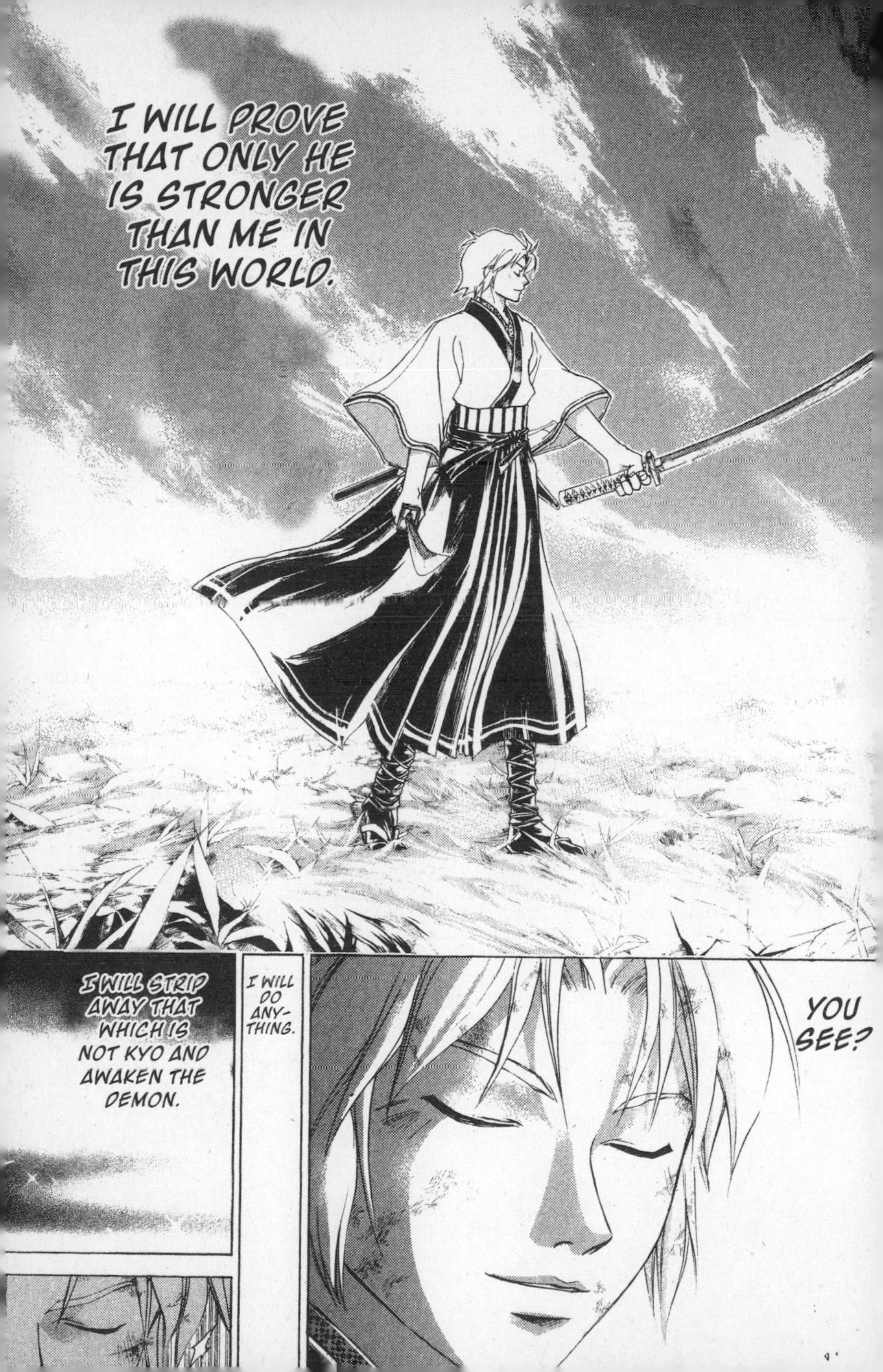
I WILL PROVE THAT ONLY HE IS STRONGER THAN ME IN THIS WORLD.
YOU SEE?
I WILL DO ANY-THING.
I WILL STRIP AWAY THAT WHICH IS NOT KYO AND AWAKEN THE DEMON.

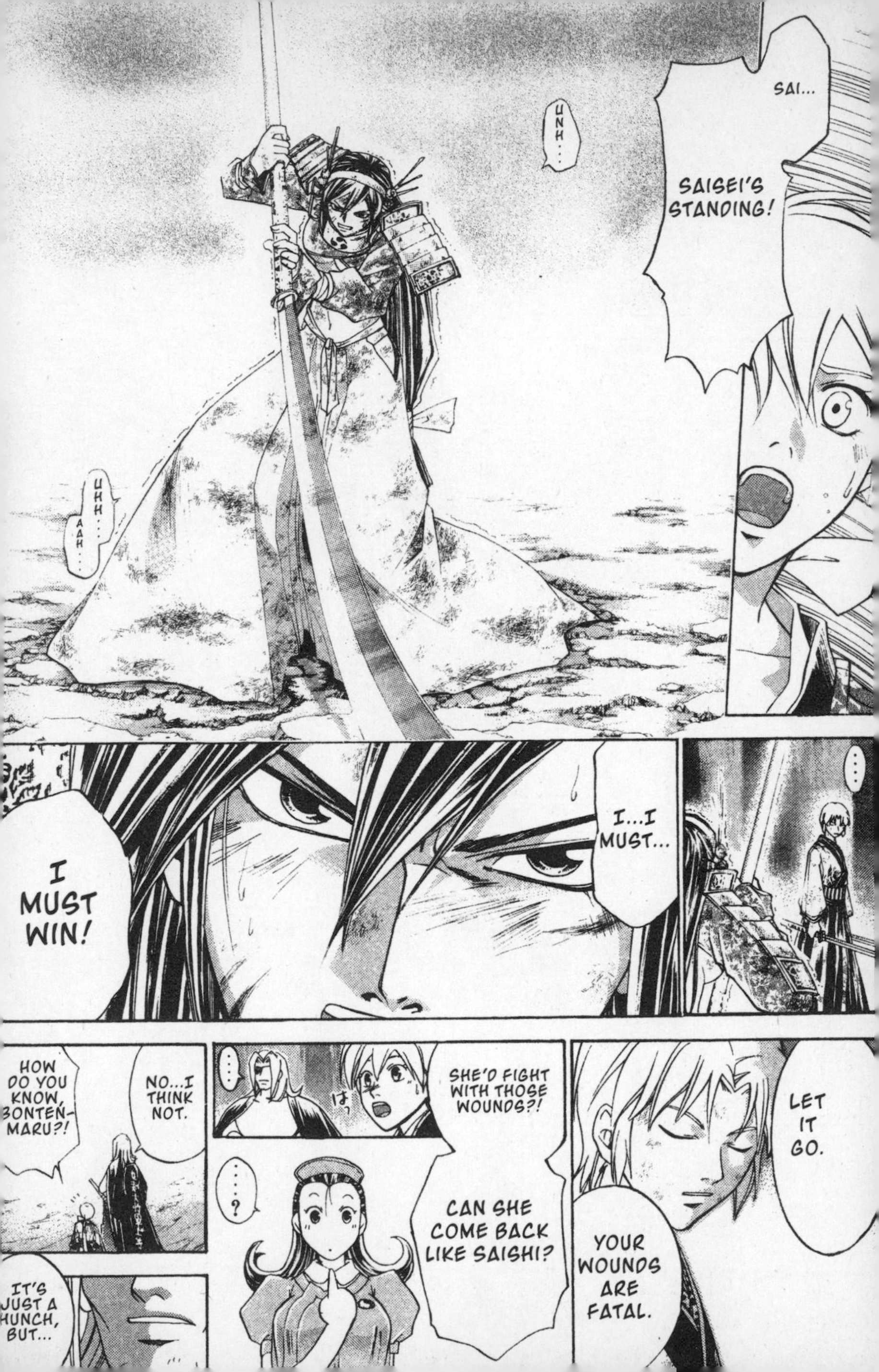
SAI...
SAISEI'S STANDING!
UNH...
UHH... AAH...
...
I...I MUST...
I MUST WIN!
LET IT GO.
YOUR WOUNDS ARE FATAL.
SHE'D FIGHT WITH THOSE WOUNDS?!
は
...
CAN SHE COME BACK LIKE SAISHI?
...?
NO...I THINK NOT.
HOW DO YOU KNOW, BONTEN-MARU?!
IT'S JUST A HUNCH, BUT...

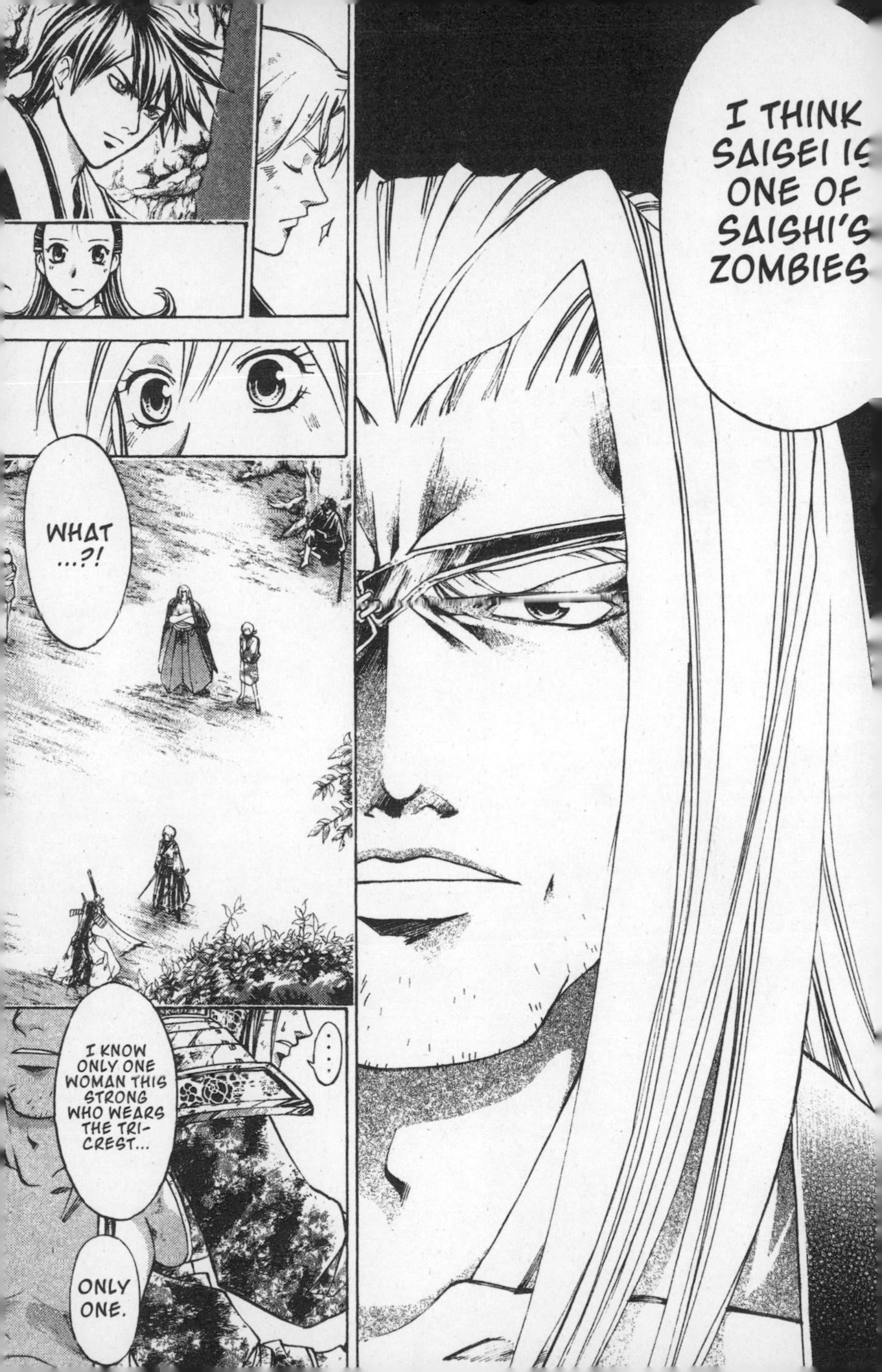
I THINK SAISEI IS ONE OF SAISHI'S ZOMBIES
WHAT ...?!
....
I KNOW ONLY ONE WOMAN THIS STRONG WHO WEARS THE TRI-CREST...
ONLY ONE.

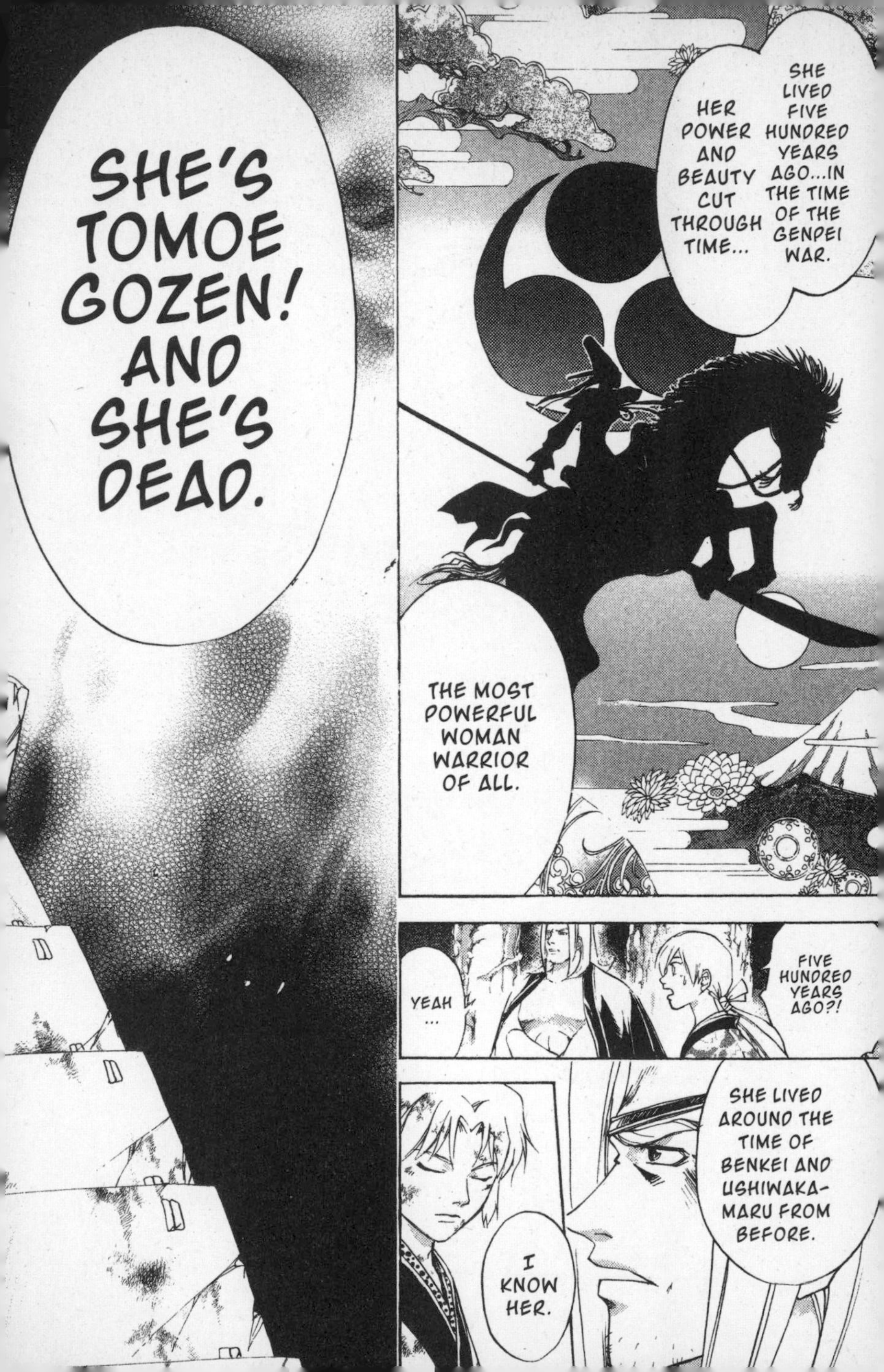
SHE LIVED FIVE HUNDRED YEARS AGO...IN THE TIME OF THE GENPEI WAR.
HER POWER AND BEAUTY CUT THROUGH TIME...
THE MOST POWERFUL WOMAN WARRIOR OF ALL.
FIVE HUNDRED YEARS AGO?!
YEAH ...
SHE LIVED AROUND THE TIME OF BENKEI AND USHIWAKA-MARU FROM BEFORE.
I KNOW HER.
SHE'S TOMOE GOZEN! AND SHE'S DEAD.

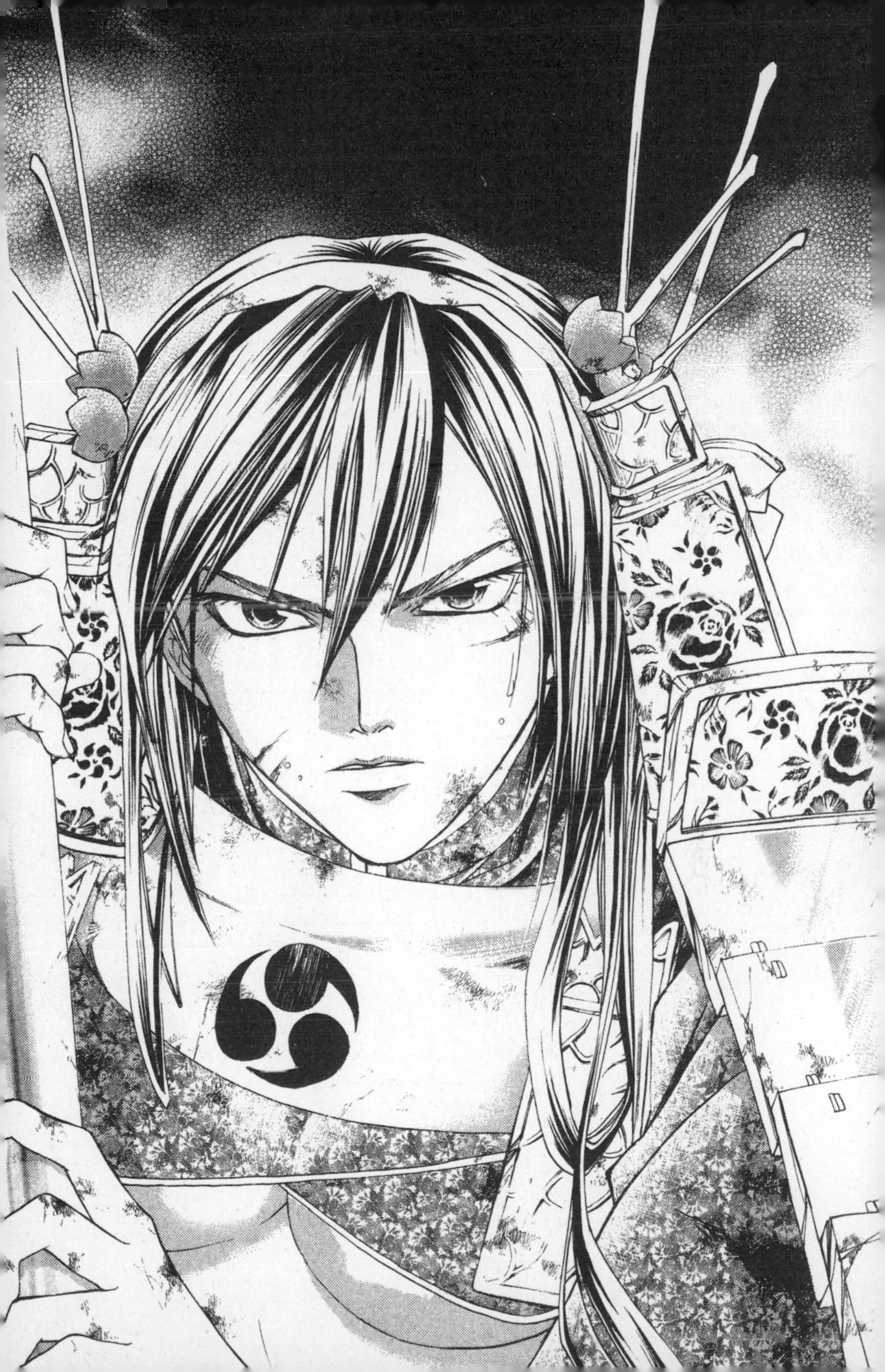

The Kamijyo Report

A big secret is revealed in our next volume! It's been a long time coming! (Of course, that's my fault...) I-I can't wait!
I'm sure you're all busy with tests, clubs, work, romance, and whatever else it is you're doing...and so am I! Let's all do our best! Yeah!
SDK is just going to get hotter from here on out...and it's more than just a manga, so be sure to keep an eye out for the anime, the game and more! See you next volume! Bye now!

DAD'S PUBLIC IMAGE

POPS! THAT'S NOT WHAT YOU SAID BEFORE! YOU'RE A LIAR!
He was mad, you know!
YOU'RE RIGHT, HIDETADA, I LIED!
POPS! GO AROUND SAYING STUFF LIKE THAT, AND PEOPLE'LL THINK YOU DON'T LIKE 'EM!
He's really hurt, you know!
RIGHT AGAIN, HIDETADA-- I DON'T LIKE HIM!
POPS!!! WHY'D YOU CUT OFF HIS HEAD?! HE DIDN'T BETRAY YOU! IT'S LIKE YOU CUT OFF ANYONE'S HEAD IF THEY DISPLEASE YOU.
YOU KNOW ME TOO WELL, HIDETADA! HE DISPLEASED ME!
MAN, I'VE HAD IT WITH YOU!
HA HA! DON'T BE SUCH A BABY, HIDETADA!
...AND THAT'S HOW BENI-TORA'S TRAVELS BEGAN! (MAYBE)

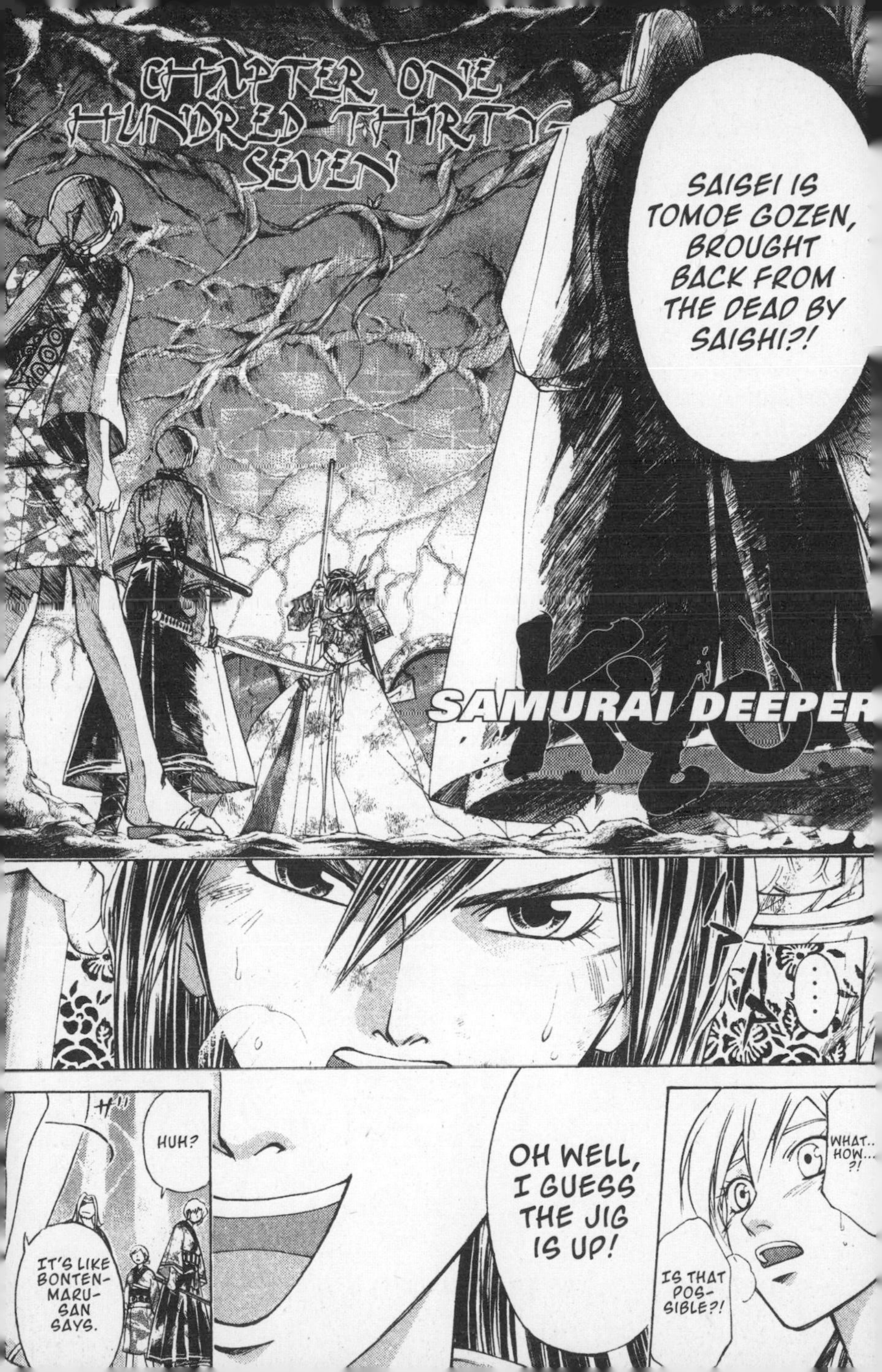
SAISEI IS TOMOE GOZEN, BROUGHT BACK FROM THE DEAD BY SAISHI?!
CHAPTER ONE HUNDRED THIRTY-SEVEN
SAMURAI DEEPER
...
WHAT.. HOW...?!
IS THAT POS-SIBLE?!
OH WELL, I GUESS THE JIG IS UP!
HUH?
IT'S LIKE BONTEN-MARU-SAN SAYS.

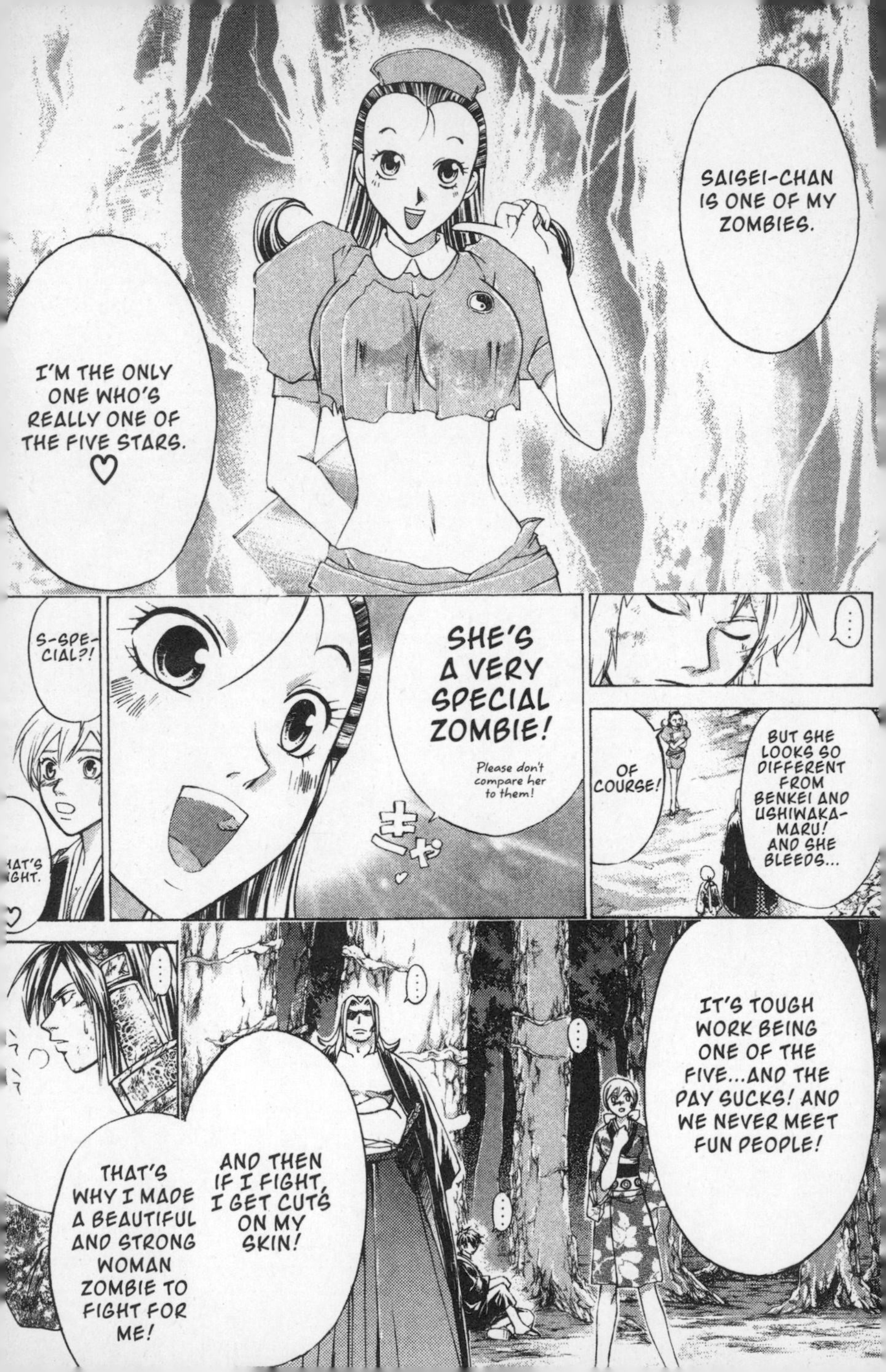
SAISEI-CHAN IS ONE OF MY ZOMBIES.
I'M THE ONLY ONE WHO'S REALLY ONE OF THE FIVE STARS. ♡
...
BUT SHE LOOKS SO DIFFERENT FROM BENKEI AND USHIWAKA-MARU! AND SHE BLEEDS...
OF COURSE!
SHE'S A VERY SPECIAL ZOMBIE!
Please don't compare her to them!
S-SPE-CIAL?!
HAT'S IGHT. ♡
IT'S TOUGH WORK BEING ONE OF THE FIVE...AND THE PAY SUCKS! AND WE NEVER MEET FUN PEOPLE!
...
...
...
AND THEN IF I FIGHT, I GET CUTS ON MY SKIN!
THAT'S WHY I MADE A BEAUTIFUL AND STRONG WOMAN ZOMBIE TO FIGHT FOR ME!
...

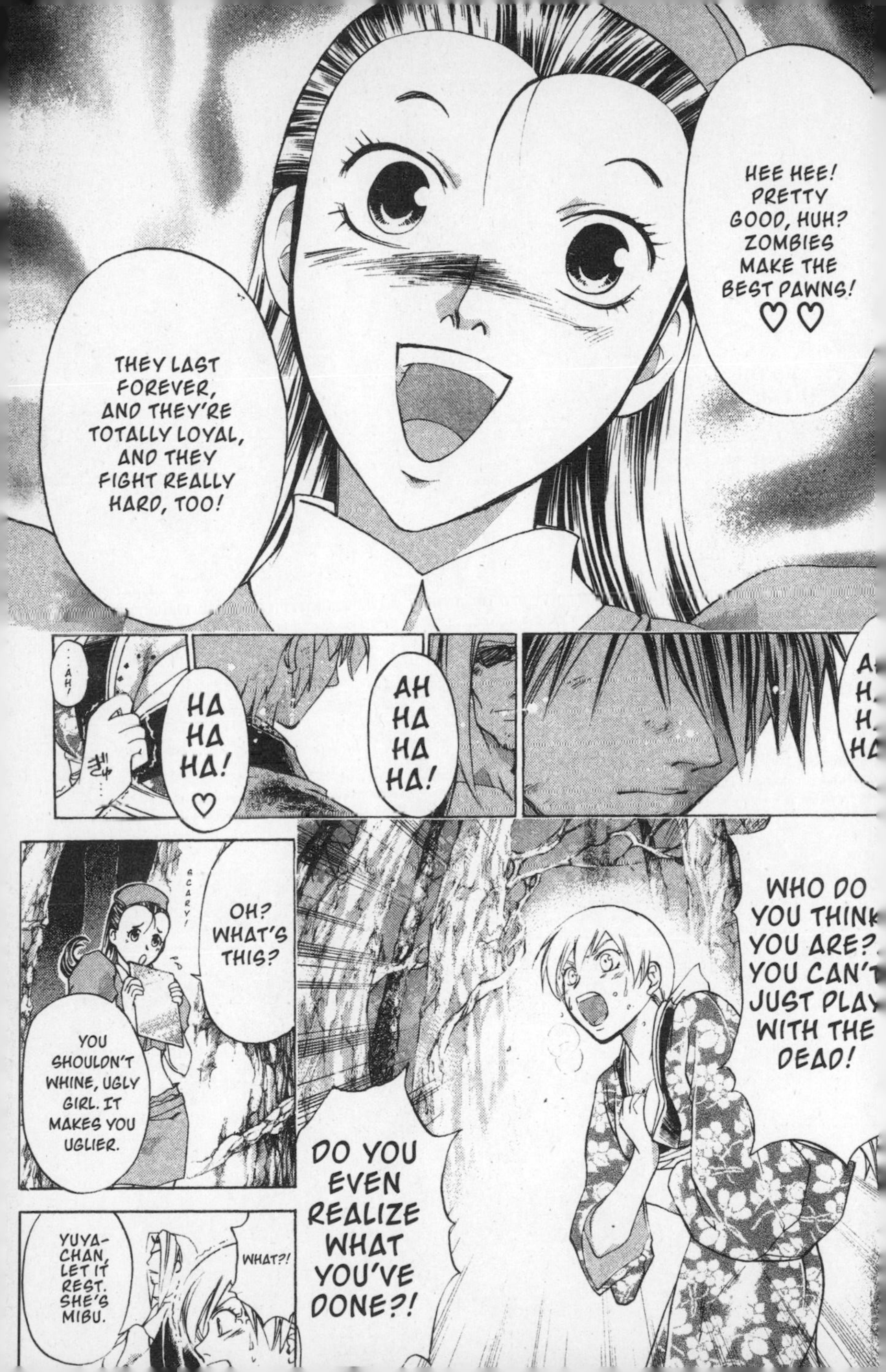
HEE HEE! PRETTY GOOD, HUH? ZOMBIES MAKE THE BEST PAWNS! ♡♡
THEY LAST FOREVER, AND THEY'RE TOTALLY LOYAL, AND THEY FIGHT REALLY HARD, TOO!
AH HA HA HA!
HA HA HA! ♡
...AH!
WHO DO YOU THINK YOU ARE?! YOU CAN'T JUST PLAY WITH THE DEAD!
DO YOU EVEN REALIZE WHAT YOU'VE DONE?!
OH? WHAT'S THIS?
SCARY!
YOU SHOULDN'T WHINE, UGLY GIRL. IT MAKES YOU UGLIER.
WHAT?!
YUYA-CHAN, LET IT REST. SHE'S MIBU.

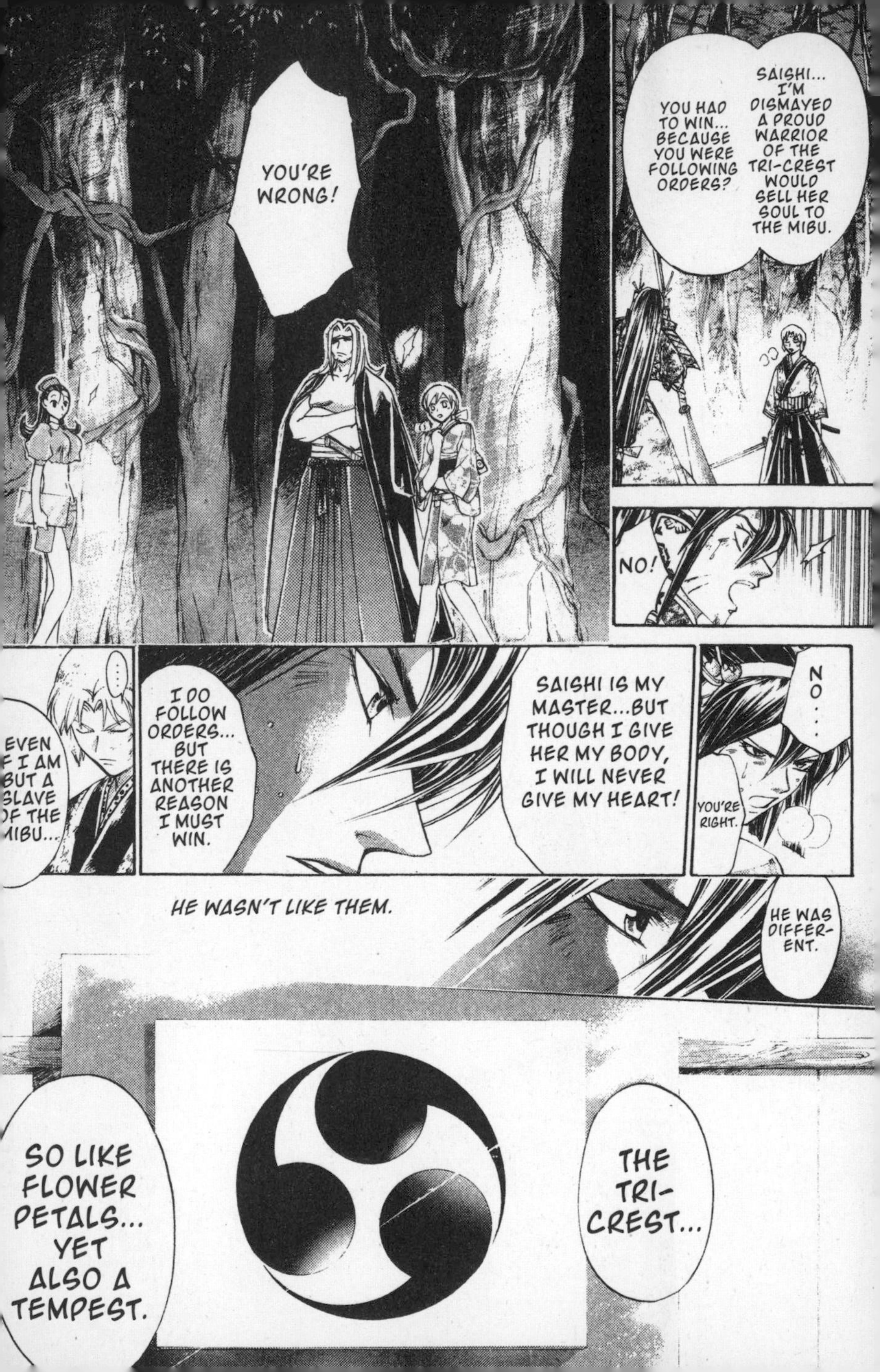
SAISHI... I'M DISMAYED A PROUD WARRIOR OF THE TRI-CREST WOULD SELL HER SOUL TO THE MIBU.
YOU HAD TO WIN... BECAUSE YOU WERE FOLLOWING ORDERS?
NO!
YOU'RE WRONG!
NO...
YOU'RE RIGHT.
SAISHI IS MY MASTER...BUT THOUGH I GIVE HER MY BODY, I WILL NEVER GIVE MY HEART!
I DO FOLLOW ORDERS... BUT THERE IS ANOTHER REASON I MUST WIN.
...
EVEN IF I AM BUT A SLAVE OF THE MIBU...
HE WAS DIFFER-ENT.
HE WASN'T LIKE THEM.
THE TRI-CREST...
SO LIKE FLOWER PETALS... YET ALSO A TEMPEST.

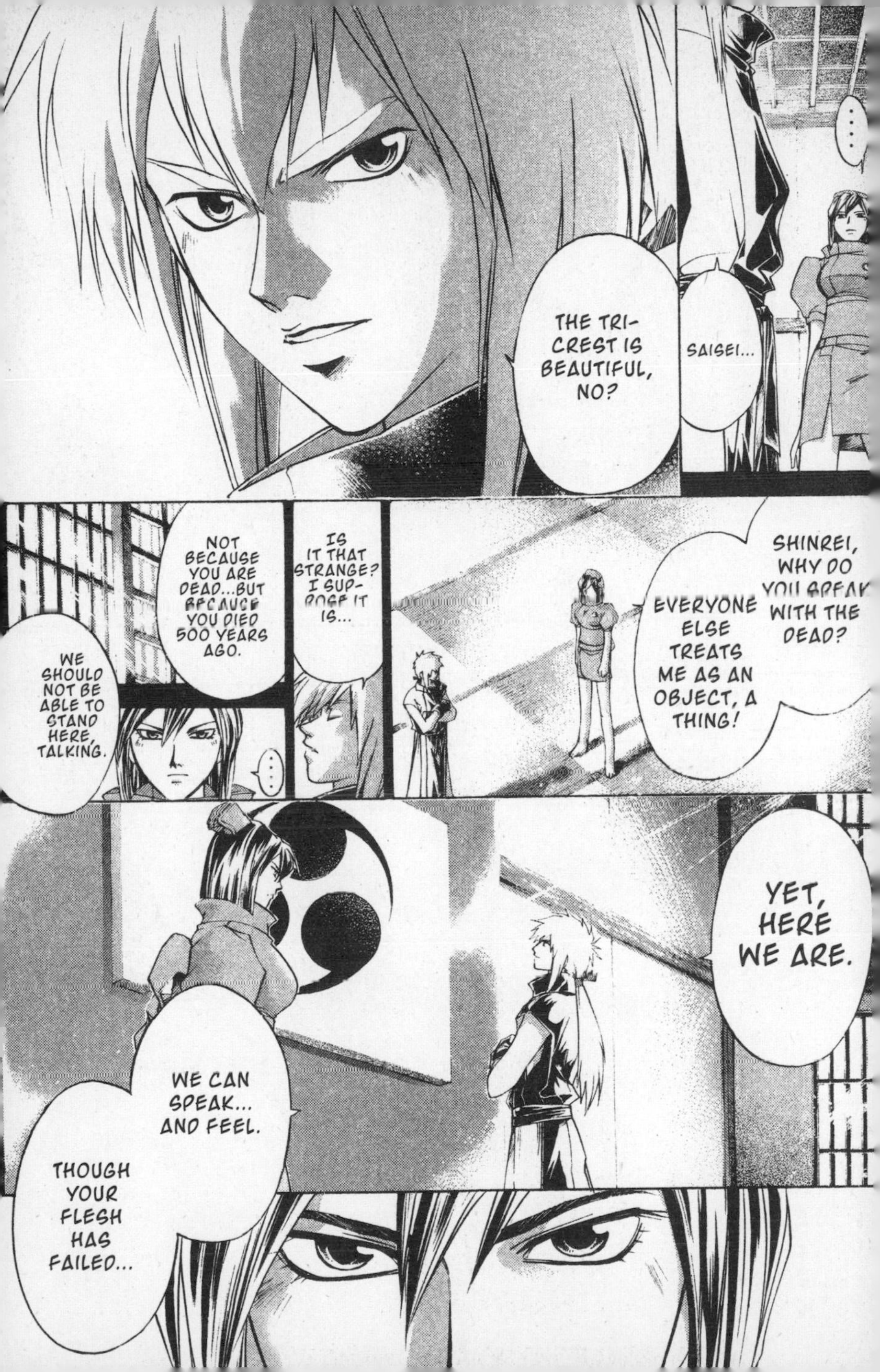
...
SAISEI...
THE TRI-CREST IS BEAUTIFUL, NO?
SHINREI, WHY DO YOU SPEAK WITH THE DEAD?
EVERYONE ELSE TREATS ME AS AN OBJECT, A THING!
IS IT THAT STRANGE? I SUPPOSE IT IS...
NOT BECAUSE YOU ARE DEAD...BUT BECAUSE YOU DIED 500 YEARS AGO.
WE SHOULD NOT BE ABLE TO STAND HERE, TALKING.
...
YET, HERE WE ARE.
WE CAN SPEAK... AND FEEL.
THOUGH YOUR FLESH HAS FAILED...

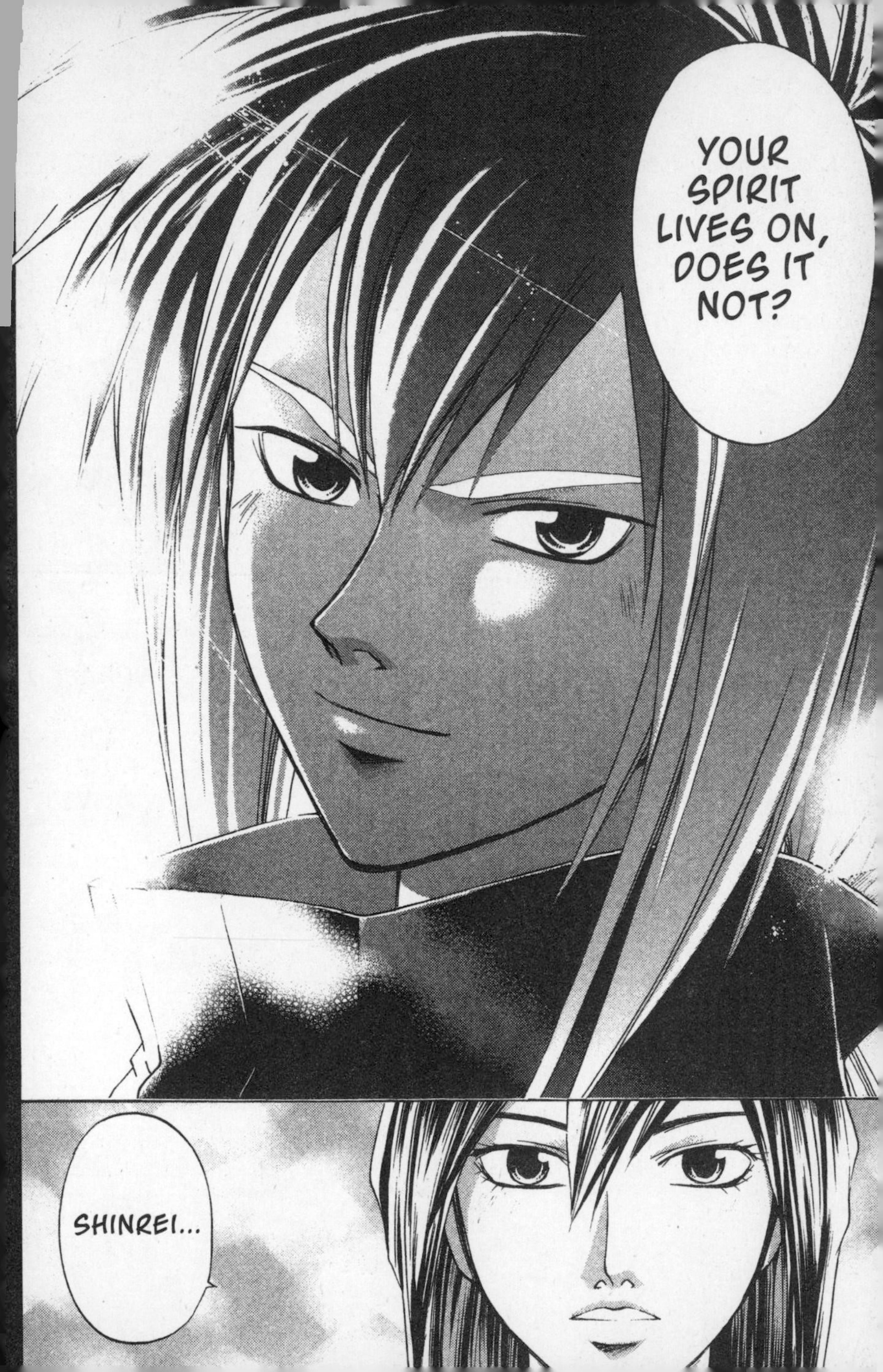
YOUR SPIRIT LIVES ON, DOES IT NOT?
SHINREI...

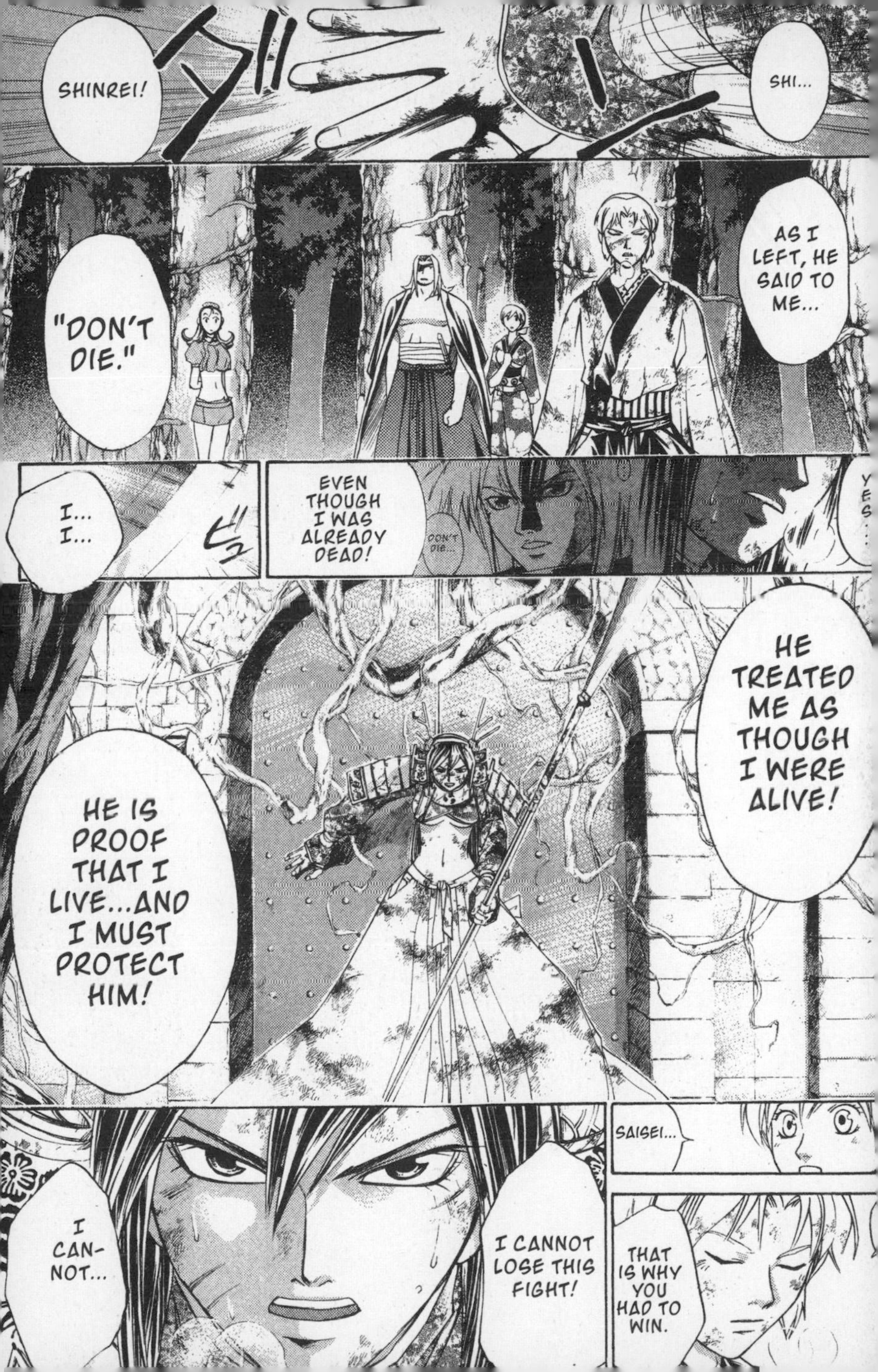
SHI...
SHINREI!
AS I LEFT, HE SAID TO ME...
"DON'T DIE."
YES...
EVEN THOUGH I WAS ALREADY DEAD!
DON'T DIE...
I... I...
HE TREATED ME AS THOUGH I WERE ALIVE!
HE IS PROOF THAT I LIVE...AND I MUST PROTECT HIM!
SAISEI...
THAT IS WHY YOU HAD TO WIN.
I CAN-NOT...
I CANNOT LOSE THIS FIGHT!

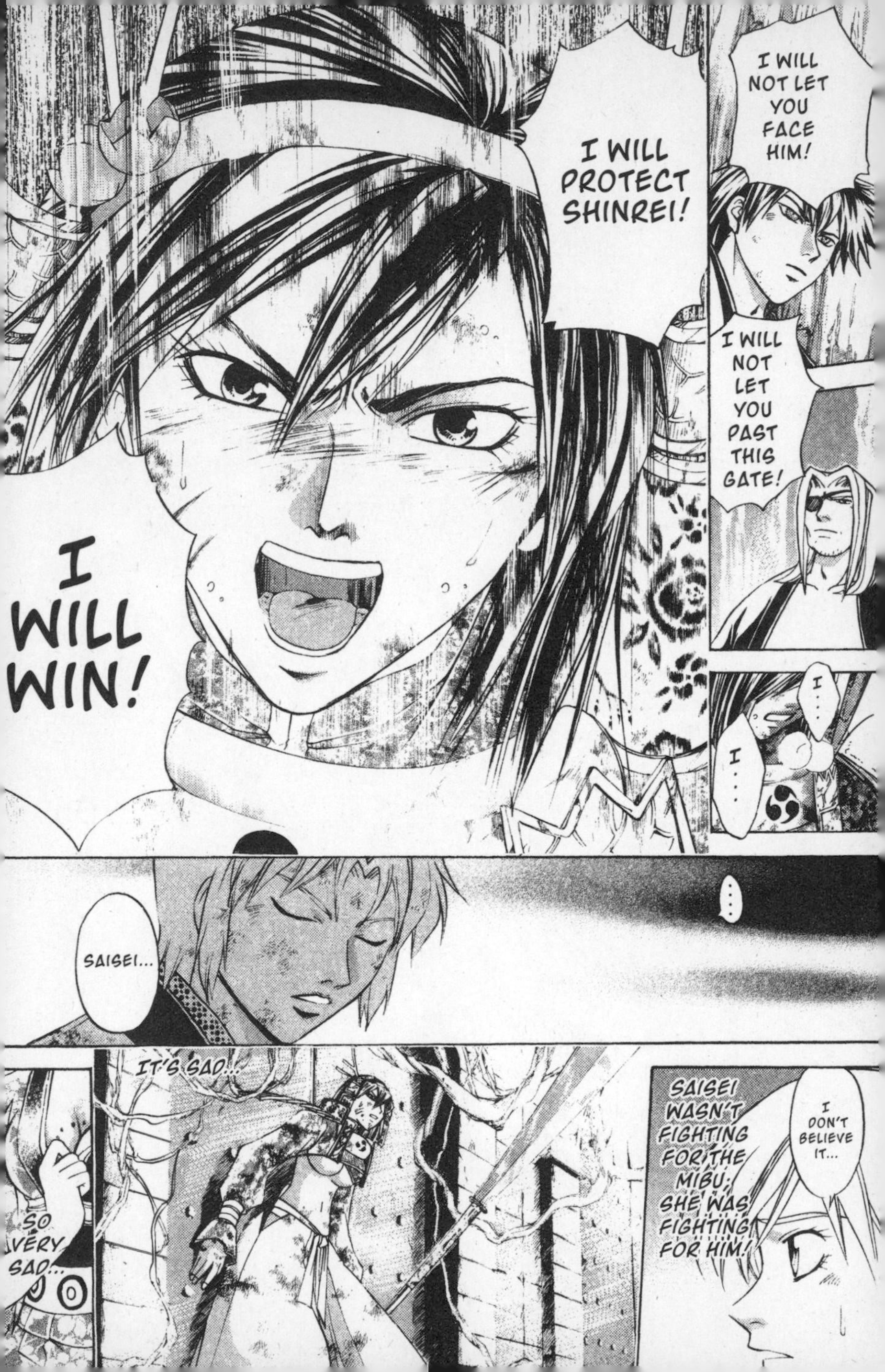
I WILL NOT LET YOU FACE HIM!
I WILL NOT LET YOU PAST THIS GATE!
I...
I...
I WILL PROTECT SHINREI!
I WILL WIN!
...
SAISEI...
I DON'T BELIEVE IT...
SAISEI WASN'T FIGHTING FOR THE MIBU; SHE WAS FIGHTING FOR HIM!
IT'S SAD...
SO VERY SAD...

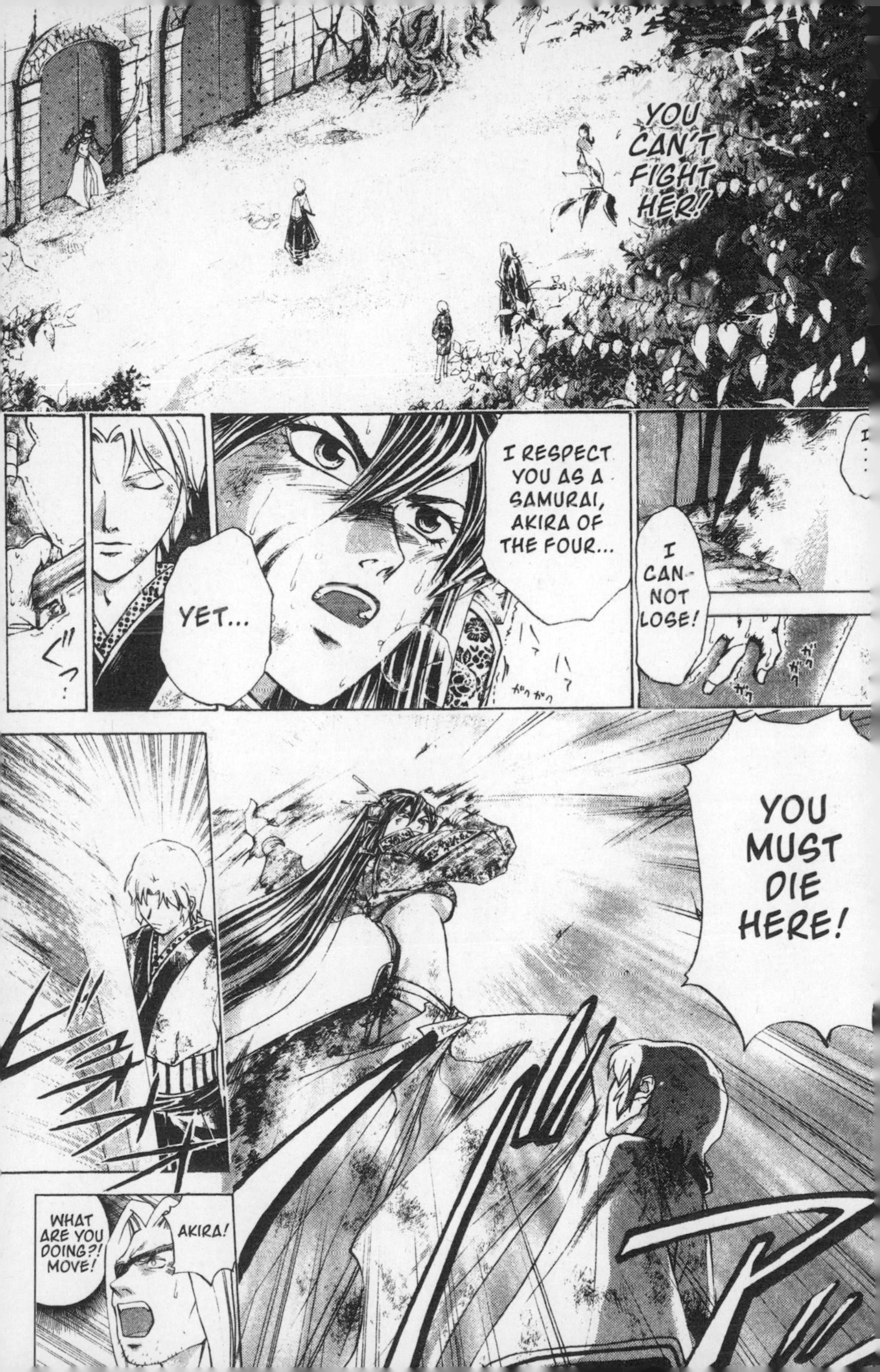
YOU CAN'T FIGHT HER!
I...
I CAN NOT LOSE!
I RESPECT YOU AS A SAMURAI, AKIRA OF THE FOUR...
YET...
YOU MUST DIE HERE!
AKIRA!
WHAT ARE YOU DOING?! MOVE!

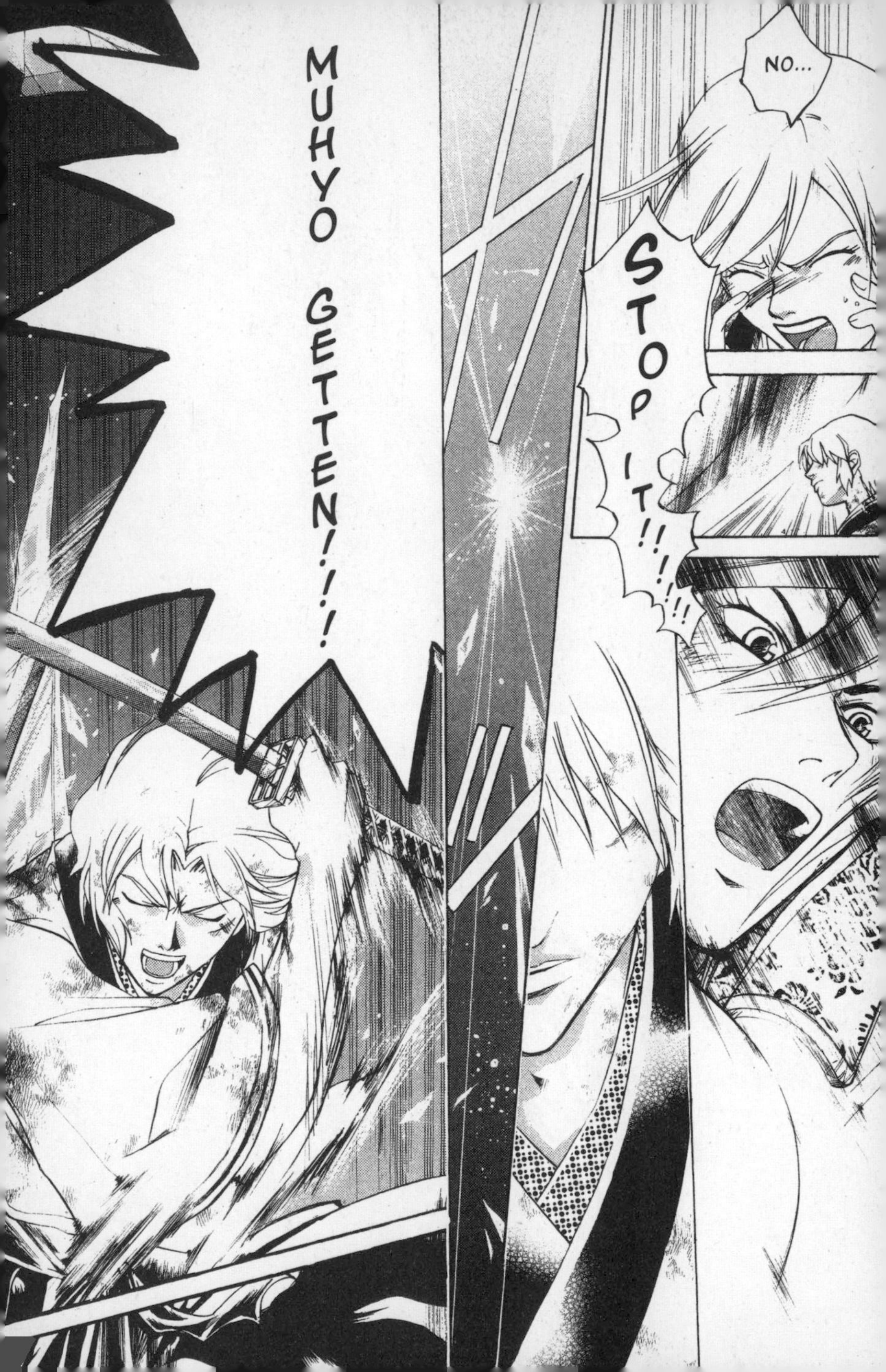
NO...
STOP IT!!!!!!
MUHYO GETTEN!!!

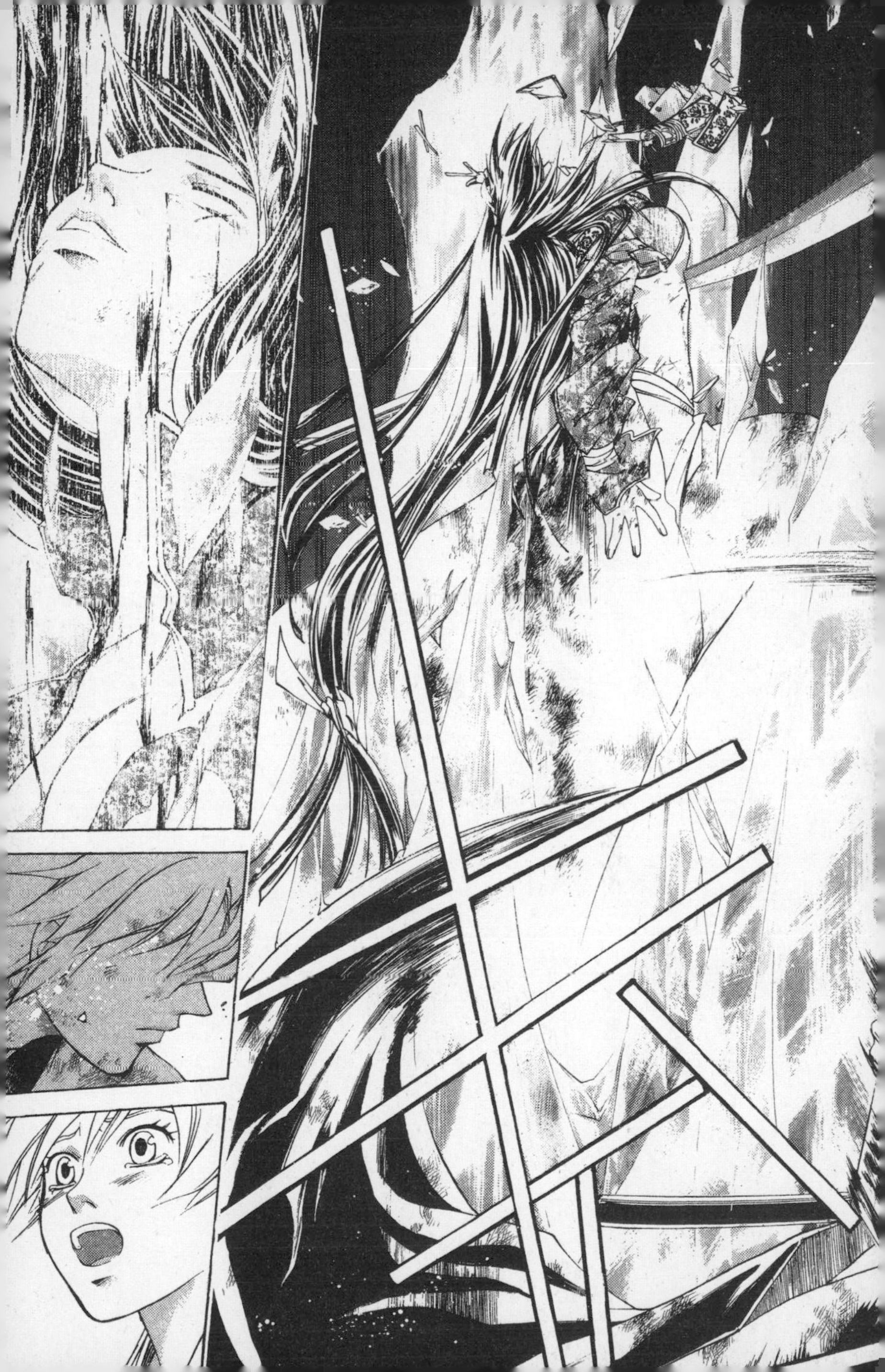

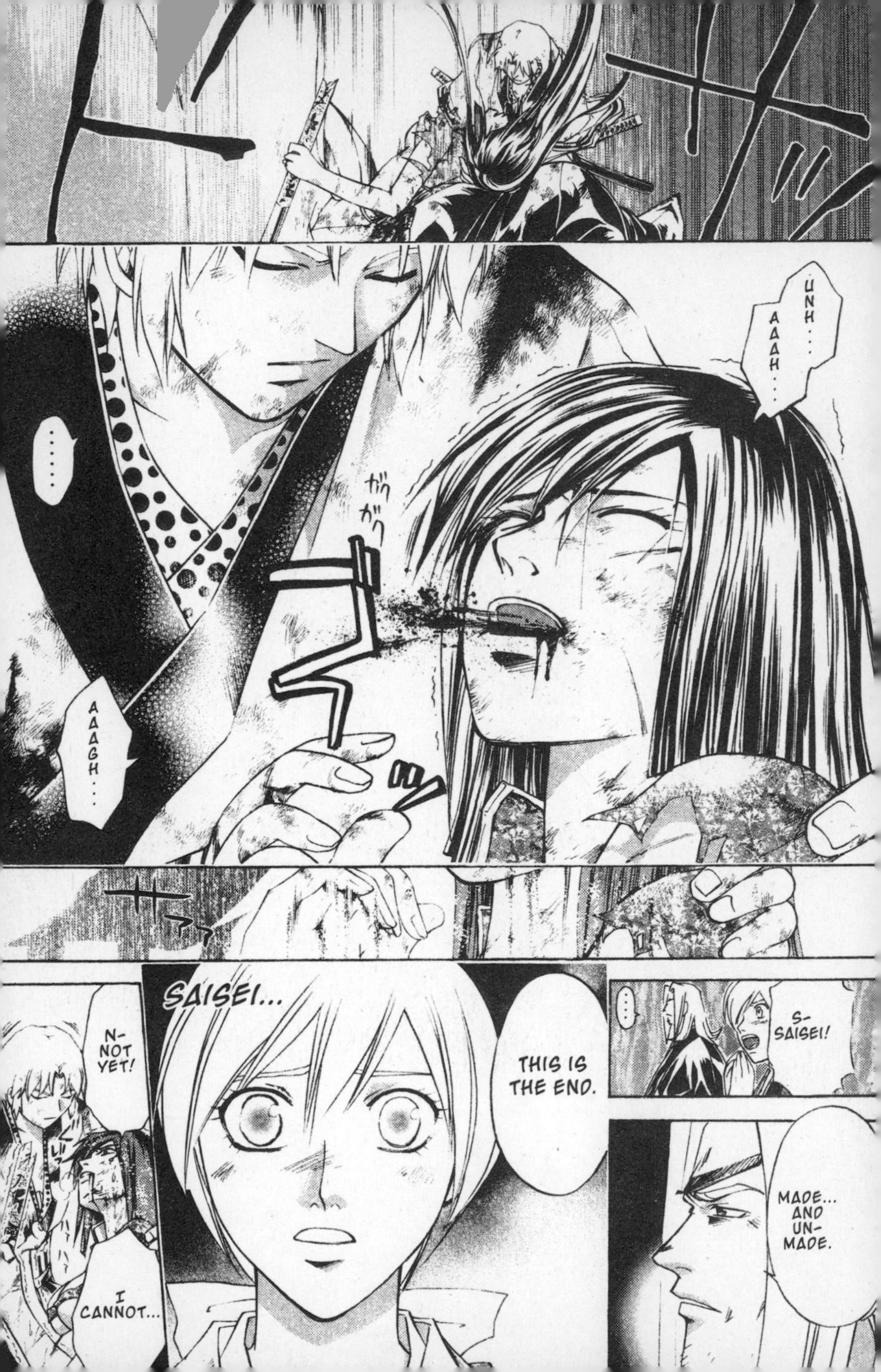

UNH... AAAH...
ガクガク
......
AAAGH...
S-SAISEI!
....
MADE... AND UN-MADE.
THIS IS THE END.
SAISEI...
N-NOT YET!
I CANNOT...

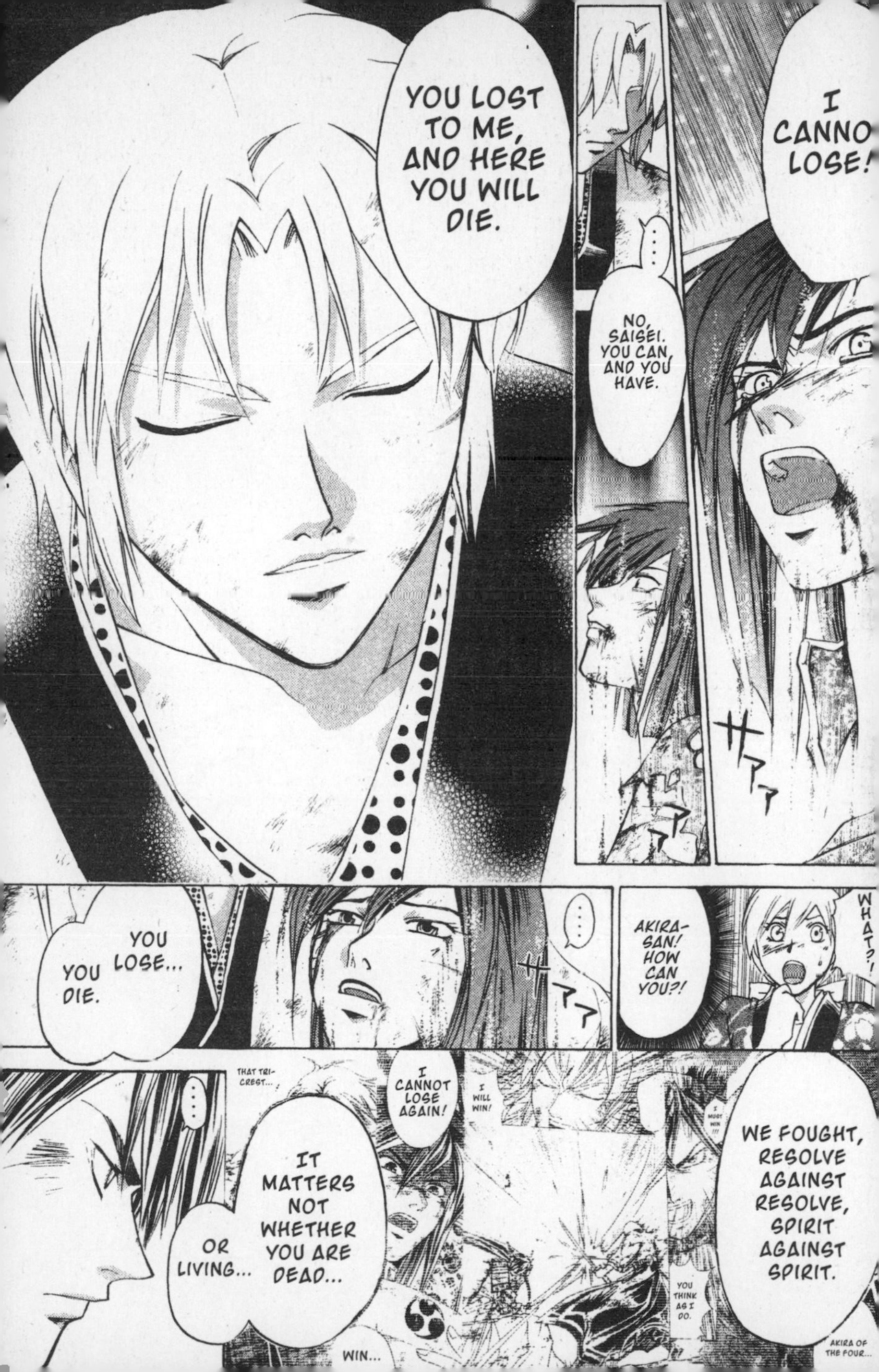
I CANNO LOSE!
...
NO, SAISEI. YOU CAN, AND YOU HAVE.
YOU LOST TO ME, AND HERE YOU WILL DIE.
WHAT?!
AKIRA-SAN! HOW CAN YOU?!
...
YOU LOSE... YOU DIE.
WE FOUGHT, RESOLVE AGAINST RESOLVE, SPIRIT AGAINST SPIRIT.
AKIRA OF THE FOUR...
I MUST WIN!!!
YOU THINK AS I DO.
I WILL WIN!
I CANNOT LOSE AGAIN!
THAT TRI-CREST...
IT MATTERS NOT WHETHER YOU ARE DEAD...
OR LIVING...
WIN...
...

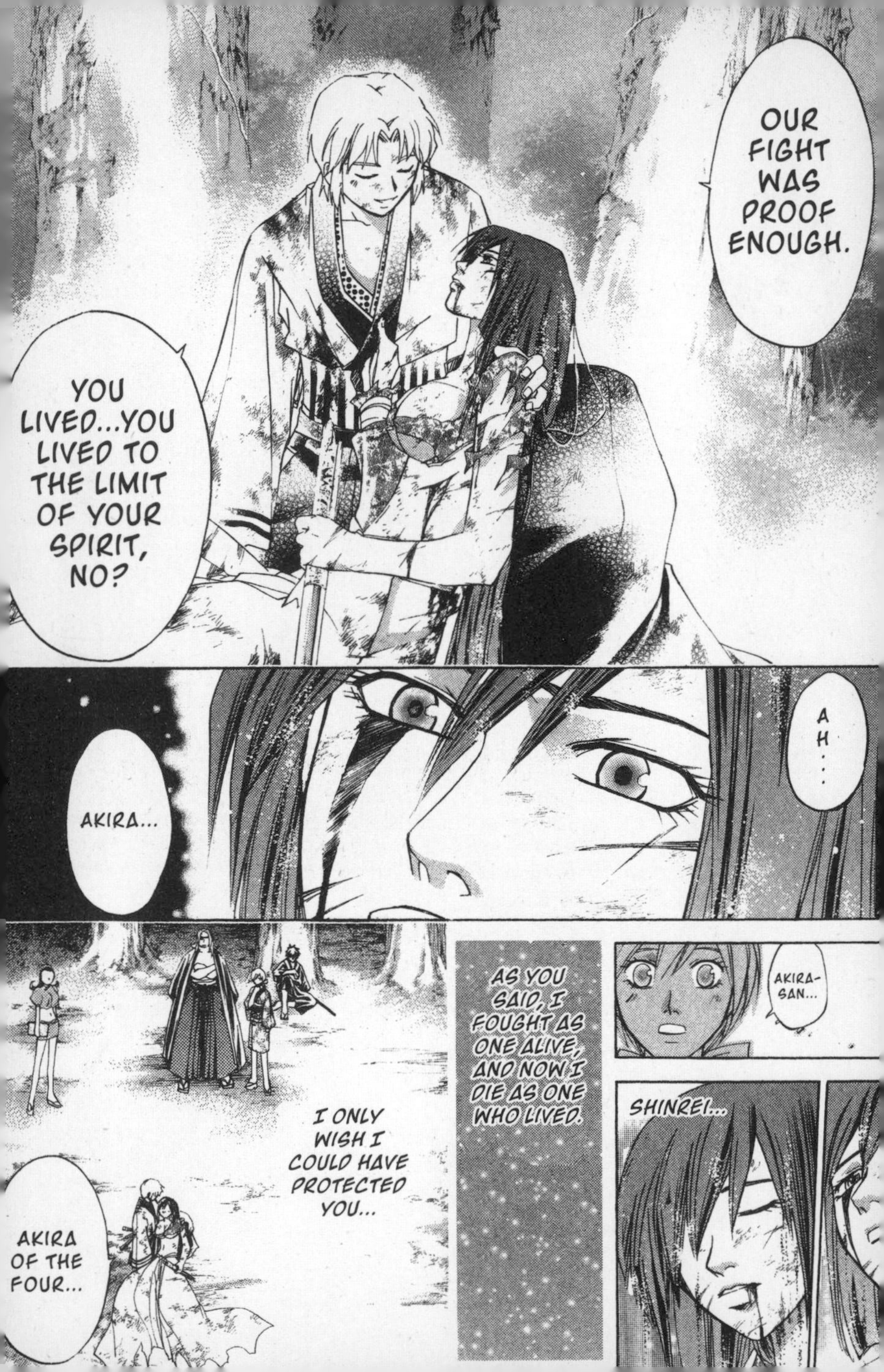
OUR FIGHT WAS PROOF ENOUGH.
YOU LIVED...YOU LIVED TO THE LIMIT OF YOUR SPIRIT, NO?
AH...
AKIRA...
AKIRA-SAN...
SHINREI...
AS YOU SAID, I FOUGHT AS ONE ALIVE, AND NOW I DIE AS ONE WHO LIVED.
I ONLY WISH I COULD HAVE PROTECTED YOU...
AKIRA OF THE FOUR...

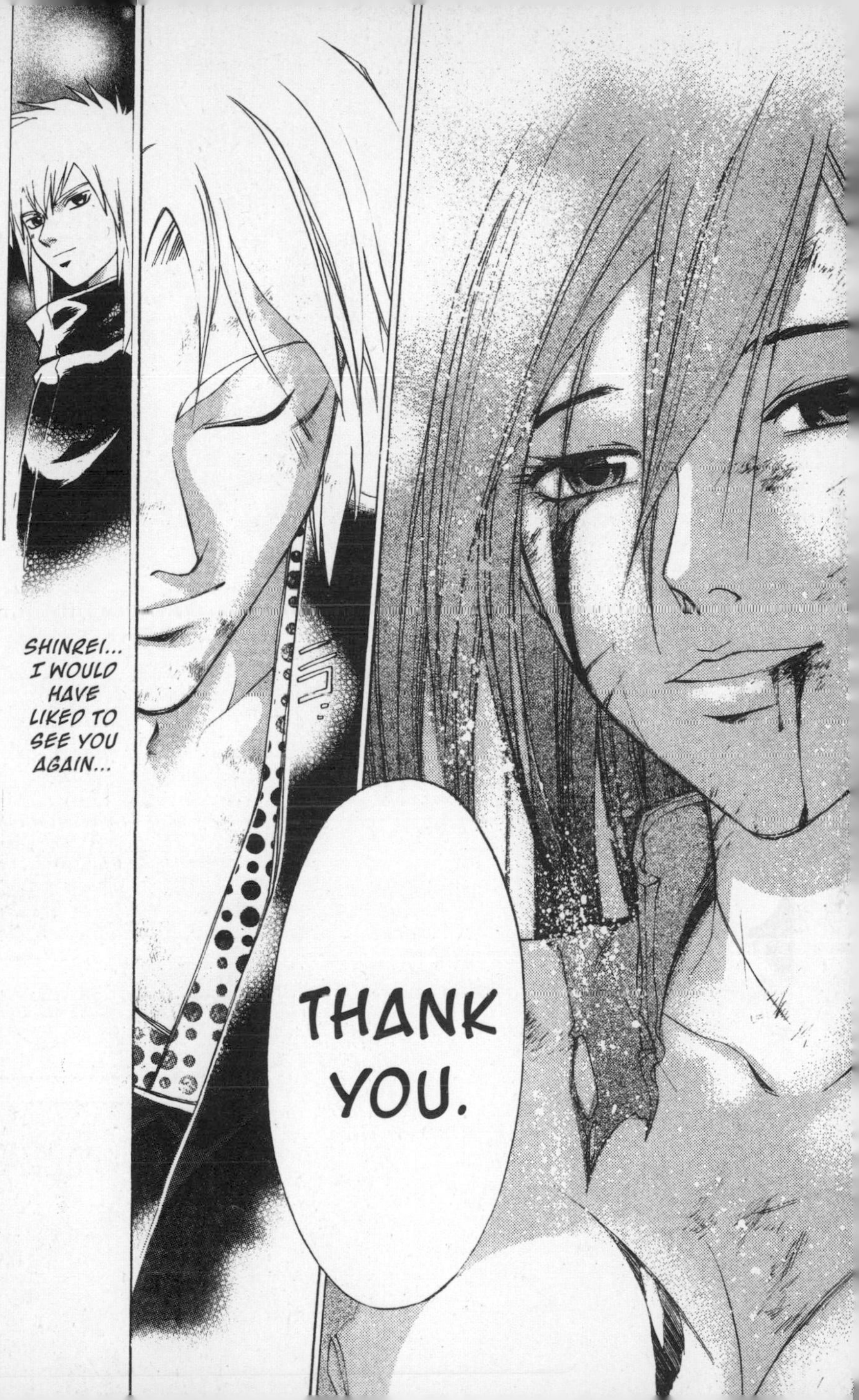
THANK YOU.
SHINREI... I WOULD HAVE LIKED TO SEE YOU AGAIN...

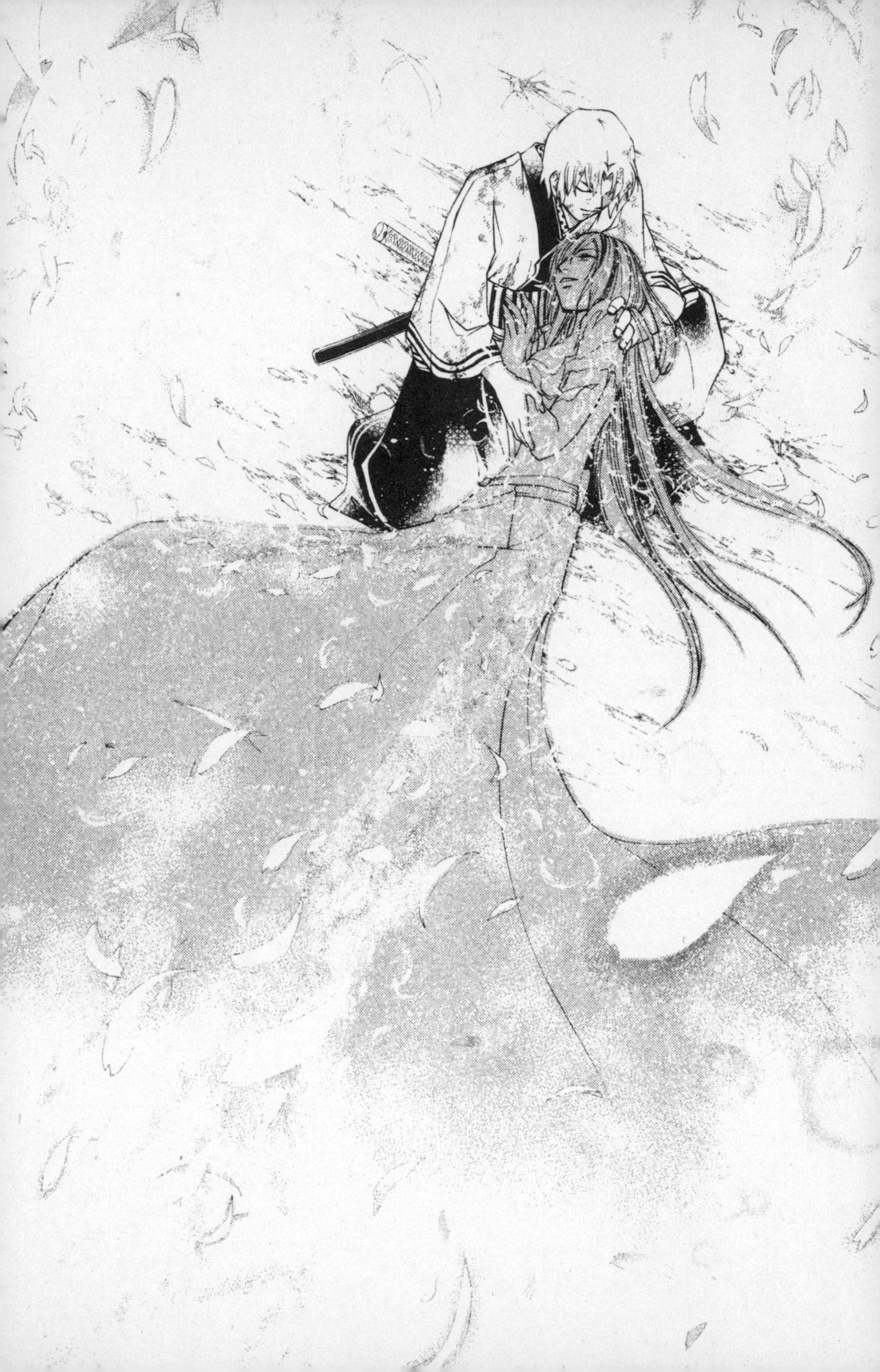

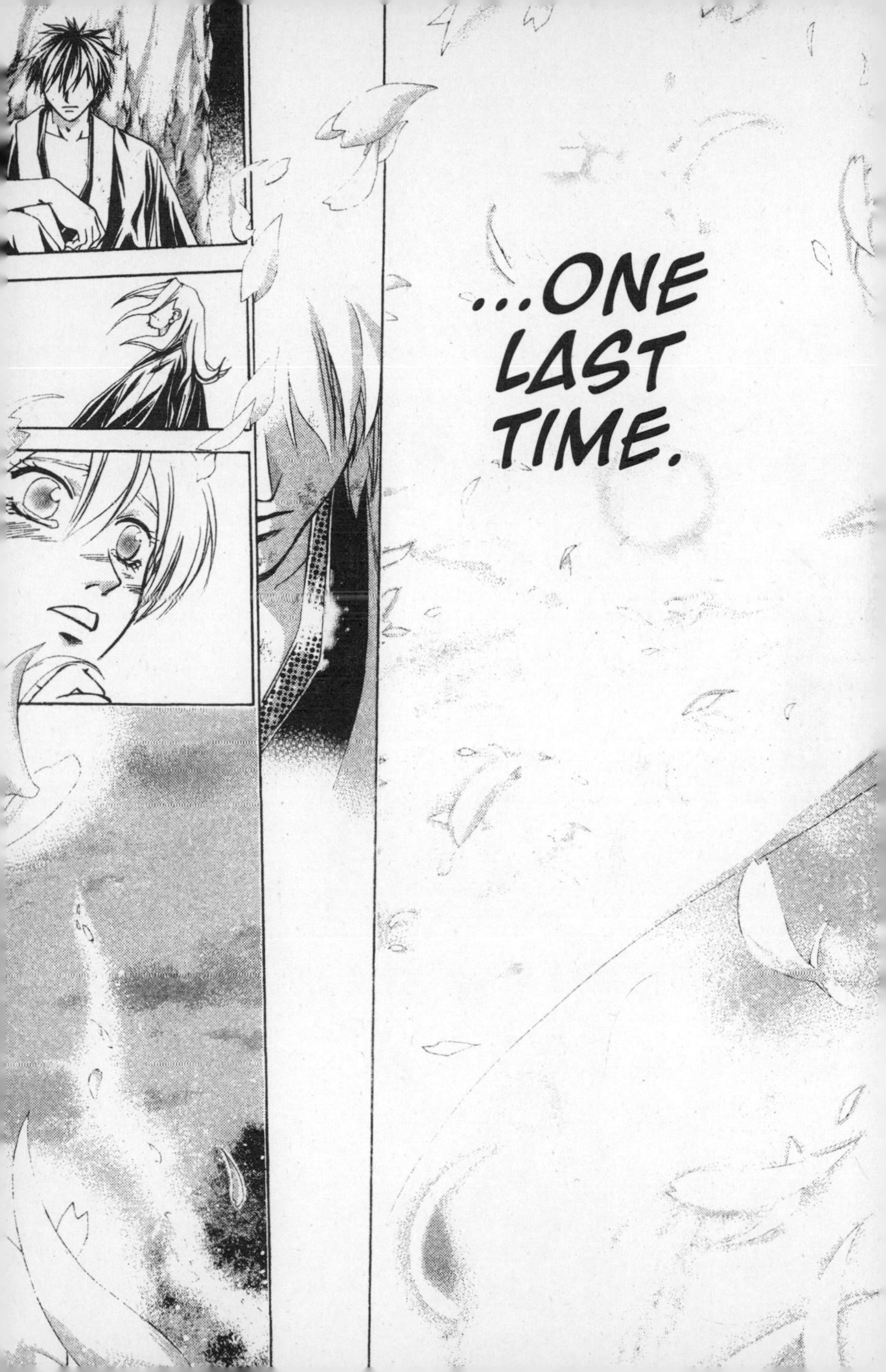
...ONE LAST TIME.

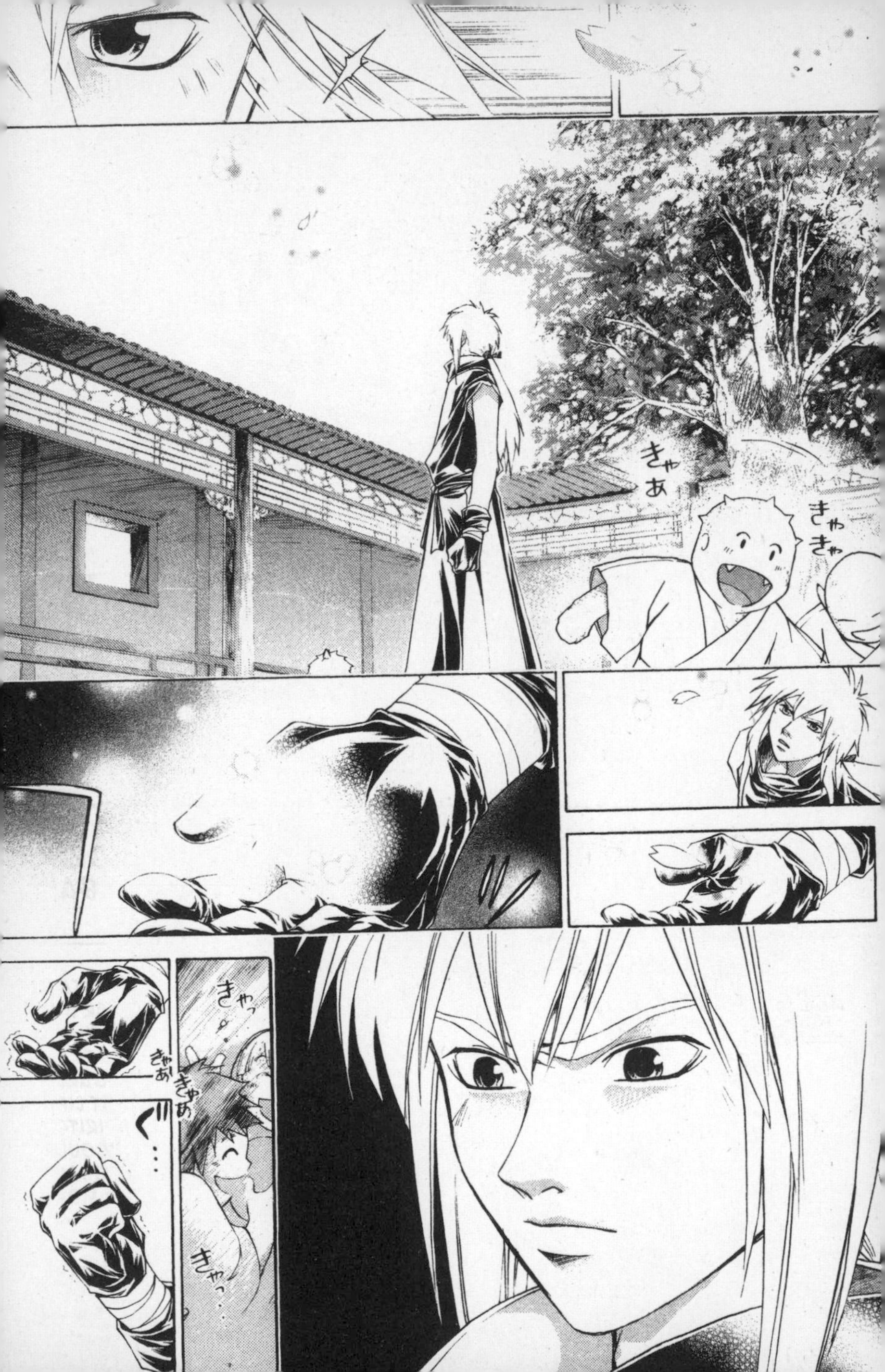
きゃきゃ
きゃあ
きゃっ
きゃあ
きゃあ
きゃっ…
く…

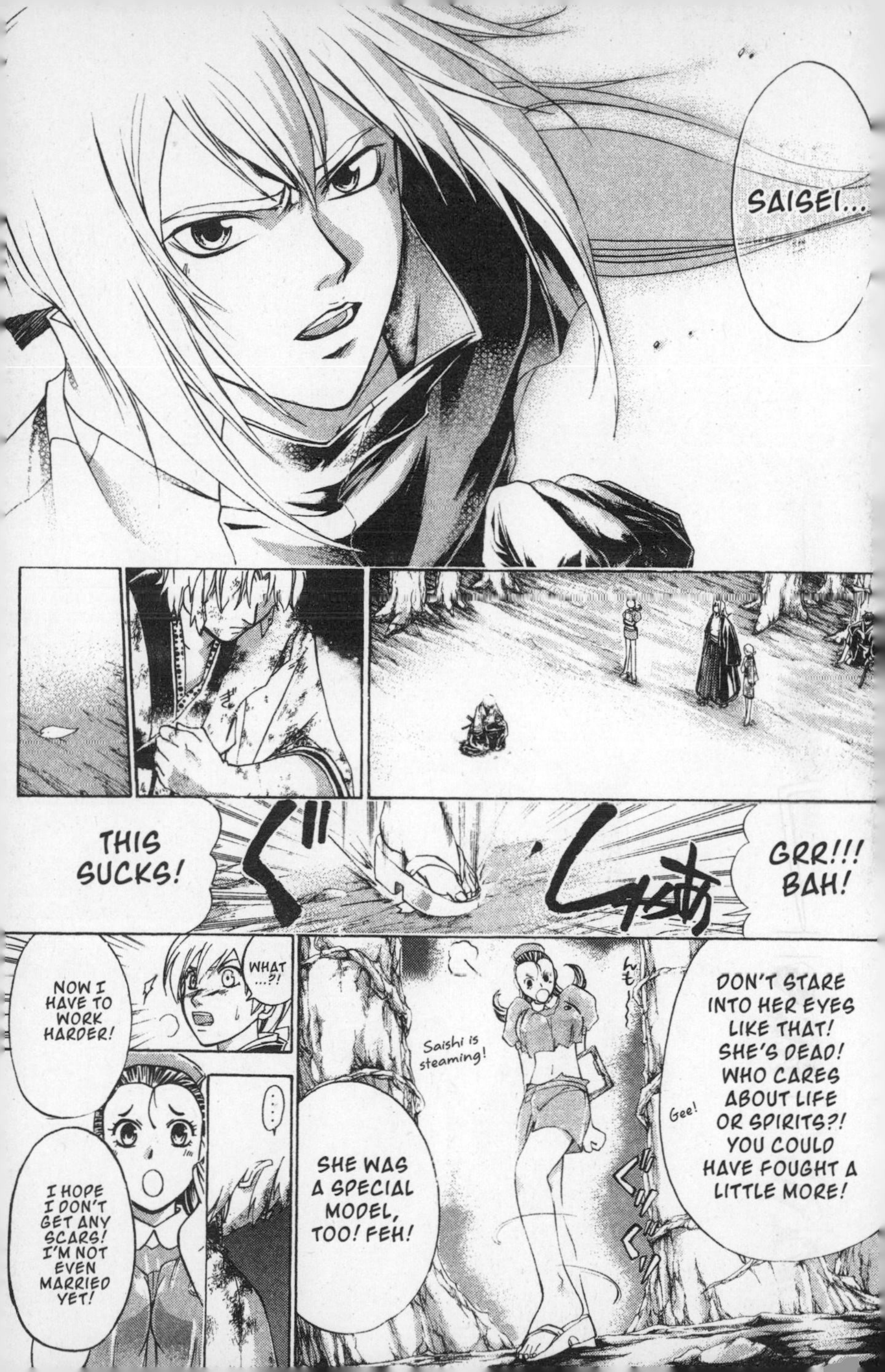
SAISEI...
GRR!!! BAH!
THIS SUCKS!
DON'T STARE INTO HER EYES LIKE THAT! SHE'S DEAD! WHO CARES ABOUT LIFE OR SPIRITS?! YOU COULD HAVE FOUGHT A LITTLE MORE!
Gee!
Saishi is steaming!
SHE WAS A SPECIAL MODEL, TOO! FEH!
WHAT ...?!
NOW I HAVE TO WORK HARDER!
...
I HOPE I DON'T GET ANY SCARS! I'M NOT EVEN MARRIED YET!

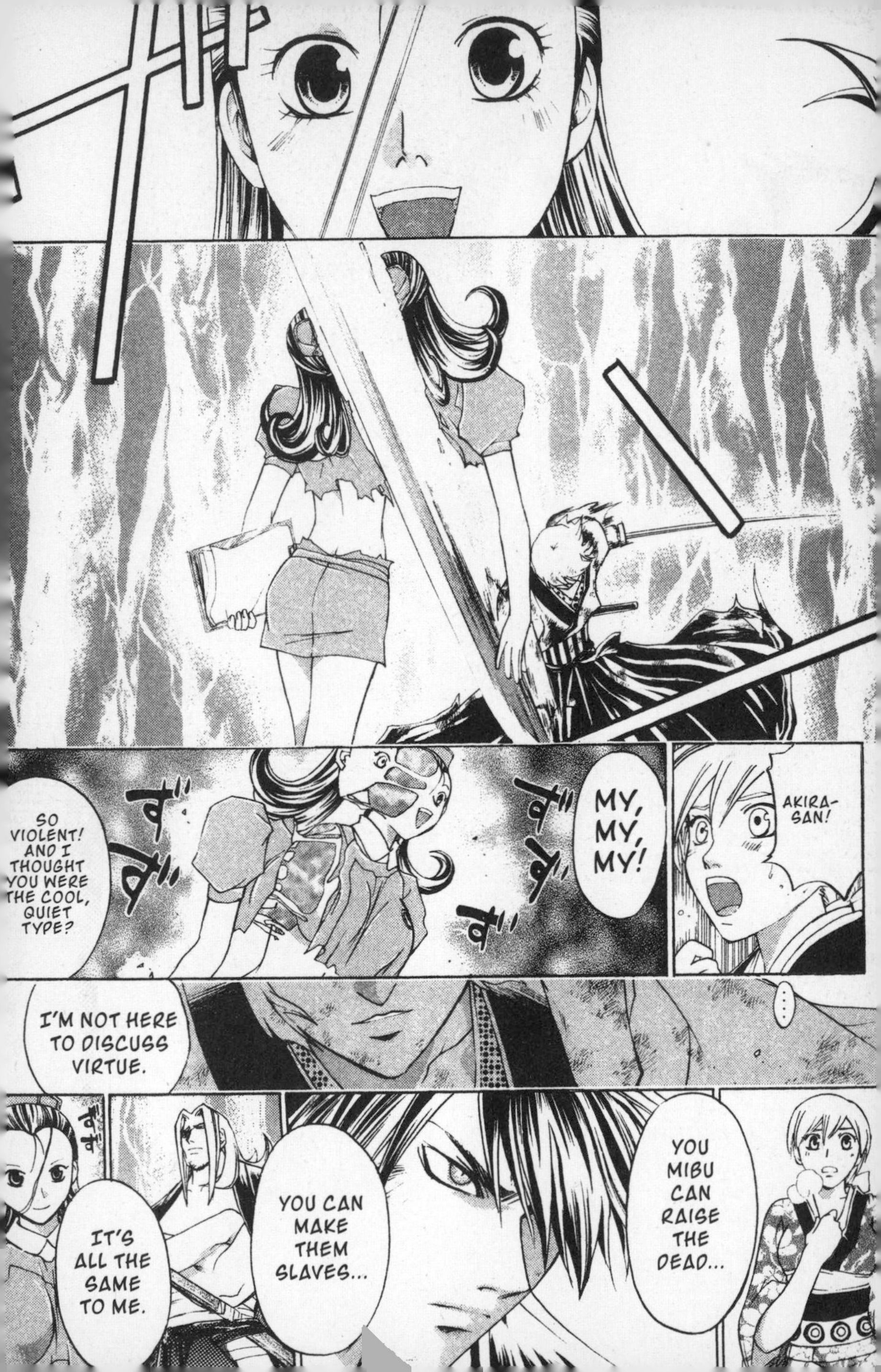
AKIRA-SAN!
MY, MY, MY!
ずず
ずず
SO VIOLENT! AND I THOUGHT YOU WERE THE COOL, QUIET TYPE?
...
I'M NOT HERE TO DISCUSS VIRTUE.
YOU MIBU CAN RAISE THE DEAD...
YOU CAN MAKE THEM SLAVES...
IT'S ALL THE SAME TO ME.

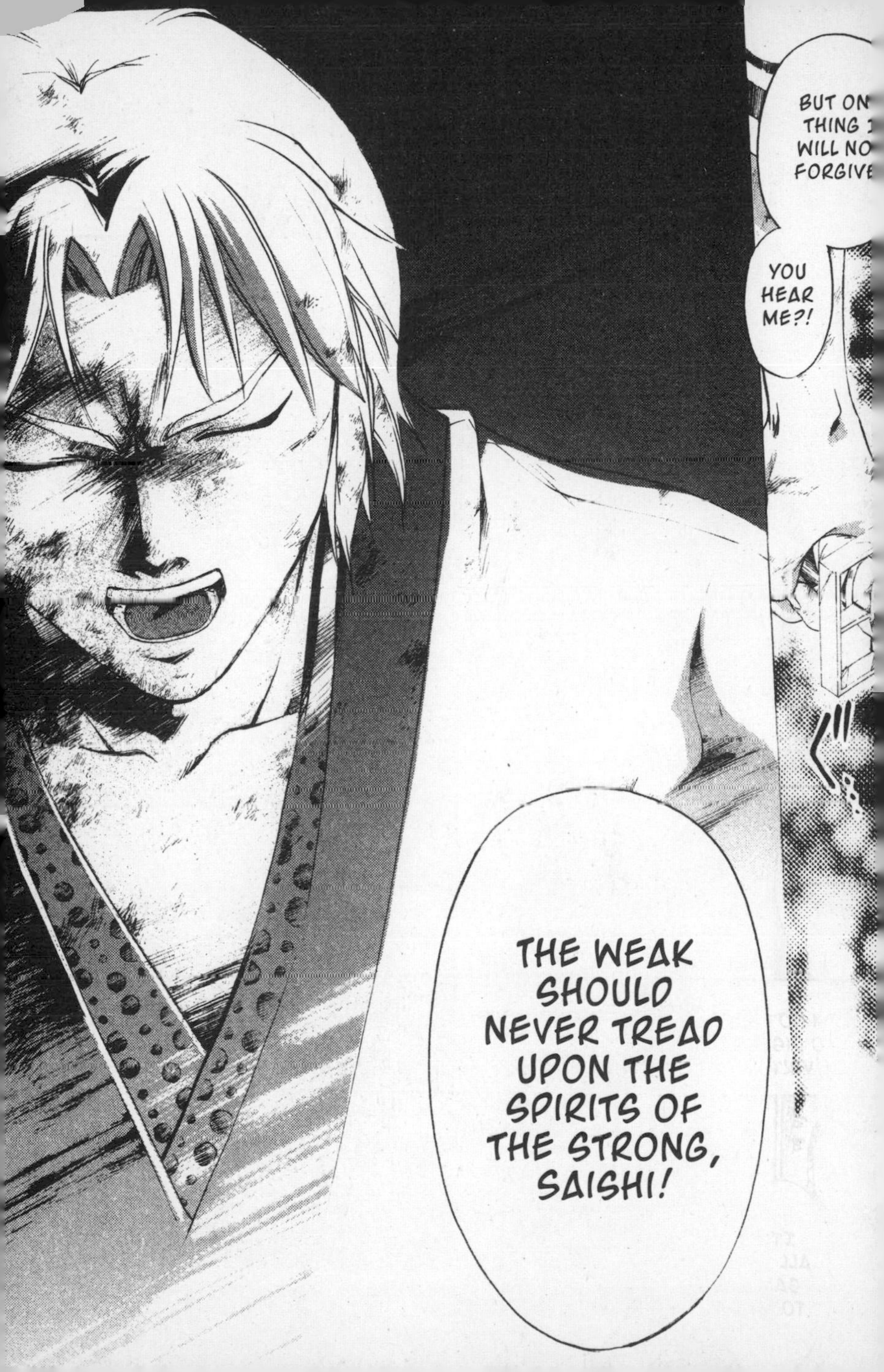
BUT ON THING I WILL NO FORGIVE
YOU HEAR ME?!
THE WEAK SHOULD NEVER TREAD UPON THE SPIRITS OF THE STRONG, SAISHI!

The Kamijyo Report

NINJA ARMY

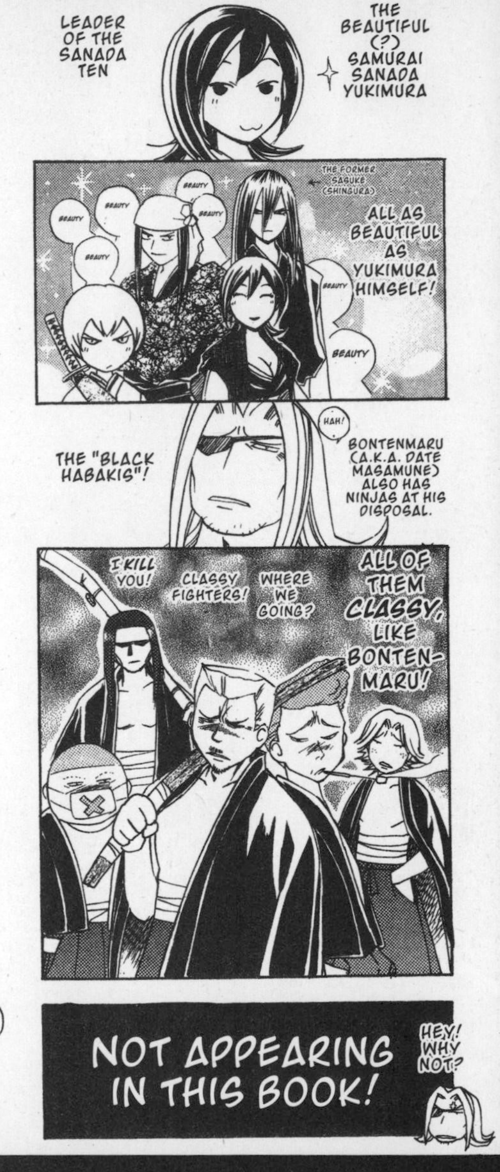
LEADER OF THE SANADA TEN
THE BEAUTIFUL (?) SAMURAI SANADA YUKIMURA
THE FORMER SASUKE (SHINGURA)
ALL AS BEAUTIFUL AS YUKIMURA HIMSELF!
BEAUTY
BEAUTY
BEAUTY
BEAUTY
BEAUTY
BEAUTY
BEAUTY
HAH!
BONTENMARU (A.K.A. DATE MASAMUNE) ALSO HAS NINJAS AT HIS DISPOSAL.
THE "BLACK HABAKIS"!
ALL OF THEM CLASSY, LIKE BONTEN-MARU!
WHERE WE GOING?
CLASSY FIGHTERS!
I KILL YOU!
HEY! WHY NOT?
NOT APPEARING IN THIS BOOK!

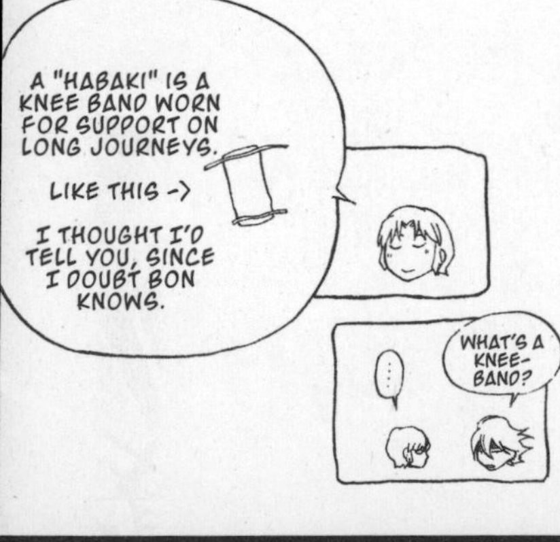
A "HABAKI" IS A KNEE BAND WORN FOR SUPPORT ON LONG JOURNEYS.
LIKE THIS ->
I THOUGHT I'D TELL YOU, SINCE I DOUBT BON KNOWS.
WHAT'S A KNEE-BAND?
...

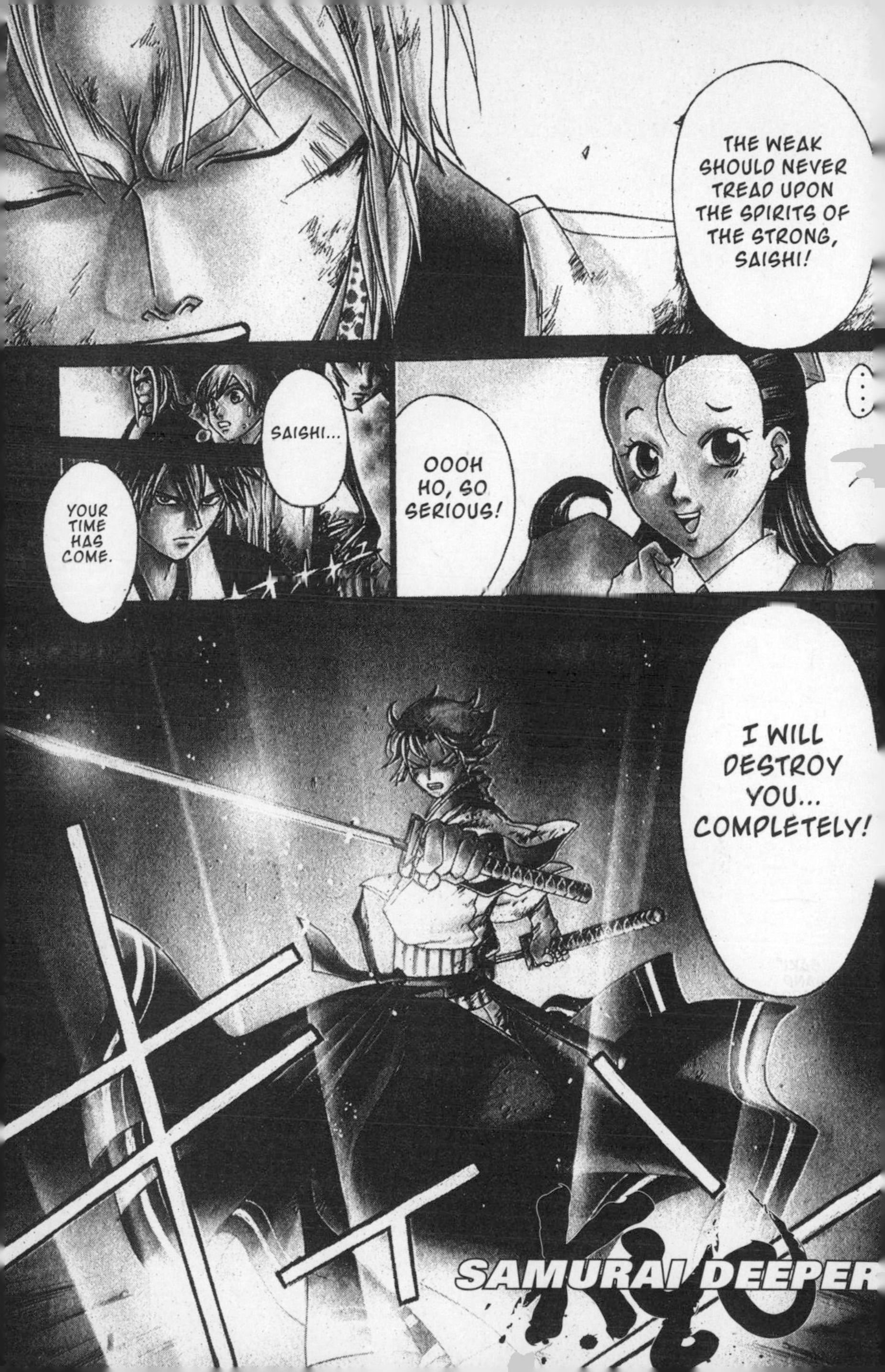
THE WEAK SHOULD NEVER TREAD UPON THE SPIRITS OF THE STRONG, SAISHI!
...
OOOH HO, SO SERIOUS!
SAISHI...
YOUR TIME HAS COME.
I WILL DESTROY YOU... COMPLETELY!
SAMURAI DEEPER

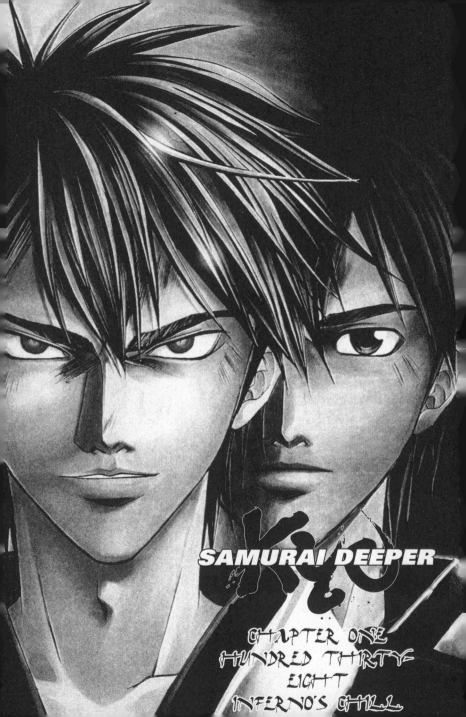

SAMURAI DEEPER *Kyo*

CHAPTER ONE
HUNDRED THIRTY-
EIGHT
INFERNO'S CHILL

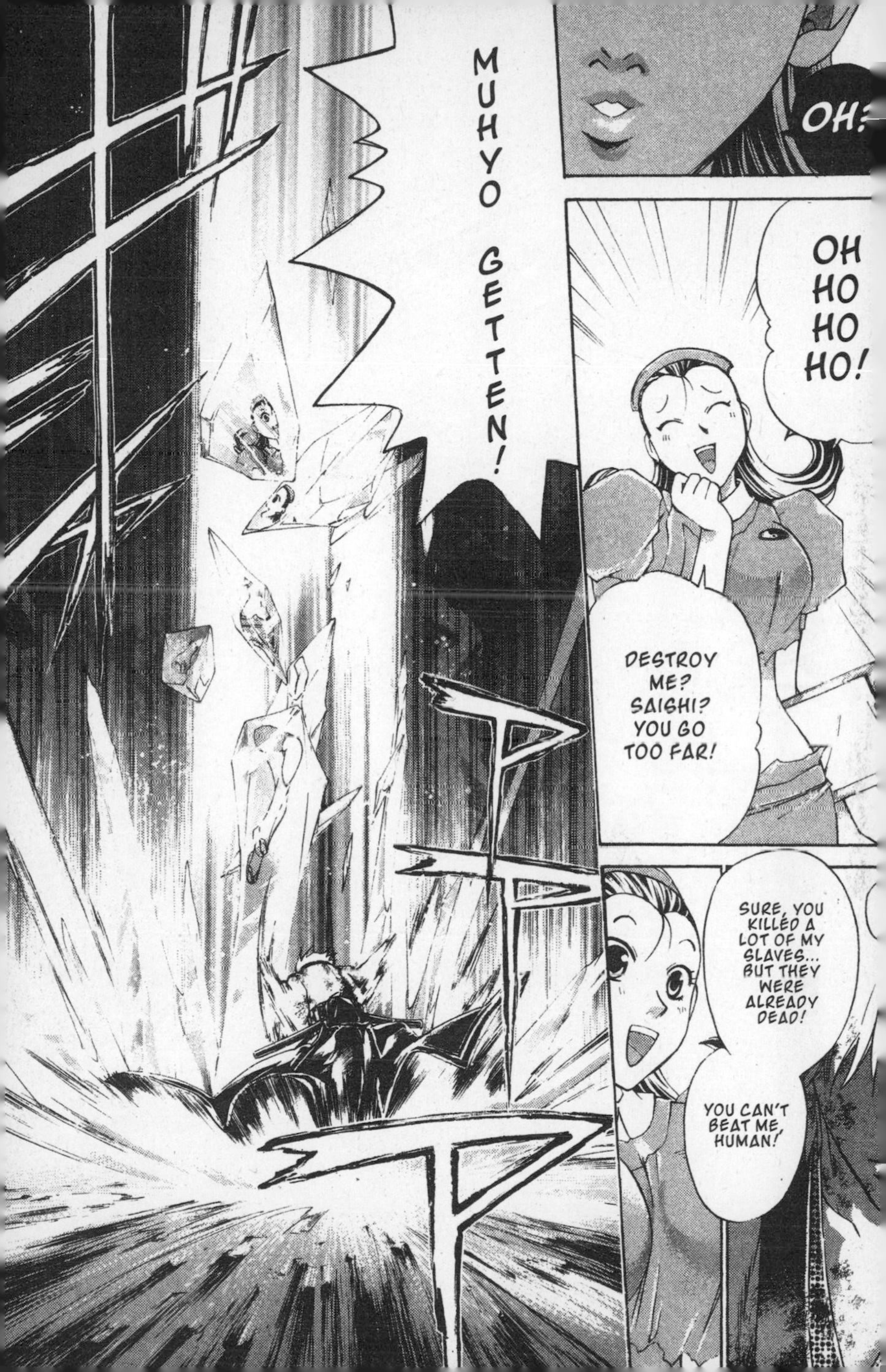
OH?
OH HO HO HO!
DESTROY ME? SAISHI? YOU GO TOO FAR!
SURE, YOU KILLED A LOT OF MY SLAVES... BUT THEY WERE ALREADY DEAD!
YOU CAN'T BEAT ME, HUMAN!
MUHYO GETTEN!

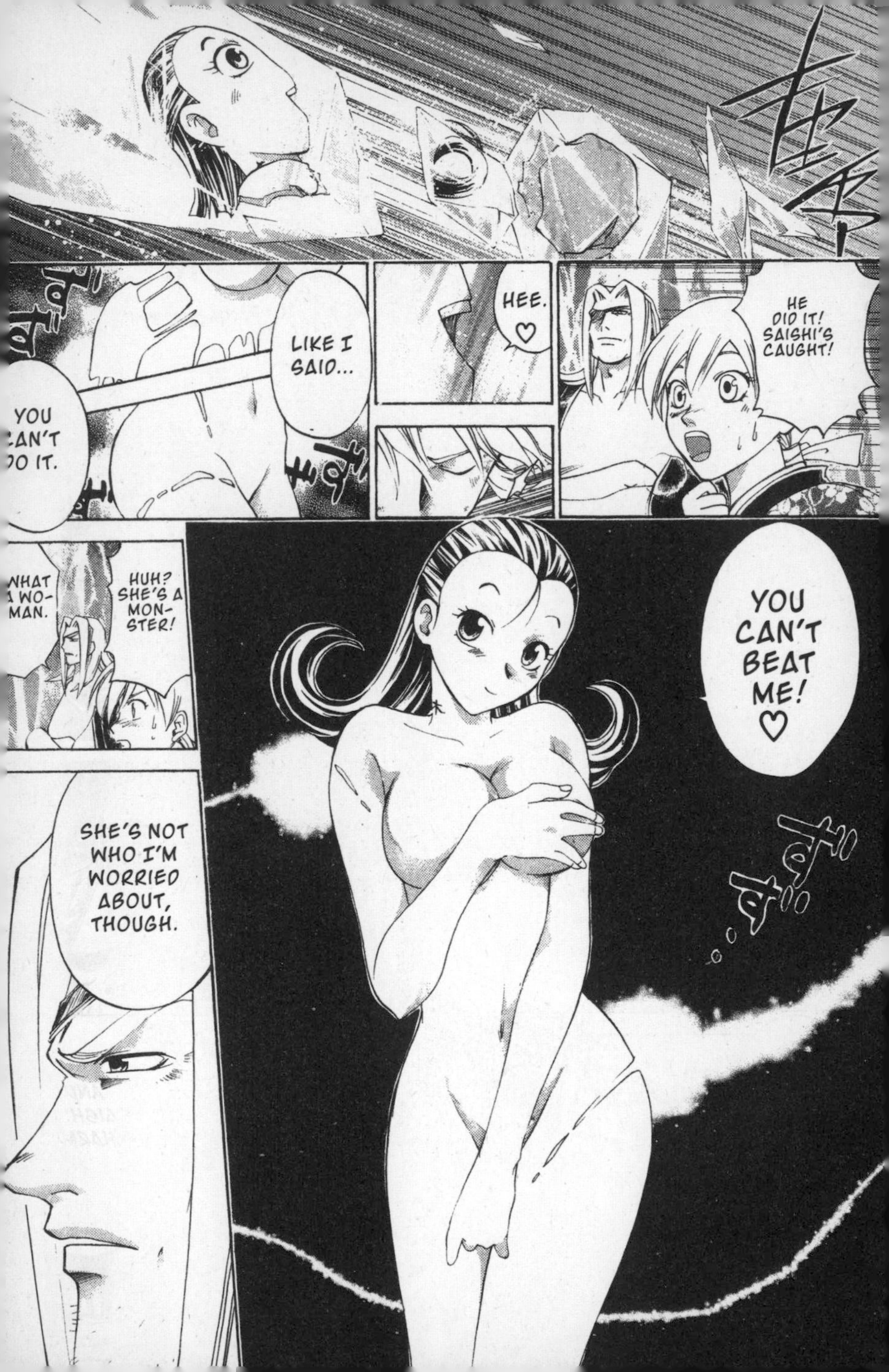
HE DID IT! SAISHI'S CAUGHT!
HEE. ♡
LIKE I SAID...
YOU CAN'T DO IT.
YOU CAN'T BEAT ME! ♡
HUH? SHE'S A MONSTER!
WHAT A WOMAN.
SHE'S NOT WHO I'M WORRIED ABOUT, THOUGH.

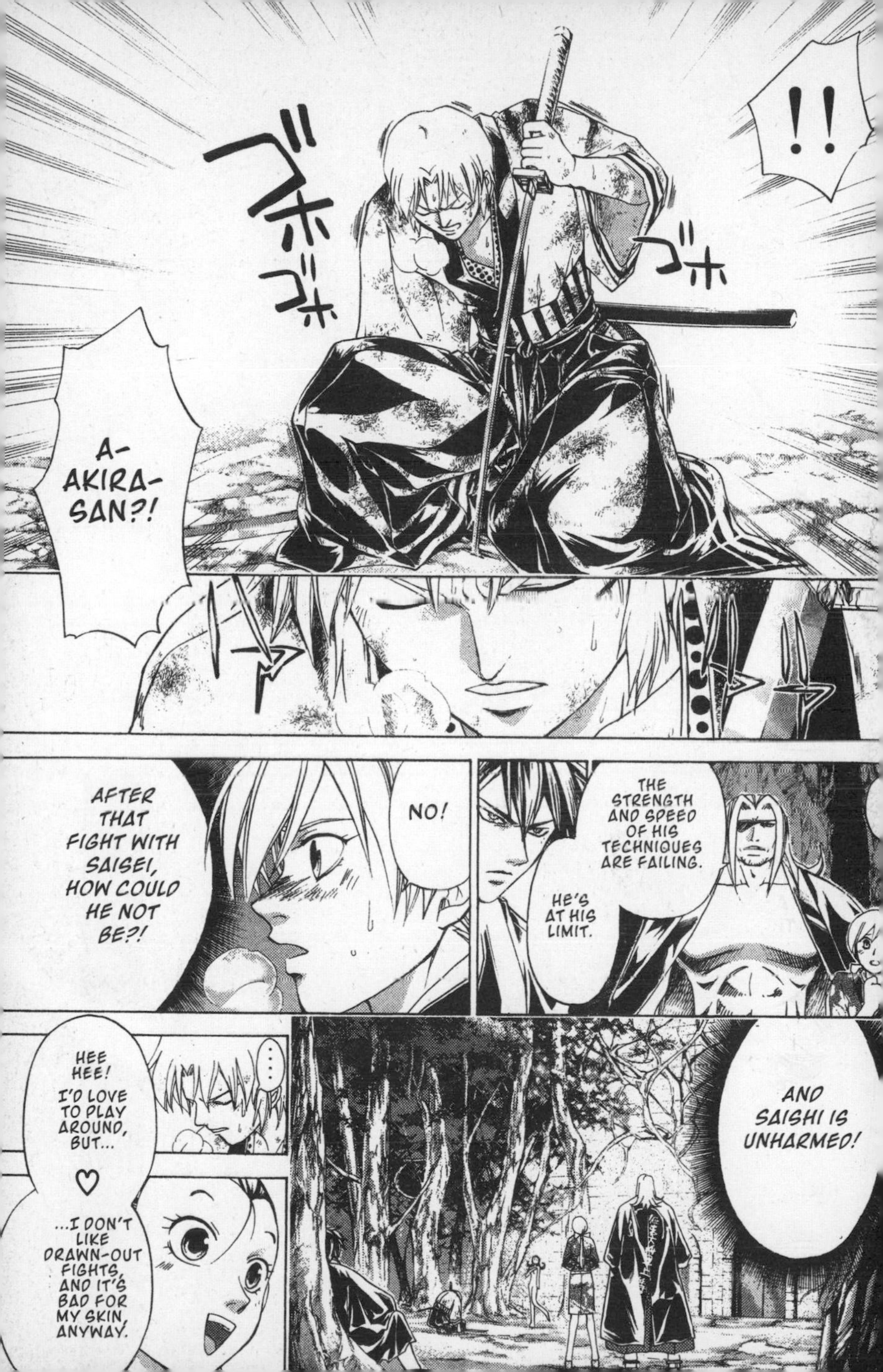

!!
ゴホ
ゴホゴホ
A-AKIRA-SAN?!
THE STRENGTH AND SPEED OF HIS TECHNIQUES ARE FAILING.
HE'S AT HIS LIMIT.
NO!
AFTER THAT FIGHT WITH SAISEI, HOW COULD HE NOT BE?!
AND SAISHI IS UNHARMED!
HEE HEE! I'D LOVE TO PLAY AROUND, BUT...
...
♡
...I DON'T LIKE DRAWN-OUT FIGHTS, AND IT'S BAD FOR MY SKIN, ANYWAY.

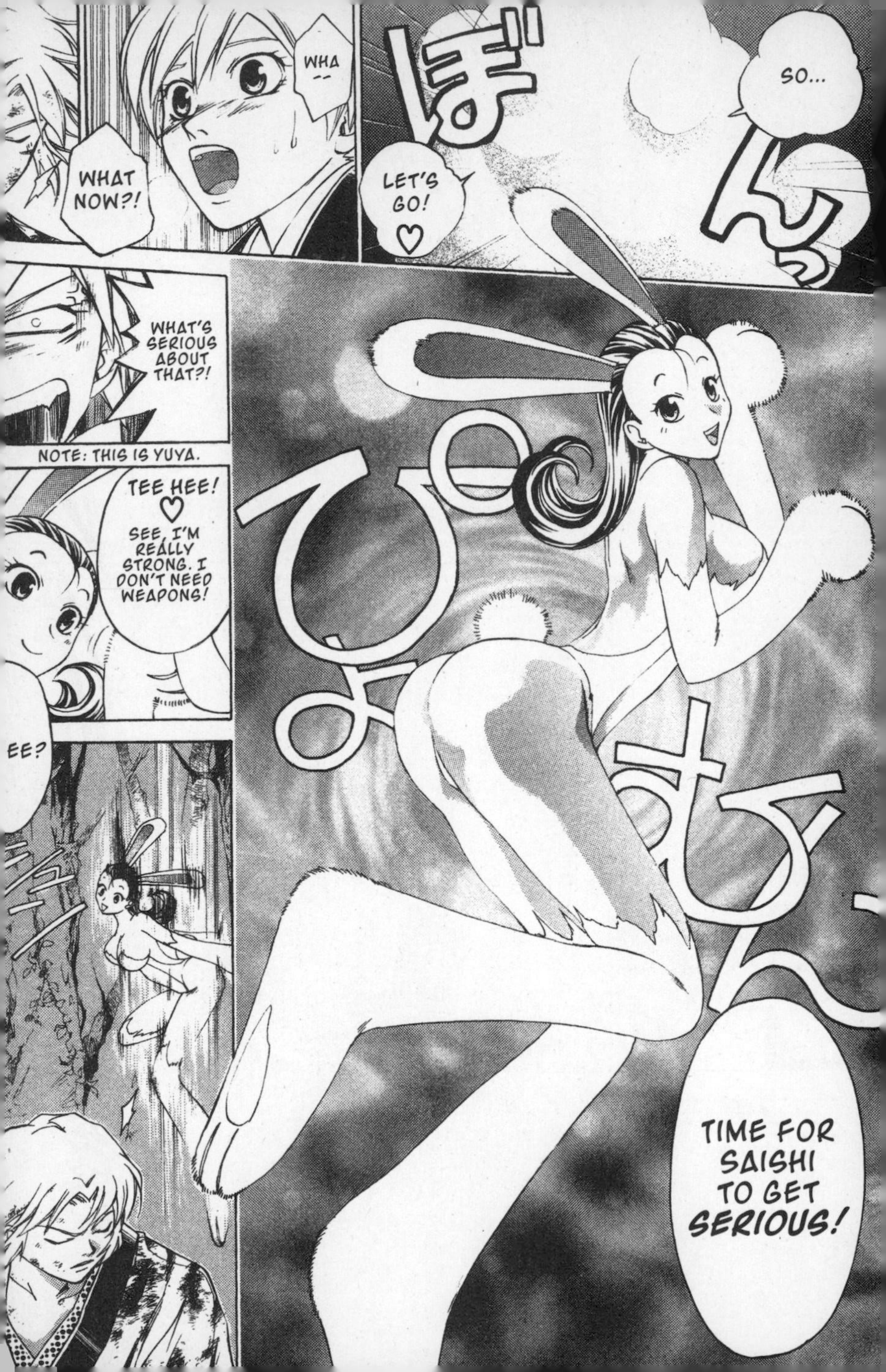

SO...
ぼんっ
LET'S GO! ♡
WHA --
WHAT NOW?!
ぴょ
TIME FOR SAISHI TO GET SERIOUS!
WHAT'S SERIOUS ABOUT THAT?!
NOTE: THIS IS YUYA.
TEE HEE! ♡ SEE, I'M REALLY STRONG. I DON'T NEED WEAPONS!
EE?

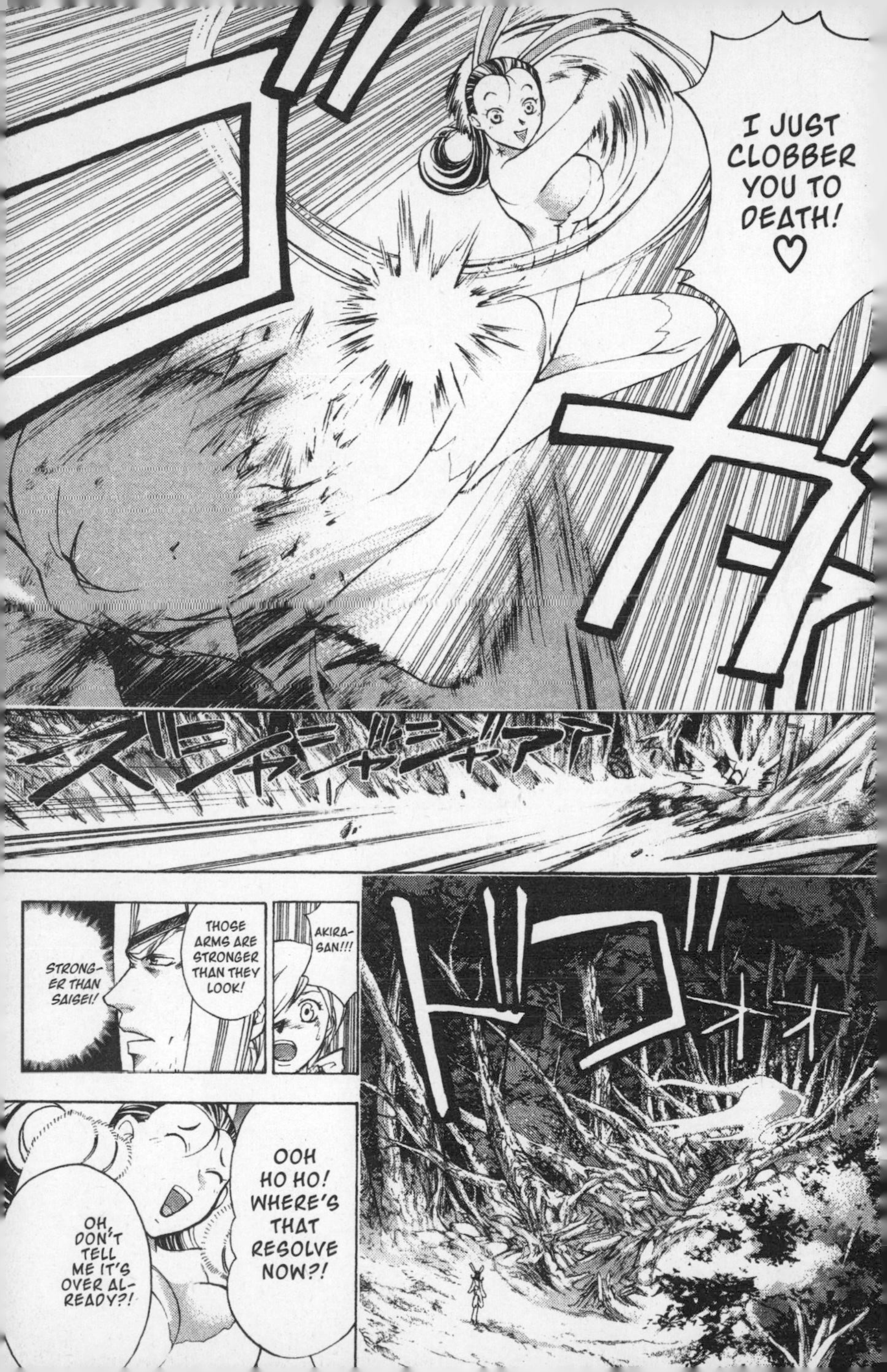
I JUST CLOBBER YOU TO DEATH! ♡
AKIRA-SAN!!!
THOSE ARMS ARE STRONGER THAN THEY LOOK!
STRONGER THAN SAISEI!
OOH HO HO! WHERE'S THAT RESOLVE NOW?!
OH, DON'T TELL ME IT'S OVER ALREADY?!

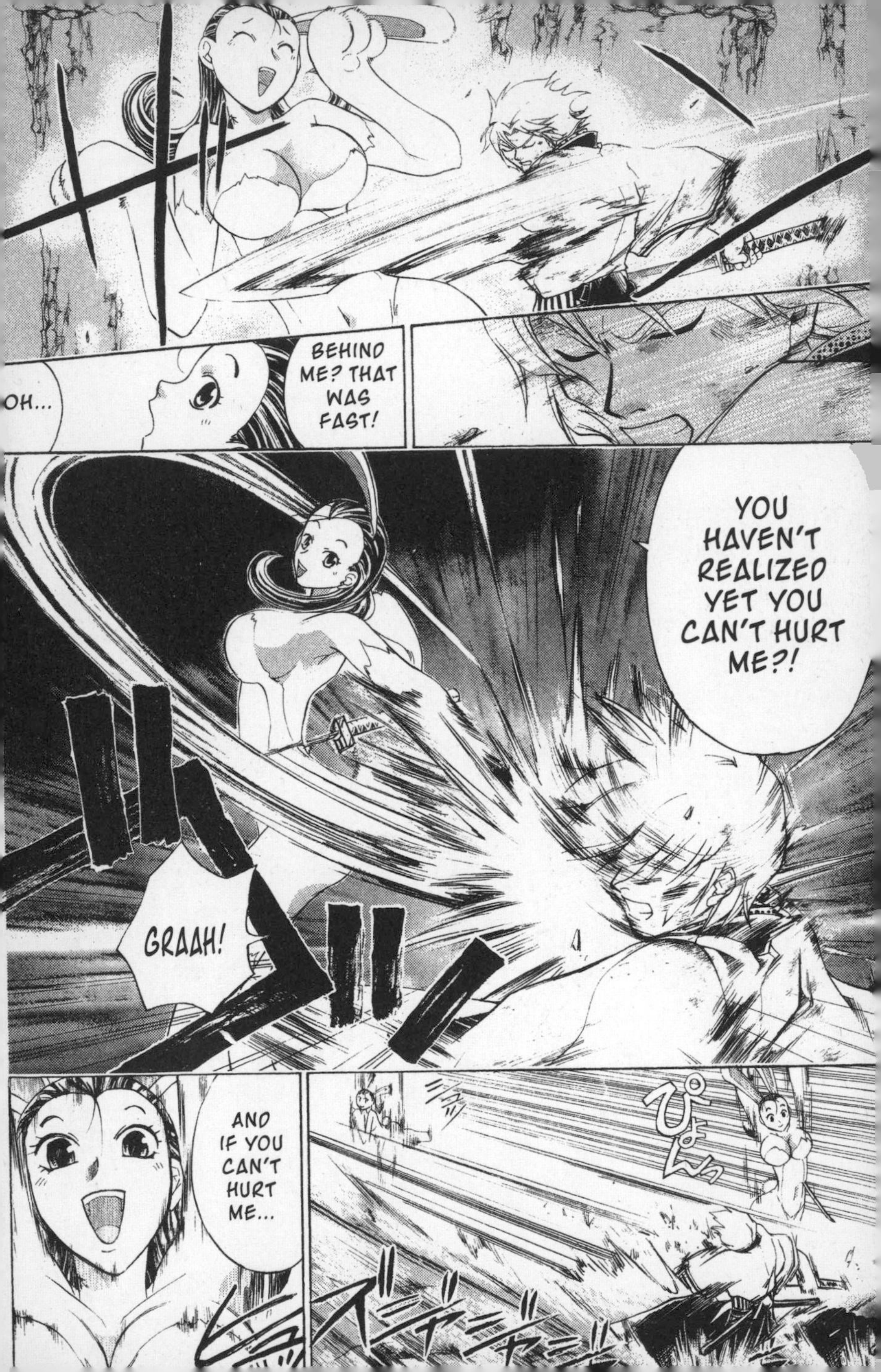
BEHIND ME? THAT WAS FAST!
OH...
YOU HAVEN'T REALIZED YET YOU CAN'T HURT ME?!
GRAAH!
ぴょん
AND IF YOU CAN'T HURT ME...

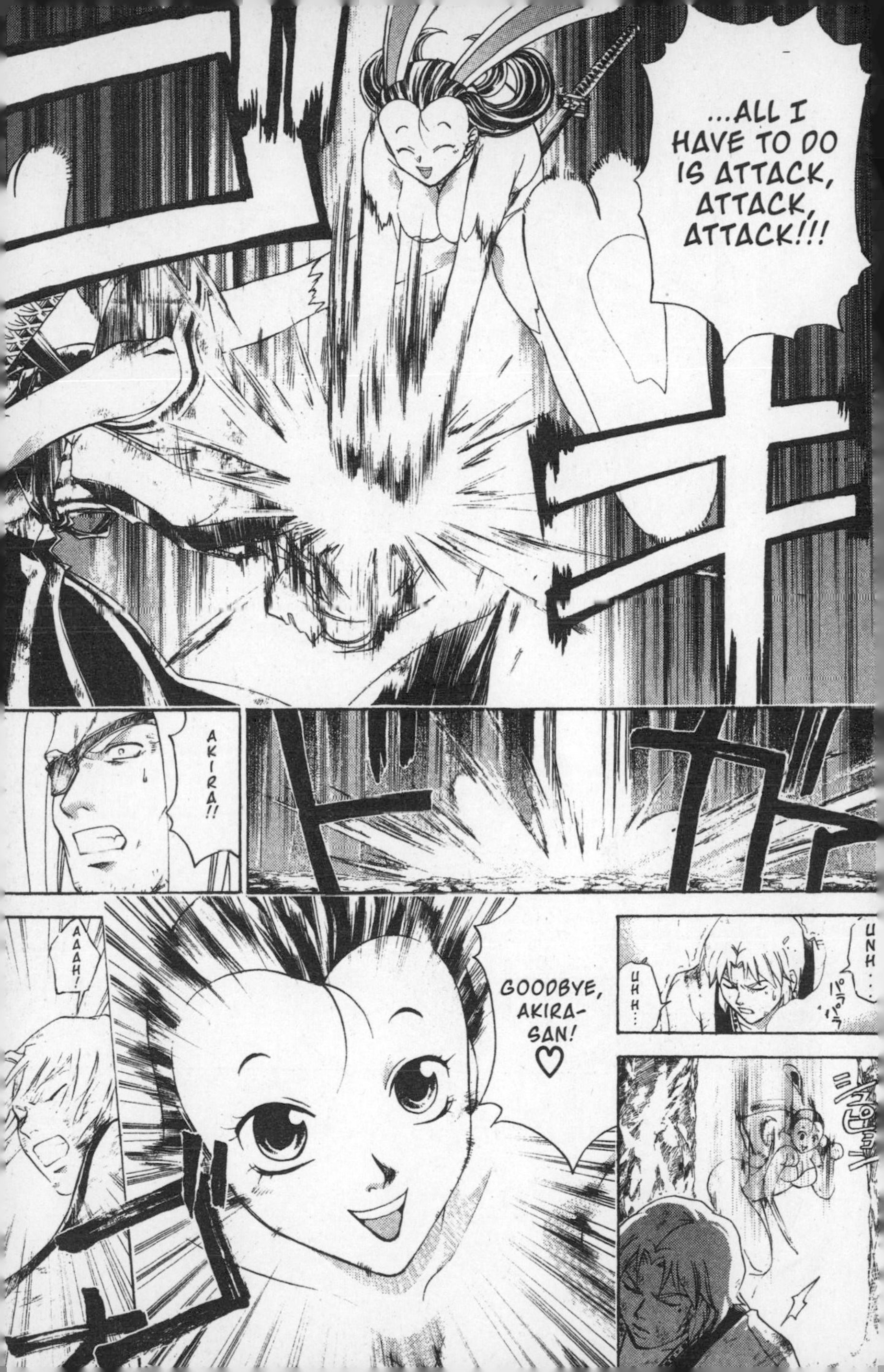
...ALL I HAVE TO DO IS ATTACK, ATTACK, ATTACK!!!
AKIRA!!
UNH...
UHH...
GOODBYE, AKIRA-SAN! ♡
AAAH!

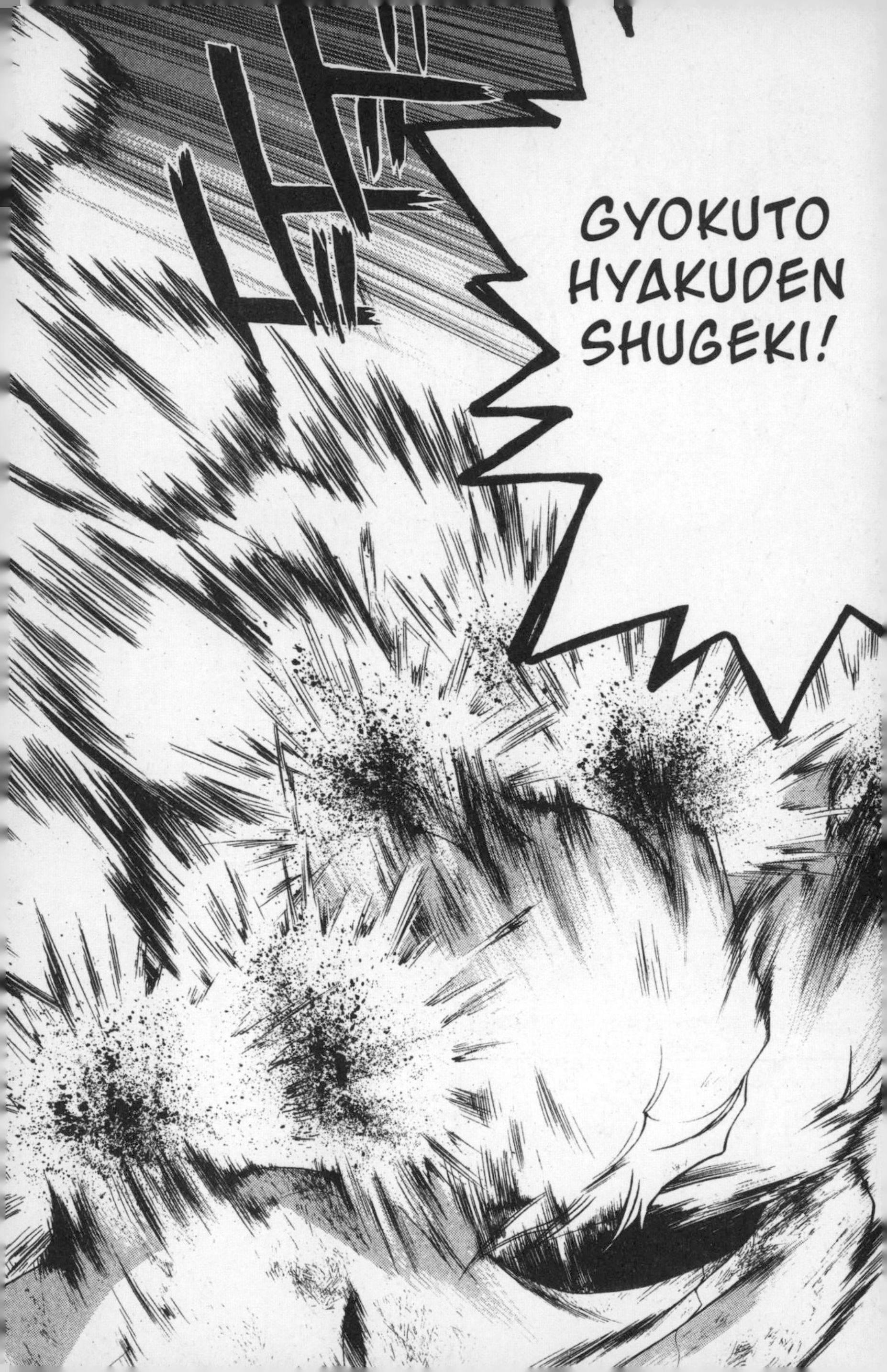
GYOKUTO
HYAKUDEN
SHUGEKI!

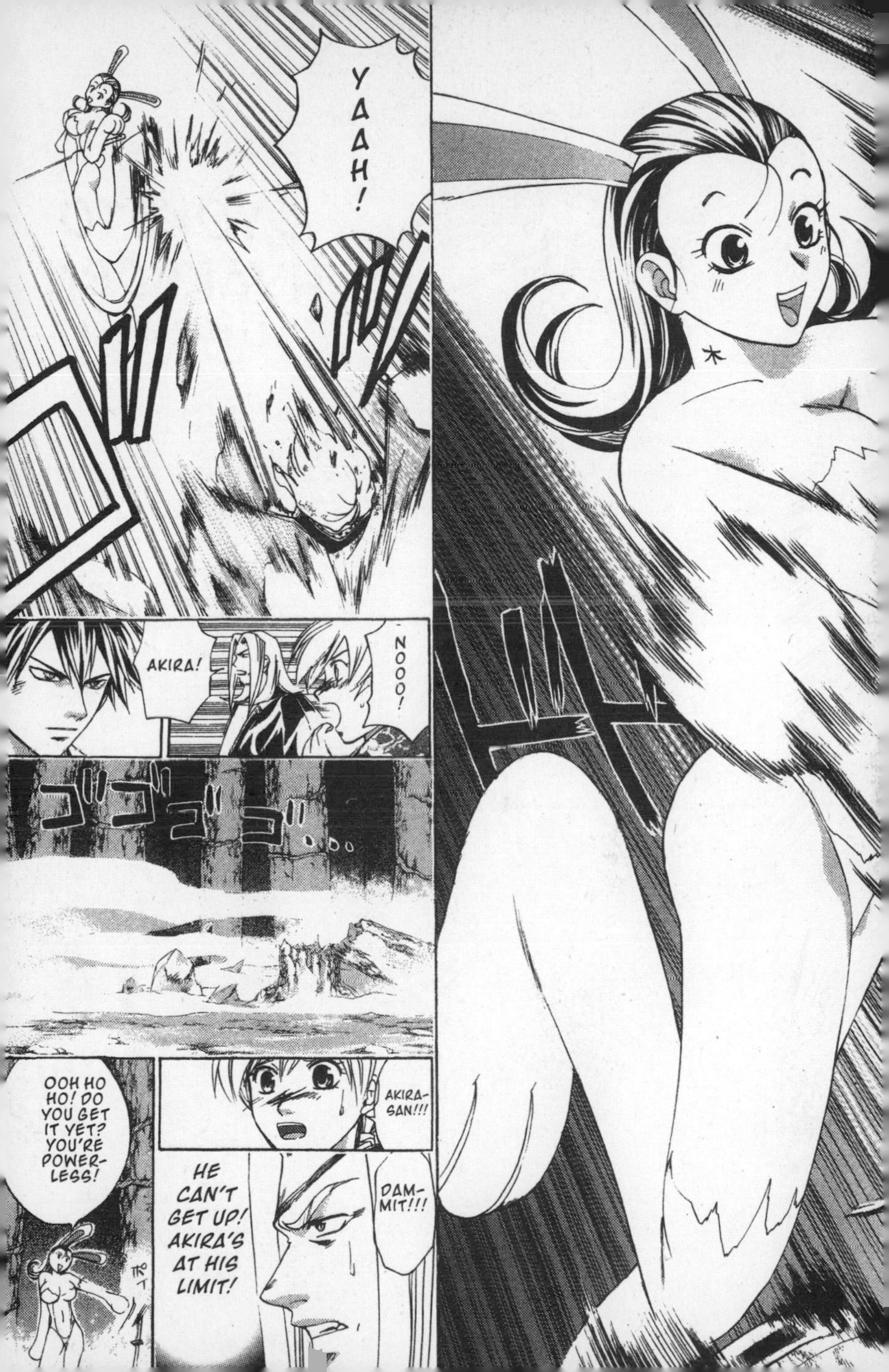
YAAAH!
NOOO!
AKIRA!
ゴゴゴゴゴ...
AKIRA-SAN!!!
DAM-MIT!!!
HE CAN'T GET UP! AKIRA'S AT HIS LIMIT!
OOH HO HO! DO YOU GET IT YET? YOU'RE POWER-LESS!

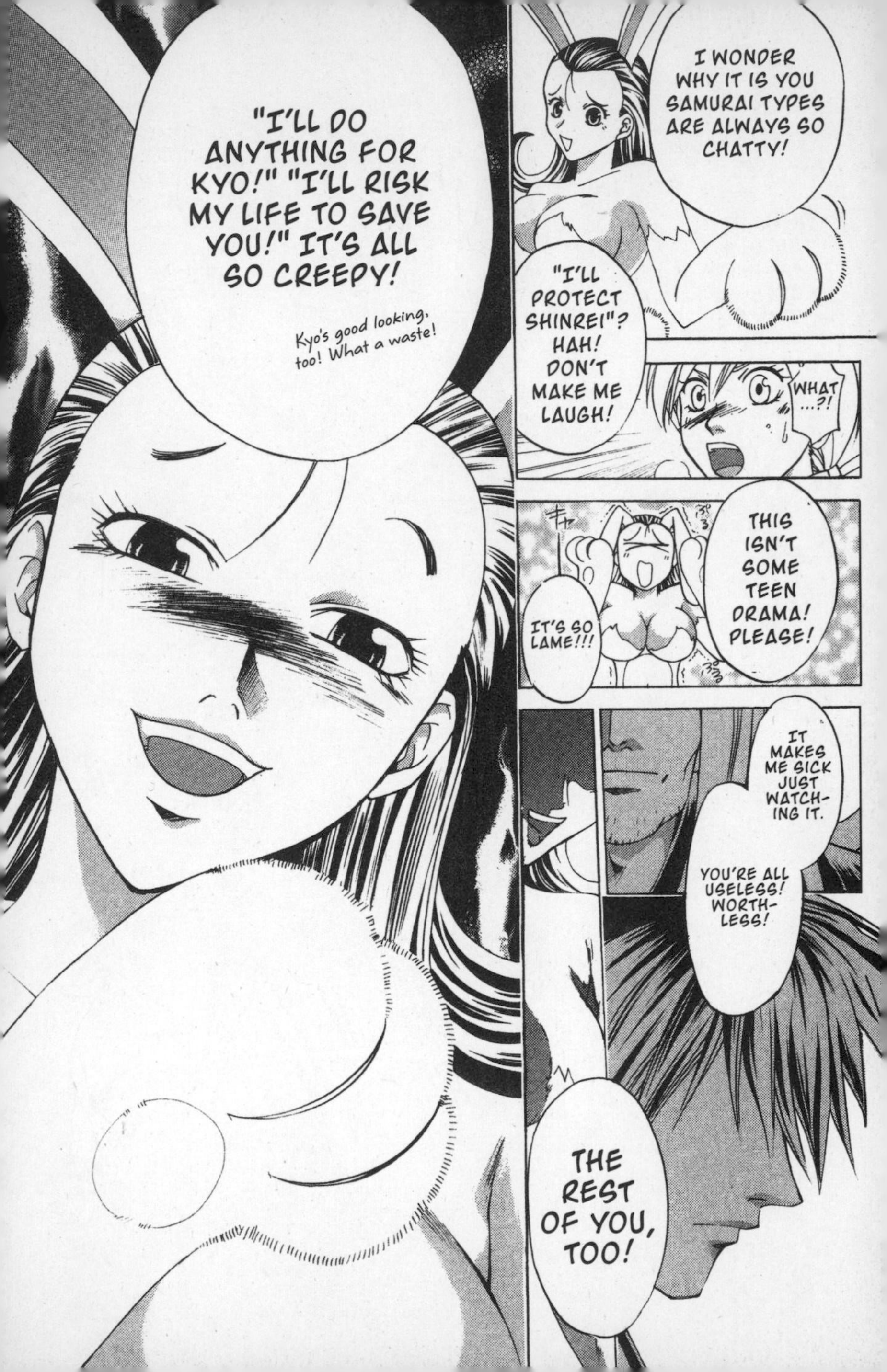
I WONDER WHY IT IS YOU SAMURAI TYPES ARE ALWAYS SO CHATTY!
"I'LL PROTECT SHINREI"? HAH! DON'T MAKE ME LAUGH!
WHAT ...?!
THIS ISN'T SOME TEEN DRAMA! PLEASE!
IT'S SO LAME!!!
IT MAKES ME SICK JUST WATCHING IT.
YOU'RE ALL USELESS! WORTHLESS!
THE REST OF YOU, TOO!
"I'LL DO ANYTHING FOR KYO!" "I'LL RISK MY LIFE TO SAVE YOU!" IT'S ALL SO CREEPY!
Kyo's good looking, too! What a waste!

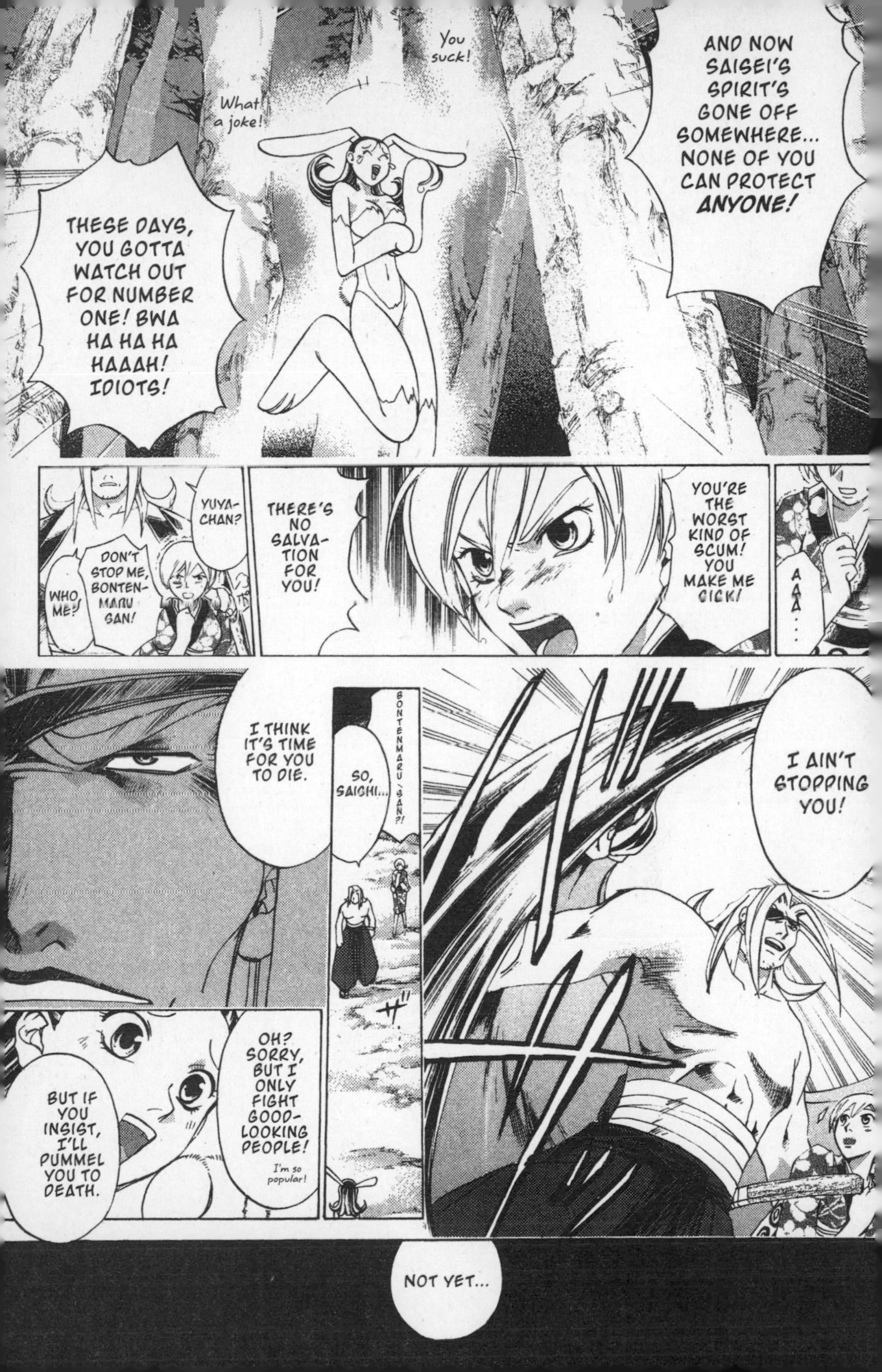
AND NOW SAISEI'S SPIRIT'S GONE OFF SOMEWHERE... NONE OF YOU CAN PROTECT ANYONE!
You suck!
What a joke!
THESE DAYS, YOU GOTTA WATCH OUT FOR NUMBER ONE! BWA HA HA HA HAAAH! IDIOTS!
A A A...
YOU'RE THE WORST KIND OF SCUM! YOU MAKE ME SICK!
THERE'S NO SALVATION FOR YOU!
YUYA-CHAN?
DON'T STOP ME, BONTEN-MARU-SAN!
WHO, ME!?
I AIN'T STOPPING YOU!
BONTENMARU-SAN?!
SO, SAICHI...
I THINK IT'S TIME FOR YOU TO DIE.
OH? SORRY, BUT I ONLY FIGHT GOOD-LOOKING PEOPLE!
I'm so popular!
BUT IF YOU INSIST, I'LL PUMMEL YOU TO DEATH.
NOT YET...

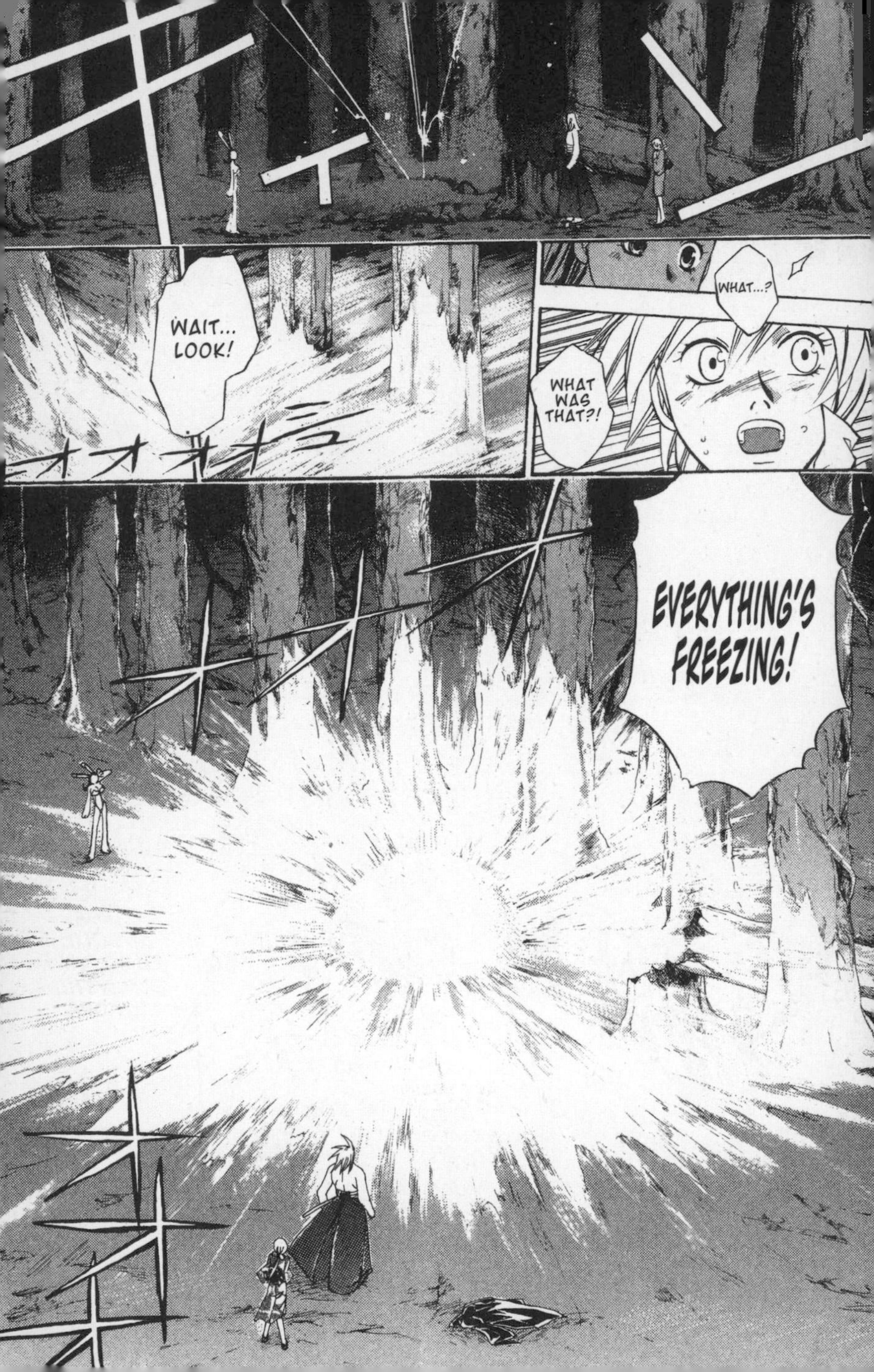
WHAT...?
WHAT WAS THAT?!
WAIT... LOOK!
EVERYTHING'S FREEZING!

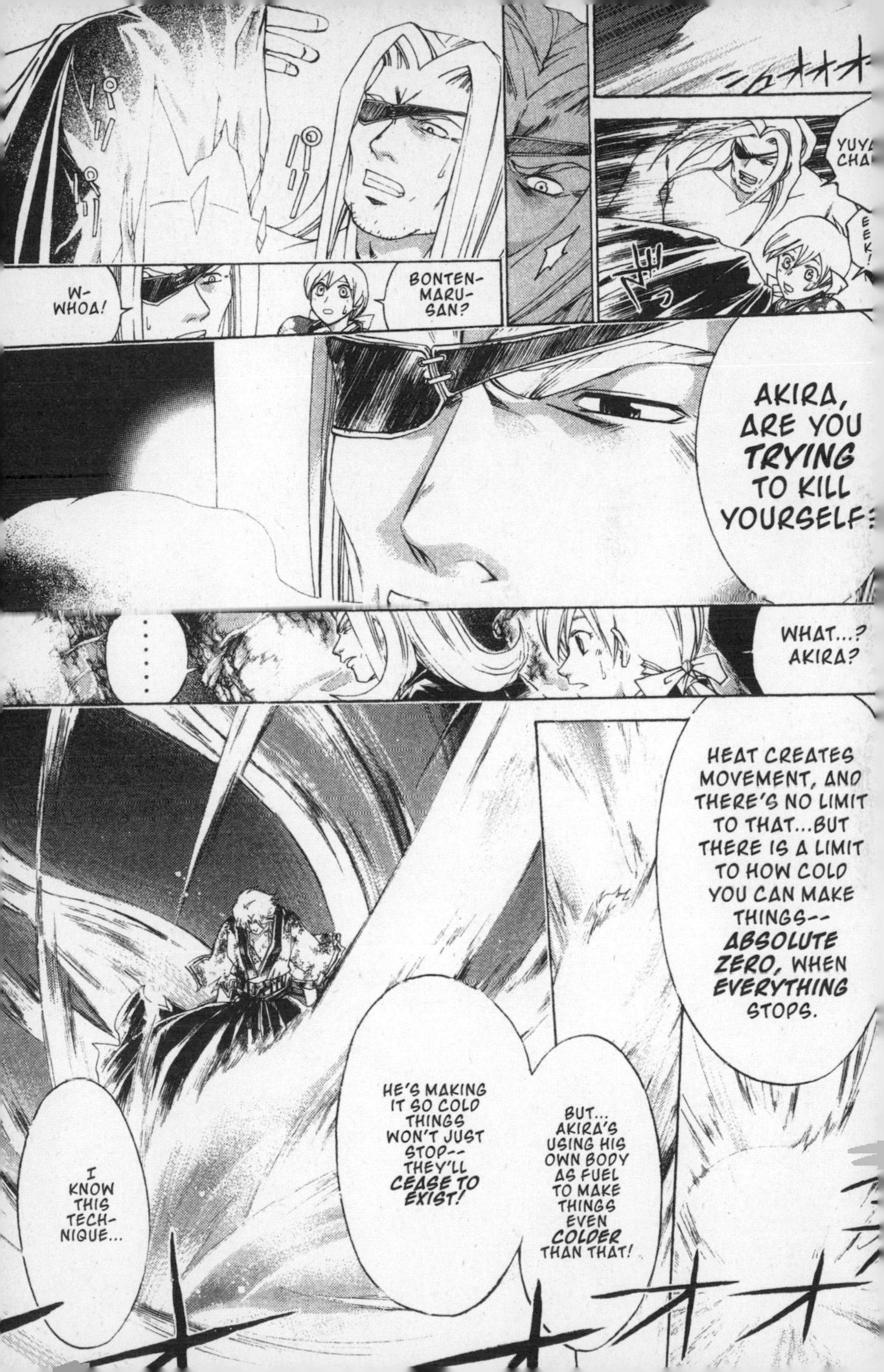
YUYA CHA
EEK!
BONTEN-MARU-SAN?
W-WHOA!
AKIRA, ARE YOU TRYING TO KILL YOURSELF!?
WHAT...? AKIRA?
......
HEAT CREATES MOVEMENT, AND THERE'S NO LIMIT TO THAT...BUT THERE IS A LIMIT TO HOW COLD YOU CAN MAKE THINGS-- ABSOLUTE ZERO, WHEN EVERYTHING STOPS.
BUT... AKIRA'S USING HIS OWN BODY AS FUEL TO MAKE THINGS EVEN COLDER THAN THAT!
HE'S MAKING IT SO COLD THINGS WON'T JUST STOP-- THEY'LL CEASE TO EXIST!
I KNOW THIS TECH-NIQUE...

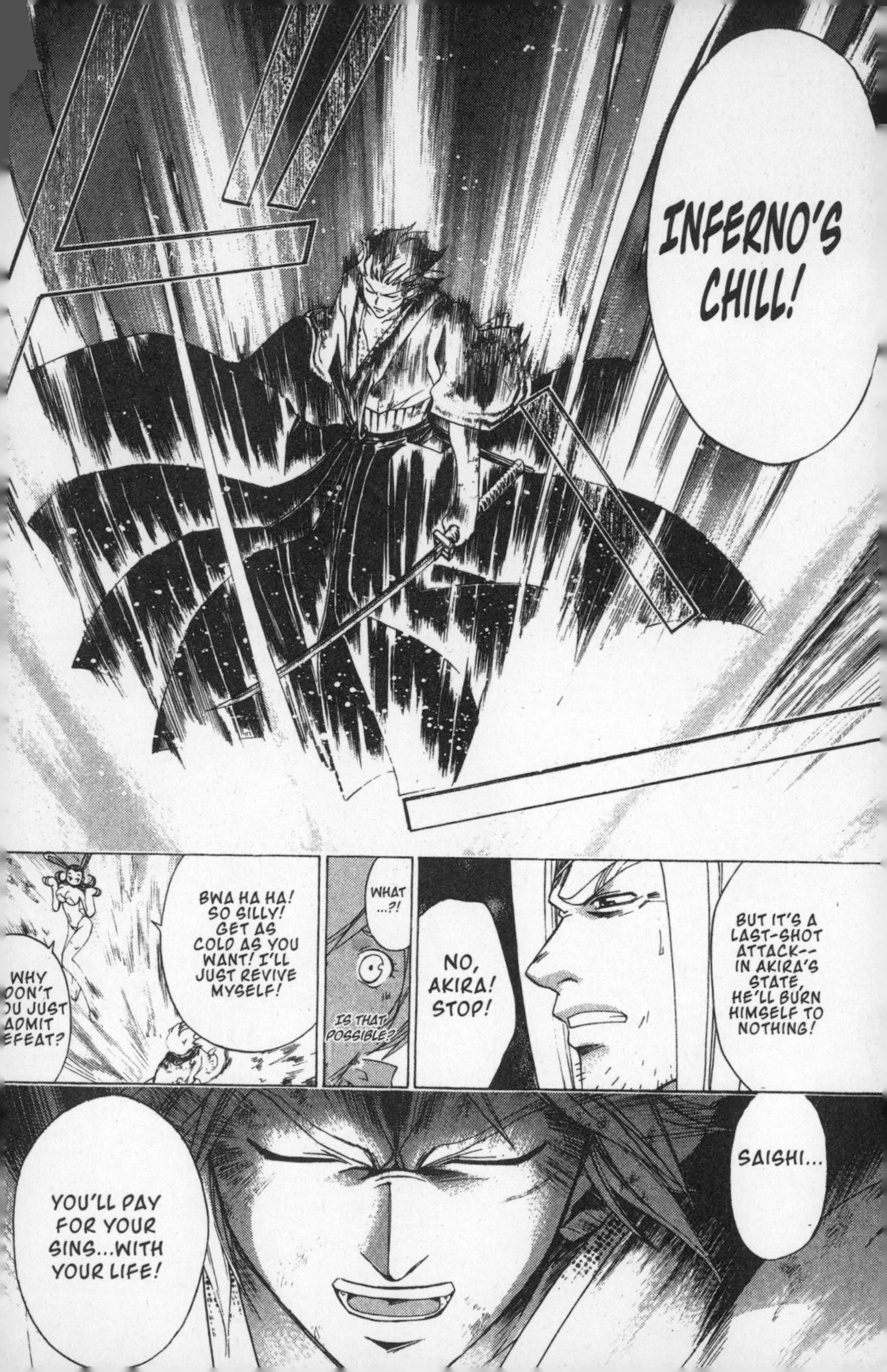
INFERNO'S CHILL!
BUT IT'S A LAST-SHOT ATTACK-- IN AKIRA'S STATE, HE'LL BURN HIMSELF TO NOTHING!
NO, AKIRA! STOP!
WHAT ...?!
IS THAT POSSIBLE?
BWA HA HA! SO SILLY! GET AS COLD AS YOU WANT! I'LL JUST REVIVE MYSELF!
WHY ON'T U JUST ADMIT EFEAT?
SAISHI...
YOU'LL PAY FOR YOUR SINS...WITH YOUR LIFE!

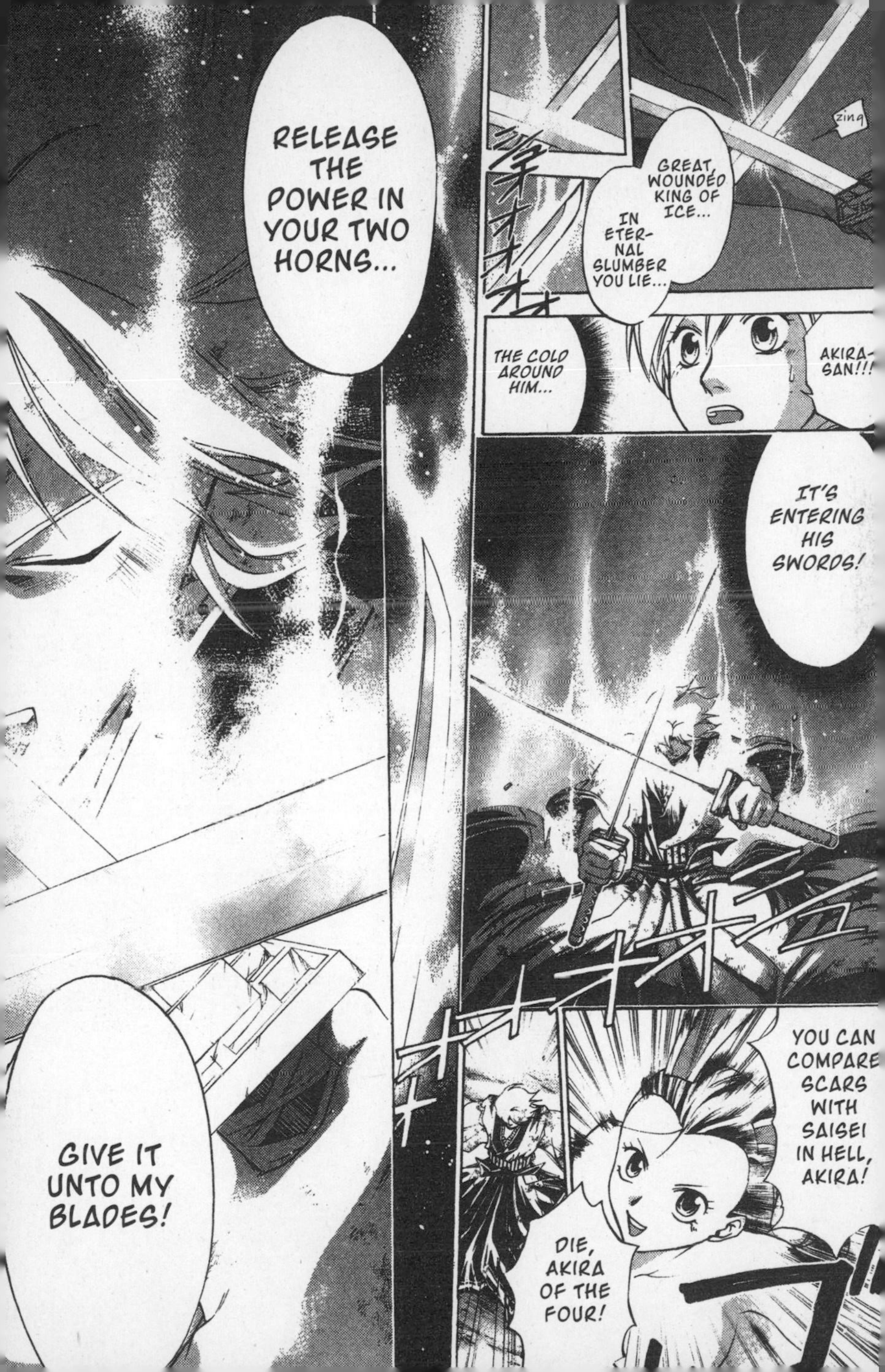
zing
GREAT, WOUNDED KING OF ICE...
IN ETERNAL SLUMBER YOU LIE...
AKIRA-SAN!!!
THE COLD AROUND HIM...
IT'S ENTERING HIS SWORDS!
YOU CAN COMPARE SCARS WITH SAISEI IN HELL, AKIRA!
DIE, AKIRA OF THE FOUR!
RELEASE THE POWER IN YOUR TWO HORNS...
GIVE IT UNTO MY BLADES!

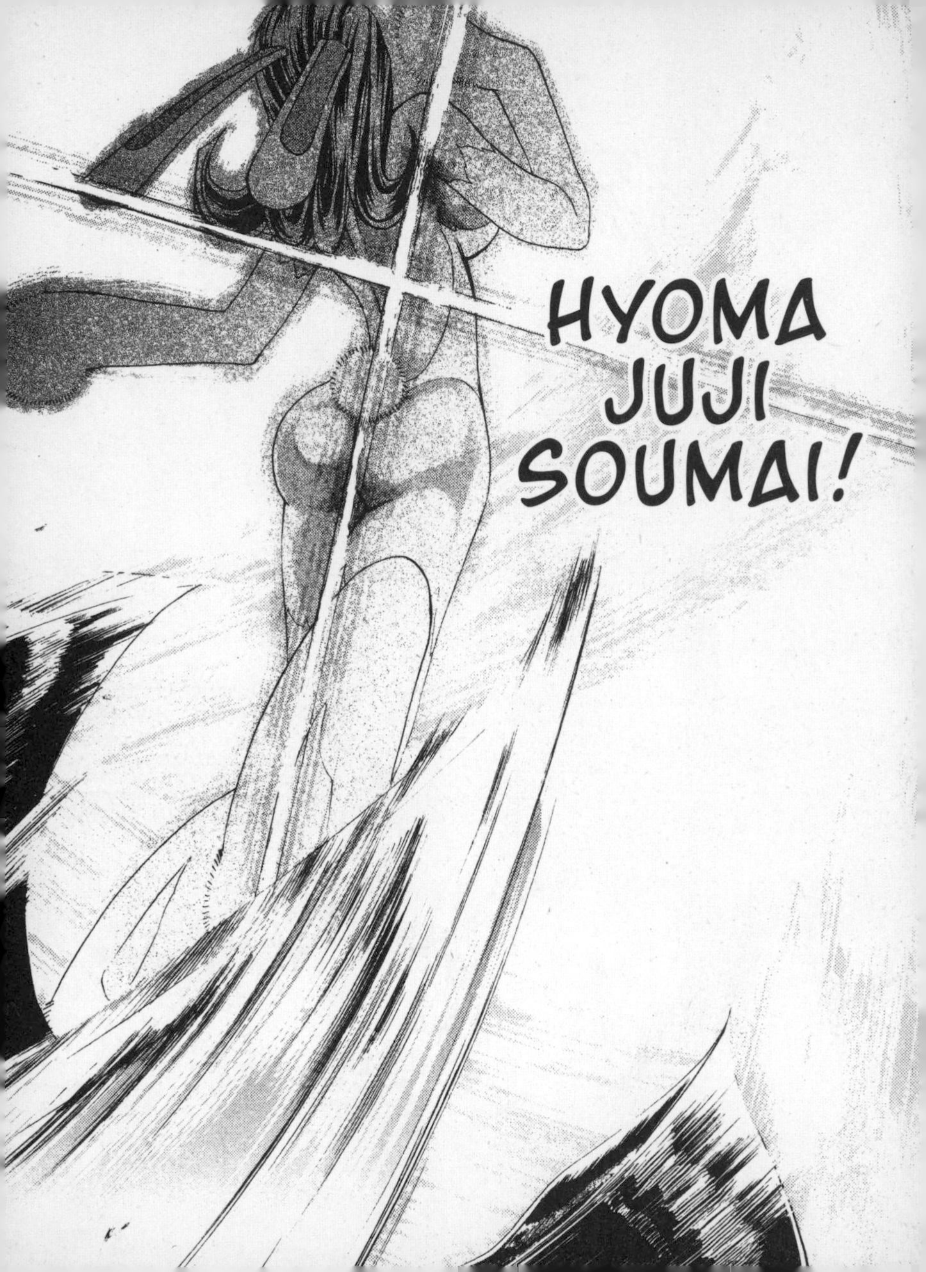
HYOMA
JUJI
SOUMAI!

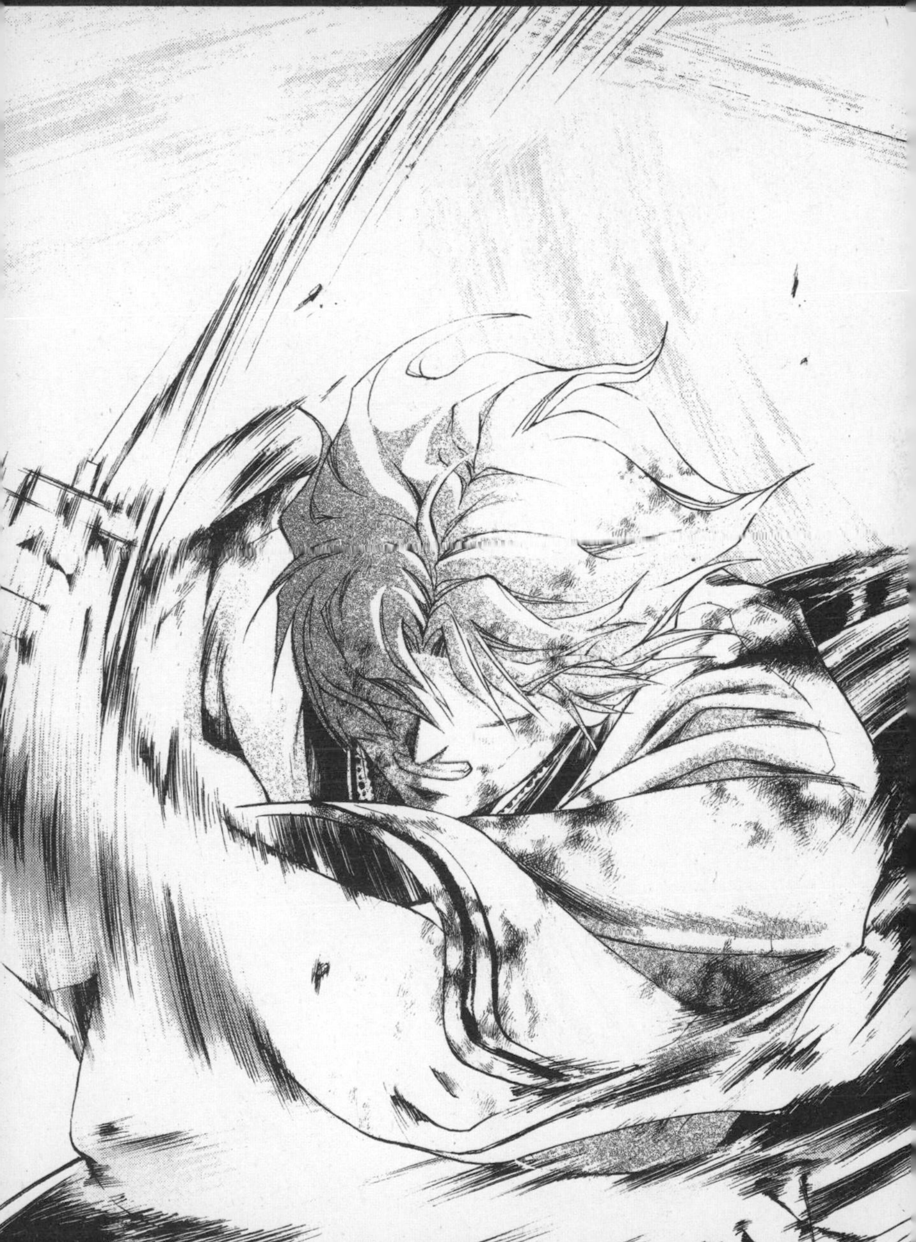

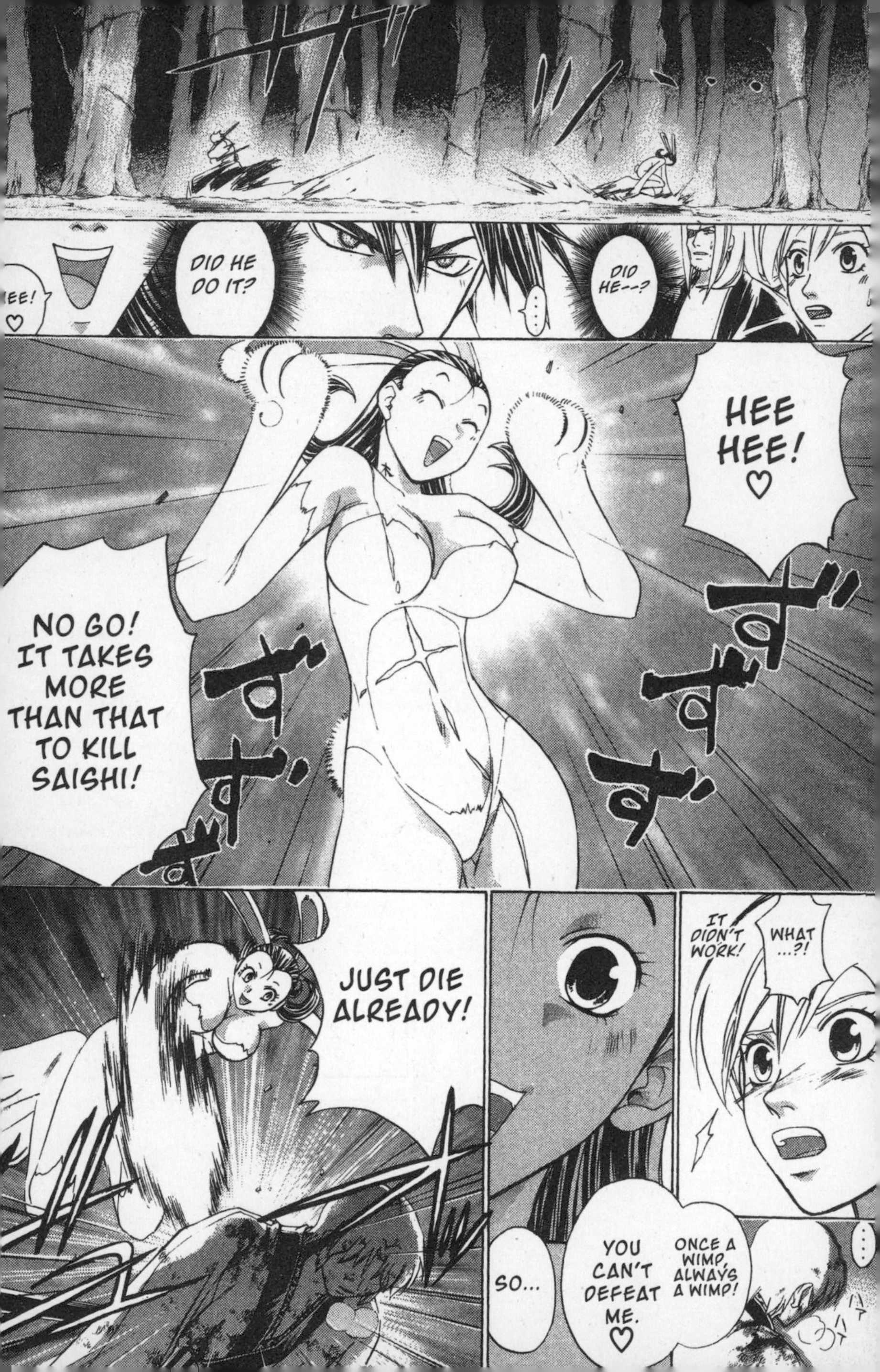

DID HE--?
...
DID HE DO IT?
EE! ♡
HEE HEE! ♡
ずずず
NO GO! IT TAKES MORE THAN THAT TO KILL SAISHI!
ずずず
WHAT ...?!
IT DIDN'T WORK!
...
ハァ ハァ
ONCE A WIMP, ALWAYS A WIMP!
YOU CAN'T DEFEAT ME. ♡
SO...
JUST DIE ALREADY!

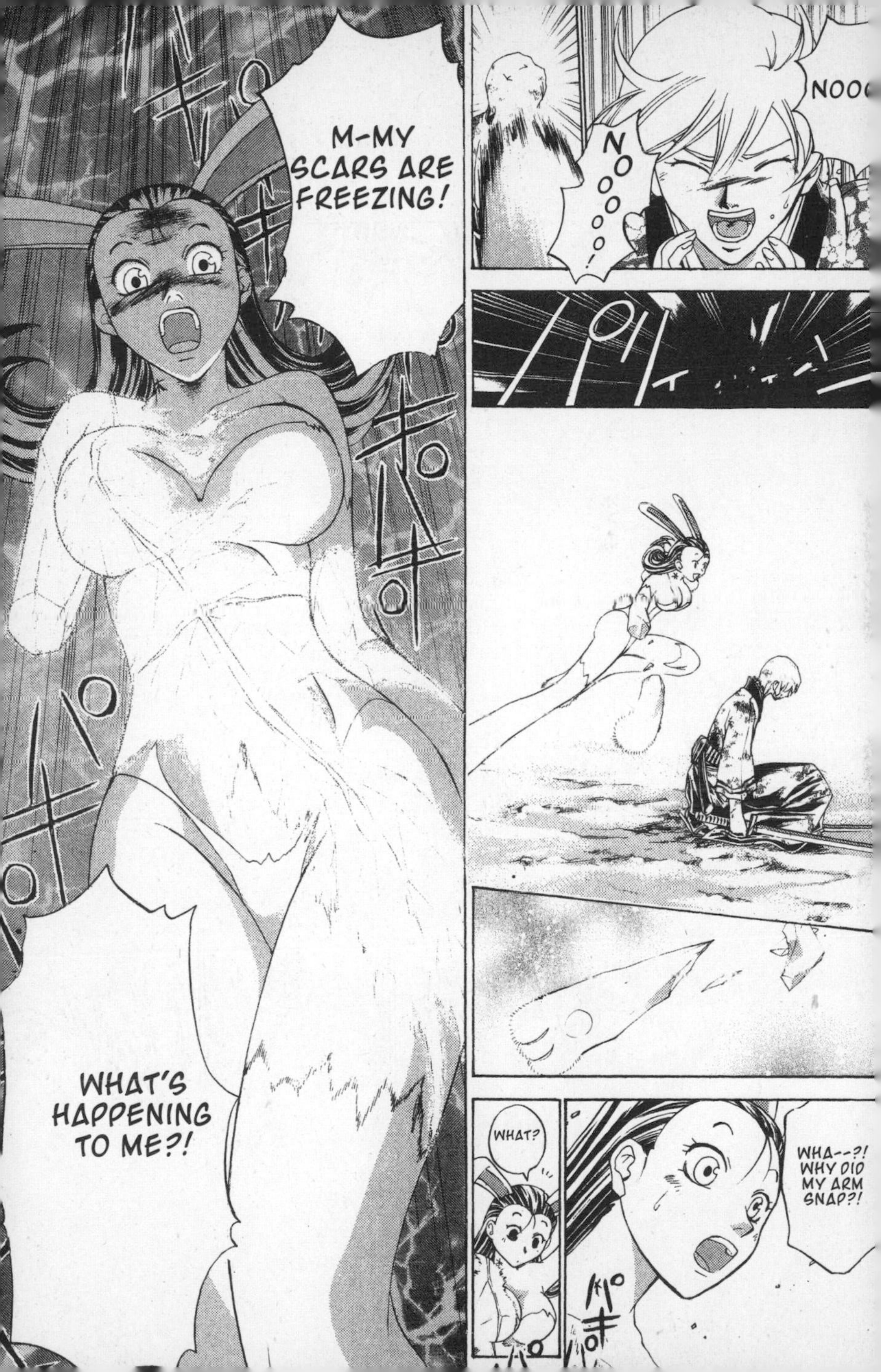
NOO
NOOOOOO!
WHA--?! WHY DID MY ARM SNAP?!
WHAT?
M-MY SCARS ARE FREEZING!
WHAT'S HAPPENING TO ME?!

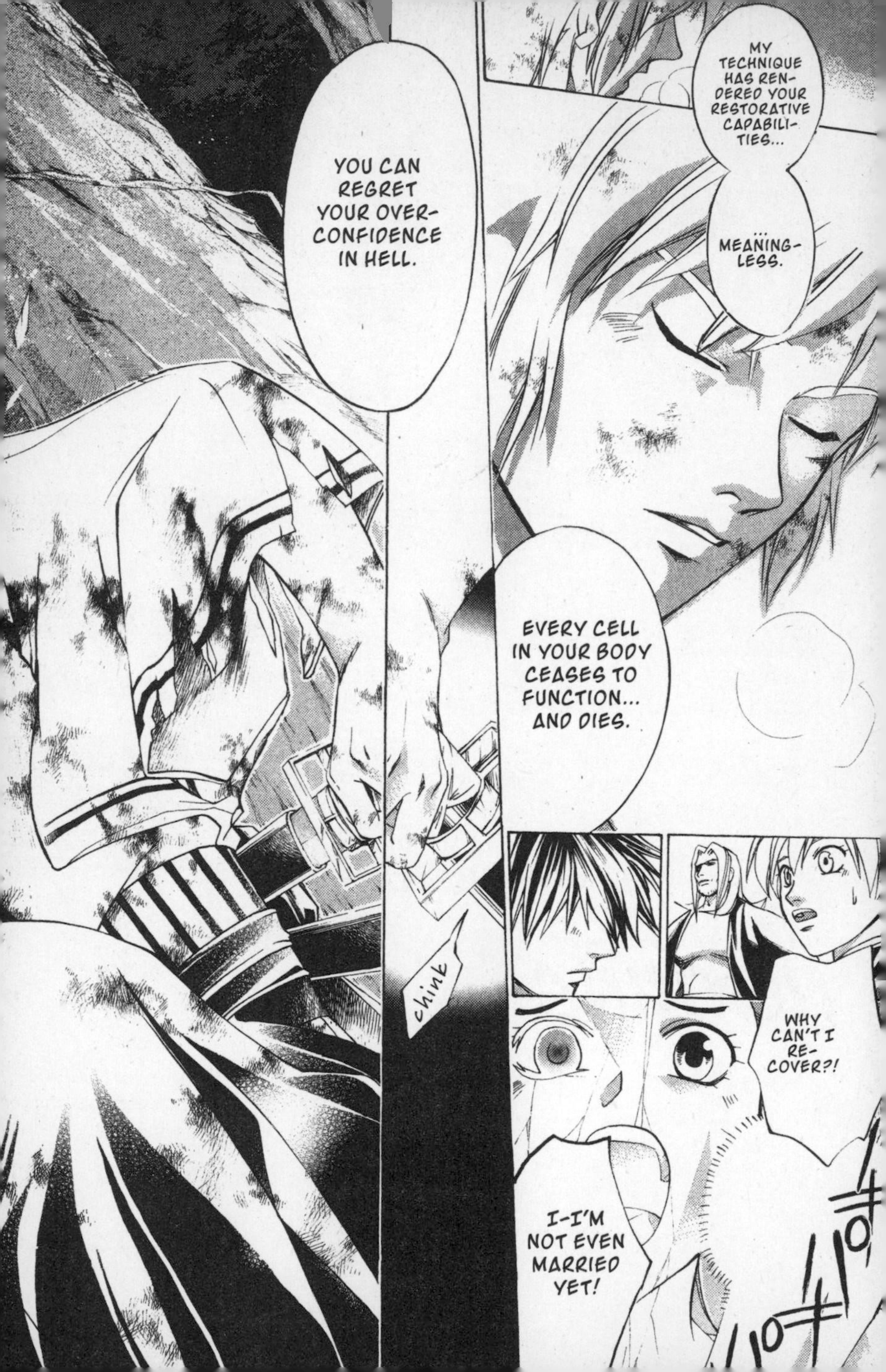
MY TECHNIQUE HAS REN-DERED YOUR RESTORATIVE CAPABILI-TIES...
...MEANING-LESS.
EVERY CELL IN YOUR BODY CEASES TO FUNCTION... AND DIES.
WHY CAN'T I RE-COVER?!
I-I'M NOT EVEN MARRIED YET!
YOU CAN REGRET YOUR OVER-CONFIDENCE IN HELL.
chink

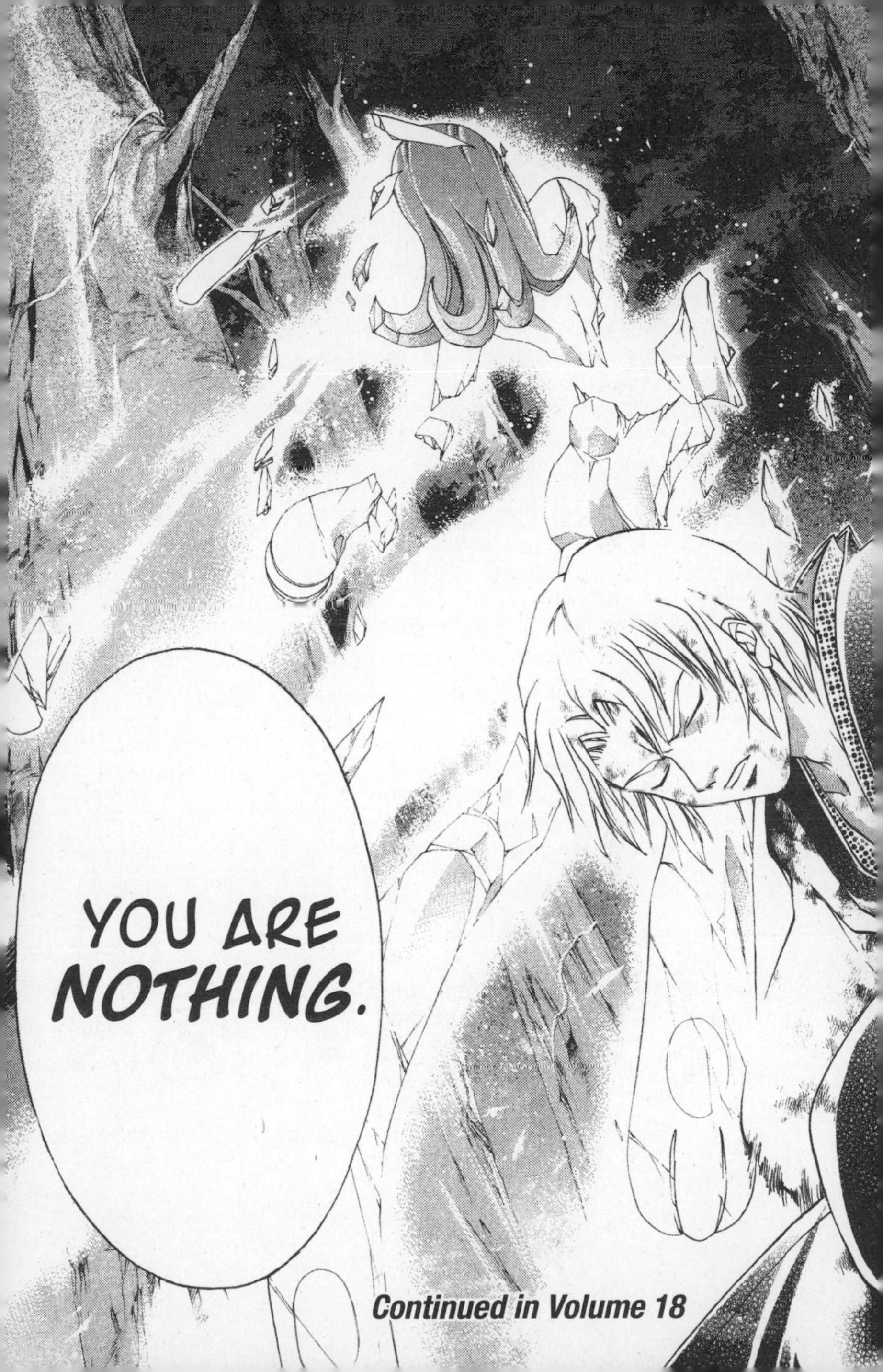
YOU ARE NOTHING.
Continued in Volume 18

Character Profile

Akira ("A" below)

I am Akira of the Four Emperors, male, height 165 cm, weight 53 kg, blood type A, job: samurai. I like deep thinking. I dislike wasteful things and losing. I'll eat anything, provided it's balanced. What am I scared of? Are you kidding? I fear nothing. What's my type? I dislike weak creatures.

Kamijyo ("K" below)

Akira's profile at last! It's been a long wait! There were a lot of requests, but it was hard to convince him. By the way, how old are you?

A: I don't remember the years before Kyo found me that well, so I'm not sure...

K: You lie! You must have some idea...

A: (Humph!) You have some basis for that bold claim? Don't you know it's rude to ask so many questions? Not to mention you forgot to ask Bontenmaru's blood type! It's "O"! That's twice you've made that mistake. Loser.

K: S-sorry! (Yipes!) Any final words?

A: I never agreed to be your ally. My plans here are not finished... Enjoy your life while you can.

K: (What a jerk...)

Akira of the Four

Akimine-kun's... Q&A Corner

Q: If you went blind, would you give up doing manga?

A: I would draw by smell.

Q: Do you choose the illustration to use for the cover?

A: Of course! But I do get help from Mr. H and Mr. S (editors for the manga) and Mr. Y (in charge of the books) and a designer.

Q: What's your favorite cover from vols. 1 through 16?

A: There isn't one I can say "this is the one!" but if I had to choose...maybe vol. 10 and vol. 13?

Q: What's your favorite time of the year?

A: I like summers that aren't hot, and winters that aren't cold.

Q: Aren't you going to make a website?

A: I dunno, I'm pretty super-analog. I'll spend my time making these bonus pages!

Q: Do you buy *Shonen Magazine*?

A: I get free copies! That's what happens when you draw manga! Heh heh heh! Pretty cool, huh? :)

To be continued! (I think.)

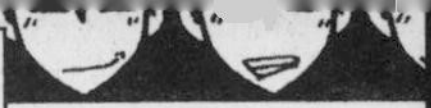

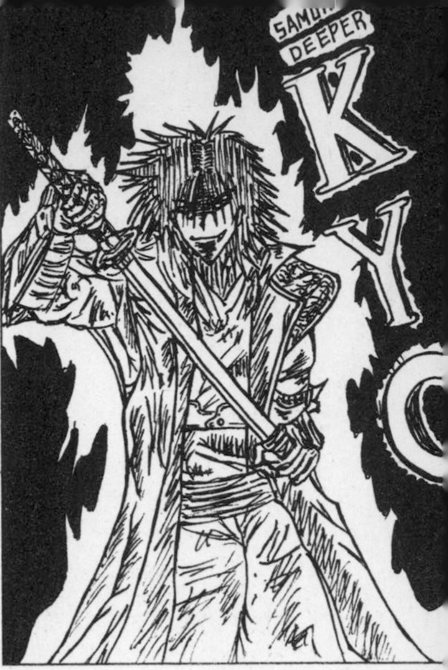
DEEPER
KYO

Whoo! Strong! [Yu Ito / Miyagi]

This guy's a teacher?! [Sammi / New Zealand]

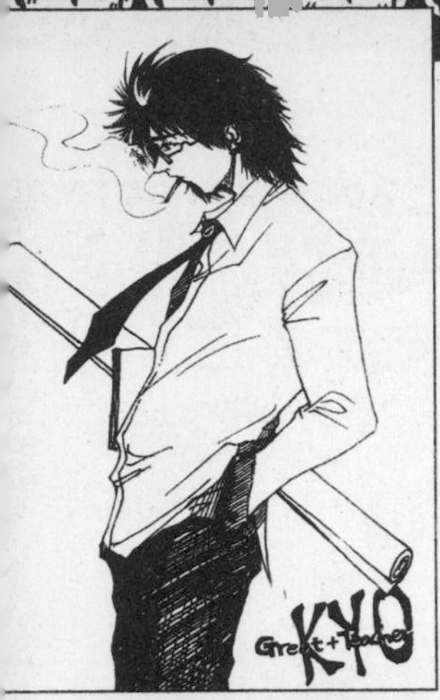
KYO
Great + Teacher

SPECIAL BIG SECTION! MAYBE *YOUR* POST-CARD'S HERE!

Draw Like Kamijyo

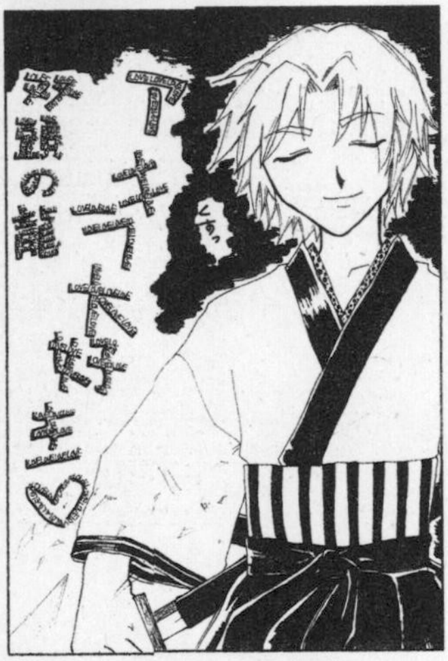
アキラ大好き♡

He doesn't look happy! [Tama / Hokkaido]

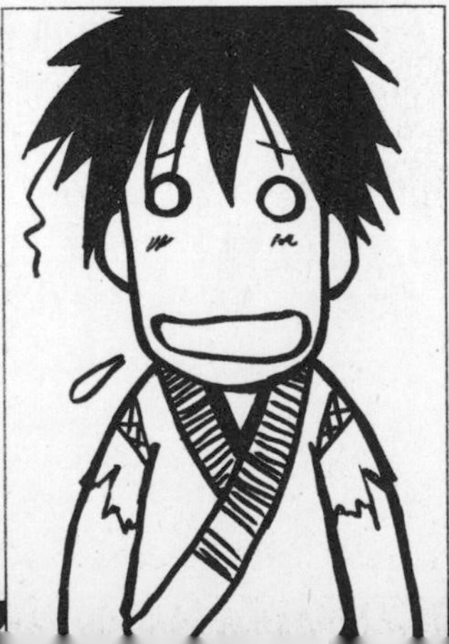

Very original! [Kinase / Gifu]

Bad guy love! :) [Ya-san / Chiba]

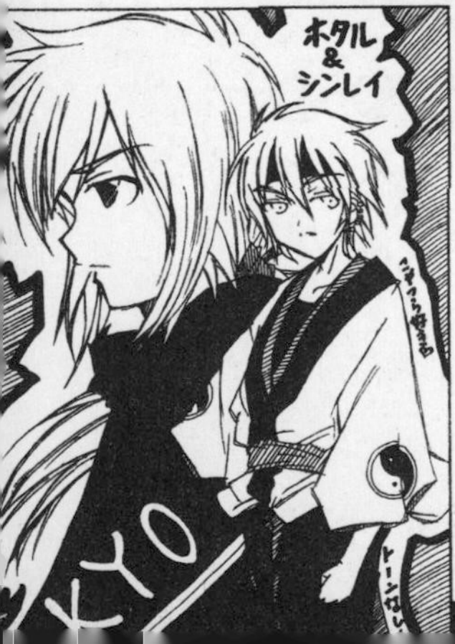
ホタル
&
シンレイ
KYO

Nice, inspiring composition!
[Piyoko / Yamanashi]

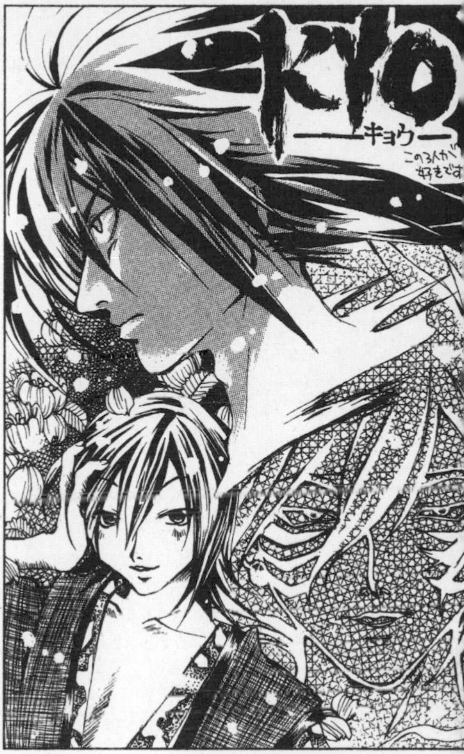
KYO
キョウ
この2人が
好きです

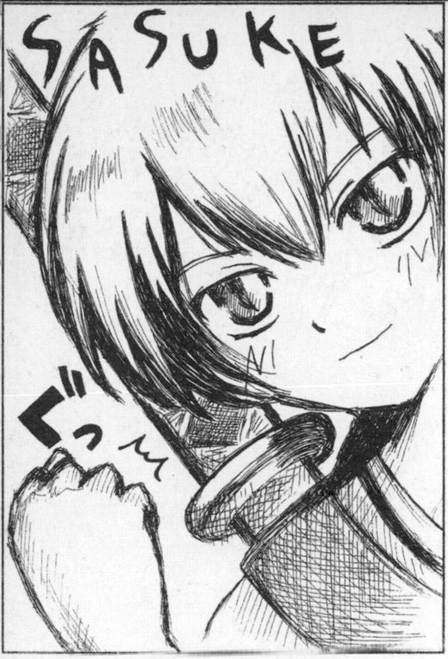
SASUKE
ぐっ

Sasuke the Kid
[Shin Yayoko / Hiroshima]

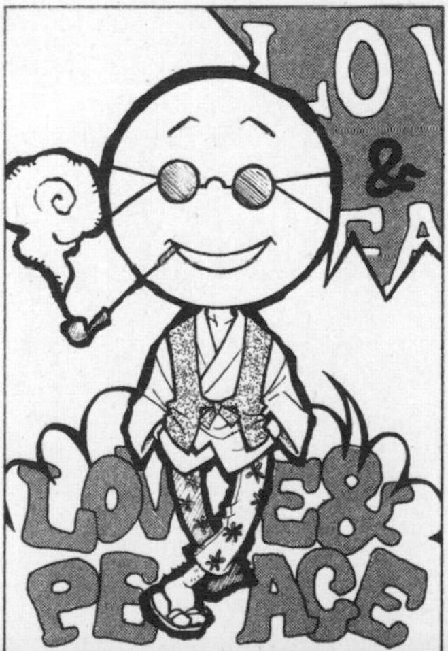
LOVE &
PEACE

Who i
it? Th
glasse
are a
good
clue.
[Koji
Omach
Tokyo

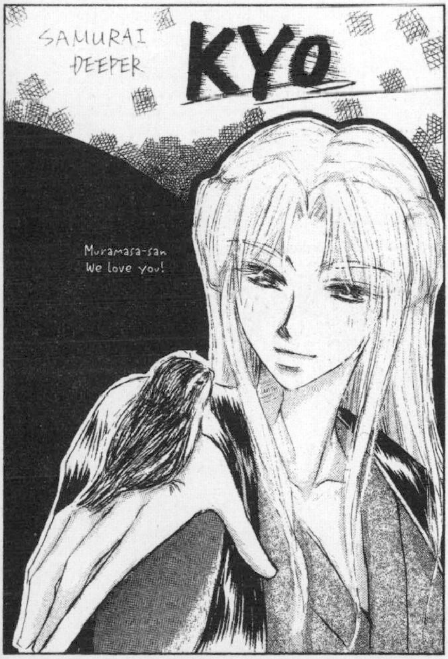
SAMURAI DEEPER
KYO
Muramasa-san
We love you!

Nice, gentle pen strokes.
[Yuto Kijo / Nara]

♡

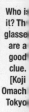

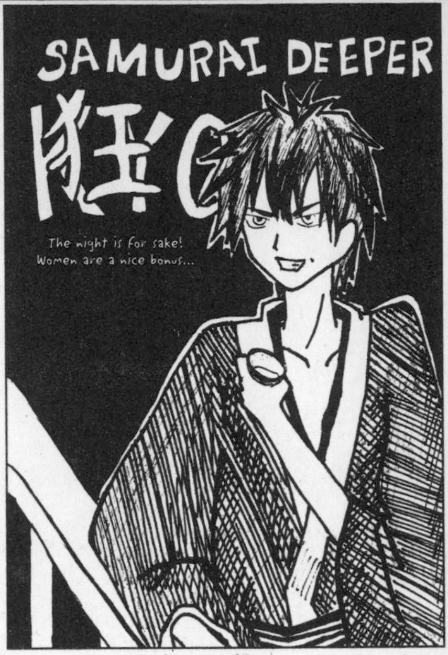
SAMURAI DEEPER
The night is for sake!
Women are a nice bonus...

I should have known!
[Ai Itonaga / Yamaguchi]

He's sleeping standing up. ;)
[Kusa / Hyogo]

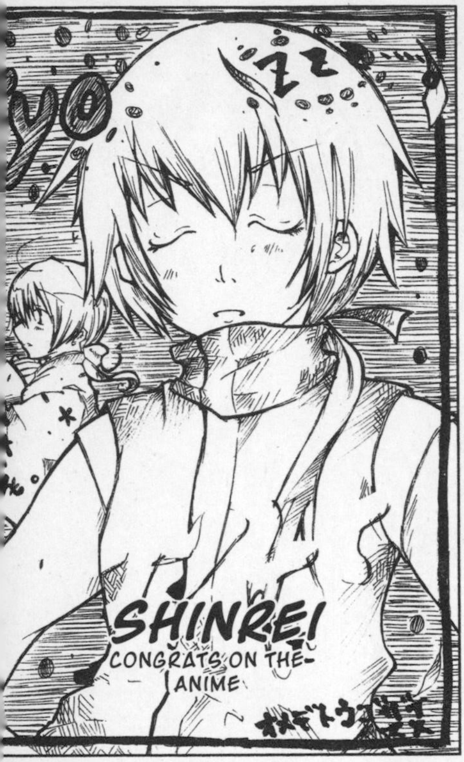
ZZZ
SHINREI
CONGRATS ON THE ANIME

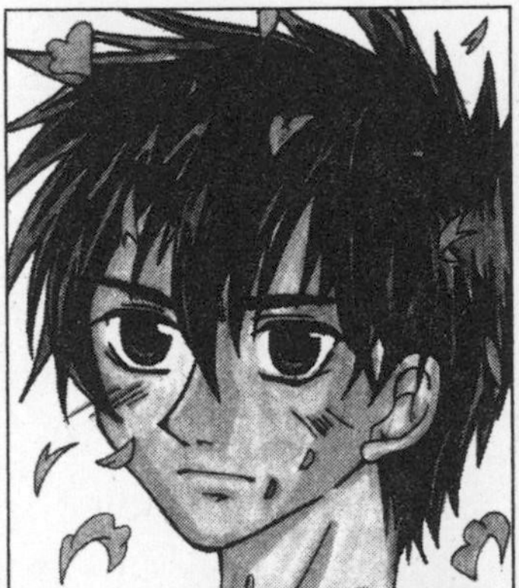
I love Kyoshiro!

Sorry this isn't in color!
[Enari / Osaka]

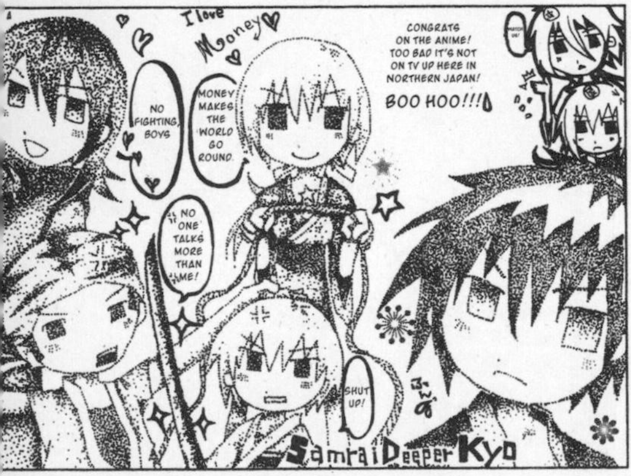
CONGRATS ON THE ANIME! TOO BAD IT'S NOT ON TV UP HERE IN NORTHERN JAPAN!
BOO HOO!!!
I love Money
MONEY MAKES THE WORLD GO ROUND.
NO FIGHTING, BOYS
NO ONE TALKS MORE THAN ME!
SHUT UP!
SamraiDeeperKyo

Whew! Good work!
[Muramasa-san Come Back?! / Iwate]

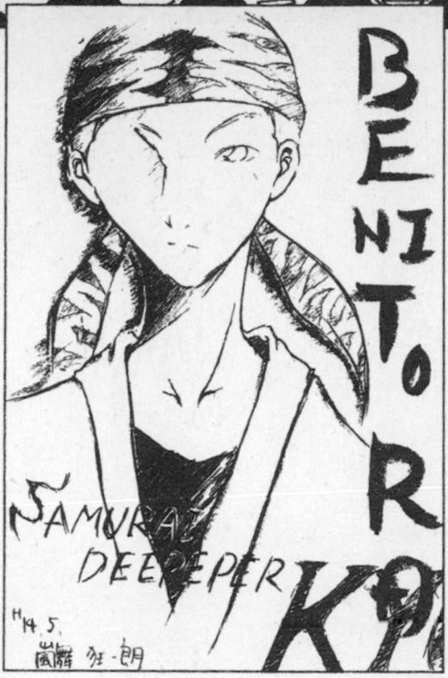
BENITORA
SAMURAI DEEPER KYO
H14.5.

He's coo even whe he's serio [Kyo ichi Arash mai Koch

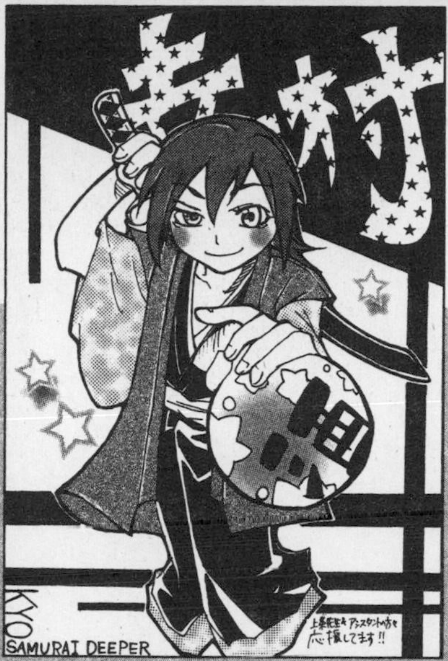
KYO SAMURAI DEEPER
上条先生&アシスタントの方々
応援してます!!

I wonder what star-sake tastes like? [Hari Hyotsu / Aichi]

Yukimura Special Gallery

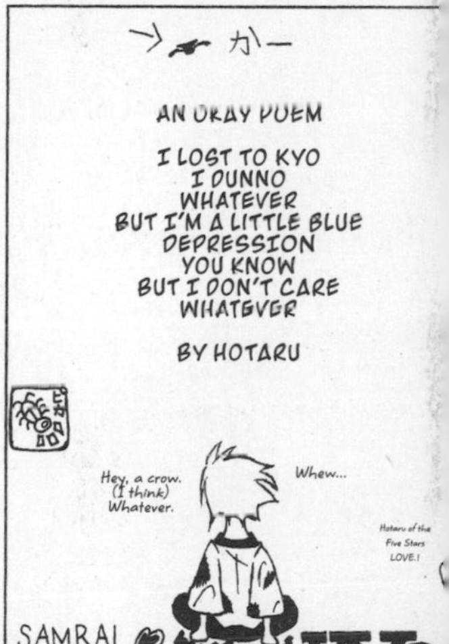
カー
AN OKAY POEM
I LOST TO KYO
I DUNNO
WHATEVER
BUT I'M A LITTLE BLUE
DEPRESSION
YOU KNOW
BUT I DON'T CARE
WHATEVER
BY HOTARU
Hey, a crow. (I think) Whatever.
Whew...
Hotaru of the Five Stars LOVE!
SAMRAI DEEPER KYO

I found the crow! [Tomoka/Hyougo]

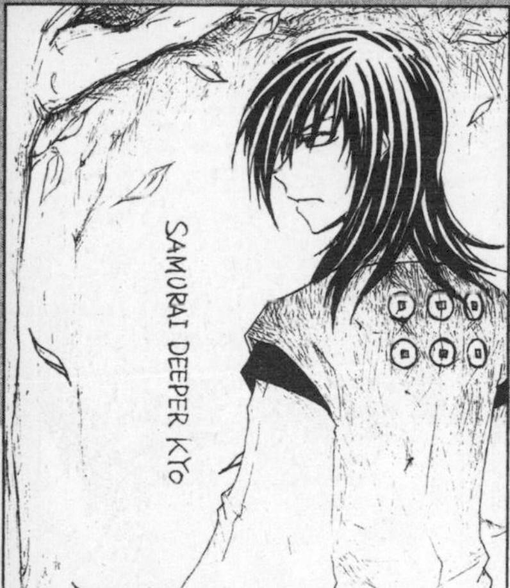
SAMURAI DEEPER KYO

When he's cool, he's cool! [Kaiki / Niiigata]

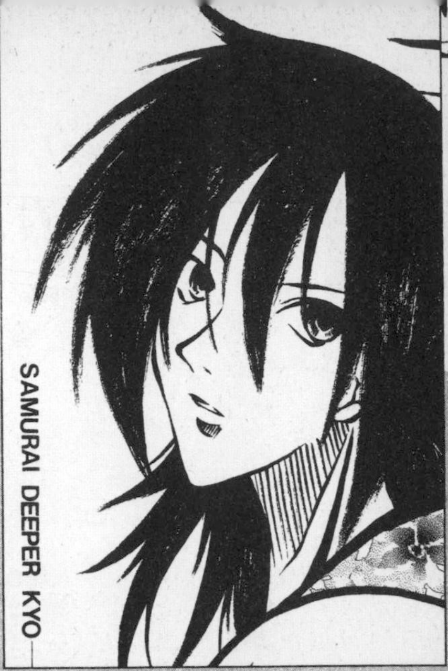
SAMURAI DEEPER KYO

Nice blacks!
[Isao Yoshida / Kanagawa]

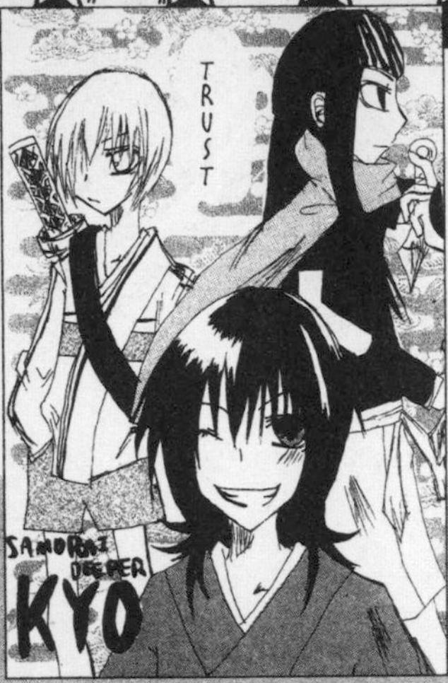
TRUST
SAMURAI DEEPER KYO

ome
what
ay...
chiya
nai /
nma]

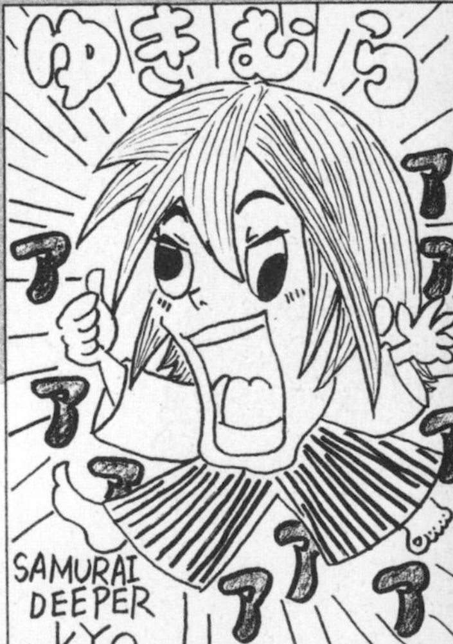
ゆきむら
アアアアアアアアアア
SAMURAI DEEPER KYO

Woot!
[Asami Sawada / Aichi]

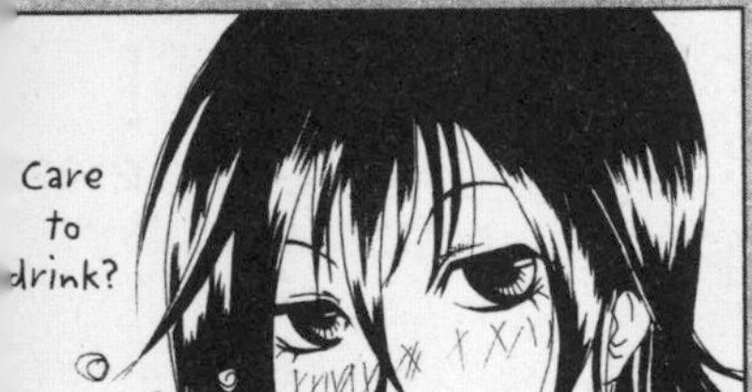
Care to drink?
SAMURAI DEEPER KYO
酒

Don't be lured by his sexy ways!
[Juran / Kagoshima]

A message from Akimine Kamijyo ♡

Next volume: Sasuke Special! Now accepting submissions for: Minor Female Characters!

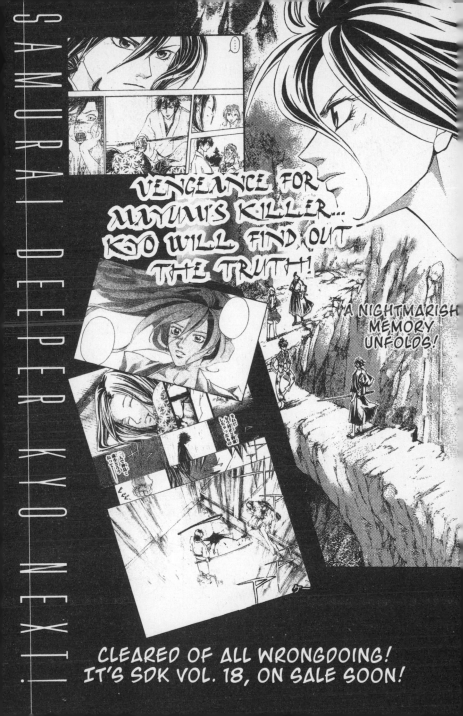

SAMURAI DEEPER KYO NEXT!

VENGEANCE FOR MURAMAS'S KILLER... KYO WILL FIND OUT THE TRUTH!

A NIGHTMARISH MEMORY UNFOLDS!

CLEARED OF ALL WRONGDOING! IT'S SDK VOL. 18, ON SALE SOON!

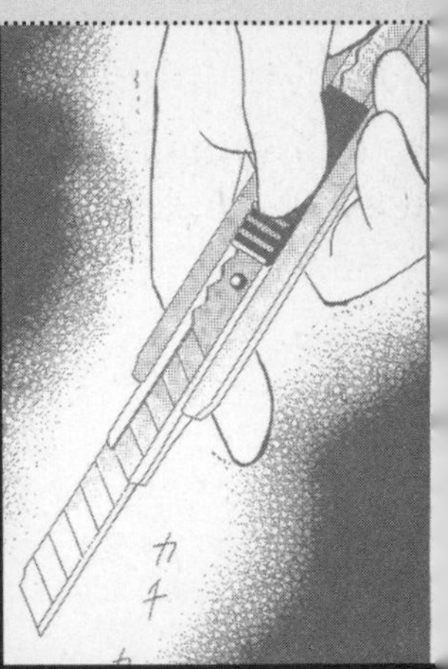

Ayumu struggles with her studies, and the all-important high school entrance exams are approaching. Fortunately, she has help from her best bud Shii-chan, who is at the top of the class. But when the test results come back, the friends are surprised: Ayumu surpasses Shii-chan's scores and gets into the school of her choice—without Shii-chan! Losing her friend is so painful for Ayumu that she starts cutting herself to ease her sorrow. Finally, Ayumu seeks comfort in a new friend, Manami. But will Manami prove to be the friend that Ayumu truly needs? Or will Ayumu continue down a dark path?

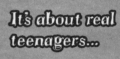

It's about real teenagers...

It's about real high school...

It's about real life.

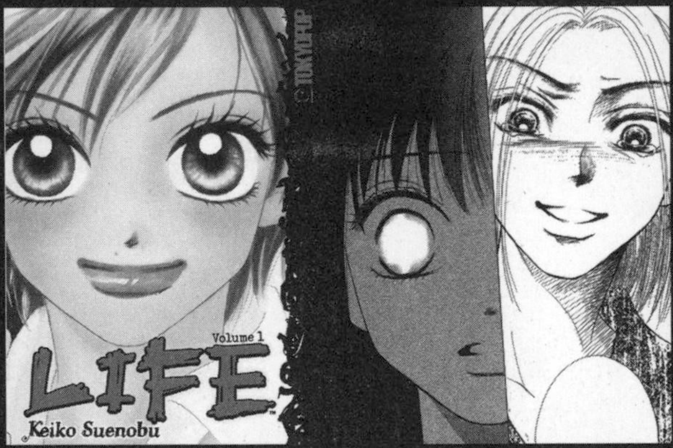
©TOKYOPOP
Volume 1
LIFE
Keiko Suenobu

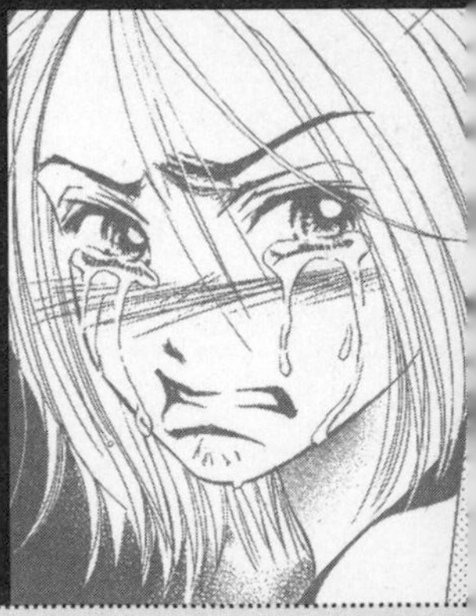

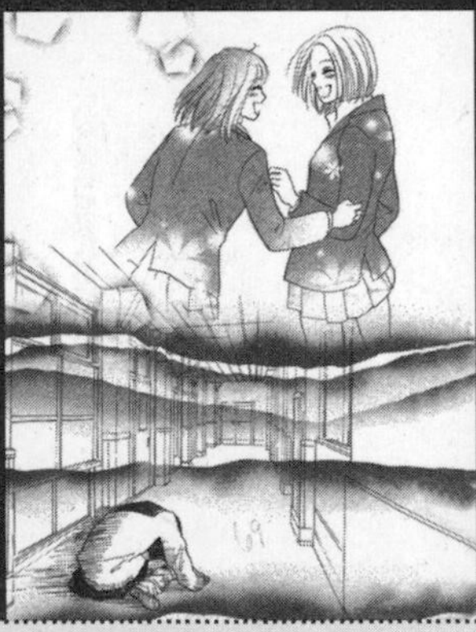

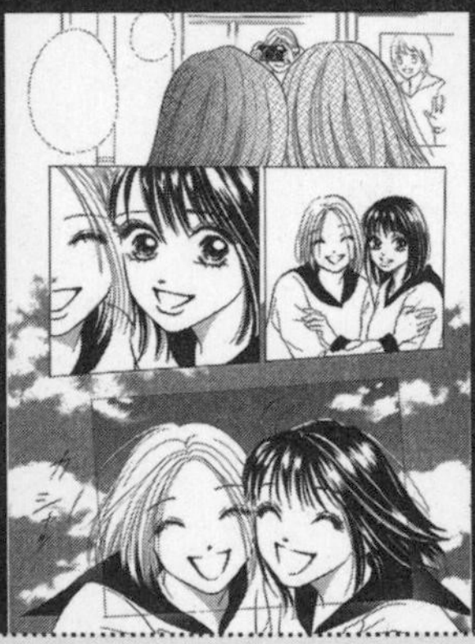

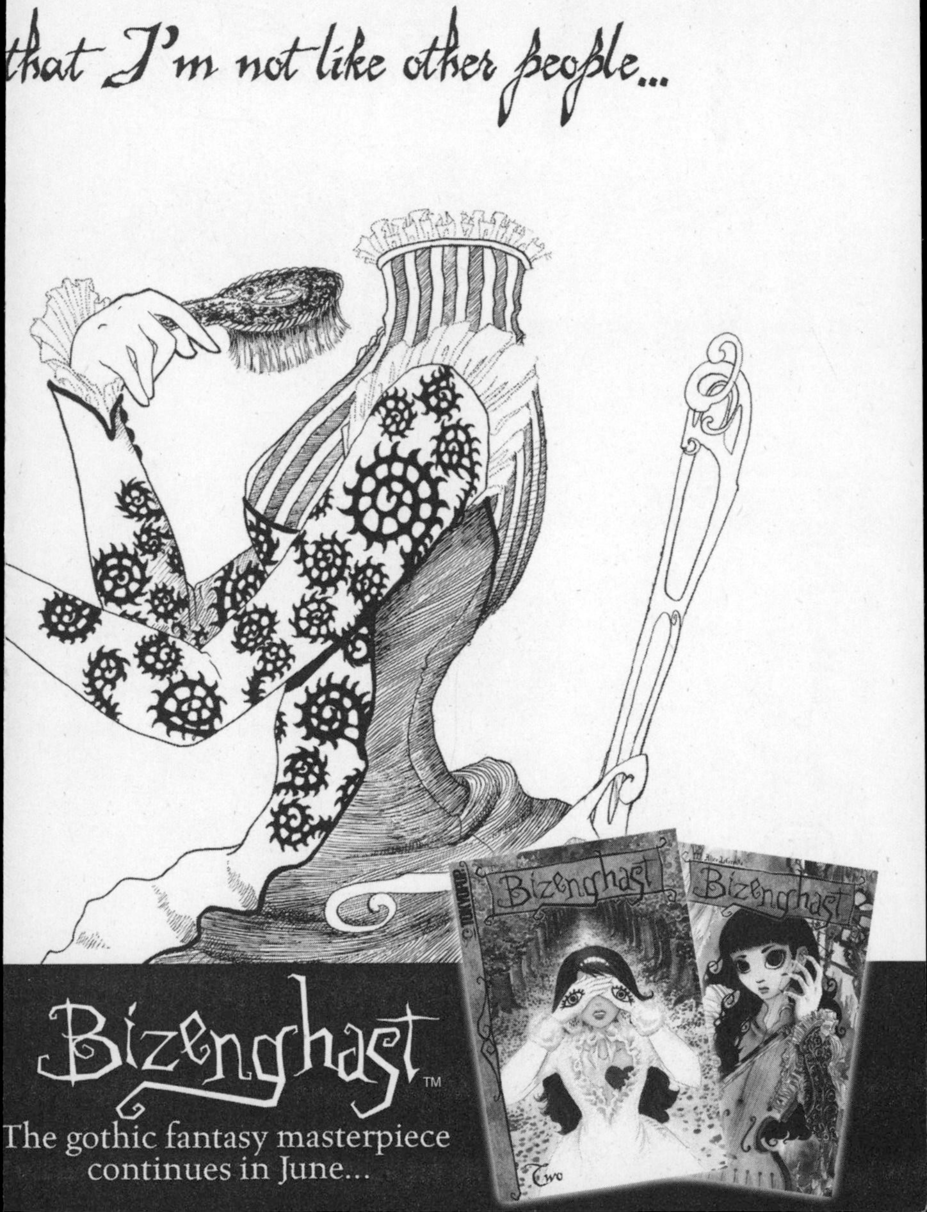
that I'm not like other people...
Bizenghast
Bizenghast
Bizenghast™
The gothic fantasy masterpiece continues in June...

THIS FALL, TOKYOPOP CREATES A FRESH, NEW CHAPTER IN TEEN NOVELS...

For Adventurers...

Witches' Forest:
The Adventures of Duan Surk

By Mishio Fukazawa

Duan Surk is a 16-year-old Level 2 fighter who embarks on the quest of a lifetime—battling mythical creatures and outwitting evil sorceresses, all in an impossible rescue mission in the spooky Witches' Forest!

BASED ON THE FAMOUS
FORTUNE QUEST WORLD

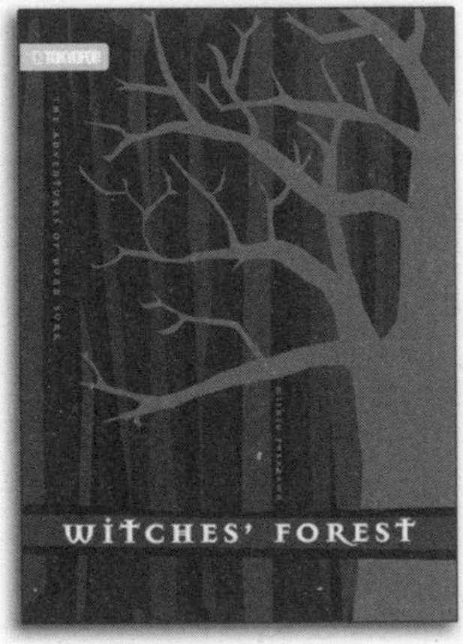
TOKYOPOP
WITCHES' FOREST

For Dreamers...

Magic Moon

By Wolfgang and Heike Hohlbein

Kim enters the engimatic realm of Magic Moon, where he battles unthinkable monsters and fantastical creatures—in order to unravel the secret that keeps his sister locked in a coma.

THE WORLDWIDE BESTSELLING FANTASY
THRILLOGY ARRIVES IN THE U.S.!

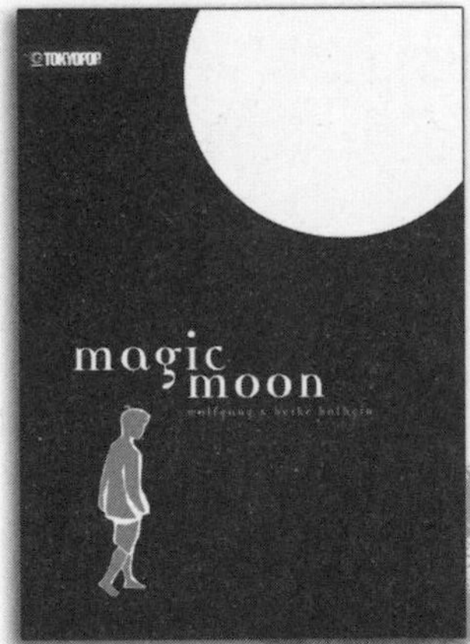
TOKYOPOP
magic moon

TOKYOPOP PRESENTS

POP FICTION

For Believers...

Scrapped Princess: A Tale of Destiny

Scrapped
PRINCESS

By Ichiro Sakaki

A dark prophecy reveals that the queen will give birth to a daughter who will usher in the Apocalypse. But despite all attempts to destroy the baby, the myth of the "Scrapped Princess" lingers on...

THE INSPIRATION FOR THE HIT ANIME AND MANGA SERIES!

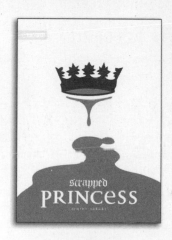

For Thinkers...

Kino no Tabi: Book One of The Beautiful World

TOKYOPOP
KINO NO TABI
The Beautiful World
Keiichi Sigsawa

By Keiichi Sigsawa

Kino roams the world on the back of Hermes, her unusual motorcycle, in a journey filled with happiness and pain, decadence and violence, and magic and loss.

THE SENSATIONAL BESTSELLER IN JAPAN HAS FINALLY ARRIVED!

STOP!

This is the back of the book.
You wouldn't want to spoil a great ending!

This book is printed "manga-style," in the authentic Japanese right-to-left format. Since none of the artwork has been flipped or altered, readers get to experience the story just as the creator intended. You've been asking for it, so TOKYOPOP® delivered: authentic, hot-off-the-press, and far more fun!

DIRECTIONS

If this is your first time reading manga-style, here's a quick guide to help you understand how it works.

It's easy... just start in the top right panel and follow the numbers. Have fun, and look for more 100% authentic manga from TOKYOPOP®!

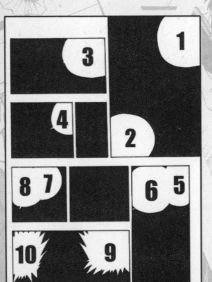